Great Southern Landings

AN ANTHOLOGY *of* ANTIPODEAN TRAVEL

edited by Jan Bassett

Melbourne

OXFORD UNIVERSITY PRESS

Oxford   Auckland   New York

OXFORD UNIVERSITY PRESS AUSTRALIA

Oxford   New York
Athens   Auckland   Bangkok   Bombay
Calcutta   Cape Town   Dar es Salaam   Delhi
Florence   Hong Kong   Istanbul   Karachi
Kuala Lumpur   Madras   Madrid   Melbourne
Mexico City   Nairobi   Paris   Singapore
Taipei   Tokyo   Toronto

and associated companies in
Berlin   Ibadan

OXFORD is a trade mark of Oxford University Press

National Library of Australia
Cataloguing-in-Publication data:

Great southern landings: an anthology of Antipodean travel.
    Bibliography.
    Includes index.
    ISBN 0 19 553582 0.

1. Australia — Description and travel. 2. Australia —
Description and travel — Fiction. 3. Australia — Discovery
and exploration. 4. Australia — Discovery and exploration —
Fiction. I. Bassett, Jan, 1953– .

919.404

Edited by Jo McMillan
Cover design by Guy Mirabella
Designed by Sandra Nobes
Typeset by Desktop Concepts P/L, Melbourne
Printed in Hong Kong
Published by Oxford University Press,
253 Normanby Road, South Melbourne, Australia

CONTENTS

CONTENTS

CONTENTS

CONTENTS

INTRODUCTION

Thousands of travellers from the northern hemisphere, from François Pelsaert, commander of the ill-fated *Batavia*, which was shipwrecked off the coast of present-day Western Australia in 1629, to countless current writers, have left records of their impressions of the Antipodes ('Australasia in relation to Europe') in extant books and journals. Others who have travelled only in their minds have written about imaginary voyages to, and utopias set in, the same area, some of them doing so years before poor Pelsaert ran aground. The first of these apparently was Joseph Hall, whose utopia (or, more properly, dystopia) originally appeared, anonymously and in Latin, under the title *Mundus Alter et Idem*, meaning 'the world different and the same', in about 1605. This anthology is made up of extracts from a wide variety of such travellers' accounts.

Deriving from the Greek terms for opposite and foot, the Middle English noun 'antipodes' was being used by 1549 to refer to 'places on the surface of the earth directly opposite to each other'. The adjective 'antipodean', which had appeared by 1651, came especially to mean Australasian by about the middle of the nineteenth century. 'Australasia', of course, encompasses Australia, New Zealand, and neighbouring islands. Although she suspected that 'Antipathies' was not quite right, Lewis Carroll's Alice certainly knew that, whatever the word should have been, it referred to these lands. Even after European 'discovery' and settlement, the Antipodes remained partly an imaginary place. 'These Antipodes call to one's mind old recollections of childish doubt and wonder', the naturalist Charles Darwin wrote in his diary on 19 December 1835, shortly after passing the 'meridian of the Antipodes' while voyaging on the *Beagle*. 'Only the other day I looked forward to this airy barrier as a definite point in our voyage homewards; but I now find it, and all such resting-places for the imagination, are like shadows, which a man moving towards cannot catch!'[1]

The Great South Land, the Antipodes, *Terra Australis*, Australasia (a term much disliked by New Zealanders, who have in the past actively campaigned for its abolition), Down Under, and Under the Southern Cross are all Eurocentric terms, as indeed are the names Australia (from the Latin *australis*, meaning southern) and New Zealand (named after the Netherlands province of Zeeland). For Australians and New Zealanders, the logical Great South Land would be Antarctica (another 'opposite' place), the real Antipodes Europe. But that is not the way in which these words have been used. It should be noted, though, that few Australians or New Zealanders today would call themselves Antipodeans or their countries part of the Antipodes, except in a humorous, self-depreciatory manner. One of Australia's best-known expatriates, Clive James, for example, in a 1976 'postcard from Sydney', says of the name of the pilot flying him back to his home city, Barry Tingwell: 'The sheer Australianness of that name was as antipodean as a sand-fly bite or a sting from a jelly-blubber.'[2] It seems to me, as an Australian by birth and residence, that there is something appealingly Pythonesque about the idea of being one of the 'opposite feet' people.

Two-thirds of the travellers from the northern hemisphere represented here came from Britain, the remainder mainly from other parts of Europe, the United States, and India. Tales of their travels in all of the Australian States (formerly colonies) and New Zealand are included. Many thought of the two countries together; quite a number, especially in the days of sea travel, visited both. Wishing to look through fresh eyes, I have left out descriptions written by Australians or New Zealanders themselves, with the exception of those of a few Australian expatriates. It is said that there is no greater stranger than a former lover. Perhaps a similar transformation takes place in the relationship between the expatriate and his or her birthplace. As I was particularly interested in the 'minds of travellers', I have generally excluded migrants' stories. The hopes, fears, expectations, and perceptions of the person 'who has left the land of his fathers, to rear his family and lay his bones in a different soil' are likely to differ greatly from those of the traveller who intends returning home in the foreseeable future.[3] Therefore, with sadness, I set aside works such as Edward Gibbon Wakefield's fictitious, but highly influential, embodiment of his theory of 'systematic colonisation', *A Letter from Sydney* (1829), written in Newgate Gaol while he served a sentence for his abduction of a fifteen-year-old heiress. Visitors who changed their minds and stayed, or later returned permanently, such as the Quaker 'traveller under concern',

Frederick Mackie, drawn back to South Australia to marry a woman he had met on his travels, remained eligible. I have not attempted to differentiate between travellers and tourists, as Paul Fussell and others have done, but have largely removed explorers from consideration. 'Explorers are quite different from travellers', writes Robin Hanbury-Tenison in his introduction to *The Oxford Book of Exploration* (1993). 'They are driven by a desire to discover which transcends the urge to conquer, the pursuit of trade, the curiosity of the scientist, the zeal of the missionary, or the simple search for adventure which first sent them abroad.'

Fact and fiction blur in many of these texts. William Dampier, the first English person to visit and write about Australia, and the imaginary Lemuel Gulliver are said by Jonathan Swift, in *Gulliver's Travels* (1726), to be cousins. Richard and Harriet Somers from D.H. Lawrence's novel *Kangaroo* (1923) strongly resemble the author and his wife. Zdzisław Najder says of Joseph Conrad's volume of 'memories and impressions', *The Mirror of the Sea* (1906): 'The book is not an autobiography in the sense of a factual report. When we try to pin down biographical data and connect the events in Conrad's reminiscences with documented facts, an identification often turns out to be impossible. Many "remembered" events simply do not have plausible counterparts in Conrad's life.'[4] Unlikely though it may now seem, many early readers of the imaginary voyages and utopias believed them to be authentic. Historians, too, have been fooled by these and other narratives. Even the historian Ernest Scott, an authority on the European discovery of Australia, apparently thought that *Fragmens du Dernier Voyage de La Pérouse* (1797) was an actual journal rather than the Pacific utopia that it is. One of the most intriguing hoaxes involves John Sherer's *The Gold-Finder of Australia: How He Went, How He Fared, and How He Made His Fortune* (1853), described by a well-known Australian historian in 1973 as 'the most colourful and realistic first-hand report of those amazing days'.[5] Sherer had in fact never visited Australia; his book is 'a clever pastiche of existing travellers' accounts and interpolated fictional narratives'.[6] The relatively recent discovery that it was not genuine is interesting, but in some senses irrelevant. The book's immediate popularity and apparent authenticity probably inspired many people to try to emulate the 'gold-finder's' success.

This collection is designed to be as eclectic as possible, not to prove any particular thesis. It is intended to be representative rather than comprehensive, entertaining rather than educational. I chose the extracts, all of which are taken from published sources, primarily for

their intrinsic interest, rather than their literary value or historical significance, although many also share these qualities. Ranging from the
illuminating to the laughable, these writings, which have reflected and
helped to shape Australian and New Zealand cultural identities, make
fascinating reading at a time when both countries are attempting
increasingly to stand on their own feet and redefine themselves. Part of
their value lies in the fact that visitors have often been prepared to look
at subjects that their hosts either have taken for granted or not wished
to see.

Anthony Trollope and Mark Twain are two of many famous figures
whose well-known visits are represented in this book. Other visits
made by such people, sometimes before they became household names,
are also included, notable examples being Herbert Hoover's 'years of
adventure' as a mining engineer in Western Australia, long before he
became president of the United States, Agatha Christie's 1922 visit,
made before she became the undisputed 'queen of crime', and Anthony
Eden's brief journalistic stint in Australia in the 1920s, decades before
his prime ministership of Britain. (There is no section on politicians as
such, partly because many of their autobiographies are tedious or
ghosted or both—I have tried to keep the number of 'ghosts' in the
book to a minimum.) Where possible I have passed over hackneyed
accounts. Thus, instead of using James Cook's descriptions, I have chosen pieces written by an artist, Sydney Parkinson, and an Italian-American sailor, James Matra, both of whom also took part in the 1768–71
voyage on the *Endeavour*. The elusive Elim H. D'Avigdor, the 'Wanderer' responsible for writing *Antipodean Notes* (1888), is one of
numerous long-forgotten visitors whose writings are also included. At
times I have emphasised the historical at the expense of recent works,
reasoning that the general reader is less likely to stumble across William
Cuff's *Sunny Memories of Australasia* (1904) on the shelves of the local
library than Paul Theroux's markedly less cheerful book about 'paddling the Pacific', *The Happy Isles of Oceania* (1992). Hence the former's inclusion and the latter's exclusion.

Women were among the earliest and most enthusiastic travellers, in
mind or body, to the Antipodes. Mary Ann Parker, who visited New
South Wales in 1791, only three years after European settlement
began, has been labelled 'Australia's first tourist'.[7] Therese Huber's
Adventures on a Journey to New Holland, written in German in 1793
and first published, under her second husband's name, in 1801, is
believed to be the first novel set in the new penal colony. Not counting
Lady Mary Fox, who was said to be the editor of an *Account of an*

Expedition to New South Wales (1837), but was really a front for Arch-bishop Whately, women wrote about a fifth of the extracts in this anthology, possibly a slightly higher proportion than for the genre as a whole. Others whose words are included range from the Frenchwoman Rose de Freycinet, who stowed away on her husband's ship in 1817, dressed as a man, to the beautiful British model and sixties icon, Jean Shrimpton, whose stockingless knees shocked Melbourne matrons a century-and-a-half later. A surfeit of 'family ties', in particular, stopped many other female would-be travellers from following them and forced others to delay their plans. That 'zestful missionary', as historian Jane Robinson calls her, Cornishwoman Lucy Broad, had to wait for years before she could indulge her 'thirst for speed' on her bicycle and pursue her love of 'escapades' at the end of the nineteenth century. After her father's death she had moved out of home and successively 'mothered' three of her brothers. 'But all the time I had been fighting a burning desire in my own heart that craved for the whole world and had special leanings towards the Foreign Mission field, which had to be silenced because of the dear mother's opposition', she writes in *A Woman's Wan-derings the World Over* (1909). 'Now when she was also called to her rest and I was free from pressing family claims, I set out.'[8] In addition, even those who travelled did not always have 'rooms of their own' allowing them to write books.

When deciding on the book's format I succumbed to what I recent-ly heard the Australian poet Chris Wallace-Crabbe describe as 'cate-goresis', that seductive but somewhat childish desire to compile lists. I have grouped extracts into various categories, usually depending upon the writers' occupations, the purposes of their visits, their activities during their stays, or the main focus of their relevant writings, whichever seemed most appropriate. Hence Eden is to be found with other journalists, Hoover, *qua* mining engineer, among the gold-seekers, and Sherlock Holmes's creator, Sir Arthur Conan Doyle, who toured Australia and New Zealand in 1920–21 to lecture on spiritual-ism, at the end of a mixed bunch of missionaries. Many of the travellers have had numerous strings to their bows. My categories, into which most authors of the genre do fall, are provided only as rough guides.

A survey of some of the convalescents, representatives of a sizeable number of travellers to Australia and New Zealand, especially during the nineteenth century, when long sea voyages were prescribed for ail-ments ranging from the effects of overwork to galloping consumption (tuberculosis), illustrates the problems of such categorisation. Straight-forward cases include that of Augustus Prinsep, whose travels in Van

Diemen's Land (present-day Tasmania) in 1829–30 apparently did little to improve his health, given that he died shortly afterwards during another voyage, leaving his grieving widow to edit his Antipodean journal for publication. Less clearcut is that of the 'blind traveller', James Holman (1786–1857), who had lost his sight at the age of twenty-five, but who probably was, strictly speaking, post-convalescent when he made his 'Australasian' visit during the third (1827–32) of his four major overseas journeys. Considering some of his exploits, he just as easily could have been tagged an adventurer. Various travellers from other categories also could be classed as convalescents. The consumptive Frank Fowler, a twenty-two-year-old English journalist who decided that a 'run round the world' to New South Wales would improve his health, played a lively role in Sydney literary circles between 1855 and 1858. Tuberculosis, alas, finally killed him in 1863, several years after his return to London.

This book begins with an excerpt from the 1609 translation of Hall's *Mundus Alter et Idem* and ends with an essay written in 1992 by the Australian expatriate John Pilger. Many of the extracts in between date from the 'heyday of travel and travel writing', which, according to Fussell, spans the nineteenth and early twentieth centuries, a period that roughly coincides with the first century or so of European settlement in Australia and New Zealand.[9] Some forms of Antipodean travel have been largely limited to particular times, others not. Predictably, all but one of the gold-seekers in these pages visited or wrote about Australia during the golden days of the 1850s. The sailors' extracts range from an account of Pelsaert's unexpected 1629 visit to a piece from Eric Newby's book on the last great grain race, which took place in 1939 and makes a fitting symbolic ending to the era of sail. Adventurers seem to be a perennial group, the earliest here being the 1791 visitor Mary Ann Parker, the latest Robin Hanbury-Tenison, who, with his wife, rode on horseback through New Zealand in 1988. Within each section extracts are, as far as possible, arranged in chronological order of real or imagined visits. (Dates in round brackets after extract headings refer to when visits were made.) Such an arrangement highlights some extraordinary shifts in thinking, perhaps none more extreme than that between the attitudes of George Campbell, who viewed Australian fauna through the sights of a gun in the 1870s, and David Attenborough, who gazed reverentially at the same through the lens of a camera almost a century later.

Like Hall's Mercurius Britannicus, most travellers to the Antipodes have found themselves in a world partly the same as their own. Not surprisingly, many have written portraits, wittingly or otherwise, of themselves or their societies. They have much in common with the Indian Muslim man travelling to England via Cape Town and Ireland at the end of the eighteenth century, of whom Michael Pearson writes in a recent article about the meanings of journeys: 'By defining the Other, he was defining himself. Our traveller kept seeing similarities and differences ... [He] was concerned to define the foreign sights against what he knew, as do all travellers.'[10] Very much is in the eyes of the beholders, as is amply evident if one reads Harry Price's and Peter Conrad's radically different word-pictures of the same mountain. In their Australian diary, Sidney and Beatrice Webb probably reveal more about themselves than the country they were visiting. Hampered by what A.G. Austin identifies as natures that were incompatible with those of Australians, imaginations that faltered beyond England, and a lack of preparation, the highly intelligent Webbs unexpectedly proved to be poor observers of Australian society. Therese Huber shows little interest in describing New Holland, concentrating instead on using it as a background for a discussion of revolution. Writers of utopias, especially, use the Antipodes, unknown or known, as places in which to locate societies that mirror their own. Despite its probable location in the area of present-day South Australia, Swift's Lilliput is intended, of course, to represent England.

Such travellers have also found themselves in a world of difference. Many have expected to find a topsy-turvy place, having had similar childhood experiences to that of Bruce Chatwin's narrator in *The Songlines* (1987). 'I also knew from my great-aunt Ruth, that Australia was the country of the Upside-downers', he recalls. 'A hole bored straight through the earth from England, would burst out under their feet.'[11] Their expectations have often become self-fulfilling prophecies. The sense of inversion that is one of the most powerful themes in Antipodean travel writing is neatly exemplified by Agatha Christie. 'In England one becomes used to trees having dark trunks and light leafy branches; the reverse in Australia was quite astonishing', she writes in her autobiography. 'Silvery white-barks everywhere, and the darker leaves, made it like seeing the negative of a photograph. It reversed the whole look of the landscape.'[12] Paradoxes and contradictions abound. At times I felt that this anthology could have been entitled *Travellers' Adventures in an Antipodean Wonderland* or *Australia and New Zealand Through Many Looking-Glasses*.

Or *in* many looking-glasses. Reading these travel accounts, especially if one is an Australian or New Zealander, is reminiscent of looking at oneself in a hall of mirrors, not like that in the palace of Versailles, but in a Luna Park version, lined with all sorts of mirrors, large and small, curved and flat, one-way and two-way. In some areas the lighting is bright and cheerful, in others dark and mysterious, and it is not always easy to distinguish reflection from reality. Some features are exaggerated, others diminished, making one, at times, barely recognisable. There are also moments when one suddenly can see familiar territory from new and unexpected perspectives. Regardless of the accuracy of the images or the educational value of the exercise, however, in general the experience itself is fun.

Jan Bassett

Note to Readers

Original spellings have been retained in these extracts. Some footnotes have been deleted.

Notes

1   Charles Darwin, *The Voyage of the 'Beagle'* (Heron Books, np, 1968), p. 417. See list of sources for publication history.
2   See extract in this book.
3   Quotation from George Bennett, *Wanderings in New South Wales, Batavia, Pedir Coast, Singapore, and China: Being the Journal of a Naturalist in Those Countries, During 1832, 1833, and 1834*, vol. 1 (Richard Bentley, London, 1834), p. 50.
4   See Joseph Conrad, *The Mirror of the Sea* and *A Personal Record*, edited and with an introduction by Zdzisław Najder (Oxford University Press, Oxford, 1981), p. xi. *The Mirror of the Sea* was first published in 1906.
5   See general editor's note in John Sherer (ed.), *The Gold-Finder of Australia: How He Went, How He Fared, and How He Made His Fortune* (Penguin, Harmondsworth, 1973, facsimile, originally published by Clarke, Beeton, & Co., London, 1853).
6   David Goodman, 'Reading Gold-Rush Travellers' Narratives', in *Australian Cultural History*, no. 10, 1991, *Travellers, Journeys, Tourists*, p. 101.
7   See Gavin Fry's introduction to Mary Ann Parker, *A Voyage Round the World* (Hordern House and the Australian National Maritime Museum, Sydney, 1991, facsimile, originally published by John Nichols, London, 1795), no page numbers given for introduction.

8   Lucy Broad, *A Woman's Wanderings the World Over* (Headley Brothers, London, nd [1909]), p. 12.
9   Paul Fussell (ed.), *The Norton Book of Travel* (W.W. Norton & Company, New York and London, 1987), p. 171.
10 Michael Pearson, 'Travellers, Journeys, Tourists: The Meanings of Journeys', in *Australian Cultural History*, no. 10, 1991, *Travellers, Journeys, Tourists*, p. 125.
11 Bruce Chatwin, *The Songlines* (Jonathan Cape, London, 1987), p. 5.
12 See extract in this book.

EDITOR'S
ACKNOWLEDGMENTS

I wish to acknowledge with gratitude the grants that I received for this project from the Literature Board of the Australia Council, the Commonwealth Government's arts funding and advisory body, and from Arts Victoria, a division of the Victorian Department of Arts, Sport and Tourism. I should also like to thank Olga Abrahams, Janet Bomford, Nicholas Bomford, Gary Boulter, Jude Bourguignon, Debra Burgess, Alexa Burnell, Roger Butler, Gillian Cardinal, Sonja Chalmers, David Collins, Geraldine Corridon, Des Cowley, Jill Davies, Andrew Demetriou, Jane Drury, Sue Ellison, Dr Robin Gerster, Frank Lyons, Una Lyons, Dr Michael McKernan, Jo McMillan, Sandra Nobes, Dr Ross McMullin, Neil McPhee, Professor Peter McPhee, Alan Mason, Guy Mirabella, Dr Carolyn Rasmussen, Maggie Richardson, Peter Rose, Garry Shead, Katherine Steward, Dr David Stockley, and Louise Sweetland for their much appreciated assistance. My greatest debt, as ever, is to the late Dr Lloyd Robson, for his support and encouragement during earlier stages of my career.

1

Dreamers

◆

JOSEPH HALL

(1574–1656)

English clergyman, bishop of Exeter (1627–41) and Norwich (1641–47). His dystopia, Mundus Alter et Idem, *satirising contemporary England, was first published anonymously in Latin in about 1605. An English translation by John Healey,* The Discovery of a New World, *appeared several years later.* Mercurius Britannicus, *the book's main character, spends thirty years in Terra Australis Incognita, an upside-down world made up of four regions, Tenter-belly, peopled by gluttons, Shee-landt, by women, Fooliana, by fools, and Theevingen, by thieves. Double-Sex Ile, described here, forms part of Shee-landt.*

'DOUBLE-SEX ILE'

Not farre from *Guaon*, the last Ile of the *Moluccaes*, betweene Cape *Hermose*, and Cape *Beach*, lies *Double-sex* Ile, much like vnto our Ile of *Man* on the coast of *Lancashire*. In this Ile nature hath so orderly disposed all things to one forme, that I could finde no one plant in all the soile but was of a double kinde; no tree, but beare two kindes of fruites or one fruite of two seuerall kindes & names: there was your *Peare-apple*, your *Cherry-damsen*, your *Date-alimond*, your *Chestnut-fylberd*, and a thousand of these conclusions of nature. Yea in so much that the very inhabitants of the whole Iland wore all their habits as indices of a coaptation of both sexes in one. Those that bare the most man about them, wore spurres, bootes and britches from the heeles to the hanshes: and bodies, rebatoes and periwigges from the crupper to the crown: and for those that were the better sharers in woman kind, they weare doublets to the rumpe and skirts to the remainder. Nay their very names bare notes of their perticipations of either side: There was *Mary-Philip*, *Peter-alice*, *Iane-andrew*, and *George-audry*, and many more that I remember not. All of their owne nation that haue not shewn themselues perfect both in begetting, & bringing forth, are made slaues to the rest: & when they take any that are but simply of one sexe, Lord what a coile they keepe about thē, shewing them as prodigies & monsters, as wee doe those that are borne double-headed, or other such deformed birthes. Their onely glory which they esteeme most, is that in their conceite they haue the perfection of nature amongst them alone, of all the world besides them. For seeing nature (say they) hath bestowed two hands, two feete, two eyes, two eares and two nosthrills to euery meaner perfect bodie, why should not the most excellent creature of all be perfect in two sexes also? And againe: the ancient sacrificers to *Cybele*, and the *Pathiques* of old *Rome* were faine to vse forced meanes for that which wee haue giuen vs by nature. Thus are they wont to protect their deformities: and truely you may obserue in them all, besides their shapes, both a mans wit, and a womans craft. They haue no Cattle in this countrie but *Mules* nor any wild beasts but *Hares*. They liue most vpon shelfish, for that is their best and most ordinary sustenance.

> *The Discovery of a New World*, trans. John Healey (*c.* 1609, first published in Latin *c.* 1605).

———

GABRIEL DE FOIGNY
(*c.* 1630–92)

Defrocked French priest who fled to Switzerland. His La Terre Australe Connue, *first published in Geneva in French in 1676, and later translated into many languages, was initially suppressed on grounds of alleged indecency. An English version translated and published by Dunton came out in London in 1693. After being shipwrecked, a French sailor named Jacques Sadeur lives in Australia (Dunton's Anglicisation of Terre Australe), a land located between South America and South Africa, for thirty-five years. He eventually tames a large bird and flies away on its back. Although Sadeur dies on the way home, his manuscript survives. In de Foigny's fantastic world, the people are hermaphrodites. Of particular interest are the Australian animals.*

ANIMALS IN TERRA INCOGNITA AUSTRALIS

There is none that are but never so little versed in the knowledge of Foreign Countries, but knows there are some peculiar Animals in them as different from those of other Regions, as the Lands that bear them. As for Example, *England* breeds no Wolves; nor can any Serpents live in *Ireland*, let them be transported from what other place soever. The Woods and Forests of the same Country are infested neither with

Worms nor Spiders. The Isles of the *Orcades* have no Flies; *Candia* has no venemous Creatures; and Poison it self, when transported into the Isles of the *Trinity*, loses its venome, and is no longer mortal when in those Countries.

It is certain, that the biggest Animals are not always the most hurtful; and those small Vermine, which the *Australians* can hardly tell how to conceive, though they have nothing rare in them but their life, yet do so much mischief in divers parts of *Europe*, that they often cause Famine, Plague, and other considerable Calamities, as might be proved by infinite number of experiences; for which reason I must needs reckon it to be one of the greatest happinesses of the *Australians*, that they are exempted from all manner of Insects. There is not to be found any venomous Beast in all their Countrey; and therefore they often lie down, and sleep on the bare ground, not only without any danger, but with great pleasure: And 'tis from thence they likewise gather a great part of those fair and delicious Fruits that there abound. They used for a long time, to keep three sorts of four-footed Beasts, and they still keep so many sorts in several parts: The least of them may be compared to our Apes, but their Faces are not hairy, their Eyes are even with their Head, their Ears are pretty long, and their Mouth and Nose are like a Man's. They have longer Claws than other Apes, with five Fingers each, with which they hold and carry what they will, with as much ease and dexterity as Men. They are very active, and turn their bodies into a great many postures, that require as much dexterity as agility: The love they have to Men is so great, that they will starve themselves, and die for grief, if they be separated from them. When they are in the presence of any Man, they never cease giving him all the divertisement they can, by their various Motions and Postures. They are now banish't out of a great many *Sezains*, because they were too troublesome, and particularly in their Religious Assembly in the *HAB*; for as they could not keep them from going thither without locking them up, and running the risk of finding them dead with pining, when they came home; so on the other side, they could not let them go thither, without exposing themselves to be continually disturbed at their devout Contemplations, and without a visible Profanation of so venerable a place. The Animals of the second sort, are something like our Hogs, save only that their Hair is as soft as Silk, and their Snouts are longer by half than those of Swine. They call them Hums; they have the instinct to work, and turn up the Earth in right lines, with as much, or more dexterity than our best Husbandmen, and have no need of any Leader, to guide them in beginning, continuing, and ending their furrows; yet they have destroyed them in most of the *Sezains*, because of the nastiness they fill all places with, and because they are useful but seven or eight days in a year; and that they must be kept shut up all the rest of the year, to prevent the dammages, and distastful annoyances they will otherwise cause.

The third sort of Animals are like our *Dromedaries*, save only that their Heads are more like those of Horses, their Backbones are sunk inwards their whole length, and the Birds that are raised above it, form a kind of Heart, whose point is turned downwards, in the upper hollow of which, two Men may easily lie down; these Beasts are called *Suefs*, and will carry with ease eight Men of that Country, that weigh at least as much as twelve *Europeans*, and they are used likewise for the carriage of heavy Burdens, and of such things as are most necessary in the Commerce of Life.

A New Discovery of Terra Incognita Australis, or the Southern World (1693, first published in French 1676).

———

JONATHAN SWIFT
(1667–1745)

Anglo-Irish poet and satirist, ordained in 1694 and dean of St Patrick's from 1713. In Swift's best-known work, Gulliver's Travels, first published anonymously in 1726, Lemuel Gulliver, a ship's surgeon, recounts his amazing experiences. At the beginning of the book, Gulliver tells of being shipwrecked on the island of Lilliput (which Swift uses to represent England), where the inhabitants are only six inches (15.24 cm) tall. Lilliput's exact location is debatable, but it appears to lie within present-day South Australia, somewhere 'perilously close to Adelaide', according to the novelist Murray Bail. Here Gulliver, who is said to be a cousin of the buccaneer William Dampier, describes his reception on Lilliput.

GULLIVER IS IMPRISONED ON LILLIPUT

It would not be proper, for some reasons, to trouble the reader with the particulars of our adventures in those seas: let it suffice to inform him, that in our passage from thence to the East Indies, we were driven by a violent storm to the north-west of Van Diemen's Land. By an observation, we found ourselves in the latitude of 30 degrees 2 minutes south. Twelve of our crew were dead by immoderate labour, and ill food, the rest were in a very weak condition. On the fifth of November, which was the beginning of summer in those parts, the weather being very hazy, the seamen spied a rock, within half a cable's length of the ship; but the wind was so strong, that we were driven directly upon it, and immediately split. Six of the crew, of whom I was one, having let down the boat into the sea, made a shift to get clear of the ship, and the rock. We rowed by my computation about three leagues, till we were able to work no longer, being already spent with labour while we were in the ship. We therefore trusted ourselves to the mercy of the waves, and in about half an hour the boat was overset by a sudden flurry from the north. What became of my companions in the boat, as well as of those who escaped on the rock, or were left in the vessel, I cannot tell; but conclude they were all lost. For my own part, I swam as Fortune directed me, and was pushed forward by wind and tide. I often let my legs drop, and could feel no bottom: but when I was almost gone, and able to struggle no longer, I found myself within my depth; and by this time the storm was much abated. The declivity was so small, that I walked near a mile before I got to the shore, which I conjectured was about eight o'clock in the evening. I then advanced forward near half a mile, but could not discover any sign of houses or inhabitants; at least I was in so weak a condition, that I did not observe them. I was extremely tired, and with that, and the heat of the weather, and about half a pint of brandy that I drank as I left the ship, I found myself much inclined to sleep. I lay down on the grass, which was very short and soft, where I slept sounder than ever I remember to have done in my life, and as I reckoned, above nine hours; for when I awaked, it was just daylight. I attempted to rise, but was not able to stir: for as I happened to lie on my back, I found my arms and legs were strongly fastened on each side to the ground; and my hair, which was long and thick, tied down in the same manner. I likewise felt several slender ligatures across my body, from my armpits to my thighs. I could only look upwards, the sun began to grow hot, and the light offended mine eyes. I heard a confused noise about me, but in the posture I lay, could see nothing except the sky. In a little time I felt something alive moving on my left leg, which advancing gently forward over my breast, came almost up to my chin; when bending mine eyes downwards as much as I could, I perceived it to be a human creature not six inches high, with a bow and arrow in his hands, and a quiver at his back. In the meantime, I felt at least forty more of the same kind (as I conjectured) following the first.

I was in the utmost astonishment, and roared so loud, that they all ran back in a fright; and some of them, as I was afterwards told, were hurt with the falls they got by leaping from my sides upon the ground. However, they soon returned, and one of them, who ventured so far as to get a full sight of my face, lifting up his hands and eyes by way of admiration, cried out in a shrill, but distinct voice, *Hekinah degul*; the others repeated the same words several times, but I then knew not what they meant. I lay all this while, as the reader may believe, in great uneasiness: at length, struggling to get loose, I had the fortune to break the strings, and wrench out the pegs that fastened my left arm to the ground; for, by lifting it up to my face, I discovered the methods they had taken to bind me; and, at the same time, with a violent pull, which gave me excessive pain, I a little loosened the strings that tied down my hair on the left side, so that I was just able to turn my head about two inches. But the creatures ran off a second time, before I could seize them; whereupon there was a great shout in a very shrill accent, and after it ceased, I heard one of them cry aloud, *Tolgo phonac*; when in an instant I felt above an hundred arrows discharged on my left hand, which pricked me like so many needles; and besides, they shot another flight into the air, as we do bombs in Europe, whereof many, I suppose, fell on my body (though I felt them not), and some on my face, which I immediately covered with my left hand. When this shower of arrows was over, I fell a groaning with grief and pain, and then striving again to get loose, they discharged another volley larger than the first, and some of them attempted with spears to stick me in the sides; but, by good luck, I had on me a buff jerkin, which they could not pierce. I thought it the most prudent method to lie still, and my design was to continue so till night, when, my left hand being already loose, I could easily free myself: and as for the inhabitants, I had reason to believe I might be a match for the greatest armies they could bring against me, if they were all of the same size with him that I saw. But Fortune disposed otherwise of me. When the people observed I was quiet, they discharged no more arrows: but, by the noise increasing, I knew their numbers were greater; and about four yards from me, over-against my right ear, I heard a knocking for above an hour, like people at work; when, turning my head that way, as well as the pegs and strings would permit me, I saw a stage erected about a foot and a half from the ground, capable of holding four of the inhabitants, with two or three ladders to mount it: from whence one of them, who seemed to be a person of quality, made me a long speech, whereof I understood not one syllable. But I should have mentioned, that before the principal person began his oration, he cried out three times *Langro dehul san* (these words and the former were afterwards repeated and explained to me): whereupon immediately about fifty of the inhabitants came, and cut the strings that fastened the left side of my head, which gave me the liberty of turning it to the right, and of observing the person and gesture of him who was to speak. He appeared to be of a middle age, and taller than any of the other three who attended him, whereof one was a page who held up his train, and seemed to be somewhat longer than my middle finger; the other two stood one on each side to support him. He acted every part of an orator, and I could observe many periods of threatenings, and others of promises, pity and kindness. I answered in a few words, but in the most submissive manner, lifting up my left hand and both mine eyes to the sun, as calling him for a witness; and being almost famished with hunger, having not eaten a morsel for some hours before I left the ship, I found the demands of nature so strong upon me, that I could not forbear showing my impatience (perhaps against the strict rules of decency) by putting my finger frequently on my mouth, to signify that I wanted food. The *Hurgo* (for so they call a great lord, as I afterwards learnt) understood me very well. He descended from the stage, and commanded that several ladders should be applied to my sides, on which above an hundred of the inhabitants mounted, and walked towards my mouth, laden with baskets full of meat, which had been provided and sent thither by the King's orders upon the first intelligence he received of me. I observed there was the flesh of several animals, but could not distinguish them by the taste. There were shoulders, legs and loins, shaped like those of mutton, and very well dressed, but smaller than the wings of a lark. I ate them by two or three at a mouthful, and took three loaves at a time, about the bigness of musket bullets. They supplied me as fast as they could, showing a thousand marks of wonder and astonishment at my bulk and appetite. I then made another sign that I wanted drink. They found by my eating that a small quantity would not suffice me; and being a most ingenious people, they slung up with great dexterity one of their largest hogsheads, then rolled it towards my hand, and beat out the top; I drank it off at a draught, which I might well do, for it hardly held half a pint, and tasted like a small wine of Burgundy, but much more delicious. They brought me a second hogshead, which I drank in the same manner, and made signs for more, but they had none to give me. When I had performed these wonders, they shouted for joy, and danced upon my breast, repeating several times as they did at first, *Hekinah degul.* They made me a sign that I should throw down the two hogsheads, but first warned the people below to stand out of the way, crying aloud, *Borach mivola*, and when they saw the vessels in the air, there was an universal shout of *Hekinah degul*. I confess I was often tempted, while they were passing backwards and forwards on my body, to seize forty or fifty of the first that came in my reach, and dash them against the ground. But the remembrance of what I had felt, which probably might not be the worst they could do, and the promise of honour I made them, for so I interpreted my submissive behaviour, soon drove out those imaginations. Besides, I now considered myself as bound by the laws of hospitality to a people who had treated me with so much expense and magnificence. However, in my thoughts I could not sufficiently wonder at the intrepidity of these diminutive mortals, who durst venture to mount and walk on my body, while one of my hands was at liberty, without trembling at the very sight of so prodigious a creature as I must appear to them. After some time, when they observed that I made no more demands for meat, there appeared before me a person of high rank from his Imperial Majesty. His Excellency having mounted on the small of my right leg, advanced forwards up to my face, with about a dozen of his retinue. And producing his credentials under the Signet Royal, which he applied close to mine eyes, spoke about ten minutes, without any signs of anger, but with a kind of determinate resolution; often pointing forwards, which, as I afterwards found, was towards the capital city, about half a mile distant, whither it was agreed by his Majesty in council that I must be conveyed. I answered in few words, but to no purpose, and made a sign with my hand that was loose, putting it to the other (but over his Excellency's head, for fear of hurting him or his train) and then to my own head and body, to signify that I desired my liberty. It appeared that he understood me well enough, for he shook his head by way of disapprobation, and held his hand in a posture to show that I must be carried as a prisoner. However, he made other signs to let me understand that I should have meat and drink enough, and very good treatment. Whereupon I once more thought of attempting to break my bonds, but again, when I felt the smart of their arrows upon my face and hands, which were all in blisters, and many of the darts still sticking in them, and observing likewise that the number of my enemies increased, I gave tokens to let them know that they might do with me what they pleased. Upon this, the *Hurgo* and his train withdrew with much civility and cheerful countenances. Soon after I heard a general shout, with frequent repetitions of the words, *Peplom selan*, and I felt great numbers of the people on my left side relaxing the cords to such a degree, that I was able to turn upon my right, and to ease myself with making water; which I very plentifully did, to the great astonishment of the people, who conjecturing by my motions what I was going to do, immediately opened to the right and left on that side, to avoid the torrent which fell with such noise and violence from me. But before this, they had daubed my face and both my hands with a sort of ointment very pleasant to the smell, which in a few minutes removed all the smart of their arrows. These circumstances, added to the refreshment I had received by their victuals and drink, which were very nourishing, disposed me to sleep. I slept about eight hours, as I was afterwards assured; and it was no wonder, for the physicians, by the Emperor's order, had mingled a sleepy potion in the hogsheads of wine.

Gulliver's Travels (1726).

———

ANONYMOUS

Purporting to be the journal of a member of the French expedition led by Jean-François Galaup de La Pérouse, stolen in Botany Bay in 1788, shortly before La Pérouse's ships disappeared, Fragmens du Dernier Voyage de La Pérouse *was first published in French in 1797. For almost two centuries readers, including the historian Ernest Scott, mistakenly believed it to be genuine. In the following extract, taken from John Dunmore's 1987 translation, the unknown author, who was inspired by classical and Rousseauan ideas, describes some of the customs of the inhabitants of the mysterious Blue Island.*

FESTIVAL ON BLUE ISLAND

La Peyrouse went ashore. It was his intention to meet once more the young person towards whom the senior elder showed such respect and such love. I went with him, together with four cadets and a few officers. Chance revealed to us what we would never have learned and what seemed impossible to discover.

It seemed certain, from some very plausible conjectures, that they celebrate only once a year the three-day festival we witnessed: it unveiled for us all the mysteries of this island. At the request of our good friends, expressed by gestures, we attended the fête they were preparing. This is what happened.

It took place near the shore. Scattered groups of natives were walking about, armed with clubs, their hair unkempt, and wearing fierce expressions of such realism that we were momentarily struck by fear and were reassured only by our numbers and our weapons.

They performed dances on the shores as wild as those of the natives of New Zealand; they crouched in a circle and mimed some strange gluttony: they devoured raw meat and uncooked herbs; they split into two groups and acted a bloody battle, and the women whose manners had been so gentle, covered in mosses and leaves, indulged in every kind of disorder.

Suddenly all this agitation ceased. A longboat in the European style appeared in the distance; curiosity broke up the groups of savages; the object grew larger. Imagine our surprise: we saw four individuals in European clothes. There was a woman among them: she was holding her arms out towards the shore in an attitude of supplication. Shouts of rage resounded; stones and arrows were flung towards the boat. The illusion was so complete that we were about to march to the rescue of the people in the boat when the good elders stopped us with a laugh: we soon realised that a play was being enacted.

They undoubtedly keep for these annual celebrations the clothes worn by the actors in the boat: they are obviously those the French wore when they landed on the island.

The insults and the angry gestures ceased when the natives saw the woman; a few chiefs stepped forward onto the shoreline and forbade any hostile action: silence reigned throughout the assembly and the sound of an oboe was heard from the boat. Although it was absurdly distorted we could nevertheless make out a certain passage which resembled our old music, Rameau's march of the natives.

The actors on the shore pretended to be moved; they threw down their arms and welcomed with expressions of admiration and joy the strangers who were now landing.

They were led to a wood; the musician played some new tunes: everything seemed to soften around him. Fruits were brought, huts were constructed with leaves and branches. The first act of this play ended with daylight.

We returned to the shore the next day. A mass of objects, no doubt from the wrecked ship, had been ferried during the night to a rock out at sea; they were brought to the shore and the natives re-enacted scenes of their early curiosity: axes, adzes, saws, wheelbarrows, iron, etc., etc., were submitted to their gaze. One cannot conceive how true to life their acting was and the skill of their impersonations. Soon the three

Europeans taught them the use of these tools: the art of building solid and attractive houses and of clothing oneself, dancing, music, and a more polished, more civilised way of life. All the actors then put on the clothes they wore when we first arrived and brought the second day to a close with singing and dancing.

The pageant came to an end on the following day with all the skills of gardening and agriculture, and with some kind of deification in which they prostrated themselves at the feet of the Europeans who then, breaking a lance—symbol of kingship—embraced the civilised natives and presented to them as chiefs twenty-four elderly men holding white sticks. The tools of the past, the heaps of weapons and clubs, the containers of times of ignorance, their rough and dirty clothing, everything was torn, broken up and burned on a pyre.

The three-day festival finally came to an end with a sorrowful and lugubrious procession to the cemetery of their benefactors; and these good people howled and wept tears of love, despair and gratitude over their friends' remains.

It must be said that there was little in the way of art in this simple play, but the pantomime was admirable, and the mood of the final act made us quietly shed tears.

Happy country! Happy people! They are at the stage of learning, of attaining a civilisation made for mankind. This is the condition that is best for us, if we give up all our works of fiction, our follies, our pomp, our systems, our dreaming. La Peyrouse has said it a hundred times: if it were not for what my honour requires, for the account of my stewardship which I must give to the King who entrusted these ships to my care, I would leave our Europe for ever to live in this true abode of happiness and peace. One day maybe …

Fragmens du Dernier Voyage de La Pérouse, trans. John Dunmore (1987, first published in French 1797).

RICHARD WHATELY

(1787–1863)

Anglican archbishop of Dublin from 1831 until his death and vocal opponent of transportation during the 1830s. He is considered to have been responsible for writing a utopia entitled Account of an Expedition to the Interior of New Holland, *supposedly an explorer's journal edited by a Lady Mary Fox, which was first published in 1837. The explorer and his compan-*

ions leave Bathurst in August 1835 and travel to central Australia, where
they find a 'civilized' nation of between three and four million people of
European, mostly English, descent. The nation, remarkably, has had no con-
tact with other 'civilized' people for almost three centuries. Much confusion
arises over the meaning of the word 'ball'.

'PLAYING AT BEING SAVAGES'

While the travellers were at Bath,—which is a city rather distinguished,
like its namesake in England and in Germany, for gaiety, as being a place
of resort to strangers on account of the mineral waters,—they were
invited to several public entertainments of various kinds, and of different degrees of solemnity and splendour. One lady with whom, among
others, they were conversing on the subject of one of these which they
were about to attend, on being asked, among other inquiries, whether a
ball possessed as much attraction for young people as, they told her, it
does in Europe, replied in the affirmative; though, for her own part, she
said, she liked archery better; but different young people, said she, differ, you know, in their tastes in respect of amusements.

When the gay party had been assembled,—which was on a lawn of
considerable extent, partially shaded with some fine mimosa and eucalyptus (gum-tree), under whose shade tents were erected,—the travellers witnessed with much interest the several diversions that were
going on; and, among others, their notice was called by the lady with
whom they had been conversing the day before to several 'games of
ball' of various kinds that were going on; some played by gentlemen
alone, some by ladies, and some by both together; and many of them
bearing more or less resemblance to the English games of cricket,
bowls, trap-ball, tennis, billiards, &c. as well as to others which are
common enough among children in England, but quite unknown
among adults.

The travellers laughed heartily (as the ladies did also, on receiving
an explanation) at the mutual mistake they had made about balls: but,
on making more particular inquiries about dancing, they learned that
this was an amusement confined to children; scarcely any ever joining
in that sport except those under thirteen or fourteen years old, and any
lively and good-humoured friend of the children, who joined their
game for their amusement. The sport was in fact 'playing at being savages,' the dances consisting in a ludicrous imitation of those of the aborigines. These, it is well known, are much given to dancing, in which
they display considerable ingenuity as well as agility and good ear; and

their dances are not merely a recreation, but are also mixed up with their most important institutions and transactions, being performed with much solemnity at their 'corrobories,' or grand meetings, for the purpose of deliberating on affairs of state, and performing certain superstitious rites of divination.

A group of romping boys and girls, who were at play in one corner of the field, were accordingly requested to exhibit to the strangers the spectacle of a dance; and some of the most forward and lively of the boys entered into the proposal with much glee. Two of the party took on themselves, by general consent, the arrangement and direction of the whole, and seemed to officiate as masters of the ceremonies, or, as they called themselves, 'Corrobory chiefs.' They were, it seems, visitors from one of the back-settlements, and had had frequent opportunities of witnessing the native dances. The sport partook somewhat of the nature of a masquerade; some whimsical changes being made in the costume of the dancers, in order to give the livelier representation of the strange originals. Much merriment took place, and many curious feats of grotesque agility were displayed, to the great diversion both of the juvenile performers and the bystanders. This sport was followed by the throwing of the spear, after the manner of the natives; an art in which many of the Southlanders are very expert, especially those who live on the margins of the lakes, where the striking of fish is a favourite diversion, as the salmon-spearing is in some parts of Scotland. The throwing of the spear at a mark, however, and also archery, are games not confined, as dancing is, to children.

The Southlanders expressed surprise that adult Europeans, even of the higher classes, should retain the amusement of dancing, 'like the savages;' an amusement which seemed to them, from habit, as childish as many of their sports, on the other hand, had appeared to their visitors. Both parties were somewhat at a loss to explain to each other the grounds of their respective notions as to what was or was not puerile. 'There is no disputing,' said one of the most intelligent of their hosts, 'about tastes; but in many points, I believe, ours are to be accounted for by that early and deep-seated association in our minds, which you have in many instances noticed, between certain practices or habits and savage life. You have remarked several times how frequently the phrase is in our mouths, that to do so and so is "like the savages;" and this may perhaps account for the ridiculous appearance which, as you perceive, one of your balls, as you call them, would have in our eyes.'

Lady Mary Fox (ed.), *Account of an Expedition to the Interior of New Holland* (1837).

JULES VERNE
(1828–1905)

French novelist. Sometimes known as the 'father of science fiction', Verne combined adventure and science in his very popular works. In Twenty Thousand Leagues Under the Sea, *first published in 1869, he tells the tale of Professor Pierre Aronnax, a professor of natural history, his servant Conseil, and a Canadian harpooner named Ned Land, who set out to hunt down a frightening sea monster, which proves to be a huge submarine, the* Nautilus. *The commander of the latter, the strange Captain Nemo, captures the trio and takes them on an extraordinary voyage, part of which is described in the following extract.*

'TORRES STRAITS'

During the night of the 27th or 28th of December, the *Nautilus* left the shores of Vanikoro with great speed. Her course was south-westerly, and in three days she had gone over the 750 leagues that separated it from La Perouse's group and the south-east point of Papua.

Early on the 1st of January 1868, Conseil joined me on the platform.

'Master, will you permit me to wish you a happy new year?'

'What! Conseil; exactly as if I was at Paris in my study at the Jardin des Plantes? Well, I accept your good wishes, and thank you for them. Only, I will ask you what you mean by a "Happy new year," under our circumstances? Do you mean the year that will bring us to the end of our imprisonment, or the year that sees us continue this strange voyage?'

'Really, I do not know how to answer, master. We are sure to see curious things, and for the last two months we have not had time for ennui. The last marvel is always the most astonishing; and if we continue this progression, I do not know how it will end. It is my opinion that we shall never again see the like. I think, then, with no offence to master, that a happy year would be one in which we could see everything.'

On January 2, we had made 11 340 miles, or 5250 French leagues, since our starting-point in the Japan Seas. Before the ship's head stretched the dangerous shores of the coral sea, on the north-east coast of

Australia. Our boat lay along some miles from the redoubtable bank on which Cook's vessel was lost, June 10, 1770. The boat in which Cook was struck on a rock, and if it did not sink, it was owing to a piece of the coral that was broken by the shock, and fixed itself in the broken keel.

I had wished to visit the reef, 360 leagues long, against which the sea, always rough, broke with great violence, with a noise like thunder. But just then the inclined planes drew the *Nautilus* down to a great depth, and I could see nothing of the high coral walls. I had to content myself with the different specimens of fish brought up by the nets. I remarked, among others, some germons, a species of mackerel as large as a tunny, with bluish sides, and striped with transverse bands, that disappear with the animal's life. These fish followed us in shoals, and furnished us with very delicate food. We took also a large number of giltheads, about one and a half inches long, tasting like dorys; and flying pyrapeds like submarine swallows, which, in dark nights, light alternately the air and water with their phosphorescent light. Among the molluscs and zoophytes, I found in the meshes of the net several species of alcyonarians, echini, hammers, spurs, dials, cerites, and hyalleæ. The flora was represented by beautiful floating sea-weeds, laminariæ, and macrocystes, impregnated with the mucilage that transudes through their pores; and among which I gathered an admirable *Nemastoma Geliniarois,* that was classed among the natural curiosities of the museum.

Two days after crossing the coral sea, January 4, we sighted the Papuan coasts. On this occasion, Captain Nemo informed me that his intention was to get into the Indian Ocean by the Strait of Torres. His communication ended there.

The Torres Straits are nearly thirty-four leagues wide; but they are obstructed by an innumerable quantity of islands, islets, breakers, and rocks, that make its navigation almost impracticable; so that Captain Nemo took all needful precautions to cross them. The *Nautilus*, floating betwixt wind and water, went at a moderate pace. Her screw, like a cetacean's tail, beat the waves slowly.

Profiting by this, I and my two companions went up on to the deserted platform. Before us was the steersman's cage, and I expected that Captain Nemo was there directing the course of the *Nautilus*. I had before me the excellent charts of the Strait of Torres made out by the hydrographical engineer Vincendon Dumoulin. These and Captain King's are the best charts that clear the intricacies of this strait, and I consulted them attentively. Round the *Nautilus* the sea dashed furiously. The course of the waves, that went from south-east to north-west at the rate of two and a half miles, broke on the coral that showed itself here and there.

'This is a bad sea!' remarked Ned Land.

'Detestable indeed, and one that does not suit a boat like the *Nautilus*.'

'The captain must be very sure of his route, for I see there pieces of coral that would do for its keel if it only touched them slightly.'

Indeed the situation was dangerous, but the *Nautilus* seemed to slide like magic off these rocks. It did not follow the routes of the *Astrolabe* and the *Zélée* exactly, for they proved fatal to Dumont d'Urville. It bore more northwards, coasted the Island of Murray, and came back to the south-west towards Cumberland Passage. I thought it was going to pass it by, when, going back to north-west, it went through a large quantity of islands and islets little known, towards the Island Sound and Canal Mauvais.

I wondered if Captain Nemo, foolishly imprudent, would steer his vessel into that pass where Dumont d'Urville's two corvettes touched; when, swerving again, and cutting straight through to the west, he steered for the Island of Gilboa.

It was then three in the afternoon. The tide began to recede, being quite full. The *Nautilus* approached the island, that I still saw, with its remarkable border of screw-pines. He stood off it at about two miles distant. Suddenly a shock overthrew me. The *Nautilus* just touched a rock, and stayed immovable, lying lightly to port side.

When I rose, I perceived Captain Nemo and his lieutenant on the platform. They were examining the situation of the vessel, and exchanging words in their incomprehensible dialect.

She was situated thus:—Two miles, on the starboard side, appeared Gilboa, stretching from north to west like an immense arm. Towards the south and east some coral showed itself, left by the ebb. We had run aground, and in one of those seas where the tides are middling,—a sorry matter for the floating of the *Nautilus*. However, the vessel had not suffered, for her keel was solidly joined. But if she could neither glide off nor move, she ran the risk of being for ever fastened to these rocks, and then Captain Nemo's submarine vessel would be done for.

I was reflecting thus, when the Captain, cool and calm, always master of himself, approached me.

'An accident?' I asked.

'No; an incident.'

'But an incident that will oblige you perhaps to become an inhabitant of this land from which you flee?'

Captain Nemo looked at me curiously, and made a negative gesture, as much as to say that nothing would force him to set foot on *terra firma* again. Then he said—

'Besides, M. Aronnax, the *Nautilus* is not lost; it will carry you yet into the midst of the marvels of the ocean. Our voyage is only begun, and I do not wish to be deprived so soon of the honour of your company.'

'However, Captain Nemo,' I replied, without noticing the ironical turn of his phrase, 'the *Nautilus* ran aground in open sea. Now the tides are not strong in the Pacific; and if you cannot lighten the *Nautilus*, I do not see how it will be reinflated.'

'The tides are not strong in the Pacific: you are right there, Professor; but in Torres Straits, one finds still a difference of a yard and a half between the level of high and low seas. To-day is January 4, and in five days the moon will be full. Now, I shall be very much astonished if that complaisant satellite does not raise these masses of water sufficiently, and render me a service that I should be indebted to her for.'

Having said this, Captain Nemo, followed by his lieutenant, re-descended to the interior of the *Nautilus*. As to the vessel, it moved not, and was immovable, as if the coralline polypi had already walled it up with their indestructible cement.

'Well, sir?' said Ned Land, who came up to me after the departure of the Captain.

'Well, friend Ned, we will wait patiently for the tide on the 9th instant; for it appears that the moon will have the goodness to put it off again.'

'Really?'

'Really.'

'And this Captain is not going to cast anchor at all, since the tide will suffice?' said Conseil simply.

The Canadian looked at Conseil, then shrugged his shoulders.

'Sir, you may believe me when I tell you that this piece of iron will navigate neither on nor under the sea again; it is only fit to be sold for its weight. I think, therefore, that the time has come to part company with Captain Nemo.'

'Friend Ned, I do not despair of this stout *Nautilus*, as you do; and in four days we shall know what to hold to on the Pacific tides. Besides, flight might be possible if we were in sight of the English or Provençal coasts; but on the Papuan shores, it is another thing; and it will be time enough to come to that extremity if the *Nautilus* does not recover itself again, which I look upon as a grave event.'

'But do they know, at least, how to act circumspectly? There is an island; on that island there are trees; under those trees, terrestrial animals, bearers of cutlets and roast-beef, to which I would willingly give a trial.'

'In this, friend Ned is right,' said Conseil, 'and I agree with him. Could not master obtain permission from his friend Captain Nemo to put us on land, if only so as not to lose the habit of treading on the solid parts of our planet?'

'I can ask him, but he will refuse.'

'Will master risk it?' asked Conseil, 'and we shall know how to rely upon the Captain's amiability.'

To my great surprise Captain Nemo gave me the permission I asked for, and he gave it very agreeably, without even exacting from me a promise to return to the vessel; but flight across New Guinea might be very perilous, and I should not have counselled Ned Land to attempt it. Better to be a prisoner on board the *Nautilus* than to fall into the hands of the natives.

At eight o'clock, armed with guns and hatchets, we got off the *Nautilus*. The sea was pretty calm; a slight breeze blew on land. Conseil and I rowing, we sped along quickly, and Ned steered in the straight passage that the breakers left between them. The boat was well handled, and moved rapidly.

Ned Land could not restrain his joy. He was like a prisoner that had escaped from prison, and knew not that it was necessary to re-enter it.

'Meat! We are going to eat some meat; and what meat!' he replied. 'Real game! no, bread, indeed.'

'I do not say that fish is not good; we must not abuse it; but a piece of fresh venison, grilled on live coals, will agreeably vary our ordinary course.'

'Gourmand!' said Conseil, 'he makes my mouth water.'

'It remains to be seen,' I said, 'if these forests are full of game, and if the game is not such as will hunt the hunter himself.'

'Well said, M. Aronnax,' replied the Canadian, whose teeth seemed sharpened like the edge of a hatchet; 'but I will eat tiger—loin of tiger—if there is no other quadruped on this island.'

'Friend Ned is uneasy about it,' said Conseil.

'Whatever it may be,' continued Ned Land, 'every animal with four paws without feathers, or with two paws without feathers, will be saluted by my first shot.'

'Very well! Master Land's imprudences are beginning.'

'Never fear, M. Aronnax,' replied the Canadian; 'I do not want twenty-five minutes to offer you a dish of my sort.'

At half-past eight the *Nautilus* boat ran softly aground, on a heavy sand, after having happily passed the coral reef that surrounds the Island of Gilboa.

Twenty Thousand Leagues Under the Sea (1869).

———

SAMUEL BUTLER
(1835–1902)

English writer. Cambridge-educated Butler bred sheep on the South Island of New Zealand from 1859 to 1864, before returning to England. The narrator of Butler's satirical romance, Erewhon, *first published in 1872, crosses an unexplored mountain range in a colony that is based upon New Zealand and discovers the society of Erewhon (an anagram of nowhere). Later he attempts to escape with his native love Arowhena in a balloon of his own construction. Butler also wrote a sequel,* Erewhon Revisited *(1901).*

ESCAPE FROM EREWHON

I sat quietly, and awaited the hour fixed for my departure—quiet outwardly, but inwardly I was in an agony of suspense lest Arowhena's absence should be discovered before the arrival of the King and Queen, who were to witness my ascent. They were not due yet for another two hours, and during this time a hundred things might happen, any one of which would undo me.

At last the balloon was full; the pipe which had filled it was removed, the escape of the gas having been first carefully precluded. Nothing remained to hinder the balloon from ascending but the hands and weights of those who were holding on to it with ropes. I strained my eyes for the coming of the King and Queen, but could see no sign of their approach. I looked in the direction of Mr Nosnibor's house—there was nothing to indicate disturbance, but it was not yet breakfast time. The crowd began to gather; they were aware that I was under the displeasure of the court, but I could detect no signs of my being unpopular. On the contrary, I received many kindly expressions of regard and encouragement, with good wishes as to the result of my journey.

I was speaking to one gentleman of my acquaintance, and telling him the substance of what I intended to do when I had got into the presence of the air god (what he thought of me I cannot guess, for I am sure that he did not believe in the objective existence of the air god, nor that I myself believed in it), when I became aware of a small crowd of people running as fast as they could from Mr Nosnibor's house towards the Queen's workshops. For the moment my pulse ceased beating, and then, knowing that the time had come when I must either do or die, I called vehemently to those who were holding the ropes (some thirty men) to let go at once, and made gestures signifying danger, and that there would be mischief if they held on longer. Many obeyed; the rest were too weak to hold on to the ropes, and were forced to let them go. On this the balloon bounded suddenly upwards, but my own feeling was that the earth had dropped off from me, and was sinking fast into the open space beneath.

This happened at the very moment that the attention of the crowd was divided, the one half paying heed to the eager gestures of those coming from Mr Nosnibor's house, and the other to the exclamations from myself. A minute more and Arowhena would doubtless have been discovered, but before that minute was over, I was at such a height above the city that nothing could harm me, and every second both the town and the crowd became smaller and more confused. In an incredibly short time, I could see little but a vast wall of blue plains rising up against me, towards whichever side I looked.

At first, the balloon mounted vertically upwards, but after about five minutes, when we had already attained a very great elevation, I fancied that the objects on the plain beneath began to move from under me. I did not feel so much as a breath of wind, and could not suppose that the balloon itself was travelling. I was, therefore, wondering what this strange movement of fixed objects could mean, when it struck me that people in a balloon do not feel the wind inasmuch as they travel with it and offer it no resistance. Then I was happy in thinking that I must now have reached the invariable trade wind of the upper air, and that I should be very possibly wafted for hundreds or even thousands of miles, far from Erewhon and the Erewhonians.

Already I had removed the wrappings and freed Arowhena; but I soon covered her up with them again, for it was already very cold, and she was half stupefied with the strangeness of her position.

And now began a time, dream-like and delirious, of which I do not suppose that I shall ever recover a distinct recollection. Some things I can recall—as that we were ere long enveloped in vapour which froze upon my moustache and whiskers; then comes a memory of sitting for hours and hours in a thick fog, hearing no sound but my own breathing and Arowhena's (for we hardly spoke) and seeing no sight but the car beneath us and beside us, and the dark balloon above.

Perhaps the most painful feeling when the earth was hidden was that the balloon was motionless, though our only hope lay in our going forward with an extreme of speed. From time to time through a rift in the clouds I caught a glimpse of earth, and was thankful to perceive that we must be flying forward faster than in an express train; but no sooner was the rift closed than the old conviction of our being stationary returned in full force, and was not to be reasoned with; there was another feeling also which was nearly as bad; for as a child that fears it has gone blind in a long tunnel if there is no light, so ere the earth had been many minutes hidden, I became half frightened lest we might not have broken away from it clean and for ever. Now and again, I ate and gave food to Arowhena, but by guess-work as regards time. Then came darkness, a dreadful dreary time, without even the moon to cheer us.

With dawn the scene was changed; the clouds were gone and morning stars were shining; the rising of the splendid sun remains still impressed upon me as the most glorious that I have ever seen; beneath us there was an embossed chain of mountains with snow fresh fallen upon them; but we were far above them; we both of us felt our breathing seriously affected, but I would not allow the balloon to descend a single inch, not knowing for how long we might not need all the buoyancy which we could command; indeed I was thankful to find that after nearly four-and-twenty hours, we were still at so great a height above the earth.

In a couple of hours we had passed the ranges, which must have been some hundred and fifty miles across, and again I saw a tract of level plain extending far away to the horizon. I knew not where we were, and dared not descend, lest I should waste the power of the balloon, but I was half hopeful that we might be above the country from which I had originally started. I looked anxiously for any sign by which I could recognize it, but could see nothing, and feared that we might be above some distant part of Erewhon, or a country inhabited by savages. While I was still in doubt, the balloon was again wrapped in clouds, and we were left to blank space and to conjectures.

The weary time dragged on. How I longed for my unhappy watch! I felt as though not even time was moving, so dumb and spellbound were our surroundings. Sometimes I would feel my pulse, and count its beats for half an hour together; anything to mark the time—to prove that it was there, and to assure myself that we were within the blessed range of its influence, and not gone adrift into the timelessness of eternity.

I had been doing this for the twentieth or thirtieth time, and had fallen into a light sleep; I dreamed wildly of a journey in an express train, and of arriving at a railway station where the air was full of the sound of locomotive engines blowing off steam with a horrible and tremendous hissing; I woke frightened and uneasy, but the hissing and crashing noises pursued me now that I was awake, and forced me to own that they were real. What they were I knew not, but they grew gradually fainter and fainter, and after a time were lost. In a few hours the clouds broke, and I saw beneath me that which made the chilled blood run colder in my veins. I saw the sea, and nothing but the sea; in the main black, but flecked with white heads of storm-tossed, angry waves.

Arowhena was sleeping quietly at the bottom of the car, and as I looked at her sweet and saintly beauty, I groaned, and cursed myself for the misery into which I had brought her; but there was nothing for it now.

I sat and waited for the worst, and presently I saw signs as though that worst were soon to be at hand, for the balloon had begun to sink. On first seeing the sea I had been impressed with the idea that we must have been falling, but now there could be no mistake, we were sinking, and that fast. I threw out a bag of ballast, and for a time we rose again, but in the course of a few hours the sinking recommenced, and I threw out another bag.

Then the battle commenced in earnest. It lasted all that afternoon and through the night until the following evening. I had seen never a sail nor a sign of a sail, though I had half blinded myself with straining my eyes incessantly in every direction; we had parted with everything but the clothes which we had upon our backs; food and water were gone, all thrown out to the wheeling albatrosses, in order to save us a few hours or even minutes from the sea. I did not throw away the books till we were within a few feet of the water, and clung to my manuscripts to the very last. Hope there seemed none whatever—yet, strangely enough we were neither of us utterly hopeless, and even when the evil that we dreaded was upon us, and that which we greatly feared had come, we sat in the car of the balloon with the waters up to our middle, and still smiled with a ghastly hopefulness to one another.

Erewhon (1901 edition, first published 1872).

2

Sailors

♦

FRANÇOIS PELSAERT

(c. 1591–1630)

Dutch East India Company officer. Sailing from Holland for Batavia (present-day Jakarta) with more than 300 soldiers, crew, and passengers on board, the Batavia, *under Pelsaert's command, struck a reef off the Houtman Abrolhos (about 75 kilometres from present-day Geraldton, Western Australia) in June 1629. Some of those on board drowned, but many reached nearby islands. While Pelsaert and some others sailed an open boat to Batavia for help, mutiny broke out among the remaining survivors on the islands, with great loss of life. After Pelsaert's return, seven of the mutineers were hanged and two were marooned on the Australian mainland. Others were later hanged at Batavia. Jan Jansz's account of Pelsaert's journal was first published in Dutch as* Ongeluckige Voyagie van't Schip Batavia *in 1647. Translated into English by Willem Siebenhaar, it appeared in the* Western Mail *as 'The Abrolhos Tragedy' in 1897. Before departing from the wreck area for Batavia in search of help, Pelsaert looked for water.*

EXPLORING THE MAINLAND (1629)

Resolution

'Since, on all the islands and cliffs round about our foundered ship "Batavia", there is no freshwater to be found, in order to feed and keep the people who are saved, therefore the Commodore has earnestly requested and proposed that an expedition should be made to the main southland to see whether it is God's gracious will that fresh water shall be found, of which so much may be taken to the people that they shall be certain of having enough provision for a considerable time; that then, meanwhile, someone shall be told off to go to Batavia, in order to let the Lord-General and his councillors know of our disaster and to ask him for early assistance. To which we the undersigned have all voluntarily consented, since necessity forces us thereto, and since, if we acted otherwise, we could not answer for our conduct before God and the high authorities. Therefore, we have unanimously agreed and resolved to try our utmost and do our duty and to assist our poor brethren in their great need. In certain knowledge of the truth we have signed this with our own hand, and have all of us sworn to it on the 8th of June, 1629', was signed—

François Pelsaert
Claes Gerritsz
Jacob Jansz Hoioogh
Claes Jansz Dor
Adriaen Jacobsz
Hans Jacobsz Binder
Jan Evertsz
Claes Willemsz Graeft
Michael Claesz

Sail for the mainland

Thereupon they commenced their voyage in the name of the Lord, and sailed into the open. In the afternoon they were in latitude 28 deg. 13 min. and shortly afterwards sighted the mainland, probably-about six miles north by west of their foundered ship, the wind blowing from the west. They were there in about 28 or 30 fathoms of water, wherefore in the evening they turned away from the land, but went near it again about midnight.

On the morning of the 9th they were still about three miles from the shore, the wind, with some rain, being mostly north-west. They guessed that during these 24 hours they had made from four to five miles in a north-westerly direction. The shore in these parts stretches mostly north-west and south-east; a bare and rocky coast, without trees, about as high as at Dover, in England. They saw an inlet and some low, sandy dunes, which they thought they could approach; but, coming close, they found that near the beach the breakers were very rough and that the sea rolled high on the land, so that they could not very well risk the landing; since the wind rose more and more.

In peril through the night

On the 10th they had to move about for a period of 24 hours on account of the strong wind and storm, which blew harder and harder from the nor-west, so that they were obliged to let go the sloop, which they had taken with them, and even to throw overboard some of their bread and other things that were in the way, as they could not otherwise bale out the water. In the night they were still in greater danger of sinking on account of the strong wind and the high seas. They had no means of keeping off the shore. They could carry no sail. They were at the mercy of the sea. That night a steady rain poured down, and they hoped that the people on the islands might also have some of it, and provide themselves with water.

On the 11th, it became calmer, and the wind turned to the west-south-west. They therefore turned northward, but the sea was just as rough and high.

On the 12th, at noon, the weather steadied down and cleared up. They were then at a latitude of 27 deg. They kept close to the shore, the wind being south-east, but they had no opportunity of nearing the land with the boat, for the breakers were too strong and the coast too steep and jagged, without any foreland or inlet, as is usually found on other coasts, so that it seemed to them, a bare and cursed country, devoid of green or grass.

On the 13th, at noon, they were at a latitude of 25 deg. 10 min. They found then that they had drifted north a good deal, and had doubled the cape, keeping mostly northward during these 24 hours, as the coast now stretched north-north-east and south-south-west. The rocks were of redstone, a good deal battered and broken. There was no foreland. These rocks were all along of very much the same height, and made landing impossible on account of the breakers and high seas.

On the 14th, in the morning, there was a gentle breeze, but during the day a calm set in. At noon they were in latitude 24 degs., keeping north with an east wind. The current still took them every day much round the north, greatly against their wish, for with but little sail they were close to the shore.

They see smoke on the shore

In the afternoon, seeing inland some smoke, they rowed thither, hoping to find an opportunity of landing. They were quite rejoiced, for they imagined that where there were people there would also be fresh water. Having reached the shore, they found the ground to be a steep and rough incline; stony and rocky, against which the breakers beat violently, so that they saw no means of landing. It made them very dejected, for they feared that they would have to depart without landing. At last six men, trusting themselves to their swimming powers jumped overboard, and reached the shore with great difficulty and peril, while the boat remained at anchor outside the breakers in 25 fathoms of water. The swimmers having reached the shore, looked the whole day for fresh water everywhere, till in the evening they became convinced that their search was vain.

They find people

They then happened upon four people, who were creeping towards them on their hands and feet. When one man, coming out of a hollow upon a height, suddenly approached them they leaped to their feet and fled full speed, which was distinctly observed by those in the boat. They were black savages, quite naked, leaving themselves uncovered like animals.

No fresh water

As those on the shore had spent the whole day without finding water, they swam aboard again towards evening being all a good deal hurt and bruised, since the breakers had dashed them roughly against the rocks. Then getting ready and lifting the grappling iron they started in search of a better opportunity, sailing along the coast all night with but little sail, and keeping outside the breakers.

On the morning of the 15th, they came to a point where a large reef extended at about a mile from the coast, and, so it seemed, another reef along the shore, so that they tried their best to steer between the two, for the water there appeared to be calm and smooth. But they did not find an entrance until the afternoon, when they saw an opening where there were no breakers. But it was very dangerous, very stony, and often not holding two feet of water. The shore here had a foreland of dunes about a mile broad, before the higher land was reached.

At last they find some

When they had gone ashore they commenced to dig holes in the said foreland, but found nothing except salt water. Some of them therefore went higher up and fortunately found some small hollows in a cliff, full of fresh water that the rain had left there. They quenched their great thirst greedily, for they had almost succumbed. Since they had left the ship they had been without wine or other drink, except a daily allowance of one or two cups of water. They also collected a fair provision, about 80 cans of water, remaining there the whole night. It seemed that the blacks had been there just before, for they found the bones of crabs and the ashes of the fire.

On the 16th, as soon as it was light, they resolved to go further inland, hoping to find more such hollows with fresh water in the mountains. But their search was vain, for they found that there had not been any rain in the mountains for a long time; nor was there any appearance of running water, for behind the mountain chain the country was flat again; bearing neither trees nor vegetation, nor grass, and being everywhere covered with high ant hills built of earth, which in the distance were not unlike Indian huts.

Great Ant Hills and Multitudes of Flies

There were also such multitudes of flies that one could not keep them out of one's mouth and eyes. They next saw eight black people, each carrying a stick in his hand. These approached them to a musket-shot's distance, but when they saw our people coming towards them they took to their heels, and would neither speak nor stop.

Jacob Kemmessensz River

Seeing that there was no chance of obtaining more water they resolved towards noon to leave and, setting sail, they passed through another opening of the aforesaid reef a little more to the north. They were then in latitude 22 degrees 17 minutes, and imagined they were approaching the river of Jacob Kemmessensz, but the wind ran to the north-east and they could not keep to the shore. They were obliged to resolve on trying to continue their voyage to Batavia as soon as possible, with God's help, in order to inform the worthy Governor and his councillors of their disaster, and to ask them for immediate assistance to rescue those who were left behind. For already they had sailed away from their ship and people more than 100 miles, without finding enough water to assist the others, and just obtaining sufficient to keep themselves on a ration of about two cupfuls daily.

'The Abrolhos Tragedy', trans. Willem Siebenhaar (1897, first published in Dutch 1647).

WILLIAM DAMPIER
(1652–1715)

English mariner and writer. Dampier's account of his voyages in the Pacific (1686–91), A New Voyage Round the World *(1697), includes a description of the north-western coast of New Holland (present-day Australia), which he and other buccaneers from the* Cygnet *had visited in early 1688. He also wrote of his second visit to the same area, during an official British expedition, in* A Voyage to New Holland 1699 *(1703, 1709). His description of Aborigines in* A New Voyage … *helped to shape European attitudes towards Aborigines for many years.*

DAMPIER'S IMPRESSIONS OF ABORIGINES (1688)

The Land is of a dry sandy Soil, destitute of Water, except you make Wells; yet producing divers sorts of Trees; but the Woods are not thick, nor the Trees very big. Most of the Trees that we saw are Dragon-Trees as we supposed; and these too are the largest Trees of any there. They are about the bigness of our large Apple-trees, and about the same heighth; and the Rind is blackish, and somewhat rough. The Leaves are of a dark Colour; the Gum distils out of the Knots or Cracks that are in the Bodies of the Trees. We compared it with some Gum-Dragon or Dragon's Blood that was aboard, and it was of the same colour and taste. The other sort of Trees were not known by any of us. There was pretty long Grass growing under the Trees; but it was very thin. We saw no Trees that bore Fruit or Berries.

We saw no sort of Animal, nor any Track of Beast, but once; and that seemed to be the Tread of a Beast as big as a great Mastiff-Dog. Here are a few small Land-birds, but none bigger than a Black-bird; and but few Sea-fowls. Neither is the Sea very plentifully stored with Fish, unless you reckon the Manatee and Turtle as such. Of these Creatures there is plenty; but they are extraordinary shy; though the Inhabitants cannot trouble them much having neither Boats nor Iron.

The Inhabitants of this Country are the miserablest People in the World. The *Hodmadods* of *Monomatapa*, though a nasty People, yet for Wealth are Gentlemen to these; who have no Houses, and skin Garments, Sheep, Poultry and Fruits of the Earth, Ostrich Eggs, &c. as the *Hodmadods* have: And setting aside their Humane Shape, they differ but little from Brutes. They are tall, strait-bodied, and thin, with small long Limbs. They have great Heads, round Foreheads, and great Brows. Their Eyelids are always half closed, to keep the Flies out of their Eyes; they being so troublesome here, that no fanning will keep them from coming to one's Face; and without the Assistance of both Hands to keep them off, they will creep into ones Nostrils, and Mouth too, if the Lips are not shut very close; so that from their Infancy being thus annoyed with these Insects, they do never open their Eyes as other People: And therefore they cannot see far, unless they hold up their Heads, as if they were looking at somewhat over them.

They have great Bottle-Noses, pretty full Lips, and wide Mouths. The two Fore-teeth of their Upper-jaw are wanting in all of them, Men and Women, old and young; whether they draw them out, I know not: Neither have they any Beards. They are long-visaged, and of a very unpleasing Aspect, having no one graceful Feature in their Faces. Their

Hair is black, short and curl'd, like that of the Negroes; and not long and lank like the common *Indians*. The Colour of their Skins, both of their Faces and the rest of their Body, is Coal-black, like that of the Negroes of *Guinea*.

They have no sort of Cloaths, but a piece of the Rind of a Tree tied like a Girdle about their Waists, and a handful of long Grass, or three or four small green Boughs full of Leaves, thrust under their Girdle, to cover their Nakedness.

They have no Houses, but lie in the open Air without any covering; the Earth being their Bed, and the Heaven their Canopy. Whether they cohabit one Man to one Woman, or promiscuously, I know not; but they do live in Companies, 20 or 30 Men, Women and Children together. Their only Food is a small sort of Fish, which they get by making Wares of Stone across little Coves or Branches of the Sea; every Tide bringing in the small Fish, and there leaving them for a Prey to these People, who constantly attend there to search for them at Low-water. This small Fry I take to be the top of their Fishery: They have no Instruments to catch great Fish, should they come; and such seldom stay to be left behind at Low-water: Nor could we catch any Fish with our Hooks and Lines all the while we lay there. In other Places at Low-water they seek for Cockles, Muscles, and Periwincles: Of these Shell-fish there are fewer still; so that their chiefest dependance is upon what the Sea leaves in their Wares; which, be it much or little they gather up, and march to the Places of their Abode. There the old People that are not able to stir abroad by reason of their Age, and the tender Infants, wait their return; and what Providence has bestowed on them, they presently broil on the Coals, and eat it in common. Sometimes they get as many Fish as makes them a plentiful Banquet; and at other times they scarce get every one a taste: But be it little or much that they get, every one has his part, as well the young and tender, the old and feeble, who are not able to go abroad, as the strong and lusty. When they have eaten they lie down till the next Low-water, and then all that are able march out, be it Night or Day, rain or shine, 'tis all one; they must attend the Wares, or else they must fast: For the Earth affords them no Food at all. There is neither Herb, Root, Pulse nor any sort of Grain for them to eat, that we saw; nor any sort of Bird or Beast that they can catch, having no Instruments wherewithal to do so.

I did not perceive that they did worship any thing. These poor Crea-tures have a sort of Weapon to defend their Ware, or fight with their Enemies, if they have any that will interfere with their poor Fishery. They did at first endeavour with their Weapons to frighten us, who lying ashore deterr'd them from one of their Fishing-places. Some of them had wooden Swords, others had a sort of Lances. The Sword is a piece of Wood shaped somewhat like a Cutlass. The Lance is a long strait Pole sharp at one end, and hardened afterwards by heat. I saw no Iron, nor any other sort of Metal; therefore it is probable they use Stone-Hatchets, as some *Indians* in *America* do …

How they get their Fire I know not; but probably as *Indians* do, out of Wood. I have seen the *Indians* of *Bon-Airy* do it, and have my self tried the Experiment: They take a flat piece of Wood that is pretty soft, and make a small dent in one side of it, then they take another hard round Stick, about the bigness of one's little Finger, and sharpening it at one end like a Pencil, they put that sharp end in the hole or dent of the flat soft piece, and then rubbing or twirling the hard piece between the Palms of their Hands, they drill the soft piece till it smoaks, and at last takes Fire.

These People speak somewhat thro' the Throat; but we could not understand one word that they said. We anchored, as I said before, *January* the 5th, and seeing Men walking on the Shore, we presently sent a Canoa to get some Acquaintance with them: for we were in hopes to get some Provision among them. But the Inhabitants, seeing our Boat coming, run away and hid themselves. We searched afterwards three Days in hopes to find their Houses; but found none: yet we saw many places where they had made Fires. At last, being out of hopes to find their Habitations, we searched no farther; but left a great many Toys ashore, in such places where we thought that they would come. In all our search we found no Water, but old Wells on the sandy Bays.

A New Voyage Round the World (1729 edition, first published 1697).

————

JAMES MATRA
(1748?–1806)

Italian-American sailor. Matra visited New Zealand and New Holland in 1769–70 while serving as a midshipman on James Cook's Endeavour *voyage (1768–71). He is believed to have been responsible for writing* A Journal of a Voyage Round the World in His Majesty's Ship Endeavour *(1771), which was published, much to the dismay of Cook, Joseph Banks, and Admiralty authorities, anonymously and unofficially several months after the*

Endeavour's return to England and well before the publication of the official journal of the expedition in 1773. In the following extract Matra makes some observations about New Zealand.

MAORI BUILDINGS (1770)

In this part of New Zealand we saw many towns, whose inhabitants had either fled or been exterminated; some of them appeared to have been deserted or uninhabited four or five years, being overgrown with shrubs and high grass. On a small island, lying SE from the place where we anchored, was one of these deserted towns, most agreeably situated, and consisting of about eighteen houses, placed in a circular form; it was surrounded and defended by a wall curiously constructed, by driving two rows of long stakes or spars into the ground, at convenient distances, and afterwards filling the intermediate space with what we called broom-stuff, being a small kind of brush, made into bundles like faggots, and placed on end, in double rows, supported by others lying parallel with the ground: in this manner the wall is raised six or seven feet in height, and, notwithstanding the simplicity of its structure, it is not easily broken or destroyed, especially when guarded by men, who fight not only to preserve freedom and property, but their own bodies from being cruelly butchered and eaten.

At a little distance from this town we saw the remains of a more regular fortification, situated on a high hill, near a pleasant bay. The hill itself was almost inaccessible, and on its top was a level flat, large enough for a town, which was surrounded by a fence made from spars two feet in circumference, drove deep into the earth, and about twenty feet in height: these were placed in contact with each other, and without them was a ditch about ten feet in breadth: within the fence were several large reservoirs for water, and stages adjoining to the spars for supporting those who were placed to guard the town, which appeared to have been spacious enough to contain two or three hundred houses, though none were then remaining. The sides of the hill in every part were so steep, that nobody could ascend them, except by crawling on his hands and knees.

At the bottom of this hill we observed the ruins of a town, which had belonged to the proprietors of this castle, and which was the place of their common residence; for, besides their town, the natives have always a separate fort or strong hold, which serves them for a place of retreat, and a magazine for securing their dried fish, fern root, and other provisions; and, to prevent its being taken by surprize, they always leave a sufficient number of armed men therein, and thither they all retreat upon an alarm; always keeping in readiness a sufficient quantity of water in reservoirs, and regular piles of spears and stones dispersed along the stage adjoining to the fence; the height of these stages being fitted to afford those on guard sufficient shelter behind the fence, and so much elevation, as not to be impeded by it in flinging their stones or using their spears, &c.

A Journal of a Voyage Round the World in His Majesty's Ship Endeavour (1771).

———

MIHO BACCICH

(1859–1935)

Dalmatian sailor. He was one of sixteen crew members who sailed, along with their captain, on the first and last voyage of the barque Stefano *from Wales in August 1875, bound for Hong Kong with a cargo of coal. Ten of those on board, including Miho Baccich, struggled ashore after their vessel was wrecked off the Western Australian coast, probably on Black Rock near Point Cloates. Baccich described the shipwreck and subsequent events in the following letter. He later returned to his home town of Dubrovnik, before settling in New Orleans where he became a businessman. Coincidentally, two of his daughters were born in different years on the anniversary of the wrecking of the* Stefano.

MIHO BACCICH'S LETTER TO HIS PARENTS

Fremantle, Western Australia
May 16, 1876

Dear Parents,

I'm sure that you, as well as the others that know me, think of me as a dead man, and believe me, I wasn't too far from that. Now I'll tell you about the terrible tragedy which occurred from October 27, 1875, until April 18, 1876.

Last year on October 27 at 2 a.m., the barque *Stefano* under the command of Captain Vlaho Miloslavich was wrecked on a reef near the North West Cape of Australia. As soon as the barque struck, it heeled over to the right side and in less than three hours the ship broke up completely into large and small wreckage. We did everything possible to launch the lifeboats, but it was all in vain because the sea was so rough. At the captain's order, a small dinghy was lowered over the stern and the captain, lieutenant, one seaman, and I got aboard. But what happened then? The moment the boat touched the sea, it overturned. I was lucky to grab the keel; the others I never saw again. Thus, frightened, in the dark night, I floated for ten hours. Finally I succeeded in getting ashore where, almost half-dead, I threw myself on the bare, hot sand, hoping to see some of my companions. Soon I was able to see Karlo Costa floating on the ship's ladder, then the boatswain and other sailors came floating on various parts of the wrecked ship. Ten of us were saved. All, half-dead, stretched out near me; we stayed there, naked, all the day, unable to walk because our feet were becoming swollen. The next day we decided to search for food and drink and we found various kinds of it floating up to us from the ship. We decided to build a hut out of the pieces broken off from the shipwreck. Next morning we saw some naked savages, men and women. At first we were frightened that they were cannibals, but they didn't do us any harm.

Finally we went in search of a river which was only a few miles ahead, as the officer had told us. We walked for six days, and if we hadn't met some savages who helped us by showing us a water well, we would all have died of thirst in the middle of all that sand. We stayed by the water for three days and then we moved on because we were told we were only two miles distant from the river. We went on foot for three days but we didn't find any water, so we turned back. We lived for three months eating only raw shellfish and having no fire to cook with. We drank plain water. You should know that we lost all our strength during that period and looked like skeletons; we were dying quickly. It stormed at Christmas and it lasted for three days. During that time we didn't have any food, as we couldn't find anything to eat. Two men died at that time, and after a few days six more also died. My companion and I survived, probably because we had more strength. But later we, too, nearly died of hunger. When the black savages came again, we clasped our hands, begging them to give us something to eat. They were deeply concerned and took us with them and gave us some fish to eat and some water to drink. We stayed with them for three months, totally naked, looking for food almost all the time. We saw several ships passing by, but they couldn't see us.

At last, on April 18, 1876, an English cutter came near the coast. The photo, enclosed in this letter, shows the captain of this ship, Captain Charles Tuckey, who saved our lives. We sailed for seventeen days with them until we came to the port of Fremantle, which has about six hundred inhabitants.

The English, hearing about our terrible accident, took us ashore and gave us food and money. In this small port, we found a rich gentleman from the island of Šipan, who has been here for seventeen years. He is married and has five children. His present name is Mr Vincent, but his real name is Vicko Vukovich. He gave us some clothes and some money, too. We are staying at his place now. His wife is treating us like her own children. He owns several ships. Soon we will embark on a schooner under his command for five liras per month.

He is sending two letters to his relatives because he hasn't heard anything about them and I beg you to inquire and let me know whether there are some of his relatives still alive so that he could help them.

The Englishman, the master of the cutter, after having questioned me about navigation, praised me in front of many fine gentlemen and asked if I would join his ship as an officer. I thanked him and told him I had already been assigned to a ship owned by my family, but I promised to visit him on my way back to Fremantle (which will be in exactly two months' time). He agreed and stated in front of all those gentlemen that he himself will pay for my officer's exam. Noticing his kindness, I asked him teasingly why he favored me so. He replied, 'First of all, you're very professional, and you're not like the local seamen, who are always drunk, which I really don't like.'

I now speak English very well. It was said here that the natives had been nourishing us so that they could eat us. All the citizens here are anxious to meet us, so they keep on inviting us for lunch or dinner. They have taken a lot of photos of us and everyone wants one. I'm sending you one which is not the best of my photos because my eyes are still hurting me. I'll also send you the photo of our countryman and his wife as well as the photo of all the survived crew of the *Stefano*, which is me and my friend Jurich from Pelješac.

I hope you're happy to know your son loves you and will never forget you.

You'll get my letters every four weeks because I can mail them only once a month. People here collected twenty pounds to help us. On the twenty-first of this month there will be a drama performed showing the terrible tragedy which occurred on the night of October 27, 1875. The money collected from selling the tickets will also be given to us. As soon as we get it I'll let you know the exact sum. I'll write to my Uncle Nikola today so that he, too, gets some news of me. Write to me whether the number of my brothers and sisters has increased.

We are immensely happy and very grateful for being saved, especially since the natives have previously eaten several persons. We could have died as well. The two of us were the first ones that have escaped from the natives' hands. I have so many things to write to you, but it's enough for today. I'll write to you more about me in my next letter.

Give my regards to Uncle Ivan and his family as well as to all the others who thought me dead. Give my regards to Kate; has she gone to the nunnery yet? I've no space to write you more. Goodbye,

Yours faithfully,
Miho Baccich

Gustav Rathe, *The Wreck of the Barque* Stefano *off the North West Cape of Australia in 1875* (1992).

———

JOSEPH CONRAD

(1857–1924)

British master mariner and novelist. Polish-born Conrad went to sea in 1874, but left it in 1894 and settled in England, where he devoted himself to writing. He had made several brief visits to Australia between 1879 and 1892. The sea provides the setting for most of his works, including the autobiographical Mirror of the Sea *(1906), a series of 'sea sketches', most of which were originally published in various papers and popular magazines from 1904 to 1906. They are, in the words of the subtitle, 'memories and impressions', rather than strictly factual accounts.*

MEMORIES AND IMPRESSIONS OF SYDNEY

These towns of the Antipodes, not so great then as they are now, took an interest in the shipping, the running links with 'home,' whose numbers confirmed the sense of their growing importance. They made it part and parcel of their daily interests. This was especially the case in Sydney, where, from the heart of the fair city, down the vista of important streets, could be seen the wool-clippers lying at the Circular Quay—no walled prison-house of a dock that, but the integral part of one of the finest, most beautiful, vast, and safe bays the sun ever shone upon. Now great steam-liners lie at these berths, always reserved for the sea-aristocracy—grand and imposing enough ships, but here to-day and gone next week, whereas the general cargo, emigrant, and passenger clippers of my time, rigged with heavy spars, and built on fine lines, used to remain for months together waiting for their load of wool. Their names attained the dignity of household words. On Sundays and holidays the citizens trooped down, on visiting bent, and the lonely officer on duty solaced himself by playing the cicerone—especially to the citizenesses with engaging manners and a well-developed sense of the fun that may be got out of the inspection of a ship's cabins and state-rooms. The tinkle of more or less untuned cottage pianos floated out of open stern-ports till the gas lamps began to twinkle in the streets, and the ship's night-watchman, coming sleepily on duty after his unsatisfactory day slumbers, hauled down the flags and fastened a lighted lantern at the break of the gangway. The night closed rapidly upon the silent ships with their crews on shore. Up a short, steep ascent by the King's Head pub., patronized by the cooks and stewards of the fleet, the voice of a man crying 'Hot saveloys!' at the end of George Street, where the cheap eating-houses (sixpence a meal) were kept by Chinamen (Sun-kum-on's was not bad), is heard at regular intervals. I have listened for hours to this most pertinacious pedlar (I wonder whether he is dead or has made a fortune) while sitting on the rail of the old *Duke of S——* (she's dead, poor thing! a violent death on the coast of New Zealand), fascinated by the monotony, the regularity, the abruptness of the recurring cry, and so exasperated at the absurd spell, that I wished the fellow would choke himself to death with a mouthful of his own infamous wares.

A stupid job, and fit only for an old man, my comrades used to tell me, to be the night-watchman of a captive (though honoured) ship. And generally the oldest of the able seamen in a ship's crew does get it. But sometimes neither the oldest nor any other fairly steady seaman is forthcoming. Ships' crews had the trick of melting away swiftly in those days. So, probably on account of my youth, innocence, and pensive habits (which made me sometimes dilatory in my work about the rigging), I was suddenly nominated, in our chief mate Mr B——'s most sardonic tones, to that enviable situation. I do not regret the experience. The night humours of the town descended from the street to the waterside in the still watches of the night: larrikins rushing down in bands to settle some quarrel by a stand-up fight, away from the police, in an indistinct ring half hidden by piles of cargo, with the sounds of blows, a groan now and then, the stamping of feet, and the cry of 'Time!' rising suddenly above the sinister and excited murmurs; night-prowlers, pursued or pursuing, with a stifled shriek followed by a profound silence, or slinking stealthily alongside like ghosts, and addressing me from the quay below in mysterious tones with incomprehensible propositions. The cab-men, too, who twice a week, on the night when the ASN Company's passenger-boat was due to arrive, used to range a battalion of blazing lamps opposite the ship, were very amusing in their way. They got down from their perches and told each other impolite stories in racy language, every word of which reached me distinctly over the bulwarks as I sat smoking on the main-hatch. On one occasion I had an hour or so of a most intellectual conversation with a person whom I could not see distinctly, a gentleman from England, he said, with a cultivated voice, I on deck and he on the quay sitting on the case of a piano (landed out of our hold that very afternoon), and smoking a cigar which smelt very good. We touched, in our discourse, upon science, politics, natural history, and operatic singers. Then, after remarking abruptly, 'You seem to be rather intelligent, my man,' he informed me pointedly that his name was Mr Senior, and walked off—to his hotel, I suppose. Shadows! Shadows! I think I saw a white whisker as he turned under the lamp-post. It is a shock to think that in the natural course of nature he must be dead by now. There was nothing to object to in his intelligence but a little dogmatism maybe. And his name was Senior! Mr Senior!

The position had its drawbacks, however. One wintry, blustering, dark night in July, as I stood sleepily out of the rain under the break of the poop something resembling an ostrich dashed up the gangway. I say ostrich because the creature, though it ran on two legs, appeared to help its progress by working a pair of short wings; it was a man, however, only his coat, ripped up the back and flapping in two halves above his shoulders, gave him that weird and fowl-like appearance. At least, I suppose it was his coat, for it was impossible to make him out distinctly. How he managed to come so straight upon me, at speed and without a stumble over a strange deck, I cannot imagine. He must have been able to see in the dark better than any cat. He overwhelmed me with panting entreaties to let him take shelter till morning in our forecastle. Following my strict orders, I refused his request, mildly at first, in a sterner tone as he insisted with growing impudence.

'For God's sake let me, matey! Some of 'em are after me—and I've got hold of a ticker here.'

'You clear out of this!' I said.

'Don't be hard on a chap, old man!' he whined, pitifully.

'Now, then, get ashore at once. Do you hear?'

Silence. He appeared to cringe, mute, as if words had failed him through grief; then—bang! came a concussion and a great flash of light in which he vanished, leaving me prone on my back with the most abominable black eye that anybody ever got in the faithful discharge of duty. Shadows! Shadows! I hope he escaped the enemies he was fleeing from to live and flourish to this day. But his fist was uncommonly hard and his aim miraculously true in the dark.

There were other experiences, less painful and more funny for the most part, with one amongst them of a dramatic complexion; but the greatest experience of them all was Mr B——, our chief mate himself.

He used to go ashore every night to forgather in some hotel's parlour with his crony, the mate of the barque *Cicero,* lying on the other side of the Circular Quay. Late at night I would hear from afar their stumbling footsteps and their voices raised in endless argument. The mate of the *Cicero* was seeing his friend on board. They would continue their senseless and muddled discourse in tones of profound friendship for half an hour or so at the shore end of our gangway, and then I would hear Mr B—— insisting that he must see the other on board his ship. And away they would go, their voices, still conversing with excessive amity, being heard moving all round the harbour. It happened more than once that they would thus perambulate three or four times the distance, each seeing the other on board his ship out of pure and disinterested affection. Then, through sheer weariness, or perhaps in a moment of forgetfulness, they would manage to part from each other somehow, and by and by the planks of our long gangway would bend and creak under the weight of Mr B—— coming on board for good at last.

On the rail his burly form would stop and stand swaying.

'Watchman!'

'Sir.'

A pause.

He waited for a moment of steadiness before negotiating the three steps of the inside ladder from rail to deck; and the watchman, taught by experience, would forbear offering help which would be received as an insult at that particular stage of the mate's return. But many times I trembled for his neck. He was a heavy man.

Then with a rush and a thump it would be done. He never had to pick himself up; but it took him a minute or so to pull himself together after the descent.

'Watchman!'

'Sir.'

'Captain aboard?'

'Yes, sir.'

Pause.

'Dog aboard?'

'Yes, sir.'

Pause.

Our dog was a gaunt and unpleasant beast, more like a wolf in poor health than a dog, and I never noticed Mr B—— at any other time show the slightest interest in the doings of the animal. But that question never failed.

'Let's have your arm to steady me along.'

I was always prepared for that request. He leaned on me heavily till near enough the cabin-door to catch hold of the handle. Then he would let go my arm at once.

'That'll do. I can manage now.'

And he could manage. He could manage to find his way into his berth, light his lamp, get into his bed—ay, and get out of it when I called him at half-past five, the first man on deck, lifting the cup of morning coffee to his lips with a steady hand, ready for duty as though he had virtuously slept ten solid hours—a better chief officer than many a man who had never tasted grog in his life. He could manage all that, but could never manage to get on in life.

Only once he failed to seize the cabin-door handle at the first grab. He waited a little, tried again, and again failed. His weight was growing heavier on my arm. He sighed slowly.

'D——n that handle!'

Without letting go his hold of me he turned about, his face lit up bright as day by the full moon.

'I wish she were out at sea,' he growled, savagely.

'Yes, sir.'

I felt the need to say something, because he hung on to me as if lost, breathing heavily.

'Ports are no good—ships rot, men go to the devil!'

I kept still, and after a while he repeated with a sigh:

'I wish she were at sea out of this.'

'So do I, sir,' I ventured.

Holding my shoulder, he turned upon me.

'You! What's that to you where she is? You don't—drink.'

And even on that night he 'managed it' at last. He got hold of the handle. But he did not manage to light his lamp (I don't think he even tried), though in the morning as usual he was the first on deck, bull-necked, curly-headed, watching the hands turn-to with his sardonic expression and unflinching gaze.

I met him ten years afterwards, casually, unexpectedly, in the street, on coming out of my consignee office. I was not likely to have forgotten him with his 'I can manage now.' He recognized me at once, remembered my name, and in what ship I had served under his orders. He looked me over from head to foot.

'What are you doing here?' he asked.

'I am commanding a little barque,' I said, 'loading here for Mauritius.' Then, thoughtlessly, I added: 'And what are you doing, Mr B—?'

'I,' he said, looking at me unflinchingly, with his old sardonic grin—'I am looking for something to do.'

I felt I would rather have bitten out my tongue. His jet-black, curly hair had turned iron-grey; he was scrupulously neat as ever, but frightfully threadbare. His shiny boots were worn down at heel. But he forgave me, and we drove off together in a hansom to dine on board my ship. He went over her conscientiously, praised her heartily, congratulated me on my command with absolute sincerity. At dinner, as I offered him wine and beer he shook his head, and as I sat looking at him interrogatively, muttered in an undertone:

'I've given up all that.'

After dinner we came again on deck. It seemed as though he could not tear himself away from the ship. We were fitting some new lower rigging, and he hung about, approving, suggesting, giving me advice in his old manner. Twice he addressed me as 'My boy,' and corrected himself quickly to 'Captain.' My mate was about to leave me (to get married), but I concealed the fact from Mr B——. I was afraid he would ask me to give him the berth in some ghastly jocular hint that I could not refuse to take. I was afraid. It would have been impossible. I could not have given orders to Mr B——, and I am sure he would not have taken them from me very long. He could not have managed *that*, though he had managed to break himself from drink—too late.

He said good-bye at last. As I watched his burly, bull-necked figure walk away up the street, I wondered with a sinking heart whether he had much more than the price of a night's lodging in his pocket. And I understood that if that very minute I were to call out after him, he would not even turn his head. He, too, is no more than a shadow, but I seem to hear his words spoken on the moonlit deck of the old *Duke* ——:

'Ports are no good—ships rot, men go to the devil!'

The Mirror of the Sea (1906).

JOSHUA SLOCUM

(1844–1909?)

New England sea captain. Born in Nova Scotia into a seafaring family, Captain Joshua Slocum became the first person to sail alone around the world, after having been told that such a feat was impossible. During the 46 000-mile voyage in the Spray, *which lasted from 1895 to 1898, he visited New South Wales, Victoria, Tasmania, and Queensland, among other places. His account of the voyage was first published in serial form in a monthly magazine in 1899–1900, before appearing as a book in 1900. An immediate bestseller, it became required reading in many American schools and is considered to be a classic of its kind. Slocum and the* Spray *disappeared on the high seas in 1909.*

'PERILS OF A CORAL SEA'

On the following day the *Spray* rounded Great Sandy Cape, and, what is a notable event in every voyage, picked up the trade-winds, and these winds followed her now for many thousands of miles, never ceasing to blow from a moderate gale to a mild summer breeze, except at rare intervals.

From the pitch of the cape was a noble light seen twenty-seven miles; passing from this to Lady Elliott Light, which stands on an island as a sentinel at the gateway of the Barrier Reef, the *Spray* was at once in the fairway leading north. Poets have sung of beacon-light and of pharos, but did ever poet behold a great light flash up before his path on a dark night in the midst of a coral sea? If so, he knew the meaning of his song.

The *Spray* had sailed for hours in suspense, evidently stemming a current. Almost mad with doubt, I grasped the helm to throw her head off shore, when blazing out of the sea was the light ahead. 'Excalibur!' cried 'all hands,' and rejoiced, and sailed on. The *Spray* was now in a protected sea and smooth water, the first she had dipped her keel into since leaving Gibraltar, and a change it was from the heaving of the misnamed 'Pacific' Ocean.

The Pacific is perhaps, upon the whole, no more boisterous than other oceans, though I feel quite safe in saying that it is not more pacific except in name. It is often wild enough in one part or another. I once knew a writer who, after saying beautiful things about the sea, passed through a Pacific hurricane, and he became a changed man. But where, after all, would be the poetry of the sea were there no wild waves? At last here was the *Spray* in the midst of a sea of coral. The sea itself might be called smooth indeed, but coral rocks are always rough, sharp, and dangerous. I trusted now to the mercies of the Maker of all reefs, keeping a good lookout at the same time for perils on every hand.

Lo! the Barrier Reef and the waters of many colors studded all about with enchanted islands! I behold among them after all many safe harbors, else my vision is astray. On the 24th of May, the sloop, having made one hundred and ten miles a day from Danger Point, now entered Whitsunday Pass, and that night sailed through among the islands. When the sun rose next morning I looked back and regretted having gone by while it was dark, for the scenery far astern was varied and charming.

Sailing Alone Around the World (1900).

———

HARRY PRICE
(1877–1965)

British seaman. Born in Birmingham to Welsh parents, Harry Price joined the Royal Navy in 1893. He kept a charming illustrated journal, published in facsimile in 1980, while serving on HMS Ophir *from February to November 1901, during the royal tour made by the Duke and Duchess of York (later King George V and Queen Mary) throughout much of the British Empire, including Australia and New Zealand. While in Hobart in early July, Price triumphantly ascended Mount Wellington. Artistic (or patriotic) licence saw the flag mentioned in the following extract transformed into its British counterpart in an accompanying illustration.*

'THE ASCENT OF MOUNT WELLINGTON'

I started about 1 p.m. and after buying a cheap flag which I meant to fix on the highest point, (the flag by the way was a French flag the only one available all the others having been sold) It was a walk of about six miles; to the foot of the mountain, I may here mention that a road led about two thirds of the way up, but as I never asked for information, I was ignorant of the fact until afterwards But anyhow I struck a timper track and started upwards in good sprits, but bad boots, These boots where the cause of much misery and hardship; in fact they where only a kind of leather slipper, served out to the seamen of the 'Ophir', so as not to make a noise, when running about the ship, on the day's we where supposed to wear boots, Sundays.ect And the sailors gave them the glorified name of the 'Royal Pumps.' Well after following the timber track for about a mile; passing many fallen monarchs of the forrest, it ended in a couple of small paths, hardly traceable in places, I followed the one I thought best and soon found myself in the thick of the forrest. The scenery was grand, nearly all the trees, were stripped of their bark, and stood up like columns of light against the dark background, on some of the trees the bark hung in long festunes from the branches a hundred feet from the ground, and the gentle breeze swung it backward's and forward, like an immense pendulum, making a peculiar rattling sound, as it touched the neighbouring tree trunks. The under groath now began to get so thick it was well nigh impassable, and I noticed that a large number of the fallen trees had been brought down by fire; but no trace of fire could be seen in the underwood. It was astonishing how the fire had hardened the burnt trees. In some places the remnants of a tree stood up several feet burnt out to a fine point as hard and sharp as a needle. The ground began to change, it rar up much steeper, the trees smaller, and in place of the tangled underwood, were rocks; all sizes, intermingled with a long dry tough grass, that came in very handy in hauling one's self from rock to rock, I now paused to take a breath, and look round. I could not see the top of the mountain, it was enveloped in clouds, but I had a splendid view of the town, the harbour, and the shipping. But I had no time to loose if I was going to reach the summit, which I had told my shipmates I intended doing. So I once more started upward's, it was now about 5 p.m. as near as I could guess; as I had no watch, and felt like sitting down to a good tea, I now began to find snow in between the rocks, and I began to get so thirsty that from time I quenched it with pieces of frozen snow, The rocks now got bigger and bigger, and the side of the mountain steeper; and now and then the clouds would drift by and expose the mountain top to view, but it seemed a long way off yet; but I still struggled on the snow getting deeper the crust of which was frozen hard, and would bear ones weight but now and then it would give way and I found myself in different depths up to ten or twelve feet. but I managed to extract myself each time from these awkward positions. My feet now began to get in a shocking state, the snow turned my

'Royal pumps' into raw hide again, and made It a very slippery job climbing from rock to rock. The patches of snow where now 20 or 30 ft in extent, and I crossed these on my hands and knees, not knowing to what depth I may descend, if the hard crust gave way, I now came to a wall of rock sixty feet high, and as I saw no other way of getting up proceeded to climb it inch by inch, foot by foot until I reached the top. Snow was now falling in sheets, winding about in all directions, and I waited till it lifted a little, when I saw what appeared to be the summit a few hundred feet in front and above me. I now began to feel the cold, but I pushed on as it was rapidly getting dark, and passing an half dead tree broke off a branch about 15 feet in length to act as a flag staff. When I reached what I thought was the top the view was rather clear, and I perceived the rocks ran up much higher yet, but I struggled on determined not to give in, After climbing another pile of rocks, I was enveloped in another snow cloud, as cold as ice; and the wind blew half a gale, the snow drifting by in heaps, all was black now except the snow; I found shelter between two large rocks, and waited for it to blow over I felt like lying down and going to sleep, but having read in books, it is fatal to do so in such cases, fought hard against the feeling. But the snow blast went as quickly as it came, and the moon shone out cold and clear. So I clambered on the largest rock andd saw to my great joy that at last I was on the top, at last I had arrived at the topmost peak; so I quickly bound flag to the branch, and jammed it down between two rocks. It was as much as I could do, the cold was so intense, so I started to desend as quickly as possible, but not the same way as I came up, I soon came to a bit of a gully, the snow sloping away into the darkness beneath, I meant to cross this, but in doing so, started to slide downwards, so I turned on my back, and dug my heels deep into the snow, this checked me, but then the idea struck me, to slide down the mountain side, I was getting desperate, and would do anything to get out of the icy atmosphere. So away I slid into the darkness. I was thankfull afterwards that I did not go over a precipice; but I did not care at the time, for was I not getting to warmer air, away from the rocks, frost, and snow. I think I must have desended, several hundred feet like this when I found the bushes and rocks getting too thick to tobaggan any farther; so I started to clamber over the rocks once more; letting myself down by the grass and bushes. The moon was now shining brightly and after toiling for an hour or more, over rougher ground than any previously met with; I began to feel warmer; the thick bush, and tangled masses of vegetation again putting in an appearance, and the farther I desended into the forrest the darker it became; untill I could not see an arm's length in front of me; for the trees were so high that the moon failed to penetrate; and so I toiled on through the thick bushes, barking my shins against fallen timber falling over tree trunks, with only one, or at least a part of one shoe on, the other having dissapeared long ago; now and then a branch knocked my cap off, and I had difficulty in finding it again even with the aid of matches, which I luckily possessed, as I desended the ground got moister and in some places I went in up to my knees, a kind of stinging nettle also gave me a lot of inconvenience, and from time to time a thorn entered my feet, even penetrating the odd shoe; and I thought what a fool I was to venture on such a trip alone and at such a time, But I had the consolation that I had accomplished my task, and it was close on midnight when I stumbled across a road, yes a regular smooth flat road, and I was as happy as a king, After walking some distance, I came to an hotel, and as they had not retired I was able to get refreshments; and they seemed immencly surprised when I said I had just come from the mountain top and all alone, I left there about half past twelve and after walking another six miles, arrived on board more dead than alive, The next morning with the aid of a powerfull glass the flag could be seen from the ship, but I had to go to bed with bad feet and aching limbs I dont know much about the next few days, that is of the outside world as I was hors-de-combat. but their 'Royal Highnesses' had a good send when we left on the sixth; by the amount of noise and cheering outside. The next time I came on deck, I found we where anchored off the mouth of the river leading up to 'Port Adelaide', Their 'Royal Highnesses' left the ship the following day, and next morning we went up the river, and tied up alongside jetty.

The Royal Tour 1901 (1980).

ERIC NEWBY

(1919–)

English travel writer. In 1938 the Finnish four-masted barque Moshulu, *with Eric Newby on board as an apprentice, sailed from Belfast in ballast to South Australia. It was one of thirteen three- and four-masted barques that sailed for Europe from South Australia in early 1939 in what proved to be the last of the great grain races. The publication in 1956 of Newby's account*

*of the round trip, The Last Grain Race, marked the beginning of his career
as a much-admired travel writer. Here he describes Port 'Veek' (Port Victoria), the port on Spencer Gulf on the western coast of the Yorke Peninsula in
South Australia, where the ships gathered to load the grain before the race.*

WAITING AT PORT 'VEEK'

Port Victoria, Port 'Veek', as Tria and the rest called it, seen from off-
shore was an idea more than a place, for the heat of the sun was enormous, destroying the substance of the land itself which swam in
mirage. Avenues of distant trees loomed in the air above shimmering
lakes which dissolved and vanished, and as rapidly reappeared in different forms. *Pommern*, at anchor between our ship and the shore, was an
extraordinary sight with a twin projection of herself balanced upside
down on top of her, mast cap to mast cap.

To reach the town we used to row past the white loading-ketches
rocking at their moorings, to the wooden jetty and go up past some
iron storage sheds into the main street of Port Victoria, wider than
Knightsbridge at its widest, but unsurfaced. On either side was a façade
of single-storeyed, iron-roofed buildings so impermanent in appearance that I never overcame my surprise when passing through the
doors of the Post Office, the secretive-looking Hotel, or Kneebone's
Café, at not finding myself at the back of a film lot facing the open
country that extended to the horizon in every direction except to the
west, where the waters of the Gulf lay. It had none of the cosy resort
flavour of Port Lincoln. Port 'Veek' had a genuine air of *terribilitá* that
raised it above the level of an ordinary small town.

The great main street, in which early motor-cars lay lifeless under
the implacable sky waiting for owners who might never return, seemed
to be expecting some world-shaking event, perhaps a procession of
mindless automata to come plodding down from the wilderness and
march through the calm and silent town into the sea. Sometimes,
thankfully having a cool drink in Kneebone's, I used to gaze out at the
whirls of dust scurrying along the length of the street and imagine
them the presentiment of the event.

Perhaps for the best, this dream atmosphere was dissipated whenever the inhabitants appeared, for they were kind and hospitable to a
degree. In any event Port Victoria could never be commonplace. At
anchor in the roads during this February and March there were five
four-masted barques: *Moshulu*, *Olivebank*, *Pamir*, *Pommern*, and
Viking, perhaps the last concourse of merchant sailing ships the world

would ever see. There were no crowds of sightseers to gape at them. Here they were a part of the scenery, for the business of this town was grain. Neither was the visitor allowed to forget it. Everywhere there was bagged wheat, brought down from the back blocks and piled in great stacks until it could be run on to the jetty in open freight trucks, transferred to the loading-ketches, and taken out to the waiting ships. The stacks loomed over everything and as they grew, piled up around the little church until only the tin spire and the iron roof were visible.

I was befriended by the agent in charge of shipping *Moshulu's* cargo, John Scott-Todd, who, with his wife, entertained me whenever I came ashore. With him I visited the neighbouring farmhouses where the inhabitants introduced me to a hospitality undreamed of in England, and to a form of fox hunting by night, equally unthought of, in their vast thousand-acre paddocks. Armed with shot-guns, we stood in the backs of open trucks, sprawled precariously over the tops of the cabs, blazing away at the foxes as they ran ahead of us over the stubble, endeavouring to escape the spotlights trained on them. It would have been a source of delight to the foxes themselves and to all more legitimate hunters if they had seen our truck, when it finally hit an invisible ditch at thirty miles an hour, throwing us high into the air and breaking its front axle.

The Australians seemed a resourceful race, the young men making journeys of hundreds of miles in order to spend an hour or so with their girls, so that a young farmer would be invested with some of the splendour of a medieval paladin setting out to redeem some lofty pledge as he kicked the starter of his motor cycle in the already gathering dusk.

'Well, so long, I'm going to see my sheila in Kadina.'

'Is every girl in Australia called Sheila? I never hear anything else.'

'All girls are sheilas to us,' said the paladin, settling himself comfortably in the saddle as the engine began to roar.

'How far's Kadina?' I asked him.

'Two hundred miles—a hundred each way.'

To me it sounded a lot of miles on such an errand.

'Too right it is,' he said, 'but I want to see my sheila real bad,' and vanished into the gloom in a cloud of blue smoke.

For a month and two days we lay at Port Victoria; sometimes a mile or so off-shore, so that the white ketches could come out from the jetty under power, loaded with grain; sometimes at the outer ballast-grounds, where we continued to throw ballast over the side.

In the first four days, with ballast still in her, the lumpers stowed seven thousand sacks in Nos 2, 3, and 4 holds, using the ship's own gear and winches. In language that made our own seem commonplace they complained bitterly of the smells below. What they said has not survived; if it had it would have proved meaningless robbed of the monotonous epithet which they attributed to every noun.

'I was reading somewhere,' said Vytautas, 'that Tibetans think themselves more holee if they say "Jewel of Lotus" many times. If they say "Jewel of Lotus" enough they have vision. Perhaps lumpers think they will have mystic vision if they use that worrd.'

'My——oath, it's——hot on this——cow,' shouted one lumper to another, just at that moment.

'——,' answered his companion, 'too——right it——is.'

'I don't think it's the right word for that, Vytautas.'

'Yerss,' he replied unexpectedly, 'not so fine that worrd for God.'

Cut off from contact with the shore, we worked for six days at the outer ballast-grounds, trying to get rid of the ballast as quickly as possible and at the same time discover what had died. On the fifth day we exhumed the liquefied remains of a very large dog, and on the sixth and last, with damp cloths round our faces, we spooned up a second one which lay at the very bottom, and committed it thankfully to the sea, cursing the Belfast stevedores for their perverse sense of humour.

With the last of the ballast overside, we cleaned the bilges, cemented them, and sailed back to Port Victoria. Thenceforward, day after day, the routine was unvaried. Every morning at six the calm would be shattered by the deafening sounds of winches and donkey engines warming up for the day's work. The ketches would come alongside and the bags, each weighing about 180 lb, would be swung into *Moshulu*'s holds in slings, a dozen at a time, where the lumpers stowed them away, slitting some, allowing them to 'bleed' and bind the cargo more solidly together. The work went on every day except for Saturday afternoons and Sundays, but sometimes the wind blew force 5 and 6 from the south west and there would be no loading. In three weeks we lost three whole days this way. For the remainder of the time the lumpers crammed grain into her, and in one working week from Monday to Saturday they loaded 16 900 bags.

The Last Grain Race (1956).

3

Artists and critics

♦

SYDNEY PARKINSON

(1745?–71)

Scottish-born natural history draughtsman. Employed by Joseph Banks, Parkinson made at least 1300 drawings and sketches during James Cook's Endeavour *voyage (1768–71), but contracted dysentery at Batavia on the way home and died at sea on 26 January 1771. Parkinson's illustration of the two Aborigines referred to in the first paragraph of the following extract from his journal is the first known pictorial record made by a British artist in Australia. It is known as* Two of the Natives of New Holland, Advancing to Combat *(1770).*

BOTANY BAY (1770)

On the 28th [April], we got into a fine bay, and some of our people went on shore on one side of it, where we saw some houses. On our approaching the shore, two men, with different kinds of weapons, came out and made toward us. Their countenance bespoke displeasure; they threatened us, and discovered hostile intentions, often crying to us, Warra warra wai. We made signs to them to be peaceable, and threw them some trinkets; but they kept aloof, and dared us to come on shore. We attempted to frighten them by firing a gun loaded with small shot; but attempted it in vain. One of them repaired to a house imme-diately, and brought out a shield, of an oval figure, painted white in the middle, with two holes in it to see through, and also a wooden sword, and then they advanced boldly, ... gathering up stones as they came along, which they threw at us. After we had landed, they threw two of their lances at us; one of which fell between my feet. Our people fired again, and wounded one of them; at which they took the alarm and were very frantic and furious, shouting for assistance, calling Hala, hala, mae; that is, (as we afterwards learned,) Come hither; while their wives and children set up a most horrid howl. We endeavoured to paci-fy them, but to no purpose, for they seemed implacable, and, at length, ran howling away, leaving their wives and children, who hid themselves in one of the huts behind a piece of bark. After looking about us a lit-tle while, we left some nails upon the spot and embarked, taking with us their weapons; and then proceeded to the other side of the bay, where we had seen a number of people, as we came in, round a fire, some of whom were painted white, having a streak round their thighs, two below their knees, one like a sash over their shoulders, which ran diagonally downwards, and another across their foreheads. Both men and women were quite naked, very lean and raw-boned; their complexion was dark, their hair black and frizzled, their heads unadorned, and the beards of the men bushy. Their canoes were made of one piece of bark, gathered at the two ends, and extended in the middle by two sticks. Their paddles were very small, two of which they used at one time; and we found a large lump of yellow gum in their gigs which seemed to be for striking fish. Some of their weapons had a kind of chisel fixed at their ends, but of what substance they were formed we could not learn.

The natives often reconnoitred us, but we could not prevail on them to come near us or to be social; for, as soon as we advanced, they fled as nimbly as deer, excepting at one time when they seemed determined to face us: then they came armed with spears, having their breasts painted white; but, as soon as they saw our boat go off from the ship, they retreated. Constrained by hunger, they often came into the bay to fish; but they kept in the shallows, and as near as possible to the shore. In one of their houses, at the top of the bay, we had laid some nails, pieces of cloth and various trinkets; and though the natives had been there in our absence, yet they had not taken any of them.

This bay is in latitude 34°6', and makes a good harbour, being only two or three points open to the eastward; but the water is in general shallow; and it has several arms extending from it, which are also shallow. On these shallows we found a great number of rays, some shell-fish, and a few sharks. The rays are of an enormous size: one of them which we caught weighed two hundred and thirty-nine pounds, and another three hundred and twenty-six. They tasted very much like the European rays, and the viscera had an agreeable flavour, not unlike stewed turtle. These rays, and shell-fish, are the natives chief food.

The country is very level and fertile; the soil, a kind of grey sand; and the climate mild: and though it was the beginning of winter when we arrived, every thing seemed in perfection. There is a variety of flowering shrubs; a tree that yields gum; and a species of palm, [*Borasus flabellifer,*] the berries of which are of two sorts; one small, eaten by the hogs, and the other, as large as a cherry, has a stone in it; it is of a pale crimson colour, and has the taste of a sweet acid. We also found a species of Salvia Fortea.

We met with but one quadruped on the island, which was about the size of a hare: we found also the skin of a snake, and saw a great number of birds of a beautiful plumage; among which were two sorts of parroquets, and a beautiful loriquet: we shot a few of them, which we made into a pie, and they ate very well. We also met with a black bird, very much like our crow, and shot some of them too, which also tasted agreeably. From the number of curious plants we met with on shore, we called the bay Botany-Bay.

A Journal of a Voyage to the South Seas in His Majesty's Ship The Endeavour (1784 edition, first published 1773).

———

ROBERT ELWES

(dates unknown)

British artist. Elwes visited Van Diemen's Land, the Port Phillip District, and New South Wales during his world tour, which began when he left England, headed for Madeira, in March 1848. In his illustrated account of his trip, he tells this tale of his arrival on Flinders Island.

'THE WRECK'

About four on Sunday morning, we were rather roughly aroused by the schooner's striking heavily. At first I imagined that we had run foul of some vessel, and rushed upon deck, where I found all in confusion. We had been going about five knots an hour, when we had run on a sand-bank, and were now bumping on farther. It was not yet light, and we appeared to be surrounded by breakers; but on the starboard side the shore was plainly visible—low, flat land stretching away into the gloom, while high mountains rose behind. Right ahead was another mountain, and astern some high islands. The captain said we were in the Bay of Fires, on the north-east corner of Van Diemen's Land. He had not long left the deck, and the ship was in charge of the mate when we struck. Both had seen the mountains some time before, but not the low, flat coast. No lead was to be found; but a piece of pipe was bent on to the log-line, and gave eight feet of water alongside.

The boat being with some difficulty lowered, a kedge was carried out to the port bow, and on this we all hove, and got the schooner off for a minute; but whilst getting up the mainsail to bring her to the wind, the hawser gave way, and she struck again, throwing us all in a heap on the deck. She soon bumped herself harder on than before, and in a worse-looking place, as there appeared to be a reef about 50 fathoms ahead of her. The striking and rolling unshipped the rudder, and forced it up, knocking the wheel away; but we soon secured it, and hoisted it up with a tackle. As it became light, we saw our position better, and then found that we were on the east coast of Flinders Island, or, as it is sometimes called, Great Island; the high mountains being the Strzelecki Peaks, the mountain ahead Cape Barren Island, and those astern Babel Islands. There were sand-banks all round us, and by going up the rigging, we could see the waves breaking over them six miles to seaward, so that we were fortunate in having struck where we had; for if we had been six miles nearer our course, we should have struck so much farther from the shore. As it was, the land was within a mile of us, and the boat was now got ready for the shore.

The captain having consulted us, Mr Lover and I agreed, that as the boat would not hold us all, we did not care to go on shore first, so we were left; and Captain Carter, his wife and child, Mr Campbell, and three hands went in her. The captain also took the chronometer, gold-dust, and several other things, leaving nothing of any great value on board, except ourselves and the remainder of the crew. The gold-dust was some of the proceeds of the voyage, most of the cargo having been sold in California in exchange for 'dust.' It was in two tea-canisters, and was worth perhaps £3000. It was rather nervous work for Mr Lover and myself, and we watched the boat anxiously as it slowly buffetted the waves, and approached the shore. There is always some risk in landing on a flat beach in surf; and we knew, that if the boat was knocked to pieces, or rendered unseaworthy, we should have no means of getting on shore. I thought of a raft but we should have had a great deal of difficulty with that, as the currents ran very strong between us and the shore, and the sea was full of sharks. However, we saw the boat land safely, and its passengers walking up the beach; and now we found that, as well as the perils of water, we nearly had to encounter the dangers of fire; for Mr Lover, rambling about, looked into the captain's cabin to see, I suppose, whether the sea was coming in, and to his horror found in the bunk, where the captain and his wife slept, a lighted candle in a flat candlestick, actually standing on the bed-clothes, which were all in confusion. He called me down to look at it, and we put it out pretty quickly, and said nothing about it; but it denoted either excessive carelessness on the part of the captain, or that he wanted to burn the ship. If the rolling and bumping of the ship had upset the candle—and I cannot imagine how it did not—the bed-clothes must have caught fire.

The captain having left the ship, and the mate and men being forward, and we two having been left in the cabin with a light, the blame of course would have fallen upon us. All this looked very much as if the vessel had been run on shore on purpose; and as she was insured for more than her value, this was not unlikely.

A Sketcher's Tour Round the World (1854).

MARIANNE NORTH
(1830–90)

English flower-painter. An impressive 'Victorian Lady Traveller', to use Jane Robinson's term, North travelled extensively from 1870 to 1885, largely in order to paint as many tropical plants and flowers in their own settings as possible. She donated her paintings and the funds for a gallery (opened 1882) in which to house them to the Royal Botanical Gardens at Kew. She had visited Australia (travelling to all of the colonies except South Australia) and New Zealand in 1880–81. Here is her description of the area that she considered the 'most enticing part of Australia', from her autobiography, which was originally published in 1892.

THE ILLAWARRA DISTRICT (1880)

They [the Macarthurs] lent me a buggy with a fat horse and driver for a week, and I went through pretty scenery till I reached the top of the Illewong Mountains, and went down the wonderful bit of road to Balli [Bulli]. At the top I saw many specimens of the great Australian lily or doryanthes [Spear Lily, *Doryanthes palmeri*], but they were not in flower. I watched a spike of one, seven feet high, off and on for two months at Camden, and it never came out (the one I afterwards painted at Kew took five months after it had begun to colour before it really came to perfection). There was a fine sea-view, and lower down the road took me through the richest vegetation, quite unlike anything else south of Brisbane. Tall seaforthia palms and cabbage or fan palms [*Livistona spp.*], full of flower, many of them of great height. Often one had helped itself up in the world by means of the branches of a giant gum-tree, resting its tired head against the trunk for support, quite 200 feet above the ground in the valley below.

But it was always raining in this unexpected bit of the tropics, and I had no easy task to finish a picture there. Three times I packed up my things in disgust, and at last brought home my paper wetter with rain than with oil-paint. People were all related to one another, and all hospitable, and I drove from house to house, only regretting that the horse and buggy were not my own, when I could have stayed much longer with enjoyment. Another day I stopped to paint a gigantic fig-tree standing alone, its huge buttresses covered with tangled creepers and parasites. The village was called Fig-tree village after it, and all the population was on horseback, going to the races at Wollongong. At Mr Henry Osborne's I saw a grand specimen of the 'red cedar' [*Toona australis*]. It had leaves like the ailanthus [Tree-of-Heaven, *Ailanthus altissima*], but its wood smelt like cedar pencils, and was red as mahogany, which gave it its name. The tea-trees there were covered with tiny white bottle-brush flowers, and were rosy with their young shoots and leaves. Another sort was called the paper-bark tree, *Melaleuca leucadendron*. One could pull lumps of soft paper from it, tear it apart, and write on it without difficulty in a blotty sort of way. There were some old dead gum-trees left standing near the house to show the steps cut in them by opossum-hunting natives, who now no longer existed in those parts. The notches were probably only cut big enough to rest the great toe in, but the bark and tree had swelled as it grew older, and the holes were now large enough to hold the whole foot. Some of them had been enlarged into nests by the laughing jackass. Lots of those comical birds perched on those trees and gossiped about us, as we sat and watched them.

The garden at Doondale was a sight to see: pink and white *Azalea indica* fit for London shows, bougainvillea with three yellow blooms at once in their purple bracts, flame-trees (*Sterculia*) [probably Illawarra Flame Tree, *Brachychiton acerifolium*], gorgeous Cape lilies, and all our home-flowers in perfection. I was offered the loan of this lovely house for a month, when they were all going to another house on the cooler side of the hills. It had a valley of ferns a mile off, and one could see miles of cabbage-palms below like gigantic Turk's-head brooms, such as housemaids use to sweep away spiders with. The road along the coast to Kiama (pronounced 'Kye-aye-mar') was dreary enough, through miles of tall dead trees all ringed or burnt to death purposely by civilised man, who will repent some day when the country is all dried up, and grass refuses to grow any more.

At the lake of Illawarra we again found ourselves in the tropics, all tangled with unknown plants and greenery, abundant stag's-horns, banksias, hakea, and odd things. I put up at the house of a pretty little widow, who apologised for having a party to say goodbye to some friend. They danced till morning, soon after which she was up to see me off. Before this I had wandered on the lovely sea-sands, seeing and hearing the great waves as they dashed in and out of the blowholes. Rocks and giant fig-trees grew close to its edge, and I found basalt pillars as sharply cut as any on the Giant's Causeway itself. The road up the Kangaroo river [Valley] and over the sassafras mountain is pretty. I tried to make out the sassafras [*Doryphora sassafras*] leaves by their scent, but nearly all the leaves were much scented on that road, and it was not till some time afterwards that I made out the tree. After turning the top of the hill we came suddenly on the zamia or cycad [probably *Macrozamia communis*]—a most striking plant, with great cones standing straight up from the stem. When ripe the segments turn bright scarlet, and the whole cone falls to pieces, then they split open, and show seeds as large as acorns, from which a kind of arrowroot can be extracted, after washing out all the poison from it. The natives roast and eat the nut in the centre of the scarlet segments. There were no zamias outside that valley, which seemed to have no outlet. Like that of the Yosemite, it was discovered by a mere accident. It belonged, like the greater part of Illawarra, to the family of Osborne, who were building a large house there. It was certainly the most enticing part of Australia, and I wished I were an Osborne.

Helen Vellacott (ed.), *Some Recollections of a Happy Life* (1986).

KENNETH CLARK
(1903–83)

English patron and interpreter of the arts. Oxford-educated Clark was the director of the National Gallery in England (1933–45), before becoming the Slade professor of fine art at Oxford University (1946–50). He travelled to Australia in 1947, primarily to visit the National Gallery of Victoria in his role as Felton Bequest adviser. Chairman of the British Arts Council (1953–60), first chairman of the Independent Television Authority (1954–57), maker of numerous television programmes, including the acclaimed Civilisation *series of the late 1960s, and chancellor of York University (1969–79), Clark was awarded a life peerage in 1969. The following comments about Adelaide are taken from his account of his Australian trip in his 'self-portrait',* The Other Half *(1977), the second volume of his autobiography.*

ADELAIDE AND AUSTRALIAN ABORIGINAL ART (1947)

From Canberra I went to Adelaide, which is (or was) one of the most charming small cities in the world. I use the word city because it was conceived as such. Its founder, a young soldier named Colonel Light, looking down from a hill on to a piece of empty scrub, drew a plan, which still exists, of a *citta ideale.* Here he would place the theatre, there the art gallery, there the main street, and there the indispensable club, in which, as usual, I stayed; and of course Government House and the House of Parliament were not forgotten. There they all are, exactly as he placed them. It must be the only city of the nineteenth century planned from scratch, except, perhaps, for Hampstead Garden City, and it makes me sad that the word 'planner' has fallen into disrepute. It is surrounded by vineyards, planted by Germans. These all had German names, as elaborate as the names of the vineyards of the Rhine. During the first war it was thought patriotic to give them English names; after the war they took back their German names. Then came the second war, but nobody bothered to change their names again. The best of their wines are delicious. For some reason that I cannot now remember I had been asked to buy pictures for the Adelaide Gallery, as well as for that of Melbourne, and as the grant was quite small I was much more successful.

It was also in Adelaide that I became fully conscious of the fascination of Australian aboriginal art. I must have seen some in Melbourne, but it was more plentiful in South Australia, and the Adelaide Museum was full of it. When I say full, I mean it. Paintings and sculpture were piled on top of one another in a disgraceful manner. Apparently no one had looked at them with an appreciative eye. The bad conscience that now afflicts most decent Australians over the first settlers' treatment of the Aboriginals was just beginning to take effect in 1947, but was directed understandably against cruelty and injustice. No one had observed that these poor, harmless, stone age people had been sensitive artists. A few paintings were exhibited, and I managed to extract some more from the debris in the surrounding cases. They were more interesting than the carvings, which were not so different in style from those of New Guinea. They were done in delicate colours, perhaps because they were the only colours available, or perhaps as an expression of genuine delicacy of feeling; at all events, they were totally unlike the crude colours of 'primitive' art. Like the fauna and flora of Australia, they seemed to be completely cut off from the rest of the world. Most of them represented animals, but without any of the vitality of Stone Age art in Europe, or the Bushman's painting of South Africa. The animals were spread out quietly, and may have been painted after they had been eaten, as a sort of memorial, for the pictures always included a record of their insides as well as of their outer appearance. They were like very primitive X-rays, and, although they varied in quality, the best of them were moving works of art. They are still hardly known outside Australia, as a lunatic Act of Parliament has prohibited their export, as if they were fragments of the Parthenon frieze. In consequence there are far more of them in Australian museums than can be properly shown.

The Other Half (1986 edition, first published 1977).

———

CAROL O'BISO
(1954–)

American museum registrar. The chief registrar of the American Federation of Arts in New York from 1978 to 1985, O'Biso visited New Zealand in 1982 and 1984 to arrange the borrowing and packing of Te Maori, *a collection of Maori artefacts, for exhibition in the United States. After touring with it in America, O'Biso personally returned the collection to New Zealand in 1986 and subsequently took up residence in Auckland. The following stage in what she calls a 'magical journey' took place at Christchurch Museum in November 1982.*

'BRIEF INTERACTION'

The museum is smaller than some and larger than others. It is made of grey stone. I wait patiently with my colleagues in a hallway just inside the door. In time I hear the call. I hear the odd, eerie wail that wobbles slightly as it rises to an off-key crescendo and then begins to fall gradually away. My feet begin to move, slowly shuffling beside my colleagues and the wail continues to electrify the air until we are all inside the room. It follows us to our chairs and on its last breath there is the boom of other voices with other kinds of power. Then there is silence. Crashing silence.

Out of the silence a voice begins to speak. The voice is a man's voice and he moves forward among his people. He speaks at some length in this language that is foreign and musical and has many hard edges. I do not understand any of it but I am intrigued by its strangeness. When the man is done a second man stands up and begins to speak. He speaks in the same odd language and at different times seems angry or impassioned. He speaks violently and waves his arms. Soon he speaks in my own language but by the time the third man stands my attention has begun to wander. The speeches are familiar and there is no need to pay attention. I will not be called on to respond because I am a woman. Even though it is to me that they speak it is someone else sitting to my left who will answer for me. He is a man.

Instead of listening I begin to inspect these people. They are brown. Some more than others. Some are in their middle years and most older. All are a little too wide. Most wear ill-fitting clothes. There is one more speech and then the man to my left stands up and begins to speak to them in their mutual language. He is young and looks more Italian than I do. I trust that he is responding well for me because I have heard him speak in English and can only hope to be as eloquent.

He finishes and there are songs and prayers and then we are all led to another room where there is tea and pink cakes.

Now we are led again through intricate corridors and down a flight of stairs. The man who leads us is tall and has some authority here. He takes us to a room that is long and narrow and artificially lit. Down the center there is a long, wide counter and on the counter there are sixteen things. The things are nearly all wooden though some are bone or stone and some ivory. They are pendants, canoe prows and carvings of ancestors. Some are large and some very small. I have seen only poor photographs of these things and now I can see that they are all very beautiful or at least simple and elegant.

I begin to watch the brown people because they don't know what to do. The women stand awkwardly and clutch their white pocketbooks. The men shuffle a little from foot to foot. The fiery speeches and powerful wails are done now and here, in this clinical room with chrome sinks, they do not know what to do. The tall man speaks because he can see that it is his role to do that. He encourages everyone to look at the objects and then goes on to caution us. 'They are very fragile,' he says, 'and must be handled with extreme care and held only by their strongest points and only over the counter.' I listen to his long list of cautions. I have heard this speech before. I have made this speech before. It is a formal speech, a museum speech. The man finishes and waits expectantly as if something ought to happen. Nothing happens. I laugh out loud and everyone turns to me. I shift my body, soften it, make it casual. 'Notice,' I say, 'how everyone backs away from the table after that speech.' I am careful to keep a grin on my face. The tall man blushes but laughs with me and says no, really, it is all right to touch them, and then everything is okay and the people begin to move.

They are tentative at first, but then more and more excited. Some time goes by and discussions are had about the origins of this and the uses of that. They point and laugh and pick up the things made by their ancestors. They look and look with joy and wonder in their faces. They look in a way I have not seen faces look before and something strange begins to crawl in my body.

Soon they seem satisfied and there is another pause, another silence. Out of the silence a voice begins to speak. The voice is a man's and starts very low. He steps forward a little and everyone tries to hear what he is saying. He says it again, not louder, still in a whisper, but with more certainty this time. 'I am afraid,' he says. The man is beautiful. A beautiful brown man with white hair like down and hands that are massive but not thick. He is not tall and his trousers were made for someone tall so that they crumple, in front, over his worn shoes. He speaks gently, twisting a button on his brown cardigan and in the small, close room, no one moves.

'I'm afraid they won't come back,' he says. His voice is hoarse. He smiles at me in apology and in his eyes I see anguish. 'Something like that,' he says and nods his head towards a small wooden comb interwoven with linen threads, 'something like that might not ever come back.' His voice breaks a little and I can see that there are tears making their way down his brown cheeks. He reaches out with one hand and touches the comb, and the thing that was crawling in my body crawls up my back and down my arms and my palms begin to sweat. I am horrified now by something I cannot name and I stare from his face to his hand. Suddenly I know that what I have just seen was not a touch at all but a caress and for one very brief second I see but not with my eyes. Then I know but not with my mind and I think I will weep. My spokesman steps forward now.

He speaks quietly of their fears and nods to me indicating that I should begin my speech. My mind screams. It screams, no, this is not what is wanted here. It is not what is needed, but I speak anyway. I tell them about couriers and trucks with air-ride suspension. I tell them about foam rubber and cotton flannel and climate control. I tell them that I will personally supervise the packing of the objects. I show them glossy photographs of the packing system. I explain that I will personally escort the objects to New York, that I will unpack and inspect them in New York. I explain that I will do this at the beginning and end of each and every stop on the tour. Then I turn and say, 'Besides.' I look right at the beautiful brown man and point at him, my arm outstretched. 'Besides,' I say again, staring into his face, 'I will be thinking of you every *second* that I am with these things.' The man grabs my pointing finger and then my whole hand. He pulls me forward and embraces me so hard I cannot breathe and then he pushes me back. He holds my arms and looks into my eyes. 'Thank you,' he says very softly and kisses my cheek. 'You're welcome,' I say very softly, and for a moment he knows that I know.

Then it is over and the room starts to move. The brown people say how pleased they are to have met us and wish us well. They file out of the room and I am left with my colleagues to go about my work. Soon I am absorbed with my cameras and tape measures and papers and soon I have forgotten. I remember only that a beautiful brown man in Christchurch has asked a favor of me. I remember that I said yes.

First Light (1989 edition, first published 1987).

4

Scientists

◆

———

CHARLES DARWIN

(1809–82)

English naturalist and evolutionary theorist. While travelling as a naturalist on HMS Beagle *during its 1831–36 scientific expedition around the world, Darwin visited New Zealand ('not a pleasant place') in December 1835 and New South Wales, Van Diemen's Land, and Western Australia between January and March 1836. His observations of Australian Aborigines, flora, and fauna contributed to the development of his theory of evolution through natural selection, expressed in his* On the Origin of Species *(1859) and* The Descent of Man *(1871). Although he later reputedly dreamed of emigrating to Tasmania, which one would not have predicted from reading the following description of his visit to that island, taken from his* Beagle *journal, Darwin did not leave England again after 1836.*

DARWIN IN VAN DIEMEN'S LAND (1836)

30th. [January] —The Beagle sailed for Hobart Town in Van Diemen's Land. On the 5th of February, after a six days' passage, of which the first part was fine, and the latter very cold and squally, we entered the mouth of Storm Bay: the weather justified this awful name. The bay should rather be called an estuary, for it receives at its head the waters of the Derwent. Near the mouth, there are some extensive basaltic platforms; but higher up the land becomes mountainous, and is covered by a light wood. The lower parts of the hills which skirt the bay are cleared; and the bright yellow fields of corn, and dark green ones of potatoes, appeared very luxuriant. Late in the evening we anchored in the snug cove, on the shores of which stands the capital of Tasmania. The first aspect of the place was very inferior to that of Sydney; the latter might be called a city, this only a town. It stands at the base of Mount Wellington, a mountain 3100 feet high, but of little picturesque beauty: from this source, however, it receives a good supply of water. Round the cove there are some fine warehouses, and on one side a small fort. Coming from the Spanish settlements, where such magnificent care has generally been paid to the fortifications, the means of defence in these colonies appeared very contemptible. Comparing the town with Sydney, I was chiefly struck with the comparative fewness of the large houses, either built or building. Hobart Town, from the census of 1835, contained 13 826 inhabitants, and the whole of Tasmania 36 505.

All the aborigines have been removed to an island in Bass's Straits, so that Van Diemen's land enjoys the great advantage of being free from a native population. This most cruel step seems to have been quite unavoidable, as the only means of stopping a fearful succession of robberies, burnings, and murders, committed by the blacks; and which sooner or later would have ended in their utter destruction. I fear there is no doubt, that this train of evil and its consequences, originated in the infamous conduct of some of our countrymen. Thirty years is a short period, in which to have banished the last aboriginal from his native island,—and that island nearly as large as Ireland. The correspondence on this subject, which took place between the government at home and that of Van Diemen's Land, is very interesting. Although numbers of natives were shot and taken prisoners in the skirmishing, which was going on at intervals for several years; nothing seems fully to have impressed them with the idea of our overwhelming power, until the whole island, in 1830, was put under martial law, and by proclamation the whole population commanded to assist in one great attempt to secure the entire race. The plan adopted was nearly similar to that of the great hunting-matches in India: a line was formed reaching across the island, with the intention of driving the natives into a *cul-de-sac* on Tasman's peninsula. The attempt failed; the natives, having tied up their dogs, stole during one night through the lines. This is far from surprising, when their practised senses, and usual manner of crawling after wild animals is considered. I have been assured that they can conceal themselves on almost bare ground, in a manner which until witnessed is scarcely credible; their dusky bodies being easily mistaken for the blackened stumps which are scattered all over the country. I was told of a trial between a party of Englishmen and a native, who was to stand in full view on the side of a bare hill; if the Englishmen closed their eyes for less than a minute, he would squat down, and then they were never able to distinguish him from the surrounding stumps. But to return to the hunting-match; the natives understanding this kind of warfare, were terribly alarmed, for they at once perceived the power and numbers of the whites. Shortly afterwards a party of thirteen belonging to two tribes came in; and, conscious of their unprotected condition, delivered themselves up in despair. Subsequently by the intrepid exertions of Mr Robinson, an active and benevolent man, who fearlessly visited by himself the most hostile of the natives, the whole were induced to act in a similar manner. They were then removed to an island, where food and clothes were provided them. Count Strzelecki states, that 'at the epoch of their deportation in 1835, the number of natives amounted to 210. In 1842, that is after the interval of seven years, they mustered only fifty-four individuals; and, while each family of the interior of New South Wales, uncontaminated by contact with the whites, swarms with children, those of Flinders' Island had during eight years, an accession of only fourteen in number!'

The Beagle staid here ten days, and in this time I made several pleasant little excursions, chiefly with the object of examining the geological structure of the immediate neighbourhood. The main points of interest consist, first in some highly fossiliferous strata, belonging to the Devonian or Carboniferous period; secondly, in proofs of a late small rise of the land; and lastly, in a solitary and superficial patch of yellowish limestone or travertin, which contains numerous impressions of leaves of trees, together with land-shells, not now existing. It is not improbable that this one small quarry, includes the only remaining record of the vegetation of Van Diemen's Land during one former epoch.

The climate here is damper than in New South Wales, and hence the land is more fertile. Agriculture flourishes: the cultivated fields look well, and the gardens abound with thriving vegetables and fruit-trees. Some of the farm-houses, situated in retired spots, had a very attractive appearance. The general aspect of the vegetation is similar to that of Australia; perhaps it is a little more green and cheerful; and the pasture between the trees rather more abundant. One day I took a long walk on the side of the bay opposite to the town: I crossed in a steamboat, two of which are constantly plying backwards and forwards. The machinery of one of these vessels was entirely manufactured in this colony, which, from its very foundation, then numbered only three and thirty years! Another day I ascended Mount Wellington; I took with me a guide, for I failed in a first attempt, from the thickness of the wood. Our guide, however, was a stupid fellow, and conducted us to the southern and damp side of the mountain, where the vegetation was very luxuriant; and where the labour of the ascent, from the number of rotten trunks, was almost as great as on a mountain in Tierra del Fuego or in Chiloe. It cost us five and a half hours of hard climbing before we reached the summit. In many parts the Eucalypti grew to a great size, and composed a noble forest. In some of the dampest ravines, tree-ferns flourished in an extraordinary manner; I saw one which must have been at least twenty feet high to the base of the fronds, and was in girth exactly six feet. The fronds forming the most elegant parasols, produced a gloomy shade, like that of the first hour of night. The summit of the mountain is broad and flat, and is composed of huge angular masses of naked greenstone. Its elevation is 3100 feet above the level of the sea. The day was splendidly clear, and we enjoyed a most extensive view; to the north, the country appeared a mass of wooded mountains, of about the same height with that on which we were standing, and with an equally tame outline: to the south the broken land and water, forming many intricate bays, was mapped with clearness before us. After staying some hours on the summit, we found a better way to descend, but did not reach the Beagle till eight o'clock, after a severe day's work.

Journal of Researches into the Geology and Natural History of the various countries visited by HMS. Beagle (1845 edition, first published 1839).

———

W. H. HARVEY

(1811–66)

Irish botanist. Harvey was colonial treasurer of Cape Town from 1836 to 1842, before being appointed a professor of botany in Dublin in 1848. A specialist in algae, he visited India, Australia, New Zealand, Tonga, and Fiji between 1853 and 1856. In the following letter to his sister, the 'contented botanist', as the editor of his letters dubs him, tells of his stay on Phillip Island.

A VISIT TO PHILLIP ISLAND

Melbourne Dec 29th—1854

My dear Hannah,

I wrote last from Queen's Cliff the beginning of this month & threw it into the Post office to go by some chance ship & whether my letter be still lying in the office, or on its way to Dublin, I know not.— In the mean time I have recd your welcome letters from Dublin & Plassey to the beginning of October by which I have good accounts of all our circle, but poor little Beck, but as she seemed to be recovering by the latest date, I hope & trust she is long since well of the *erycipolus*. — Soon after sending off my letter, the Wyvern made her appearance & I went on board on the 7th but owing to contrary wind, did not sail for Western Port till the 8th I believe I wrote before that the Govr. had kindly sent this vessel specially to take me to Western Port.— My accomodation on board was magnificent, first astern cabin, to sleep in — then a saloon to lounge & read in & finally a large spare cabin to myself for spreading plants & papers—I commenced at once to take possession by hanging lines across the Cabin & spreading papers all about & also on the decks above to dry in the sun.—The Commander had brought his wife with him for the trip & we got on right well together We weighed anchor soon after daylight on the 8th & drifted out with the tide with scarcely any wind, & this soon deserted us, so that we only got as far as Cape Schank—some 25 miles—by sundown—This cape is a bald rocky headland covered with trees & in front of it is a detached columnar rock called the Pulpit—but looking more like a large ship—Mrs Keys amused herself by catching fish—& I was either shifting my plants, or falling asleep over a novel on the sofa all the sunny day.—At night, we lay off the shore & at daylight steered again for Western Port, but with scarcely any wind, creeping, creeping slowly along the coast.—We soon sighted the West end of Phillip's Island (our destination)—with a large haystack looking islet in front called 'the Knobby'—& entered the harbour about 11 oclock A.M.— Presently we saw the houses on Phillip Island; & I went ashore in the boat to see whether this was Mr MacHaffie's station & to ask whether I could be allowed to billet myself on him for a fortnight or so—I found Mrs McH—at home & she assured me her husband would take me in &c—& that I could have every facility for my plants &c &c—so I returned to the Wyvern & landed after dinner with bag & baggage weighing nearly 5 Cwt—which the sailors had to carry on their backs from the shore over the sandhills & a ¼ of a mile to the house—poor things!—I have called Mr McH's dwelling a 'house'—but it is in Colonial phrase only a '*hut*', being a 3 roomed 'wattle & dab' erection—like a very small cottage—Half the hut forms the living room where meals are taken & where all household affairs, except cooking (which is done in another detached hut) go on—Here I laid down my plants by day at a corner of the table & slept by night on one of the stretchers, which served as sofas by day—My luggage was partly stowed away in the wool shed & partly thrust under the sofas.—One of the bedrooms was a nursery for a precious baby of 6 months old—the other was occupied by Mr & Mrs McH—Capt. & Mrs Keys landed with me & spent the evening at the Hut.—The Capt. went out quail shooting but though the birds were very plentiful & we heard many shots, he came home at sundown with empty pockets to be laughed at by his wife & the company.—The next day was Sunday—the vessel sailed away by daylight & in the afternoon Mr McHaffie & I walked out to view some of the places which he thought would be best worthy my exploring.—We first crossed the island about 2 miles to the South shore & then walked westward toward the 'Knobby' & so home by the beaches on the northern coast which latter we fixed on as the best ground—The surf is too great on the South shore for much work.—In calm weather it tumbles in just as it does at Kilkee incessantly & in storms it must be magnificent—In many places the beaches were strewed with wrecks, no lack of drift timber for all purposes.—We also picked up several pretty *sponges* of sundry kinds & I have since collected a barrel full, which I hope soon to send home.—

The Island contains nearly 37 square miles or 24 000 acres which Mr McH has all to himself at a trifling quit rent from Govt He is what is called a '*squatter*'—when he came to the Island 12 years ago, it was so densely covered with 'scrub' & small trees that it was scarcely possible to walk in any direction without the greatest difficulty & every one thought him mad for going there with his sheep—But by judicious annual burnings, he has completely cleared away the scrub, in place of which has sprung up a thick covering of grass & he has now about 16 000 sheep & 140 horses pasturing on the Island & there is ample food for 4000 sheep more.—He has the Island fenced off into 3 divisions or 'runs'—one of which is burned every summer—so that the whole Island is burnt once in 3 years.—This keeps down the scrub & clears away the coarse grass which the sheep reject & favours the springing of fresh juicy herbage—One end of the island is abundantly supplied with excellent water (a rare thing in Australia) the other end is but badly supplied—He has introduced *deer* which are increasing & some earlier *Crusoe* had let hogs run wild.—These are rather a nuisance as they are apt to eat the young lambs & he has been obliged to shoot or poison them.—They make no use of the slaughtered wild pig—strange to say.—The small Kangaroo or Wallaby is plentiful—though I only saw one, which waited till I came within 20 yards & then hopped away in double quick time.—The advantages of living in an Island are manifold—Having no neighbours, his cattle cannot trespass & as they cannot swim to the mainland, neither can they escape.—There are no native dogs & no natives—& no thieves, save when some little coasting vessel happens to cast anchor in the island when the hungry sailors sometimes take a sheep or two.—He only requires to keep two men & a boy to manage the flocks—& himself & his nephew as overseers—If he were on shore he would require at least 20 Shepherds & perhaps not have the work as well done.—I just arrived at the conclusion of the annual shearing—at which time he hires 6 shearers to come from Melbourne.—This year he has 120 bales of wool of the value of upwards of £3000—nearly all clear profit—I believe he has made his fortune for Mrs McH says they will go home finally in a year & a half, as she thinks it foolish to remain in the lurch away from their friends, when they can live comfortably at home.—She will not let him build, or improve the *hut*, but he should be *too comfortable* & unwilling to move.—She has only been out here 2 or 3 years.—He went home to marry her after a 15 years engagement!—She is a very nice person & often reminded me of Eliza Prin of Mount St—I have told her she is to come to the Quay if ever they visit Dublin as they may do & I am sure you will like her.— She has lost 2 previous babies & has only the one.—She used frequently sit by me, while I was laying down seaweeds & we chatted very pleasantly on various matters.—Nothing could exceed their kindness to me, the whole time I was with them—a fortnight.— I had the use of every thing & all the available room & liberty to have my wet papers on lines all round the sitting room till it looked like one of R Webb's drying rooms!—I have made a very good collection of Algae at the Island & discovered one very curious new Genus, which I call '*Bob-tails*' colloquially—but am going to call it *Bellotia* botanically in memory of Lieut Bellot the young French volunteer, who was lost in the search for Franklyn.—It belongs to '*Sporochnea*' & is very like except in colour (which is brown) the many headed *cotton grass* of your bogs—The 'bobs' are quite as large.—It is the most remarkable Algae I have yet found in Australia & as it is to be named after a Frenchman I intend to send it to a friend in Paris, to be noticed before the French Institute & published first in that City.—The Island consists altogether of trap rocks I have not seen any regular columns—but in several places the flat rocky surface between tide marks is broken in a semi crystalline way, into hexangular pieces like the tops of the columns in the Giants causeway.—In some spots the honey combing is quite regular, each being about 2 feet in diameter.—There are alternate reefs & beaches round the Island.—I got most on the latter the reefs being too shallow & with too few deep pools to yield many good Algae.—The shores are thickly strewn with sponges, of all shapes & textures & with immense quantities of a sea squirt or (Ascidian)—which looks extremely like a dried Normandy pippin or a wizzened potatoe!—It is either solitary or in masses with a thick brown hide & its mouths are surrounded with 4 or 5 fleshy plates which look like the withered blossom at the top of the Apple.—On the end of one of the reefs, a much larger species of a similar animal is abundant. It is funnel shaped one or two feet high—excessively tough, stiff & shaggy—& adheres most firmly to the rocks—standing high & dry at low tides—A species of burrowing Echinus or urchins, something like those at Miltown, is found in the rock pools.—I have preserved a pair for R Ball—& also picked up a dead *Cidaris* on the shore for the same gentleman —

So my time passed rapidly away—fully occupied with my collections & at the end of the fortnight to my no small regret—the Wyvern came to take me back & I left the Island not half explored—But we cant do every thing & I must not delay too long in one place.—I went on board on Xmas eve sailed early Xmas morning & anchored in Port Phillip that evening—opposite a mountain called Arthurs seat, at the foot of which dwells another 'squatter' a Mr Burrell, with a cattle run of 25 square miles.—He has no near neighbour, but has a family of 10 children a wife & sister in law & a very agreeable family they are—We spent Stephen's day with them very pleasantly—They gave Capt. Keys & me horses & 4 of the sons also mounted took us up to the top of the 'Seat'—which is nearly 2000 feet high & commands a very extensive view of land & water.—The day was hazy so we missed the more distant part.—the mountain is covered with wood, but not densely & there is considerable variety of trees.—The she oaks & Banksias were particularly fine & so was the wild 'cherry' (with the stone on the outside) of which you have heard—The fruit thereon was ripening, but is much more like a yewberry in appearance than a cherry—The tree itself is like a *Savine* in appearance & of a beautiful bright yellow green colour— The botanical structure of this fruit is a *dry fruit* (called the stone) sitting on a fleshy fruit stalk (called the cherry).—We came down the Mt. by a different route to the beach & had a gallop home along the sands.—At night we returned on board, but had so little wind next day that we did not anchor at Melbourne till late in the evening—nor did I land till midday the following day (yesterday) when I again established myself at Wm Robinson's & got my letters which had been lying for me.—I shall stay here a week or so, putting my Victoria collections to rights & leave them for shipment before starting for V. D Land where I mean to spend the next 3 months—returning to Melbourne in *April*, if spared so long.—I am at present, thank Goodness, in good health & spirits & not at all homesick!—what a pity!!—

Jany 5th 1855.—I wrote the enclosed a week ago & have been very busy since examining my collections & putting them in order previous to packing up & sending home.—I hope to finish by Monday evening the 8th & then be ready for the Launceston steamer which leaves in a day or two.—I hope to send bill of lading by overland mail.—I am not discribing the new species, as I cannot spare the time but I shall probably characterise the new Genera—of which there are some half dozen—I have called a very beautiful plant Apjohnia partly after Dr A —& partly after his wife who is a '*follower*' of mine.—The weather is not so abominable as [...] would make you believe—Most of the days are pleasant enough for summer—Yesterday we had a hot wind & dust storm—but I stayed at home, working with the microscope & so escaped it pretty well & the evening was cool & pleasant.—I went out to the yearly meeting of the Episcopal Church to hear the statement of accounts & 'occurrences for the progress'—There were several speakers.—The Bishop who presided gave us an interesting sketch of the past & present state of the Diocese & his prospects for the future.—When he arrived 7 years ago, there were only 3 clergymen in the Colony—now there are 47 doing duty.—still more are required & he is going to England for the purpose of further advancing this branch church.—The council here has lately passed an Act for establishing a sort of Church Constitution in which a liberal form of Govt something similar to that of the American Church will be recognised by law the Bishop specially goes home to try & get the Queen's assent to this Act which seems necessary.—I hope he may get it—but I have my fears— from my opinion the only use made in the present day of what is called the 'Royal Supremacy'—is to obstruct every useful or good movement of the times.—I hope we may live to see this relic of oppression & mistake given up for ever—But I have not time to say all I think & thou would not care to hear it either—farewell I am thank Goodness in good health & spirits not homesick or tired—I rise at 5 & go to bed before 11—Gabe Unthank is now here employed by WR. to manage his boarding house. He is very obliging and useful—RF Alexander started yesterday for the Ovens diggings—Their boarding house at Geelong was a failure—

> Thine affe WHH
>
> Wm. Robinson (of Thos. Bewley & Co) has arrived safely—

Sophie C. Ducker (ed.), *The Contented Botanist: Letters of W. H. Harvey about Australia and the Pacific* (1988).

GEORGE CAMPBELL

(1850–1912)

*British naval officer. The fourth son of the 8th duke of Argyll, Campbell
served on HMS* Challenger *during much of its 1872–76 scientific world
cruise, which included visits to Australia and New Zealand. Although not a
scientist himself, he was keenly involved in the expedition's work of sounding,
dredging, surveying, and observation. When ashore, he and his colleagues
showed a remarkable propensity for shooting at almost anything that moved,
a practice that reached its nadir in butterfly-shooting on Australia's Cape
York, a 'new sport' to Campbell. 'Many were shot at … and many were
blown to pieces.' (Not surprisingly, only one specimen was procured.) They
also shot animals, fish, and birds.*

'RAINE ISLAND, GREAT BARRIER REEF'

We steered for the entrance through the 'Great Barrier' reef, 1300 miles
away, where we arrived on the 30th, sounding the day after we left in
deeper water than we have found for a long time—2650 fms,—and six
times afterwards in somewhat lesser depths, in which we twice trawled.
On that evening we passed Raine Island, which lies on one side of the
entrance through and into the maze of reefs, and anchored close to it
on a coral patch that night. Raine Island is a small extent of sand on the
top of a coral reef, having on some parts of it a foot deep of soil, and is
marked by a large beacon-tower built with coral rock by two men-of-
war, assisted by artificers from Brisbane in '48.

Wheeling over the ship and island in countless thousands were sea-
birds, boobies, terns, frigate- and tropic- birds. And, by the way, I have
never seen more bird-life at sea than on this stretch between Api and
Raine Islands. Nearly every day long-tailed tropic-birds flew above and
around the ship in twos and threes; great flocks of tern were seen fishing—diving into the sea with a splash in the distance; occasionally a
frigate-bird soared and wheeled quietly overhead with motionless
wings, and long forked tail constantly opening and closing; stupid old
boobies, perching on our yards and boats, were caught and ruthlessly
skinned; little petrels skimmed our wake; while sharks, the brutes!
glided around us whenever we stopped—sounding or dredging.

The next morning the ship got under way, and a number of us land-ed on Raine Island—a wonderful sight indeed! As we landed the terns rose *en masse* in a cloud, really darkening the light, and perceptibly fan-ning the air with their wings as they hovered, screaming shrilly, above us. The ground, covered with long coarse grass, and, in some places, overspread with a creeping plant, was alive with young terns, cheeping and feebly falling about in the grass. There were boobies of three species, too stupid and lazy to fly away till you actually made them; even then commencing a hoarse, indignant argument—in the mean-time, I fancy, mentally gathering up their skirts—before they turned and flapped slowly away. Most of these were sitting on newly-hatched, ugly little offspring, or on eggs.

The boobies and terns were nesting, or otherwise looking after their young, indiscriminately together; but the frigate-birds had a rookery of their own, with young downy creatures standing sheepishly up, nearly ready to fly.

Dead turtle, faded skeletons with shells peeling off were lying about here and there. At one place, where they had tried to get up a steep little bank from the sand on to the grass, they were piled in a heap, hav-ing from weakness or other cause failed to get up, and so died. Why they tried this particular spot was, of course, their own lookout; but as it was the only steep bit in the whole island round, it appeared to us stupid, to say the least of it. Others were lying dead among the grass in the centre of the island. I don't know what causes turtle to die—old age, I suppose. It was a pity for us that this was not their egg-laying sea-son, for which purpose the beach seemed a perfect one.

Sam was great fun, and enjoyed life amazingly; how he dashed at the boobies, caught them, gave them a shake as he would a rat, and some-times, if the booby was a wide-awake one, and flew off just as Sam rushed up, he jumped, caught booby's feet, and booby, crying lustily, and pecking viciously, was dragged down. And the unkind manner with which he tossed the cheepers about—one shake and a flick over his shoulder—was certainly very savage; but Sam is in heart the most gentle of dogs, and when I forbade him further cruelty, not another bird did he touch. It was only Kerguelen reminiscences bubbling up and overflowing.

With us all cruising about and guns popping, the bird-population was now thoroughly aroused; the terns rising in a dense cloud as we approached, hiding the sea and sky; while their young were so thickly scattered in the grass that where they were most numerous you could not help kicking them about, although the greater number were able to run quickly. As one walked away the cloud of birds descended bodily to the earth again. Plucky little birds these, giving one the idea that they stick to their babies from parental love, while the boobies give one the notion of doing so from stupidity, keeping to their nests till driven away, when they joined their innumerable kind swiftly flying overhead.

The frigate-birds remained over their rookery, soaring far up, but swooping down occasionally, and then we shot them. Theirs is a beautiful easy flight; the narrow body terminating in long thin bill and tail poised between sharp motionless wings. I have seldom seen a frigate-bird flap its wings. One I watched a long time the other day at sea. At first a speck in the distant sky, then wheeling high over the ship in circles, and again sailing away into the distance with never a movement of the wings, and down below with us there was scarcely any wind, though, doubtless, he had plenty up there in the skies. The 'bos'un' or 'tropic-birds' flap their wings rapidly, rather like a pigeon's flight; at sea they are the most beautiful birds one seas, as the sun strikes on their snow-white plumage and long streamer tails against the blue sky. We saw no red-tailed ones.

Eleven species of birds we found at Raine Island:—three gannet, two tern (the noddy and another in far greater number), one gull, one tropic-bird, one rail, one frigate-bird, one heron, one turn-stone (in flocks). Fish were swimming about in the shallows among the coral, and two I shot.

After about three hours on shore, we went on board, and anchored again that night on a reef further up the passage. Sailing in these coral seas, within the Great Barrier reef, ships have, of course, to anchor every night. Coral reefs are scattered broadcast—some cropping up above the water, while others, the most dangerous, are always covered. A few of the higher ones have patches of sand and soil on them, covered sparsely with grass or scrub, while those beneath the surface show merely as green or brown patches on the water, or else as a foaming line of breakers, warning one by sight and sound to beware. Under way at daylight next morning we threaded the passage up to Cape York, passing endless reefs and islands; a glorious fresh breeze rattling us merrily up to the anchorage, where we arrived just at dusk.

Log-Letters from 'The Challenger' (1881 edition, first published 1877).

CARL LUMHOLTZ
(1851–1922)

Norwegian ethnographer and naturalist. Sponsored by the University of Christiania, Lumholtz, who had graduated in theology in 1876, visited Australia from 1880 to 1884 to study the Aborigines and their customs and to collect zoological specimens. A tree-kangaroo that he described while in Australia was named after him. He spent most of his time in Queensland, some of it with the Archer family at Gracemere. From August 1882 to July 1883 he was based in the Herbert River area, where he lived among Aborigines. Although subjective and unsystematic, the observations in his unfortunately titled Among Cannibals *(1889), a work that appeared in several languages, are considered to be of some significance. He also wrote about his later researches in Mexico and Borneo.*

KVINGAN AND OTHER SPIRITS

The season was already so far advanced that it was out of the question to get back to my headquarters before Christmas. The new 'land,' which we reached after a short time, presented a grand, wild, and romantic aspect. We descended from the table-land and suddenly got sight of Herbert river, flowing dark and restless far down in the depths below.

We followed the bend of the river to the east, walking on a ledge of the steep mountain nearly a thousand feet above the level of the water. Below us the mountain presented a wild, broken mass, while above it was overgrown with dense scrubs. Near the chief bend of the river we made our camp by the side of a mountain brook which plunged down over the precipice. It was no easy matter to find a place for a camp here, for it was a spot on which a person could scarcely lie in a horizontal position.

The natives had some strange superstitions in regard to this place. In the depths below dwelt a monster, *Yamina*, which ate men, and of which the natives stood in mortal fear. No one dared to sleep down there. Blacks who had attempted to do so had been eaten, and once, when a dance had been held there, some persons had been lost. I proposed to take a walk thither, but they simply shrugged their shoulders and did not answer. A gun would be of no use, they said, for the monster was invulnerable.

It was *Kvingan*, their evil spirit, who chiefly haunted this spot. His voice was often heard of an evening or at night from the abyss or from the scrubs. I made the discovery that the strange melancholy voice which they attributed to the spirit belonged to a bird which could be heard at a very great distance. But I must admit that it is the most mysterious bird's voice that I have ever heard, and it is not strange that a people so savage as the Australian natives should have formed superstitious notions in regard to it. *Kvingan* is found in the most inaccessible mountain regions, and I have heard it not only here but also in the adjoining districts. During these moonlight nights I tried several times to induce the natives to go with me to shoot the bird, but it was, of course, blasphemous to propose such a thing, and their consent was out of the question.

At other times, when they spoke of their evil spirit, I found that it manifested itself in a cicada. Their notions in regard to their evil spirit appeared to be very much confused. This insect, the cicada, produces in the summer a very shrill sound in the tree-tops, but it is impossible to discover it by the sound. It is this loud shrill sound, which comes from every direction, and which is not to be traced to any particular place, that has evidently given rise to superstitious ideas concerning it.

In the south-eastern part of Australia the evil spirit of the natives is called *Bunjup*, a monster which is believed to dwell in the lakes. It has of late been supposed that this is a mammal of considerable size that has not yet been discovered. It may be added that the devil in various parts of Australia is described as a monster with countless eyes and ears, so that he is able to see and hear in all directions. He has sharp claws, and can run so fast that it is difficult to escape him. He is cruel, and spares no one either young or old. The reason that the natives so frequently move their camp is, no doubt, owing to the fact that they are anxious to avoid the devil, who constantly discovers where they are. At times he is supposed to reveal himself to the older and more experienced men in the tribe, who accordingly are highly esteemed. The natives on the Gulf of Carpentaria say that the devil's lips are fastened by a string to his forehead.

With the exception of the instance already described, I never heard of any effort being made by the natives to propitiate the wrath of this evil being. They simply have a superstitious fear of it and of the unknown generally.

Among Cannibals (1889).

FRANCIS RATCLIFFE

(1904–70)

British biologist. In his popular account of his 'youthful wanderings in Australia', Ratcliffe, who had graduated from Oxford, where he was one of Sir Julian Huxley's students, described two surveys that he undertook for the Council for Scientific and Industrial Research, one of flying-foxes in Queensland (1929–31), the other into soil erosion from South Australia to Queensland (1935). The first part of his account, from which the following extract is taken, was written in Scotland, the second, later, in Australia, where he ultimately settled. He died in Canberra in 1970, after a distinguished scientific career.

AUSTRALIAN BUSH THROUGH ENGLISH EYES

Between the mountain and the capital [Brisbane] are fifty miles of bush, with scattered farms, a couple of townships, and a river or two spanned by wooden bridges. I travelled by service car, an interested and expectant passenger, alert to take in every detail of a very strange country. Nevertheless, all that remains in my memory of that drive is a blur of something very like disappointment. The scenes that struck me were scenes of monotony and ugliness and untidiness: the lack of colour in the eucalyptus forest, square wooden bungalows raised on stilts, flood-borne litter strewn along the river-banks, muck and driftwood and dead grass, which clung to the bridges and loaded down the branches of the waterside shrubs. Paradoxically enough it was the jungle, itself as strange to me as the eucalyptus forest, which brought relief as of something natural and familiar.

The whole thing, as I now know, was a matter of eyes. Mine were still English eyes, and as such simply could not see Australia. English eyes have set ideas about trees and about light and distances. They can appreciate the jungle, because for all its exotic show the jungle is only an exaggerated wood. Its trees, though bizarre, are in essence what trees should be—trunks supporting a leafy mass which breaks the light and casts a shadow. But among the gum-trees English eyes are as good as blind. They are almost literally blinded by the light. The thin grey foliage is carried at the end of the branches high against the sky; the fierce Australian light pours through it and floods the grass, the earth, and the trunks and limbs of the trees themselves, washing away the colour and leaving a monotone of bright yellowish grey. In time (the process in my case took a month at least) the eyes adjust themselves, taking on, so to speak, a pair of physiological dark spectacles which make allowance for the glare and reveal the bush as it really is. They then see the colours hidden behind the brightness—rather restrained colours it is true, but very well suited to the open distances.

It cannot be denied that the bush has more than its share of monotony. This again is due to the eucalypts. This genus plays a part in Australia to which there can be no parallel in any other country of the world. From Cape York in the far north to Gippsland in the south, one can travel (avoiding human settlement and the isolated patches of swamp and jungle) through an unbroken forest of eucalyptus. It will vary in form between forest proper and open parkland; but from the tropics to the temperate zone, from the low river flats to the mountaintops, the eucalyptus rules. Instead of relinquishing its dominance (as in England beech gives place to elm and oak, and the oak in turn to birch and pine) the eucalyptus keeps it in the family, and species succeeds species (there are over four hundred and fifty in all) as the country and the climate change.

Flying Fox and Drifting Sand (1963 edition, first published 1938).

DAVID ATTENBOROUGH

(1926–)

British broadcaster and writer. After being educated at Cambridge University, Attenborough served in the Royal Navy from 1947 to 1949, was an editorial assistant in a publishing house from 1949 to 1952, and then worked in various capacities with BBC Television from 1952 to 1973. Freelance from 1973, he has won many awards for his natural history documentaries. Attenborough wrote of his travels in the Northern Territory in Quest Under Capricorn *(1963).*

MAGPIE GEESE NEAR NOURLANGIE, NORTHERN TERRITORY

The South Alligator River rises a hundred miles south of Nourlangie in a wilderness of empty hills. As it winds its way northwards, it is joined by smaller streams that come tumbling down the fretted western edge of the great rock plateaux of Arnhem Land. Strengthened, the river slides on towards the coast, sometimes, in the dry season, sinking from sight beneath spits of hot white sand, sometimes swelling into stretches of deep amber water, haunted by cockatoos and crocodiles. And then, as it nears its final destination in the Timor Sea, it loses its way. It spills over the wide flats near Nourlangie and lingers, entangled by reeds and clutched by the arching roots of mangroves, in a maze of shimmering swamps.

It was late in the evening when we went down to these marshes for the first time. To reach them we had to drive across wide plains of blue earth, bare but for isolated tussocks of coarse grass. Only a month or so previously all this land had itself been submerged. But the sun, beating on the waters from a cloudless sky, had transformed the shallow tepid lagoons first into bogs and then into acres of mud. To these quagmires herds of buffalo had come, plodding hock high, to wallow in the softness. But they had not been able to enjoy the squelching bog for long. As the last drops of moisture evaporated, the sun, with the swiftness and ferocity of a fire in a potter's kiln, had baked the mud stone-hard. Now as we drove across the plains, once so viscous that they had sucked at the buffalo's legs, the rigid curling edges of the deep hoof-marks shook the wheels of our truck as violently as if we had been driving across a field of granite boulders.

We jolted slowly across the flats towards a belt of trees that marked the beginning of a permanent lagoon. A hundred yards short of them we stopped and, as the rattle of our engine died away, we heard, rising from beyond the trees, a throbbing chorus that filled the air like the sound of a gigantic swarm of bees. There was no mistaking it. It was the contented murmur of honks and grunts made by an immense flock of wildfowl.

Cautiously we walked towards the trees and picked our way through them, stepping with the greatest care lest the snap of a twig breaking underfoot should signal our presence. We reached the far edge of the thicket and peered through a chink in the veil of leaves that screened us from the swamp.

No matter how often you have seen great gatherings of waterfowl, moments such as these are unfailingly thrilling. The lagoon was vast. It stretched from within a few yards of where we crouched for at least a mile ahead. Away to the left, the sun was already setting behind a small bush-covered island, tingeing the opal-grey expanse of water with pink. And everywhere there were birds; strings of ibis flying across the red-flecked sky; black duck, pygmy geese, whistling duck, teal and shelduck, each keeping to their separate flotillas; pied herons standing in tightly packed ranks on the shores; pratincoles, small brown wading birds, pattering about in the shallows excitedly flicking their tails from side to side as they searched for insects; and most abundant of all, dominating the lagoon as their voices filled the air, magpie geese.

It was the geese which held our attention. Most of the other birds in front of us are found elsewhere in Australia, and there were few species that we had not seen before. But nowhere in the world, except in tropical Australia and New Guinea, can you see magpie geese in any number, and nowhere do they congregate in larger flocks than in the swamps around Nourlangie.

They were strange looking creatures, somewhat gawky compared with other species of geese. Their legs were unusually long, their bodies rather heavy. On top of their heads they had a curious conical hump, like a clown's cap. In colour, they were black with a broad cummerbund of white encircling their breasts and back. Most of them were dabbling in the waters, plunging down their long necks to search for the bulbs of water plants. Some had already finished feeding and were standing motionless in the water. How many there were I could not begin to judge, but in the South Alligator swamps alone there are said to be about a hundred thousand—so many that quite recently a few people in the Territory came to regard them as a pest.

Some years ago an attempt was made to grow rice at Humpty Doo, forty miles south of Darwin. Enormous areas of land were cleared and planted with rice seedlings. Wild rice has always been one of the favourite foods of the magpie goose and when the birds discovered this new and munificent addition to their feeding grounds, they descended on the fields in huge flocks. The farmers tried to scare them away with bright lights, rattles, scarecrows and hooters. But nothing was really effective. Poisoned bait was put down for them, but although many were killed, the size of the flocks was scarcely affected, for birds were continually arriving from all over the Territory. Eventually, the military were called in. Squads of machine gunners, in watches, maintained a regular fusillade over the sprouting crop. But the acreage involved was too big; the geese merely flew away from the guns and settled down again out of range. Finally the whole project was abandoned. The geese had won.

But if this was a victory for the birds, it had been preceded by a whole series of defeats. Once magpie geese lived all over Australia. They were spectacular prizes for sportsmen and were heavily hunted, many of the swamps on which they depended for food in the dry season were drained, and by the middle of this century they had been exterminated as a breeding species over most of the continent. Today they still disperse widely over Australia during the rainy season, but as the billabongs and marshes disappear with the coming of the dry, they retreat again up here to the northern coast, which is now their last refuge.

We crouched among the mangroves for some time watching the birds, but to tackle any serious filming, we needed a hide and to build it we should have to reveal ourselves. I stepped through the leaves on to the muddy shore. There was a thunder of wings and the whole flock peeled off the surface, circled and flew to a distant part of the swamp, leaving the water in front of us empty but for the ripples of their wake.

I now saw a finger of dry land, jutting out from the shore, that would provide an ideal site for an observation post. From it we could get a wide view of the swamp; behind it the bush was sufficiently thick to allow us to approach unseen; and at its farthest tip grew a paperbark tree with a branch that dangled close to the ground, forming a framework which we could easily clothe with extra leafy twigs and convert into a screen.

We built the hide that night. The next morning, before dawn, we sat down inside it and began watching and filming the geese.

Hides are seldom comfortable places and this one, although it was ideally placed, was more uncomfortable than most. The ground on which it was built, although superficially quite hard, soon softened beneath the weight of our feet, so that we and the camera tripod slowly sank deeper and deeper into mud. The leaves that hid us so effectively from the birds also served to screen us from the few cooling breezes that occasionally played over the lagoon, and the interior of the hide became as airless and stifling as a Turkish bath. In the mornings and evenings, mosquitoes droned in from the swamps and harried us unmercifully, submitting us to a torture that was the more maddening as we dared not wave our hands about or smack ourselves too vigorously, for fear of scaring the birds. But the geese made up for everything.

They grazed so close to us that we could see clearly the bright pink skin at the base of their bill and the vivid yellow of their legs. Many of them, we noticed, had spent so much time here that their white breasts were stained a scruffy chestnut by the mud in which they dabbled. Now too, we could clearly see that their feet were only half webbed—one of the characteristics that sets them apart from all other wildfowl.

Within the hide, we moved with exaggerated slowness and talked in whispers. Our behaviour was not unlike that of people in a holy place and, as the posture of the body often induces the appropriate emotion, so we felt a reverence for the scene in front of us. We were acolytes to whom a vision was being revealed; we were gazing upon another world. It was like this before man appeared on earth. Here, none of his logics or his preferences, his moralities or his rules, had any place. This world was governed only by elemental things—by the heat of the sun, the evaporation of the water, the burgeoning of the reeds and the unknowable urges of the geese.

And then, after two or three hours, a gust of wind caught the whirr of the camera and swung it across the swamp. A goose that had strayed to within a few feet of us, craned its neck in fright and flew. Within seconds the alarm had spread and soon all the geese were taking off, their contented honking replaced by the sound of their frantic wing flaps. We sat infuriated, for we had missed an important film shot. But even more saddening, the spell was broken. We had intruded, and the balance and harmony of the world on which we had been eavesdropping was shattered.

Quest Under Capricorn (1963).

5

Convalescents

♦

AUGUSTUS PRINSEP

(1803–30)

Anglo-Indian civil servant. London-born Prinsep was educated privately and at Haileybury, before following in his father's footsteps to India in 1822. His impressive career in the Indian Civil Service was cut short when he left Calcutta in March 1829 on his doctor's advice. He and his wife Elizabeth, with their baby, travelled throughout Van Diemen's Land from September 1829 to March 1830. Prinsep died at sea later that year during another voyage undertaken for health reasons. The fatiguing journey from Hobart Town to Launceston over rough roads, part of which Prinsep describes here, probably did little to improve his health. His wife, who later remarried, lived until 1885.

HOBARTON TO JERICHO

… On the 21st of February, we started in our gig to go gently the first forty miles, as far as Jericho, where our two friends F—— and G—— proposed joining us to introduce us to their acquaintances on the other side, whose estates it might be interesting to visit. We felt great curiosity to see the style of living in the bush, (to use the local term,) as we had often talked over the matter together, and considered the possibility of our doing the same thing some day, if misfortune or ill health drove us from India. We pursued the same road as in our trip to New Norfolk, as far as a mile above Roseneath Ferry, to Stony Point Ferry, where we crossed the river, and landed upon the ground I mentioned, opposite the Black Snake inn.

A beautiful crop of corn was now standing in sheaves, and the ferryman informed us that this land yielded no less than ninety bushels an acre. The road was scarcely traced here; with some difficulty we descended a steep stony pitch, to the shallow clear stream of the Jordan, over whose rocky bed we passed with some danger to our gig, if not to ourselves; and mounting the other bank, we came upon a farm house, from which we willingly received further directions about our route. After tumbling and rolling over numberless ruts and stones, and hills, for five miles more, we joined the main road from Roseneath Ferry, anticipating, most erroneously as it proved, some amendment from this junction. A little way on, we came to the town of Brighton, as yet composed only of the ale-house, and a few sheds—at least this was all within sight; but with such a want of dwellings, it was curious to see such an extent of cultivated ground. We then passed over a small rise, called Cornelian Hill, alternately hard rock, or deep sand. This hill receives its name from the quantity of cornelian stones found upon it, and some of which are extremely beautiful. I believe I have not mentioned that these abound in many parts of the country. Bagdad, a miserable inn, that looked as if next storm would with ease upset the frail wooden construction, was our first halting place, after sixteen miles' drive. For provisions we found but mouldy bread, and salt pork; and, for amusement, the endeavouring to act as peace-makers between the landlord and a party of drunken reapers. We proceeded eight miles farther, passing several neat houses and farms, less thinly scattered, till we came to the Swan Inn, at the foot of Constitution Hill, where we passed the night. We had nothing to complain of in the accommodations of this house, excepting one evil, I fear, incurable. Whether the new wood, of which the houses in the colony are built, is the cause, I know not, but they are infested with bugs; and in the Swan Inn more abundantly than usual, and of an uncommon size. Perhaps they were increased by the vicinity of the house to the overhanging wood of Constitution Hill.

We began our journey next morning about nine o'clock; the horse seemed an old traveller, and perfectly aware of the arduous toil he had to undergo. The road wound at first in a zigzag, gently amongst the trees; the waggons, which were before us, drawn by teams of oxen, urged by the shouts of the drivers, enlivened the scene; great branches and trees were lying in thick confusion about the road, so as almost to intercept our progress; on one side a deep woody ravine, with peeps of woody hills beyond. In this way we toiled up for a mile and a half to the summit, on the level of which the road runs two miles and a half, and allowing another for the descent, we travelled in all not less than five miles in crossing the hill. As we descended, the ravine spread into a pretty little valley of fields, in which was a scattered village, called the Green Ponds. Here, at the twenty ninth milestone, measured from Hobarton, twenty-seven from New-town, was another capital inn, but we had no time to stop. This valley is about seven miles in extent, the whole well cultivated; part of it is called the Cross Marsh, where there is a fine estate belonging to Mr Kemp, the principal merchant of Hobarton. At the back of his estate rise hills, like downs, naturally bare of trees, and clothed with excellent pasture for sheep, with which their sides were covered. The Jordan meanders below, on the banks of which all the farm-houses are situated, and between us and them rich fields of corn and grain stood ready for the reaper. The uncultivated parts of this valley were over-run with wattle-trees, the species of mimosa above-mentioned, making even these sandy tracts valuable. We next crossed the hills, which bounded the valley, and came to a most *unlovely* spot, called Lovely Banks; we thought it still worse, probably from our finding little at the wretched public-house, to satisfy our hunger, or that of our horse. From this a wild hilly tract of pasture country extends for eight miles, with no trace of human habitation.

Looking back from the highest hill, Spring Hill, on which is the fortieth mile-stone, we had a fine view of the whole western range from Mount Wellington; and of the eastern range from Mount Direction. Before us, to the north, the elevated plain of Jericho. This looked dreary enough, being but partially cultivated, and as usual, in the whole township, but two or three houses visible, which gazed at each other at the respectful distance of a mile or two. The Inn, however, answered its good fame, and here I was glad to rest a whole day …

Mrs Augustus Prinsep (ed.), *The Journal of a Voyage from Calcutta to Van Diemen's Land* (1833).

———

JAMES HOLMAN
(1786–1857)

English traveller. Holman entered the navy in 1798 and served on the home and North American stations, but became totally blind at the age of twenty-five. His health then was delicate and his nerves were depressed, but eventually his 'elasticity of feelings' was restored and he 'ventured, alone and sightless upon my dangerous course', travelling abroad very extensively from 1819 onwards. He undertook four major journeys, three of which he recorded in books. During his third trip (1827–32), he visited, among other places, Van Diemen's Land, New South Wales, and New Zealand. While in New South Wales, he visited the Bougainville Cataract.

A 'FEARFUL SPOT'

In the following month (July) I left Sydney again for a tour in the interior, and passing through Argyle, proceeded in a south-westerly direction to the shores of the river Morrumbidgee (Great and Good), which forms the south-western boundary of the Colony. This river, which is deep, rapid, and wide, is not fordable, and on approaching its banks I felt the wind, accompanied by occasional hail, blowing very keenly from the southward; but the view of the snowy mountains, and the ranges in its immediate vicinity, abundantly repay the traveller for the inconveniences to which the trip personally exposes him. From the Morrumbidgee I returned to Argyle, and after traversing Goulburn Plains, I made a de-tour through an inner range of hills at the back of the Blue Mountains, and thence proceeded on the route to Bathurst. On my arrival at Bathurst it was my intention to have proceeded to the northward, still keeping on the western side of the Blue Mountain range, about 150 miles, until I came to Liverpool Plains, nearly in a line with the head of the Hunter, where I proposed to cross the chain, and after lingering a short time with my friends in that neighbourhood, to make the best of my way down to Sydney. But this intention was frustrated by adverse circumstances. The continual rains had swollen the rivers and flooded the low grounds to such a degree that the country was impassable, and, although there was no scarcity of horses, and the people were so much in want of money, as to be obliged to carry on their dealings chiefly in barter, I could not procure either horses or guides for hire, to enable me even to attempt the prosecution of my desire. In this situation I was compelled to abandon my intention, and to take the new line of road over Mount Vittoria, which was at that time in forward progress, and has since been completed. Yet even here the difficulty of procuring a guide was such, that I was obliged to apply to Government for permission to be attended by one of the mounted police part of the way, which was readily granted to me. On my journey across the mountain I visited the celebrated cataract, called the Campbell Cataract, by Governor Macquarie, but afterwards re-christened the Bougainville Cataract, by Sir Thomas Brisbane; the former in honour of his lady, the latter in honour of the French Commodore who visited it. The summit of the waterfall is 2800 feet above the level of the sea, and here, much to the horror of the serjeant of police who accompanied me, I stood on the brink of the perpendicular rock that looks down into the yawning abyss, which receives the descending torrent. My companion entreated me not to approach the fearful spot, assuring me that he had been there with some distinguished persons, who would not venture to gaze into that awful depth until he had got a secure hold of them; but I requested him not to touch me, giving him an assurance that I had a complete control over my nerves, and that although I was perfectly conscious of the awful chasm at my feet, I encountered no risk whatever in advancing to the extremity of the ledge of rock. While I stood there, contemplating in sightless wonder, the sublimity of the scene, I could not help thinking of blind Gloster at the cliffs of Dover; the situation was very similar, and my imagination easily supplied equivalent figures to that of the one, who, 'half-way down hung gathering samphire, dreadful trade!'

A Voyage Round the World including Travels in Africa, Asia, Australasia, vol. IV (1835).

ROBERT GASCOYNE-CECIL
(1830–1903)

Third marquess of Salisbury and British prime minister. After being educated at Eton and Oxford University, Cecil was advised by his doctor to take a long sea voyage to cure his nervous illness. Accordingly he left England in July 1851, spent three months in Cape Town, then visited South Australia, Victoria, Van Diemen's Land, New South Wales, and New Zealand. In 1853 he returned to England, where he went on to be a Conservative MP (1853–68), secretary for India twice, foreign secretary four times, and prime minister three times (1885–86, 1886–92, 1895–1902). While in Victoria, he and a friend, Sir Montagu Chapman, an Irish baronet, visited the gold-diggings.

JOURNEY TO CASTLEMAINE (1852)

[24 March] We anchored in Hobson's Bay this morning. We had heard many terrific accounts of the carelessness with which luggage was shipped into the steamer which meets the ships, with the almost certainty of breakage. But like many tales before and since with reference to the horrors caused by the diggings, it proved utterly untrue. We got our luggage on board with perfect ease, and landed it without the slightest damage and went to Passmore's Hotel.

THURSDAY, MARCH 25.—Melbourne. Breakfasted this morning at the table d'hote. Provisions decent, but butter infamous. After breakfast Sir Montagu sallied forth to take places for us by some conveyance to the diggings.

After a desperate struggle with my carpet bag I started, together with Sir Montagu, in a spring-cart for the diggings. Our fellow passengers were five. There was a Californian digger—by his accent and some of his expressions evidently a Yankee. He was a coarse, hideous, dirty looking man, without an attempt at ornament or even neatness in his dress; yet he wore in his ears a pair of earrings about the size and shape of a wedding ring. He wore a pair of pistols in his belt, and the words 'put a bullet through his brain' were continually in his mouth. There were besides him (1) a young runaway merchant's son from Sydney, (2) a man who was going up to serve as postmaster at Mount Alexander, a very civil and quiet man; (3) a man who told us that he had walked 80 miles in 19 hours; and (4) his wife, who was fashionably timid, and supplied the shrieking whenever the cart dipped sideways into a hole. The whole road up to the diggings was a very bad one, so that she had plenty of opportunities for the indulgence of this propensity. From the conversation of these men one could gather that there had been more robberies on the road than the Governor was willing to admit. The favourite manœuvre among the thieves seems to be what they call 'picking up,' that is treating a successful digger to grog until he is drunk enough to be plundered with impunity.

We stopped several times on the road in order to refresh the inner man at coffee shops—a euphemism, generally speaking, for unlicensed (sly) grog shops. I was struck at all these places with the perfect civility with which everyone treated us—a strange contrast to all that we had heard. At one of them we saw a digger in his jumper and working dress walking arm in arm with a woman dressed in the most exaggerated finery, with a parasol of blue damask silk that would have seemed gorgeous in Hyde Park. She was a lady (so the driver told us) of Adelaide notoriety, known as Lavinia, who had been graciously condescending enough to be the better half of this unhappy digger for a few days, in order to rob him of his earnings. A ci-devant digger informed me that when he was at Bendigo a lady had offered 'to be his wife' for the moderate charge of 1/6. These women are no rarities at the diggings. About 5.30 we arrived at the Bush Inn, where we were to lodge for the night. The inn was crowded, and all our fellow travellers were refused admittance on that ground. But we, on the strength of our black coats, were admitted at once, and found the inn comfortable enough. We were shown to a private sitting-room, to which no one else was admitted, except a Dr Seymour, who came in late. He had been in India, and was rather a pleasant companion. From some cause or other I hardly slept an hour during the night.

SATURDAY, MARCH 27.— Next morning we were up punctually at six. But the driver, with characteristic Australian unpunctuality, had not even begun to catch the horses which were to take us to the mine, and which were supposed to be wandering somewhere near us in the forest. It was 8 o'clock before we got off. With a late start, an infamous road, and the fagged horses which had brought us yesterday from town, our prospects were not bright. We had 50 miles to do; and as we had five miles to walk after our arrival through the very thick of the diggings it was material that we should get there before dark. On the whole the roads that we passed to-day were the worst I had hitherto seen. There were no single places so dangerous as many I saw at the Cape; but they were more uniformly impassable. Through the Black Forest, the scene of many a tale of bushranging exploits, the road, which was a mere pathway hewn through the forest, was not only a foot deep in dust and pitted with as many holes as a rabbit warren, but it was at times so narrow that the naves of both wheels grazed the trees on each side. To complicate the navigation still more, it was intersected by large roots, and dotted over with stumps half buried in the sand. To lighten the cart we had to walk a great part of the way.

Once out of the Black Forest the road was good enough until we arrived at the Coloban (vulgo Columbine) River. But here—about 20 miles from Mount Alexander—the road grew worse and worse. The holes grew more numerous, and the hills far steeper. The dust was absolutely unbearable. It hung in a dense cloud about the cart, getting into eyes, ears, mouth, and nose, stopping respiration utterly and clinging to hair, whiskers, and beard as if it were flour. The particles were so small that they penetrated through the thickest clothing and choked up every pore of the skin. The horses were quite unable to get through it; and we more than once stuck fast in the deep holes which it concealed and which the driver, who in the course of the journey had nearly finished a great bottle of brandy, was too drunk either to get out of or to avoid. On such occasions the passengers had to get out and push the cart back into the hard road. The timid female was the only one who was left in the cart; and she gave vent to her emotions by a succession of inarticulate moans, now and then bursting forth into a fretful lecture to the driver on the evils of intemperance. Of course up most of the hills we had to walk; but at last the driver got so drunk and the horses so fagged, that there seemed no little prospect of our spending a night in the wood; and so we should had not the Californian taken the matter into his own hands.

By incessant flogging he contrived to get us into the diggings before it was quite dark. We had been more than once warned that we could not penetrate to the commissioner's tent after dark—that it would be madness at such a time to brave the dangers of random bullets, unseen pitfalls, and wandering brigands. But our experience of Australian exaggeration induced us to try. There was indeed, both then and during the whole night, a desultory feu de joie kept up from various quarters of the huge encampment; but most of the cartridges seemed to be blank. It is the habit of the diggers to discharge their firearms every night, to warn ill-disposed persons that they have got them. This platooning, together with the rows of camp fires which lined the glen, gave the mines a very military air. However, the moon was bright, and we walked our five miles along a good unbroken road, without approaching pitfalls or being molested by brigands. We had been specially warned by a post-office official just as we started on our walk, not to speak to any wandering passers-by for fear of being robbed; yet, whenever we asked our way, which we did of almost everyone we met, we were always directed civilly, and once or twice even guided for a short distance. When we reached the commissioner's camp we went into the mess tent where they had just had dinner, introduced ourselves to Mr Wright, the chief commissioner, and presented the Governor's letter. He received us very kindly and gave up to us one of his tents.

After washing ourselves—no slight luxury in this land of dust—we had some dinner in the mess tent. There were there two Independent Ministers who had arrived that evening on horseback, and whom we had fallen in with and spoken to on the road. When they found that we were the foot passengers who had spoken to them they gazed at us with breathless wonder for a moment and then let out, with exquisite naivete, that they had taken us for bushrangers. We had observed them making a most serpentine course towards the commissioner's camp, and going through a series of very complicated manœuvres without any apparent object—but we had never dreamt that we were the centres of repulsion. They were a delightful pair—so self-complacent and so simple. Their faces were just what Leech would have delighted to copy, and their conversation would have been a perfect treasure to Dickens. Their names were Higgins and McNichol—of course they went in the mess by the names of Higgins and Stiggins. The same evening the Roman Vicar Apostolic, Dr Gagen [Geoghegan] had arrived. He was a fat, droll, merry little Irish priest, very shallow and superficial, with a great deal of low cunning, and an evident desire to be 'all things to all men' by a display of liberality and a series of profane jokes.

All these assured me, especially Mr Wright, that the stories current of murder and outrage being rife at the diggings, were simple falsehoods. No homicide, either from private motives or in resistance to authority, had occurred since he had been there. Two men had been shot and nearly killed by the rashness of a frightened policeman; but they were recovering. No resistance was ever attempted either to the fines inflicted by the magistrate or to the burning of sly-grog shops by the police. The culprit always looked on himself as the victim of an inevitable fate. I observed the same on the road. To the question 'What has become of that coffee shop that stood here?' 'Oh! they've burnt it for sly-grog selling' was the regular answer, creating neither dissatisfaction nor surprise. In illustration of the extent to which exaggeration is carried in this colony, he told me that on his appointment here, as he was starting from his home a digger whom he knew told him that a horrible murder had been committed on Fryar's Creek; that one man had successively murdered his four mates in their hole; that the diggers on discovering it had tied a stone round his neck and sunk him in a waterhole, and that the police had seized the lynchers and taken them to Melbourne for trial. As he came nearer to the diggings he was told—by a respectable man—that the lynchers had been convicted at Melbourne and were on their way down under Captain Mair's charge to be hanged. He continued his journey cursing the ill-luck which gave him such an inaugural duty to perform—and arrived at Mount Alexander. What was his astonishment to find that the whole story from beginning to end was an utter fabrication! Mr Wright also told me that when the Bishop arrived at Melbourne the Vicar Apostolic left his card on him, and the Bishop actually sent it back!—a piece of bigotry I believe he has since regretted.

Ernest Scott (ed.), *Lord Robert Cecil's Gold Fields Diary* (1945 edition, first published 1935).

———

HENRY CORNISH

(1837–1915)

Anglo-Indian journalist. Born in Madras to a British Army officer father and an Indian mother, Cornish became a journalist on the Madras Times *in*

1864 and helped to found the Madras Mail *in 1868. While recuperating from illness, he visited all of the Australian colonies in the late 1870s. After leaving Australia he studied law and became a counsel of the English bar in Madras in 1882. Cornish, who eventually died in England in 1915, was convinced of the benefits of a sea voyage to Australia.*

'ADVANTAGES OF A HOLIDAY TRIP TO AUSTRALIA'
(1878)

I am on board the Peninsular and Oriental Company's steamer *Assam*, bound from Galle to King George's Sound, a straight, unbroken run, in a south-easterly direction, of 3330 miles—the longest road without a turning I have ever travelled over. It is, moreover, a lonely sea route, few sailing ships having occasion to frequent it, while the only steamers ever seen here are those carrying the monthly mails to and from England and Australia. Indeed, the only familiar object about these latitudes is the beautiful constellation of the Southern Cross which, at nights, appears high in the heavens, instead of being down low on the horizon as in the neighbourhood of the equator.

'Can't make out why I am so squeamish to-day; always thought I was a good sailor before,' I groan as I sway backwards and forwards in my berth, in response to the graceful but uncomfortable motions of the ship.

'It's the Trades,' mumbles my neighbour in the upper berth, a stout man who is half asleep. His berth creaks ominously after this effort of conversation: if it came down it would flatten me to a pancake. I am in that state of indifference, however, that I contemplate this awful possibility with calmness.

'It is not the Trades,' I answer somewhat petulantly. 'A man who has crossed the Bay of Biscay in a gale, and was none the worse for it, is not likely to be knocked over by a paltry blow like this.' And yet, on further reflection, I feel the Trades must have something to do with my unhappy condition, or why did the fat of that boiled mutton yesterday look so sickly yellow, and the capers so sickly green?

The 'Trades' referred to in the above conversation require explanation. People familiar with the sea-routes of the southern hemisphere talk thus familiarly of the south-east trade winds. At Galle, I noticed that most of the passengers bound for Australia spoke with a certain pride and fondness of these winds, as though they had a proprietary right in them. I had been prostrated by fever after leaving Aden. 'The Trades will soon set you to rights again,' says one passenger cheerily. 'A blow off Cape Leuwin will be just the thing for you,' says another. 'In three days from Galle,' remarked the doctor argumentatively, 'you will find yourself in a cooler climate, and in a fortnight you can be enjoying an Australian winter.'

What wonder, then, that I form favourable anticipations of the trade winds, and feel an anxiety to be off to the south? We have not long to wait. The transfer from the Southampton steamer of the comparatively small amount of cargo for Australia is made in a few hours, and by 8 o'clock on Thursday evening, the 30th May 1878, the *Assam* is steaming cautiously out of Galle Harbour, the buoys being lighted up to facilitate our navigation from this dangerous port. A good south-west breeze is blowing, and we start off at a speed which promises great things in the way of a rapid passage to Australia. By noon next day, or in fifteen hours, we have run 188 miles. The monsoon wind is still stronger the day after, and, being in our favour, the Captain puts on all sail, and we score a run of 306 miles in twenty-four hours. On the same day, the 1st of June, we 'cross the line,' (an event that has lost all importance on board steamers,) get beyond the influence of the south-west monsoon, and encounter a slight wind coming from the south or south-east—our friend the 'trades.' Our run in the next twenty-four hours is reduced to 258 miles; the next day we register 280, the next 241, the next less than 200, and by and bye we dwindle down to about 180. In short, thanks, to the strength of the trade winds, we find, after being at sea a week, that we have not got over much more than half of our journey, and that we shall be two or three days longer in getting to King George's Sound than we had calculated on. So much for the effect of an ill-timed south-east trade wind on the progress of a steamer bound from Galle to Australia: a wind that, while it is singularly soft, fresh, and invigorating to passengers, is almost as formidable an object for a steamer to contend against as is the south-west monsoon in the Indian Ocean.

Now for the other side of the picture. Considering the sufferings many invalids undergo in crossing the Indian Ocean and Red Sea, before getting to Europe, the rapid change of temperature that may be ensured, at this season of the year, by a few days' journey to the south, is well deserving the attention of Indian doctors. In many cases of sickness a cool temperature is one of the chief aids to recovery; and this being so, it is worth inquiring whether the sea voyage to Australia might not be oftener prescribed with advantage both to the patient's health and purse. The following readings of the thermometer, taken from the official log of the *Assam*, will best illustrate what I mean. It is only necessary to say the thermometer is hung in a small room by the Captain's cabin, sheltered, like the whole of the quarter deck, by the usual canvas awning, and that it therefore fairly represents the temperature in the shade.

READINGS OF THE THERMOMETER BETWEEN GALLE AND KING GEORGE'S SOUND.

			Range in 24 hours.		
30th May, 1878 at Galle			min. 80° to	90° max.	
31st ,, at sea, Lat 3° N	...		83	,,	88
1 June on Line	...		84	,,	85
2 ,, ... Lat 4° S	...		80	,,	85
3 ,, ... 8	...		80	,,	84
4 ,, ... 11	...		80	,,	82
5 ,, ... 14	...		80	,,	83
6 ,, ... 16	...		77	,,	80
7 ,, ... 19	...		76	,,	80
8 ,, ... 22	...		74	,,	75
9 ,, ... 94	...		66	,,	72
10 ,, ... 27	...		70	,,	76
11 ,, ... 30	...		65	,,	74
12 ,, ... 33	...		60	,,	70
13 (off the Sound) 35	...		60	,,	68

The temperature at Galle was unusually low for the season of the year, to be accounted for perhaps by the rains they had just been having there; but, taking the above figures as they stand, they demonstrate plainly enough that, at this season of the year, an invalid voyaging from Galle to the South can in a fortnight get into a temperature twenty degrees cooler than that of India. I do not pretend to say what are the advantages or disadvantages of this change of temperature; that is a matter for the doctors; I am content with pointing out the possibility of obtaining the change, and recording its beneficial effect in my own person. 'If I were an Indian officer,' said an Australian gentleman to me, 'I should spend my two months' furlough every year by running down to Australia and back.' Making some allowances for the prejudices in favour of his own country, there is really a good deal to be said in favour of his argument. No hill retreat in India supplies such a gradual and yet thorough change of temperature as a voyage to Australia and back must give. The voyage can be done well within the sixty days, for this steamer, which left Bombay on the 24th May, is due at that port again about the end of July, and, in the meantime, will give such passengers as return by her to India an opportunity of spending three weeks in Australia. This means an opportunity of taking a hasty glance at Melbourne, Sydney, Adelaide, and Tasmania, and of hunting up any friends and acquaintances one may have in the colonies. The cost of the trip can hardly be considered excessive. The return fare, first class, from Bombay to Melbourne is £72, which, it should be borne in mind, includes the cost of board and lodging for about forty-five days out of the sixty days which military men can claim as their furlough. On the whole, perhaps a man would live as cheap on a P. and O. steamer as he could at an Indian hill station in the fashionable season of the year.

Under the Southern Cross (1880 edition, first published 1879).

————

WILLIAM CUFF

(dates unknown)

British pastor. The Reverend William Cuff, an ex-president of the Baptist Union of Great Britain and Ireland, had been ministering at Shoreditch Tabernacle, London, for thirty years when he and his wife visited Australia and New Zealand at the turn of the century. A 'poor, miserable, helpless dyspeptic', he came on his doctor's orders in search of rest and health and returned 'altogether a new man', having lost his dyspepsia 'on the wild and beautiful hills of New Zealand, or on the rolling seas over which we sailed'. Perhaps it disappeared at Puketiraki.

NEW YEAR'S DAY, NEW ZEALAND (1903)

We were at Dunedin on New Year's Day, the most popular holiday of the year in New Zealand, and we were anxious to see how the people enjoyed themselves on their holiday. We started early to go to a place called Puketiraki, some miles from Dunedin, right up in the mountains, a wild and lonely place looking right down on the sea. There was to be a Maori *fête*—in their language, a *harka*, which means a war dance. Before we reached the railway station we saw that this *harka* was a very popular affair, for all Dunedin seemed to be astir; there were thousands of people at the station, and three trains had already gone to the Maori *fête*. The train we went by was a very long one, and had two engines attached to it, most of the carriages being coal and goods trucks of every description. These were provided with rough planks for seats, and covered with tarpaulin or coarse canvas for shelter from the sun or rain. Every truck was packed full of people; everybody was good-tempered and happy, and seemed quite accustomed to the fashion of truck-travelling.

What we saw when we reached Puketiraki was the most wild, weird, and savage scene we had ever witnessed; and this was our first contact with the Maoris. They are a wonderful people, and their history has yet to be written. Some books about them have already appeared, but it is a big story and needs to be well and adequately told. We saw their war dance in a lovely dell, with surroundings of beauty on every hand. It is impossible to describe this dance, but it is an awful and savage display. They always performed it before going into battle, and so worked one another up into a most terrible fury, and looked as though they would face and fight actual devils. Our British soldiers certainly had real warriors to face when they fought the Maoris of New Zealand. Here is a vivid description of a war dance by one who saw many and understood the people well:—

'The *élite* of the two tribes are now opposite to each other, all armed, all kneeling, and formed into two solid oblong masses, the narrow end of the oblong to the front. Only thirty yards divide them; the front ranks do not gaze on each other; both parties turn their eyes towards the ground, and with heads bent downwards, and a little on one side, appear to listen. You might have heard a pin drop. The uproar has turned to a calm; the men are kneeling statues; the chiefs have disappeared—they are in the centre of their tribes. Suddenly, from the extreme rear of the strangers' column is heard a scream—a horrid yell. A savage of herculean stature comes, *mere* in hand, rushing madly to the front. He seems hunted by all the Furies. Bedlam never produced so horrid a visage. Thrice, as he advances, he gives that horrid cry, and thrice the tribe give answer with a long-drawn gasping sigh. He is at the front; he jumps into the air, shaking his stone weapon; the whites only of his eyes are visible, giving a most hideous appearance to the face. He shouts the first words of the war song, and instantly his tribe spring from the ground. It would be hard to describe the scene which follows—the roaring chorus of the war song, the horrid grimaces, the eyes all white, the tongues hanging out, the furious and yet measured gesticulation, jumping, and stamping. I felt the ground plainly trembling. At last the war dance ended.'

But, then, there were plenty more Maori things to come which were very curious and very entertaining. A baby baptism according to the rites and ceremonies of the Maoris was performed, and was almost as wild and grotesque as the war dance. The ceremony was gone through with wonderful gusto, and with the loud laughter of the crowd round the dell in which it was performed. Then we saw how they cooked their food, and this time it was a whole bullock split down the middle in true English order, which was to be baked. The oven is a hole dug in the ground, and filled with large stones, which are made almost red-hot. The two sides of the ox are then laid on the hot stones, and carefully covered up with large cloths or wrappers. Then it is all closely covered over with earth, and well patted down to keep every bit of heat in. In due course the mould is cleared away, and there lie the two sides of beef as clean as a pin, and well cooked; they lie on two long poles, which are put on the top of the stones. The men lifted up the whole cooked side of beef, and put it on a raised and large platform, and there, in the presence of the whole people, cut it up, and sold it to any who would buy. There were no weights or scales; pieces were sold at so much each, by men who quite understood their business. The meat was mostly eaten on the spot; many took it away, but we were not purchasers. We understood that the Maoris have done this from time immemorial, and this cooking feat interested us above all we saw on that eventful day. We returned to Dunedin in a cattle-truck with our kind, good host and his family. New Year's Day, 1903, will never be forgotten by us, for it was crowded with strange incidents and fascinating interest. We thankfully record that we did not see one man the worse for drink during the whole day of pure, healthy enjoyment in the open air. Everywhere we were deeply impressed with the fact that the people in the Colonies know how to enjoy themselves on their holidays without getting drunk. When will our people at home learn to do the same? It will be a happy day for Old England when that day dawns.

Sunny Memories of Australasia (1904).

6

Adventurers

♦

MARY ANN PARKER

(dates unknown)

English traveller. Mary Ann Parker, 'Australia's first tourist', had travelled through France, Italy, and Spain, before she accompanied her husband Captain John Parker (1749–94) on a return voyage to New South Wales in 1791–92. Motivated by a sense of adventure and a desire to provide company for her husband, she left her two children behind in England, one of whom died in her absence. Her husband, an officer in the Royal Navy, was in command of the frigate Gorgon, *bringing members of the New South Wales Corps, and stores from CapeTown, to the new colony. A few days after her arrival back in England in mid-1792, Mary Ann was delivered of a son. An 'accomplished woman' with 'a little dash of satire in her composition, tho' not joined to the least ill nature therefore entertaining' (according to her husband's second-in-command), she wrote a book about the voyage to raise money to support herself and her children after her husband's sudden death from yellow fever in the West Indies in 1794.*

SOME IMPRESSIONS OF NEW SOUTH WALES (1791)

But to return to my narrative.—On the 30th Governor Phillip did us the honour to breakfast on-board; so did also Mr Collins, Judge Advocate; and Mr Palmer, the Commissary. The conversation was very interesting; the one party anxiously making enquiries after their relatives in England; and the other attentively listening to the troubles and anxieties which had attended the improvements made in that distant colony. When the company returned on-shore, we amused ourselves with the pleasing novelties of *Sidney Cove*, so named by the Governor in honour of Lord Sidney: from this Cove, although it is very rocky, a most pleasant verdure proceeds on each side: the little habitations on shore, together with the canoes around us, and the uncommon manners of the natives in them were more than sufficient amusements for that day; the next was occupied in receiving visits from several officers belonging to this settlement.

When we went on shore, we were all admiration at the natural beauties raised by the hand of Providence without expence or toil: I mean the various flowery shrubs, natives of this country, that grow apparently from rock itself. The gentle ascents, the winding valleys, and the abundance of flowering shrubs, render the face of the country very delightful. The shrub which most attracted my attention was one which bears a white flower, very much resembling our English Hawthorn; the smell of it is both sweet and fragrant, and perfumes the air around to a considerable distance. There is also plenty of grass, which grows with the greatest vigour and luxuriance, but which, however, as Captain Tench justly observes, is not of the finest quality, and is found to agree better with horses and cows than with sheep.

In Botany Bay there are not many land fowls: of the larger sort, only eagles were seen; of the smaller kind, though not numerous, there is a variety, from the size of a wren to that of a lark; all of which are remarkable for fine loud notes, and beautiful plumage, particularly those of the paroquet kind. Crows are also found here, exactly the same as those in England. But descriptions, infinitely beyond the abilities of her who now, solely for the benefit of her little flock, is advised to set forth this narrative, having been already published, it would be presumptive to attempt any thing farther.

Our amusements here, although neither numerous nor expensive, were to me perfectly novel and agreeable: the fatherly attention of the good Governor upon all occasions, with the friendly politeness of the officers rendered our *séjour* perfectly happy and comfortable.

After our arrival here, Governor King and his Lady, resided on shore at Governor Phillip's, to whose house I generally repaired after breakfasting on-board: indeed it always proved a home for me; under this hospitable roof, I have often ate part of a Kingaroo, with as much glee as if I had been a partaker of some of the greatest delicacies of this metropolis, although latterly I was cloyed with them, and found them very disagreeable. The presents of eggs, milk, and vegetables, which I was often favoured with from the officers on shore, were always very acceptable; and the precaution which Captain Parker had taken, previous to our departure from the Cape of Good Hope, made me fully contented with my situation.

Our parties generally consisted of Mrs King, Mr Johnson, and the Ladies who resided at the colony. We made several pleasant excursions up the Cove to the settlement called *Paramatta*. The numerous branches, creeks, and inlets, that are formed in the harbour of Port Jackson, and the wood that covers all their shores down to the very edge of the water, make the scenery beautiful: the North branch is particularly so, from the sloping of its shores, the interspersion of tufted woods, verdant lawns, and the small Islands, which are covered with trees, scattered up and down.

Upon our first arrival at *Paramatta*, I was surprised to find that so great a progress had been made in this new settlement, which contains above one thousand convicts, besides the military. There is a very good level road, of great breadth, that runs nearly a mile in a straight direction from the landing place to the Governor's house, which is a small convenient building, placed upon a gentle ascent, and surrounded by about a couple of acres of garden ground: this spot is called Rose-Hill. On both sides of the road are small thatched huts, at an equal distance from each other. After spending the day very agreeably at the Governor's, we repaired to the lodging which had been provided for us, where we had the comfort of a large wood fire, and found every thing perfectly quiet, although surrounded by more than one thousand convicts. We enjoyed our night's repose; and in the morning, without the previous aid of toilet or mirror, we set out for the Governor's to breakfast, and returned with the same party on the ensuing day.

This little excursion afforded us an opportunity of noticing the beautiful plumage of the birds in general, and of the *Emu* in particular, two of which we discovered in the woods: their plumage is remarkably fine, and rendered particularly curious, as each hen has two feathers generally of a light brown; the wings are so small as hardly to deserve the name; and, though incapable of flying, they can run with such swiftness that a grey-hound can with difficulty keep pace with them. The flesh tastes somewhat like beef.

In this cove there are some cool recesses, where with Captain Parker and the officers I have been many times revived after the intense heat of the day, taking with us what was necessary to quench our thirst.

Here we have feasted upon Oisters just taken out of the sea;—the attention of our sailors, and their care in opening and placing them round their hats, in lieu of plates, by no means diminishing the satisfaction we had in eating them. Indeed the Oisters here are both good and plentiful: I have purchased a large *three-quart* bowl of them, for a pound and a half of tobacco, besides having them opened for me into the bargain.

A Voyage Round the World in the Gorgon Man of War (1795).

ROSE DE FREYCINET
(1795–1832)

French adventurer. Paris-educated Rose de Freycinet successfully breached naval regulations to accompany her husband, Louis de Freycinet, geographer and commander of the corvette Uranie, *on a round-the-world scientific expedition (1817–20), which included a visit to New South Wales in 1818. She survived the wrecking of the* Uranie *in the Falkland Islands in 1820, but died of cholera in 1832. In a letter to her mother (who had already been informed of the plan by Louis), written some hours before she was smuggled aboard dressed as a man, Rose explains the reasons for her proposed action.*

REASONS FOR GOING (1817)

... sometimes heard you express a view whose truth strikes me at this moment: if it happens, you said, that we find ourselves really uncertain how to choose between two duties that appear to us irreconcilable, then divine Providence allows something to happen that helps us in our weakness and uncertainty. That is why, having heard that your health is now perfectly restored, I have no longer hesitated to make the decision that has caused your tears. Write and tell me that you do not blame me, that you see it as an unavoidable necessity, and that you hope it will be supported by help from Heaven. Who knows, alas! whether it was not in order to provide my dear Louis with a companion entirely free to follow him that up to now I have been denied the privilege of motherhood!

However that may be, my mind is made up: I will follow my husband in his expedition round the world; I will share his fate and soften his anxieties if there should be any ... Ah! however great the trials of such a voyage may prove for your daughter, believe that a hundred times worse would be the absence of the one she so loves—your heart will tell you how much she would suffer from that separation.

But since I can hide nothing from you I confess that I am agitated by a thousand fears. The thought of that sea frightens me; I greatly need to have my courage strengthened by Him who commands the wind and the waves. I, who trembled in a boat in the middle of Marseille harbour—how shall I fare on the ocean, when I can see nothing but sky and water and when the weather grows stormy!...

Today, one thing frightens me as much as the prospect of storms. As you will realize, I have to get on board secretly. In the last few days I have made my farewell visits to my Toulon acquaintances as if I were about to return to Marseille by tonight's coach. Yesterday evening, after I had made my arrangements for departure and settled accounts with the house where I am lodging, a trusted servant delivered my trunks, not to the coach-office, but to the ship, where the dear Commandant received them. As for me, a little before midnight I went to the house of a lady who had a hiding-place ready prepared; here I shall stay hidden, I hope, until the moment when Louis will come to take me on board.

When I got here my friend made me promise to go to bed; I agreed to this so as to leave her at liberty to go to bed herself ... Perhaps she hoped that after such an exhausting day I would be able to sleep a little. I had no hope of that: you can guess how agitated my mind was. The moment I found myself alone, the daring thing I was about to do rose up before me, presenting a thousand difficulties that had not occurred to me at first; then the afflicting thought of parting from loved ones I was leaving in France, of separating myself from them for several years, the fear of what might happen to all of us in the interval; your regrets, your worries, our dangers—ah! Mother, what a night!

As soon as I rose, I took up my pen, having dedicated this last day to writing to you, to my sister, my other relatives and to my friends. I have done nothing else all morning, leaving this letter and then returning to it whenever I felt I must tell you of my love for you. In preparation for leaving this evening, dressed as a man, I have had to have my hair cut off to disarm all suspicion. The good friend with whom I now am wanted to undertake this task herself; she could not carry it through without bursting into tears. Although she is the daughter and the wife of distinguished sailors, she is astonished and touched at my resolution. I am leaving her my hair; she willingly undertakes to have a necklace made for you and some bracelets for Caroline.

Need I repeat, my darling Mother, that you will receive our news as often as we can find an opportunity to send it? You can rely on that, and remember that you will have it much sooner and much more often than we can hope to have yours, because in all probability we shall have covered three-quarters of the whole distance we have to go, before we reach the first place that Louis has mentioned to you for addressing your letters; and God knows with what interest on our part those dear letters will be read! Write to us often, kind and beloved Mother, write us every detail of everything that concerns you. Above all, as Louis has bidden you, do not believe the ridiculous rumours that will possibly be set afoot about the expedition. Whether from malice, or love of the sensational, people usually like to spread rumours of supposed wreck. Dear Mother, let us keep on hoping, keep up our courage, and put our trust where we ought.

A few days ago I made the acquaintance of the expedition's priest: he is a respectable ecclesiastic and his society will I think be very agreeable and consoling to me during this long voyage.

All my letters are closed except this one. Now I must go. Here is Louis to take me away …

Marnie Bassett, *Realms and Islands: The World Voyage of Rose de Freycinet in the Corvette* Uranie *1817–1820* (1962).

———

THOMAS W. KNOX

(1835–96)

American traveller and writer. The widely travelled Knox is best known for his popular boy travellers series of books, which purport to be accounts of the experiences of 'those youthful veterans of travel', Frank Bassett and Fred Bronson, who were actually an imaginary pair, and their 'uncle', mentor, and travelling companion, Dr Bronson, a figure based on Knox himself. The trio offered their Australasian book, later said to be 'the first illustrated book describing Australia and the neighbouring colonies, Tasmania and New Zealand, written by an American and published by an American printer', as their contribution to the Australian centennial (1888). Frank describes the following exciting incident, which occurs while they are staying on a station in Queensland.

'A SNAKE IN FRED'S BED'

'The house was a two-story building of wood, about fifty feet by thirty, and stood upon posts, or piles, seven feet high, each post having a geranium vine growing around it. There was a wide veranda all around the house; the space on the ground was occupied with dining-room, pantry, store-room, office, and bath-room, and was easily accessible on all sides. There was a huge fireplace in the dining-room, and also one in the large sitting-room directly above it. On the same floor with the sitting-room there were four good bedrooms. One of these was given to Doctor Bronson; the others being occupied by the family, Fred and I were shown to a small house just outside the yard, where were two very good rooms, plainly but comfortably furnished. After arranging our toilets we returned to the big house, and were ready for dinner, which was shortly announced.

'We dined substantially on roast mutton, preceded by a soup of kangaroo tail, and followed by a plum-pudding which had been put up in London and sent to Australia in a tin can. We spent an hour or two in the sitting-room listening to tales of Australian bush life, and then started for bed; and thereby hangs a tale.

'Fred's room was separated from mine by a thin partition. When Mr Watson left us Fred remarked that he was quite ready for a good sleep, as he was very tired. As he spoke he turned down the bed-clothes, and then shouted for me to come quick.

'"Here's a big snake in my bed!" said he. "Come and help me kill him."

'Mr Watson heard the remark, and hastened back before I could get to where the snake was.

'"Don't harm that snake," said he; "it's a pet, and belongs to my brother. It's nothing but a carpet snake."

'With that Fred cooled down, but said he didn't want any such pet in his bed, even if it was nothing but a carpet snake. The serpent, which was fully ten feet long, raised his head lazily, and then put it down again, as if he was quite satisfied with the situation and did not wish to be disturbed.

'Mr Watson explained that the snake had no business there, and without more ado he picked the creature up by the neck and dragged it off to a barrel which he said was its proper place. After he had gone Fred and I put a board over the top of the barrel to make sure that the reptile did not give us a call during the night. Poverty is said to make one acquainted with strange bedfellows, but poverty can't surpass Australian bush life where a man finds a snake in his bed altogether too often for comfort.

'While we are on this subject,' Frank continued, 'we will have a word about the snakes of Australia. The carpet snake, to which we were so unceremoniously introduced, is the largest of the family, and is really harmless, so far as its bite is concerned, though it has powers of constriction that are not to be despised. It lives upon small game which it can easily swallow, and occasionally ventures upon a young wallaby or kangaroo. It may be kept as a pet, as you have seen; but as it can't sing, doesn't learn tricks, never undertakes to talk, and does nothing for the amusement or entertainment of its owner, I don't understand why anybody should want to pet it. But there's no accounting for tastes. It catches a few rats and other vermin, and occasionally creates havoc in the chicken-yard.

'There are five deadly serpents in Australia—the black snake, the brown snake, the tiger snake, the diamond snake, and the death-adder. The black and brown are most common, and the brown snake frequently reaches a length of nine feet. The most vicious and dangerous is the tiger snake, which seems to be allied to the *cobra-de-capello* of India, as, when irritated, it flattens and extends its neck to twice its ordinary size. It secretes its maximum amount of poison in the summer, and its bite is speedily fatal. The bite of any of the snakes here enumerated will cause death in a few hours unless the proper antidotes are applied.

'The death-adder is unlike the other snakes in one respect; it never attempts to get out of any one's way, but lies quite still until it is touched, when it instantly strikes at its victim. The best-known remedies for snake-bites are hypodermic injections of ammonia, cutting out the wound, and swallowing large quantities of brandy or other spirits.

'Mr Watson says there was once a man named Underwood, who discovered a perfectly efficacious antidote to the bite of a poisonous snake. He gave several performances in which he allowed himself to be bitten by snakes that were undoubtedly healthy and in full possession of their venomous powers. Dogs and rabbits that were bitten by the same snakes after they had tried their fangs on Underwood died very soon afterwards; and it must be remembered that the second bite of a snake is always less poisonous than the first. After being bitten by the snakes, Underwood applied a remedy which was known only to himself, and soon recovered from the effects of the bite.

'The manner of his death is a very convincing proof of the perfection of his remedy. One day, while under the influence of liquor, he allowed himself to be bitten by a snake; in consequence of his intoxication he was unable to find his antidote, and so he died of the bite. His secret perished with him; he had demanded £10 000 ($50 000) for it, which the Government refused to pay, as they thought the price exorbitant.

'Every new chum—freshly arrived men in the colonies are known as "new chums"—has a nervous apprehension about snakes when he first sets foot in the bush, and has quite likely provided himself with a pair of long boots as a protection against venomous reptiles. Within a week or so this feeling wears off, and after a while a man thinks no more about snakes than in England or the United States. Most of the deaths from snake-bites occur among the laborers in the fields, and altogether they are by no means uncommon. In some localities one might go about for years without seeing a snake, while in others the deadly reptiles are so numerous that caution must be exercised. The worst regions are said to be the cane-fields of the Mackay district and the reed-beds on the Murray River.'

The Boy Travellers in Australasia (1889).

———

DAVID W. CARNEGIE
(1871–1900)

British explorer. Carnegie, whose father was the 6th earl of Southesk, trained as an engineer, then worked on tea plantations in Ceylon, before he and a friend, Lord Percy Douglas, joined the gold-rush to Coolgardie in 1892. He worked in various mines for eighteen months, made two commissioned prospecting expeditions for a pastoral company (1894–95), and then crossed Western Australia from south to north and back, looking for gold and a possible stock route from the Kimberley area to Coolgardie, travelling 3000 miles (4800 kilometres) in thirteen months (1896–97). Since described as a 'thoroughly professional explorer', he later published an account of his five years in Australia. Carnegie's life of adventure ended abruptly when he was killed by a poisoned arrow in a native uprising in November 1900 in northern Nigeria, where he had gone as an assistant resident the previous year. During the second prospecting expedition he found himself in the following predicament.

'ALONE IN THE BUSH'

By March 4th we were satisfied that the appearance of the mine was good enough to warrant our applying for a lease of the area already marked out. So leaving Czar behind, to enable Paddy and Jim to pack water, I, riding Satan and leading Misery, loaded with specimens from the reef, set forth for Coolgardie, to apply for the lease, and get a fresh supply of provisions, of which we were sadly in need. My departure for Coolgardie was taken advantage of by several who wished to bank their gold, and thus I became an escort.

Coolgardie lay almost due south, 220 miles on the chart, but nearly 300 miles by the track, which deviated from water to water. Speed being an object, I decided to strike through the bush to George Withers' hole. Here, by the way, poor Alec Kellis had just been murdered by the blacks—not the pleasantest of news to hear, as I started on my solitary journey. I followed a horse pad for fifty-five miles, mostly through thick scrub, to Cutmore's Well, where several parties were camped, who eagerly questioned me as to the richness of the new field.

Leaving Cutmore's, I struck through the bush, and before long the sickness I had had on me for some time past, developed into a raging fever. Every bone in my body ached and shot with pain. I could neither ride nor walk for more than a few minutes at a stretch; I was unable to eat, nor cared to drink the hot water in my canteen. I struggled on, now riding, now walking, and now resting under a bush, travelling in this fashion as long as daylight lasted, from five in the morning until six at night. Afraid to let the camels go at night lest they should wander too far, or, while I was following them in the morning, my packs should be raided by the blacks, I tied them down, one on either side of my blankets; and thus I had not only a protection against the wind, but the pleasure of their companionship—no slight blessing in that solitude.

How lonely I felt, in that vast uninhabited bush! Racked by pain, I tossed from side to side, until sheer weariness kept me still; so still that the silence of death seemed to have fallen upon us; there was not a sound in all that sea of scrub, save the occasional sleepy grunt of one of the camels, until the quiet night re-echoed with the hoarse call of the 'Mopoke,' which seemed to be vainly trying to imitate the cheerful notes of the cuckoo. How could any note be true in such a spot! or how could a dry-throated bird be anything but hoarse! At last morning came, heralded by the restless shuffling of the camels, and another day's journey began.

Tying the camels down at nights necessitated the cutting of scrub and bushes for them to feed upon, and I doubt they got little enough to eat. Before long I was too weak to lift the saddles off, and could only with difficulty load and unload the bags of quartz, and, weakened as I was by illness, my labours were not light. Yet further trouble was in store for me, for presently a salt lake barred my way. Then I began to understand the meaning of the word despair. Neither kindness nor cruelty would induce my camels to cross; I was therefore forced to follow the banks of the lake, hoping to get round it, as I could see what I supposed was its end. Here I was again baffled by a narrow channel not ten yards wide. It might as well have been half a mile, for all the chance I had of crossing it. The trend of the lake was north-west by south-east, and I was now at the north-west end, but stopped, as I say, by a narrow channel connecting evidently with another lake further to the north-west.

There was nothing for it but to retrace my steps, and follow along the margin of the lake to the south-east, and eventually I got round, having been forced some ten miles out of my course.

I was fortunate in finding water without difficulty, in a small rock-hole amongst some granite hills in which 'Granite Creek' takes its rise. From these I had still eighty miles to travel before I could reach a settlement, Coongarrie (the 90 mile) being the nearest point. Could I do it? I had to succeed or perish miserably, and a man fights hard for his life. So I struggled on day and night, stopping at frequent intervals from sheer exhaustion, cursing the pitiless sun, and praying for it to sink below the horizon. Some twenty miles from Coongarrie I was relieved by striking a track, which did away with the necessity of thinking where I was going.

A few miles more, and—joy unspeakable—I found a condenser and a camp. The hospitable proprietor, whose name I never learned, did all he could to make me comfortable, and I felt inclined to stay, but despatch was imperative, for not only must be the lease be applied for forthwith, but Conley and Egan must be provisioned. At Coongarrie I gave a swagman a lift, and he helped me with the camels and loads, until at last Coolgardie was reached.

Giving my camels in charge of the first man I could find willing to look after them, an Afghan, Neel Bas by name, I finished my business at the Warden's office. Then, yielding to the persuasion of my friends in Asken and Nicholson's store, I retired to the hospital, for indeed I could fight against my sickness no longer. Here I remained some three weeks under the kind care of Miss O'Brien (now Mrs Castieau) and Miss Millar, the pioneer nurses on the goldfields. No words can express the admiration I, and all of us, felt for the pluck and goodness of these two gently nurtured ladies, who had braved the discomforts and hardships of the road from York to Coolgardie—discomforts that many of the so-called stronger sex had found too much for them—to set up their hospital tent, and soothe the sufferings of poor fever-stricken fellows.

The services of these kind ladies, and of many that subsequently followed their example, were badly needed, for the typhoid fiend was rampant—carrying off the young, and apparently strong, men at a rate too tremendous to be credible. Funerals were too common to call for even passing notice. 'Unwept, unhonoured, and unsung,' they went to a nameless grave.

My chief anxiety was for my mates. How could I send them relief, incapacitated as I was? Fortunately, my friend David Wilson offered to go for me, in consideration of a certain interest in the mine we had found. This was a great help, and now I could rest contented; not altogether though, for Neel Bas had some hesitation in giving up the camels, and had a violent row with Dave Wilson, all of which he would insist on explaining to me in broken English, as he sat cross-legs on the floor of my tent. The doctor happily arrived and kicked him out, and I was left in peace. In less than three weeks I was able to go by coach to Southern Cross, and thence by train to Perth, where, under the kind roof of Colonel Fleming, the Commandant, I soon regained my health.

When I mention that my syndicate never even offered to defray the cost of my illness, my readers will understand that my statements as to the ingratitude of those who benefit by the prospectors' toil are not unfounded. Unfortunately for me, my old mate, Lord Douglas, was absent in England, and, in consequence, much misunderstanding resulted between the syndicate and myself.

Spinifex and Sand (1898).

———

ALAN COBHAM

(1899–1973)

British aviator. Cobham served as a flying instructor in the Royal Flying Corps during the First World War, before undertaking various long-distance flights in the post-war period. Between June and October 1926 he flew in a seaplane from England to Australia and back because that seemed to offer 'a new little adventure'. The flight was marred by the death of Cobham's mechanic, A.B. Elliott, after he was shot by an unknown assailant on the ground as the pair flew over the swamps near Basra. Cobham, who acquired another mechanic en route, was greeted by huge crowds in Australia, particularly in Melbourne, where he arrived on 15 August.

ARRIVAL IN MELBOURNE (1926)

According to plan a single machine met us about fifty miles out of Melbourne, while a little further on another escort picked us up, and thus we arrived over the aerodrome at Essendon.

Now there had been a record crowd of sixty-thousand people to greet us at Sydney, but at Melbourne we were amazed to find a crowd of at least a hundred and fifty thousand; in fact, one of the largest I have ever seen in my life. I looked at Ward through the window of the cabin; he looked back at me; and I think we were both a little overcome. It was obvious that the people of Australia were more alive than most—especially those at home—to the importance of aviation to the future of the Empire. I think it was for this reason that they turned out in such overwhelming numbers to greet the little 'bus which had brought us all the way from the home country.

As I looked down on the crowd beneath me I could see that it was ready to break through the barriers, and I realised that if I did not get down at once I should not be able to land at all because the ground would soon be packed with humanity. A special clearing had been made in front of one of the hangars, to which I was supposed to taxi the machine, the plan being that railings would be erected round the aeroplane and all the addresses and such-like would be made from an adjacent platform. Before I landed I could see this would never work, and so as I neared the ground I decided to taxi as hard as I could up to the hangar immediately on landing, in the hope that the doors would be opened and I should be able to get inside the hangar before we were completely overrun.

The moment our wheels touched the ground the crowd on all sides broke the barriers and rushed at us. I turned the machine as quickly as I could and taxied full out for the hangar, while the crowd got denser and denser. They seemed to have an utter disregard for the propeller, which being an all-metal one would certainly have cut in half anyone it touched; behind, they were falling over and breaking our tail. At last the crowd became so overwhelming that we could not move, and I simply had to stop the propeller. Then there was a mighty rush, and the police and Air Force literally had to extract me from the cock-pit and carry me through that astounding throng towards the hangar. As they opened the hangar door to get me inside, the crowd squeezed in too, whereupon I was rushed to the far corner and thrust into a small iron room where I was locked in. Thus it came about that within a few moments of landing at Melbourne I found myself a prisoner in a corrugated iron room with barred windows up to which boys were clambering, and a tin roof on which more boys were dancing!

A little later Colonel Brinsmead came in with the Lord Mayor and other representatives, and they told me that all the arrangements for my official reception had been dashed aside by the enthusiasm of the crowd. I feared for my machine, and was much relieved to hear that it had been safely pushed into the hangar and that Ward was found to be still alive.

We spent a whole fortnight in Melbourne, during which time I think I worked about eighteen hours a day. Letters poured in from every part of Australia, and I felt it my duty to answer them in gratitude for their writers' kindness in taking such an interest in the enterprise. I was provided with a staff of secretaries and thus I was able to cope with the two thousand odd letters that I received.

I came to the conclusion that Australia was the most perfect country in the world for flying, and that aviation might very easily alter the whole national life of this great continent by means of the light aeroplane and the privately-owned aeroplane. The isolation problem on the out-back farms could be abolished entirely if every station had its own aircraft, because whereas at present it very often takes days to visit a friend or to get supplies, air-transport would reduce this to minutes or hours. I think I have said before that the continent is one vast natural aerodrome, and the climatic conditions—they never have fogs or blizzards or snow—permit three-hundred-and-sixty-five days flying in the year.

Australia is alive to flying, and during my visit I noticed that three light aeroplane clubs came into being; one at Sydney, another at Melbourne, and a third at Adelaide. They were all using the little De Havilland 'Moth' which had been developed at home, and in one of which in my earlier days I had managed to fly from London to Switzerland and back in a day.

During our stay at Melbourne we shifted our machine over to the Australian Air Force aerodrome at Point Cook, where every facility was given us to overhaul her. Ward set to work on the machine, assisted by Mr Capel of the Armstrong-Siddeley Company, who had come out to Australia on business.

On the return journey I hoped to put up a bit of a speed record, which would mean two big jumps a day. Now I knew this would be too much work for Ward because it entailed flying from dawn until sunset every day with but one brief halt at mid-day in which to refuel, thus leaving insufficient time for one man to attend to machine and engine in the available daylight. Therefore I asked Capel if he would care to fly back with us, for although the machine was already overloaded as a seaplane I thought that by throwing some extra clothing overboard and lightening up all round we might be able to take his extra weight.

When the day came for our departure from Melbourne we said farewell to the many new-found friends who had done all in their power for us, and with many regrets flew on to Adelaide.

Australia and Back (1926).

———

PENRYN GOLDMAN
(1911–87)

English adventurer. Although youthful, Goldman had already spent time in Canada and Africa before working his passage from England to Australia in the late 1920s. After a stay at Government House in Adelaide, he worked for six months on a sheep station near Clare, South Australia, then decided to attempt to travel from Adelaide to Darwin alone by car. He had considered, but decided against, using camels or a motorcycle. In August 1929, some eighteen years after the first successful crossing of Australia from south to north by car, Goldman set off from Government House. He drove his second-hand Austin Seven, nicknamed 'Baby', as far as Daly Waters.

'BABY—SO LONG' (1929)

DIARY entry at Daly Waters:

'I will state the plain facts, as time is short and I am unhappy. Last night's forebodings were well-founded. My mind and thoughts are upside down, but I will turn them back and relate the incidents in brief.'

The fever-stricken cook at Newcastle aroused me at 5 a.m. Baby was in splendid form, purring happily, and by six o'clock we were well away for Daly Waters, eighty-seven miles distant, the first of the three last laps to Darwin.

After covering twenty miles, I noticed that something was wrong with our balance, the left side of the back sagged badly. Another spring had gone, and I failed to understand the reason, for by now our load was light, and, apart from the usual jumpy rattle, there had been no severe jerk or impact since Newcastle. Having used all the spare springs, I was obliged, as before, to resort to wire.

Half an hour on we were just drawing out of an uneasy patch, but not too bad, when a loud clatter started up, followed by resounding thumps from under my legs. It was the main driving-shaft that had become slightly twisted and also bent, while the arch of the bend was striking against the base of the hand-brake. How could a shaft of finely tempered steel, without an abnormal strain, become twisted? I snapped the hand-brake right off, which lessened the thumping, though when we bounced the whacks continued against the floor.

Things were going beyond my understanding. We carried on, but with a growing sense of coming trouble.

I was soon held up by a tearing from within the engine. It proved to be a screw which had worked loose from the fan, and had torn a hole in the radiator. Daly Waters was still thirty-five miles ahead, and Newcastle fifty-two miles behind us, while between was not one inhabitant. All that we could do was to slowly carry on, and keep going until the lack of water circulation should finally disable the engine.

We crawled on mile after mile until, having covered fifteen, frequently stopping to cool the overheated engine, and dreading lest she might seize, we came to a wide patch of sand between a number of bush trees. I backed to assure a better run, and turned off the engine in order to obtain more power since I was in no mood for being stuck.

After a few moments' pause, I restarted her, and, letting in the clutch, moved forward with a rattle of noise. We reached to a lively speed, and entered the sandy patch. Then suddenly came a slipping movement sideways and … we crashed …

Later, I remember wondering how it was that the universe was dizzying around amid a sparkle of stars and flashlights, and who the devil was spraying hot liquid down upon my face.

I opened my eyes to a smudgy-red world. Wiping them clear, I saw my face in the splintered windscreen mirror, bleeding from a cut above my right eye, and, lying above my head, a tree.

A skid on the slippery sand must evidently have pitched us against a sapling, jamming the stump under the radiator, while the pole snapped across, knocking me silly. The burning fountain I had felt spraying on my face when I first regained consciousness was, I discovered, coming from a tin of petrol on the seat beside me, which, inflated almost to the point of exploding by the heat of the sun, had been punctured by the sapling as it fell.

The damage done to the car was irreparable, for all that had before been straight on the front bearings, was now bent. The steering was twisted, and the bent axle brought the wheels close together, throwing them out of alignment and forcing the front spring into a deep arc. The bottom of the radiator was mutilated beyond repair, and the shock-absorber looked as though it had received its last shock. I tried to insert the starting-handle but found that the grip through the radiator had been displaced, and I was obliged to smash at the base before I could work the handle in and give a twist. She started at the first turn. Where the heart beats there is life; and again I put my trust in Baby, knowing that somehow she would pull me through. I was desperate to get her into Daly Waters. I could not abandon her by the wayside.

Wondering what would happen next, I reversed the gear and tried her gently. Baby moved, and cleared the stump. I tried her forwards: she moved again, but the wheels being out of alignment, the effort to keep her straight was continuous, and the steering with three turns of play, extremely uneven. First one wheel and then another refused to respond and wobbled gaily on its own. Every tree, ant-heap, and telegraph pole appeared out to bar our passage: we dodged and swung and swayed and lurched, but Baby, as I knew she would, got us into Daly Waters.

Diary entry:

'A fighter to the last jolt, Baby is dead.'

Once again it was Baby's gameness that won over her shattered frame and delivered us out of the wilds to end, if end she must, in the protection of an uninhabited place.

'It seems hard, after forty-seven days on the way from Adelaide, and only three hundred miles left to reach Darwin, that an ordinary collision should deal us a complete knock-out blow. Three days more and I think we could have made it!'

I knew not what to do and felt sorely puzzled. The monthly boat from Darwin had sailed that morning, and I was the length of a continent removed from Adelaide, my port of return. First I had to get to Darwin, a month's wait, and then, probably, a second month on the sea. As I stood debating within myself, a voice hailed me from the relay station.

'How now, two visitors in one day! What is the world coming to? Anyway, join us in here; tea's on the table and a real cake!' It was Mr Ashton, the telegraphist, and close by I had noticed a large car under the shade of a tree. 'You and I know each other well by name, young feller, but let me introduce Mr and Mrs Wright, just arrived from Singapore, and who are making home to Melbourne by an original route, overland instead of cruising around Australia coastwise.'

'Which is your direction, due south or east?' I enquired. Mr Wright told me they were making south to Newcastle Waters, and would then strike off across Eastern Australia, and down through Queensland and

New South Wales to Victoria, not taking Central Australia as I had done. His talk thrilled me beyond measure, for it had been my intention to follow this route with Baby after Darwin, supposing I had arrived there. I have forgotten what was said, or how it came to pass, but I do recall Mr Wright saying, as he rose from the table, 'Well, if you can make up your mind to cut out Darwin, the front seat of our car is wide enough for three. We'd give you a lift across North Australia, and drop you at railhead in Queensland.'

That help should come to me in the moment of my extreme need was like the beneficent happening of a miracle, for the number of cars passing that lonely outpost in the course of a year would, I dare say, be counted on the fingers of the two hands, and yet it was with a heavy heart that I assented to turn my mind from Baby and from the goal that was so nearly realized, and to remember that she would no longer be there to patch with shoe-leather, mend with wire, or dig from sand.

Baby I discussed fully with Ashton, and confided her to his care. It was the body and chassis that had given out. I think the friction and the strain must have worn the very temper out of the steel, leaving the metal resistless to the unmerciful rigours of each day's journey. Yet, through all the gruelling, the engine had barely missed a beat nor required a spanner.

Two months later Ashton sent me a sum of forty-eight pounds on her behalf, a further tribute to the value of British engineering.

'The Wrights are ready to start; they are calling, and I must go. Farewell to our journey north and—Baby—so long.'

To Hell and Gone (1932).

––––––

ROBIN HANBURY-TENISON

(1936–)

British farmer and explorer. Hanbury-Tenison, in addition to running a hill-farm in Cornwall, has taken part in more than twenty expeditions, including the first land crossing of South America at its widest point (1958), helped to found Survival International in the 1960s to fight for the rights of threatened tribal peoples, written a number of books, and edited The Oxford Book of Exploration *(1993). After completing long horse-rides through France and along the Great Wall of China, in 1988 he and his second wife, Louella, rode on horseback through New Zealand's two main islands, partly to support the charity Riding for the Disabled. Between January and March, they travelled from near Invercargill in the South Island to just beyond Gisborne in the North, a distance of 648 miles (1202 kilometres). Hanbury-Tenison experienced a particularly exhilarating moment near Akaroa, in the South Island.*

SEALS ON THE BEACH (1988)

Akaroa was almost painfully beautiful. The harbour, formed from the flooded crater of one of the Banks Peninsula volcanoes, looked more like a lovely lake than an arm of the sea. We saw our first pohutukawa trees growing along the shore. Here, at the very southern limit of their range, they were covered in glorious red bottlebrush flowers which were reflected in the calm blue water, though in the subtropical north they flower at Christmas and are therefore known as New Zealand's Christmas tree. A French colony was on the point of being established at Akaroa in 1840, Captain Jean Langlois having thought that he had bought the whole of Banks Peninsula from the Ngai Tahu tribe. However, when he stopped at Waitangi on his return with the first sixty-three emigrants, he found that the Treaty had just been signed and New Zealand was now a British colony. The French settlers stayed in spite of this and as a result Akaroa has a delightfully Gallic feel to it. Many of the old stone and clapboard houses have been preserved and there are excellent seafood restaurants, one of which we visited with our hosts Robyn and Kit Grigg.

Their farm, over the hill at Hickory Bay, is down a private road and has an inaccessible and therefore undisturbed beach beyond the farmhouse. There we gathered large, succulent mussels by the bucketful and watched a completely unafraid yellow-eyed penguin which simply stood on a rock looking self-conscious and stared at us. As it is one of the rarest penguins in the world, there being only a few hundred left, I went back alone later to try to get some photographs. Creeping quietly between some large rocks, I made my way to a boulder in the centre, behind which I hid. Peering slowly over the top I found myself looking straight into a large whiskery face with melancholy eyes gazing myopically into mine. It was quite frightening, as for a moment I had no idea what it was. Then, slowly turning my head and looking round, I realized that I had crept into the middle of a colony of fur seals. There were at least a dozen all round me and I must have walked within inches of one on my way in. When my nearest neighbour yawned, giving a satis-tied grunt at the end, he revealed big teeth and I wondered if seals ever bit people. That was silly, I told myself. I had only to stand up and they would all flop back into the sea in a panic. I stood up. A couple of heads I had not noticed were lifted to glance incuriously at me and then lowered, but none of the seals showed the least alarm. It must have been horribly easy for the whalers and sealers to kill them when the shores teemed with seals which had never seen man before. I decided to enjoy the moment and stop worrying. It was wonderful. As my eyes became accustomed to picking out a glimpse of brown fur among the rocks and seaweed, I would see a hind flipper raised casually here and there as a stout, contented animal lay on its back in the shallows, or scratched itself with the small residual claw on its forelimb. There was a strong, acrid smell emanating from them. No-one had warned me that I might meet seals on the beach and it had not crossed my mind that I would do so. It occurred to me that all the books which say that there were only two mammals (bats) in New Zealand before man arrived were wrong.

In the Galapagos Islands I once swam underwater with a group of female sea lions. They flirted around me as I dived through a tunnel under the reef and came almost nose to nose to look into my face mask. That, too, had been an experience of pure magic until the huge shape of the male had risen like a submarine from the depths and chased me ignominiously back to the boat. Now I began to wonder if I were trespassing again and should perhaps leave while all was peaceful. I tiptoed away, receiving barely a glance as I passed. Only those lucky enough to have had similar experiences will understand the elation I felt as I ran back to tell everyone about it.

Fragile Eden (1990 edition, first published 1989).

7

Gold-seekers

◆

MRS CHARLES (ELLEN) CLACY

(dates unknown)

English traveller. Ellen and her brother left England for the Victorian gold-fields in April 1852. While in Australia she also visited New South Wales and South Australia, before departing with her newly acquired husband in November 1852. Her account of her trip, said to have been 'written on the spot', was published soon after her arrival back in England in February 1853 and became very popular. The following adventure occurred near Bendigo.

'AN ADVENTURE'

Sunday, 3.—A FINE morning. After our usual service Frank, my brother, and myself, determined on an exploring expedition, and off we went, leaving the dinner in the charge of the others. We left the busy throng of the diggers far behind us, and wandered into spots where the sound of the pick and shovel, or the noise of human traffic, had never penetrated. The scene and the day were in unison; all was harmonious, majestic, and serene. Those mighty forests, hushed in a sombre and awful silence; those ranges of undulating hill and dale never yet trodden by the foot of man; the soft still air, so still that it left every leaf unruffled, flung an intensity of awe over our feelings, and led us from the contemplation of nature to worship nature's God.

We sat in silence for some while deeply impressed by all around us, and, whilst still sitting and gazing there, a change almost imperceptibly came over the face of both earth and sky. The forest swayed to and fro, a sighing moaning sound was borne upon the wind, and a noise as of the rush of waters, dark massive clouds rolled over the sky till the bright blue heavens were completely hidden, and then, ere we had recovered from our first alarm and bewilderment, the storm in its unmitigated fury burst upon us. The rain fell in torrents, and we knew not where to turn.

Taking me between them, they succeeded in reaching an immense shea-oak, under which we hoped to find some shelter till the violence of the rain had diminished; nor were we disappointed, though it was long before we could venture to leave our place of refuge. At length, however, we did so, and endeavoured to find our way back to Eagle Hawk Gully. Hopeless task! The ground was so slippery, it was as much as we could do to walk without falling; the mud and dirt clung to our boots, and a heavy rain beat against our faces and nearly blinded us.

'It is clearing up to windward,' observed Frank; 'another half-hour and the rain will be all but over; let us return to our tree again.'

We did so. Frank was correct; in less than the time he had specified a slight drizzling rain was all of the storm that remained.

With much less difficulty we again attempted to return home, but before very long we made the startling discovery that we had completely lost our way, and to add to our misfortune the small pocket-compass, which Frank had brought with him, and which would have now so greatly assisted us, was missing, most probably dropped from his pocket during the skirmish to get under shelter. We still wandered along till stopped by the shades of evening, which came upon us—there is little or no twilight in Australia.

We seated ourselves upon the trunk of a fallen tree, wet, hungry, and, worst of all, ignorant of where we were. Shivering with cold, and our wet garments hanging most uncomfortably around us, we endeavoured to console one another by reflecting that the next morning we could not fail to reach our tents. The rain had entirely ceased, and providentially for us the night was pitch dark—I say providentially, because after having remained for two hours in this wretched plight a small light in the distance became suddenly visible to us all, so distant, that but for the intensity of the darkness it might have passed unnoticed. 'Thank God!' simultaneously burst from our lips.

'Let us hasten there,' cried Frank, 'a whole night like this may be your sister's death and would ruin the constitution of a giant.'

To this we gladly acceded, and were greatly encouraged by perceiving that the light remained stationary. But it was a perilous undertaking. Luckily my brother had managed to get hold of a long stick, with which he sounded the way, for either large stones or water-holes would have been awkward customers in the dark; wonderful to relate we escaped both, and when within hailing distance of the light, which we perceived came from a torch held by some one, we shouted with all our remaining strength, but without diminishing our exertions to reach it. Soon—with feelings that only those who have encountered similar dangers can understand—answering voices fell upon our ears. Eagerly we pressed forward, and in the excitement of the moment we relinquished all hold of one another, and attempted to wade through the mud singly.

'Stop! halt!' shouted more than one stentorian voice; but the warning came too late. My feet slipped—a sharp pain succeeded by a sudden chill—a feeling of suffocation—of my head being ready to burst—and I remembered no more.

When I recovered consciousness it was late in the morning, for the bright sun shone upon the ground through the crevices of a sail cloth tent, and so different was all that met my eyes to the dismal scene through which I had so lately passed, and which yet haunted my memory, that I felt that sweet feeling of relief which we experience when, waking from some horrid vision, we become convinced how unsubstantial are its terrors, and are ready to smile at the pain they excited.

That I was in a strange place became quickly evident, and among the distant hum of voices which ever and anon broke the silence not one familiar tone could I recognize. I endeavoured to raise myself so as to hear more distinctly, and then it was that an acute pain in the ankle of the right foot, gave me pretty strong evidence as to the reality of the last night's adventures. I was forced to lie down again, but not before I had espied a hand-bell which lay within reach on a small barrel near my bed. Determined as far as possible to fathom the mystery, I rang a loud peal with it, not doubting but what it would bring my brother to me. My surprise and delight may be easier imagined than described, when, as though in obedience to my summons, I saw a small white hand push aside the canvas at one corner of the tent, and one of my own sex entered.

She was young and fair; her step was soft and her voice most musically gentle. Her eyes were a deep blue, and a rich brown was the colour of her hair, which she wore in very short curls all round her head and parted on one side, which almost gave her the appearance of a pretty boy.

These little particulars I noticed afterwards; at that time I only felt that her gentle voice and kind friendliness of manner inexpressibly soothed me.

After having bathed my ankle, which I found to be badly sprained and cut, she related, as far as she was acquainted with them, the events of the previous evening. I learnt that these tents belong to a party from England, of one of whom she was the wife, and the tent in which I lay was her apartment. They had not been long at the diggings, and preferred the spot where they were to the more frequented parts.

The storm of yesterday had passed over them without doing much damage, and as their tents were well painted over the tops, they managed to keep themselves tolerably dry; but later in the evening, owing to the softness of the ground, one of the side-posts partly gave way, which aroused them all, and torches were lit, and every one busied in trying to prop it up till morning. While thus engaged, they heard our voices calling for help. They answered, at the same time getting ready some more torches before advancing to meet us, as there were several pit-holes between us and them. Their call for us to remain stationary came too late to save me from slipping into one of their pits, thereby spraining my ankle and otherwise hurting myself, besides being buried to my forehead in mud and water. The pit was not quite five feet deep, but, unfortunately for myself in this instance, I belong to the pocket edition of the feminine sex. They soon extricated me from this perilous situation, and carried me to their tents, where, by the assistance of my new friend, I was divested of the mud that still clung to me, and placed into bed.

Before morning the storm, which we all thought had passed over, burst forth with redoubled fury; the flashes of lightning were succeed-ed by loud peals of thunder, and the rain came splashing down. Their tents were situated on a slight rise, or they would have run great risk of being washed away; every hole was filled with water, and the shea-oak, of whose friendly shelter we had availad ourselves the evening before, was struck by lightning, and shivered into a thousand pieces. After a while the storm abated, and the warm sun and a drying wind were quickly removing all traces of it.

Frank and my brother, after an early breakfast, had set out for Eagle Hawk Gully under the guidance of my fair friend's husband, who knew the road thither very well; it was only three miles distant. He was to bring back with him a change of clothing for me, as his wife had per-suaded my brother to leave me in her charge until I had quite recovered from the effects of the accident, 'which he more readily promised,' she observed, 'as we are not quite strangers, having met once before.'

A Lady's Visit to the Gold Diggings of Australia in 1852–53 (second edition of 1853).

———

JOHN SHERER

(1810– ?)

British printer and writer. Edinburgh-born Sherer wrote numerous histories, travel books, and other works. His popular narrative, The Gold-Finder of Australia: How He Went, How He Fared, and How He Made His Fortune *(1853), the title page of which bears his name as editor, was long believed to be a genuine account of Sherer's experiences on the Australian gold-fields, described in 1973 as 'the most colourful and realistic first-hand report of those amazing days'. The 'gold-finder' apparently left England in 1851, reached the gold-fields in 1852, made his fortune, then returned home. Sherer claims that the adventures outlined in the book, one of which appears below, are 'such as have absolutely been passed through'. Alas, however, the gold-finder was fictitious, Sherer had never visited Australia, and his book is, in the words of historian David Goodman, 'a clever pastiche of existing travellers' accounts and interpolated fictional narratives'.*

DISCOVERING A POCKET

March was in the wane by the time we had sunk no fewer than nine holes, averaging from sixteen to twenty feet, with very indifferent success; but we had now become so inured to toil and disappointment that we worked like beings almost insensible to the influence of any of the passions whatever. Perhaps the most disagreeable portion connected with our employment was the being asked half-a-dozen times a day by some more lucky party how we were getting on; when we could only return the oft-told tale, that we had had very little luck yet. Now, one does not like to be always telling a tale of sorrow; yet, when the question was asked, we had no other reply to make without departing from the truth. At length, however, we were destined to tell another story. The lucky day came at last; and I shall never forget the rush of emotions which filled my breast on striking, nearly at the bottom of one of our holes, a nugget of fourteen pounds weight.

'O Gemini!' cried Raikes, letting fall the barrow from his hands at the mouth of the hole, and jumping down with an alacrity which sufficiently evinced the strength of his own feelings on the occasion. 'We have it now,' he continued, 'and we'll do well.'

It was true what he said. We found a whole 'pocketful' of gold, and for eight consecutive days took out from six to eight pounds a day. We had the prudence to keep this extraordinary change of luck quiet, having seen enough of the folly of bruiting abroad any sudden turn of fortune which had befallen a successful party, from the swarms of excavators it immediately brought around them to mine in their neighbourhood. We therefore continued to labour with the same persevering and dogged energy which had all along, since our arrival at Bendigo, characterised our proceedings. It was the more easy for us to keep our success quiet, from the fact of there being very few diggers working in the gully in which we were. Not far from us, however, was one family whose example of laborious industry had few parallels in the Diggings. Every morning by the break of day, they were all hard at work—the father digging, the mother rocking, with a baby in her arms, as her eldest boy poured the water on the earth, the 'toddlin' wee thing' of three years old even helping to bring his share of golden grist to the mill. Such industry could not help being rewarded; and, accordingly, we understood them to be doing well.

When we had fallen upon the auriferous mass at the bottom of our hole, it had the effect of suspending our labours for a few minutes, so commanding were the feelings with which we were severally assailed. These, however, soon subsided, when Brown was despatched with it to our tent, that Binks might, as soon as possible, share in the joy which its discovery gave us. During his absence, Raikes and I continued to follow the vein we had struck; and our amazement increased as we proceeded, from the quantity of smaller pieces which we found. In one spot they were stuck as thick as currants in a rich dumpling, and varying in size from that of a raisin to a pin's head.

The Gold-Finder of Australia (1853).

ANTOINE FAUCHERY

(1827?–61)

French writer and photographer. During his first visit to Australia (1852–56), Fauchery tried his hand as a digger at Ballarat for two years, founded and briefly ran a cafe in Melbourne, and spent several unsuccessful months as a storekeeper in the Daylesford area. His vivid picture of life in Melbourne and on the Victorian gold-fields, originally published in instalments in Le Moniteur Universel *in 1857, appeared as* Lettres d'un Mineur en Australie *(1857). During his second visit (1857–59), he worked in Melbourne as a photographer, producing some outstanding photographs. He later became ill in China, and died in Japan in 1861 from gastritis and dysentery.*

A 'MYSTERIOUS' INCIDENT AT THE DIGGINGS

We were leaving the place, loaded up like donkeys, and were going through the doorway, when the owner of the establishment, who had been watching us with a serious air during the course of our purchases, came rushing after us. 'Hey, there!' quoth he. All three of [us] turned around, and hearing a mysterious 'Hush!' accompanied by an imperceptible movement of his head, we came back. Another 'Hush!' greeted our return, and the proprietor left us, to our astonishment, to look carefully around outside. We couldn't understand it. *'What is the matter?'* we asked, and the only reply was a third 'Hush!' However, our man, after assuring himself no doubt that all was well, came back and disappeared under his counter. Then, after a few seconds, we saw his anxious head pop up, like a trick snuff-box, motioning to one of us to go and join him. Shall we go or not?—One man takes the risk, plunges down behind the oilcloth-covered boards, and comes out again with a scarlet face and without saying a word. The next man takes his place, and comes back with the same red face and as silently. Upon my word, I only go reluctantly where the others have been, purely for the purpose of showing that I had some courage. Under the counter I start to say something. The most energetic 'Hushes!' shut my mouth, and I reappear with a still more crimson face than my partners. I was strangled, asphyxiated; I had had a glass!

Good Lord! this Bouchardy stage-setting, these muffled tremolos from the orchestra, these uneasy glances into the wings, these strange gestures, you might almost say these trap-doors,—all this for a glass?— Yes indeed, and what awful brandy at that!

Here is the key to this mystery. The farsighted authorities, for fear of the disturbances and excesses caused by drunkenness, have utterly and absolutely forbidden, at the mines, all spiritous or fermented liquors, and they prosecute those that sell them on the sly with a severity that drives drinkers and vendors to despair. The police show no mercy; they inspect the drays and seize implacably the liquids with which they are loaded; they incessantly watch the store-keepers, who all have a few bottles hidden under that famous counter behind which your face gets so red. Sometimes the policemen disguise themselves as diggers covered with dust and mud, and with a pick on their shoulder seek to catch unawares the confidence and cupidity of the merchants, who don't always resist the temptation to gain about a thousand per cent on a drop of gin, rum or brandy; for this pure vitriol, which comes to 6 francs a quart, is sold retail to the tune of 1fr. 70c. a *nobbler* (a word coined in the colony and signifying the contents of a half-glass; the equivalent of the old gill).

To be sure, it is a cruel alternative. On the one hand, why not try to satisfy your customers, when the profits are so exorbitant and these same customers threaten to pay double the agreed price or, if you refuse too obstinately, to take their money to a less recalcitrant dealer?

On the other hand, the law is brutal. At the first denunciation by the *detectives*, the liquor is seized, and you have to pay out at the *commissioner's* office the sum of 50 pounds as a fine. If there is a second offence, there is a fresh seizure, but the fine is five times as big. A third offence, and once more there is a seizure, plus 250 pounds, plus four months' *hard labour*,—in other words, imprisonment plus work every day breaking stones on the roads under the eye of the overseers. There is no known instance of a fourth offence. For that you must surely be hanged.

Despite these little pinpricks from the authorities, people, while observing the greatest prudence, still manage to fix things up among themselves; the money comes into the till, and from one counter to another a man eventually gets drunk. At the mines, brandy is all-powerful. It is the true, the only hidden divinity that holds its sway and is revered; it is for it and by it that the fever breaks out, a fiery fever that burns before and after, that holds the knife at the corner of the woods, whose blue flames eat up heaps of that pure gold so painfully torn out of the ground.

Whatever Great Britain may say about it, and whatever she may affect to be doing when she buys from us at a high price the wines from our best vintages, Château-Margot, Château-Laffitte and Champagne-Clicot, her private and sincere liking is for our Armagnacs, our Montpelliers and even our Cognacs. When I say 'even' I am reversing in the grossest fashion the hierarchical order of the labels, to the great scandalisation of true connoisseurs, but for a good reason. The Englishman does not taste, he drinks, as he himself admits: all brandies are *the* best, and it is brandy that he prefers to other drinks, beer or wine. In the stately home as in the tavern, the bottle that holds this beloved liquor is the pole towards which all eyes turn, and in all classes of society, without distinction, a benevolent feeling, a favourable inclination is in evidence for *pale brown* or *dark brandy*.

In Paris I knew a real gentleman, in the lofty style, who spoke a queer sort of French with an admixture of English words, and who said to me in the most naïve way in the world: '*Oh! j'aimais bien les vins de France. But I like above all le vin de Saint-Georges, because there's a lot of brandy in it.*'

I shall not dwell on the enormous quantities of brandy that France sends to England and her colonies. All that I can certify is that more than anywhere else this drink is the only one appreciated and in demand at the mines; and that, although it is still found there in more than reasonable proportions, people grumble about not being able to drink it *in larger quantities and as freely as they like.*

Letters from a Miner in Australia, trans. A.R. Chisholm (1965, first published in French 1857).

———

GEORGE FRANCIS TRAIN

(1829–1904)

American entrepreneur and merchant. Born and raised in Massachusetts, Train worked as a clerk for the White Diamond Line in Boston and Liverpool before spending three profitable years in gold-rush Victoria (1853–55), during which he acted as an agent for various insurance companies, represented the White Star shipping line of Liverpool, built warehouses, sold goods ranging from clothing to wagons, and was active in community affairs in Melbourne. Some of his letters to American newspapers were later collected in An American Merchant in Europe, Asia, and Australia … *(1857). He subsequently introduced horse-drawn tramways to England and was involved in the development of railroads in the United States, but became insolvent at the age of 47. Increasingly eccentric, he continued to travel widely. Imprisoned several times in Britain and America throughout his life, Train was once described by his lawyer as 'a Vesuvius constantly erupting'. He and the many other American merchants who were attracted by the gold-rushes contributed to a much remarked upon phenomenon.*

THE 'AMERICANIZATION' OF MELBOURNE

Melbourne,
Dec. 16, 1853.

You would be surprised to see how fast this place is becoming *Americanized.* Go where you will, from Sandridge to Bendigo—from the 'Ovens' to Balaarat, you can but note some indication of the indomitable energy of our people. 'Hang a coffee bag in that place noted for the warmth of its temperature and the morals of its inhabitants, and a Yankee will be sure to find it,' says some observer of our national character!

The true American defies competition and laughs sneeringly at impossibilities. He don't believe in the word, and is prepared to show

how meaningless it is. It is not an unusual thing to hear the movers of some undertaking that has been dragging its slow carcase along, remark:— 'If you want to have the jetty finished, you must let the Americans take hold of it;' and sure enough they have obtained the contract to complete the Hobson's Bay Railroad Pier, and our country-men mechanics invariably receive the preference.

A mail or two since I wrote you about the *Tittlebat* appearance of the Melbourne fire brigade at the late fire in Collins street, and sug-gested the propriety of your sending us out a Boston tub or two, just for aggravation sake. Hardly had my letter cleared the Heads before we had another scorcher, more furious than the first, burning down some half-dozen buildings in Flinder's lane. The Americans could not endure it any longer, and on the spot determined to volunteer their services for the public good. It was too much for our weak nerves to see the reckless destruction of property, simply for want of a suitable engine. The next morning our paper was started and *sixteen thousand dollars* subscribed in less time than it takes to perform the episcopal service, for the pur-chasing of the suitable apparatus for a thoroughly efficient fire depart-ment under the volunteer system. After all the American houses had contributed their fifty pounds, the paper was passed round among the 'merchants of all nations,' who gladly gave us a helping hand. The enclosed *scrip* from the Argus will show you that this is no flash in the pan—but a genuine go ahead affair. A committee has been appointed to wait upon his excellency, with a brief outline of our system of man-aging such affairs, and to request the government to furnish us with engine houses, &c., if it met with his sanction and approval. A meeting will be called to hear the report of said committee, and if favorable, the order for the engines will be sent forthwith.

As most of the Atlantic States are represented here by mercantile houses, there is quite a difference of opinion about where, and by whom said machinery shall be made—some say Boston, (and I most respectful-ly would intimate that I am one of that number, having for many years a most religious belief in the superiority of that city over many others for clipper ships, clipper mechanics, clipper engines, clipper scholars and clipper merchants!) Some say New York, others, Philadelphia, while one or two believe in Baltimore. To settle the question, we may have to draw from each, an engine for competition sake,—each maker will then be striving to excel, and we shall accordingly get the best 'mer-chines.'

This movement will show you that the Americans are not asleep.

A few days since I was trying my *veil*, preparatory for the cloud of dust that sweeps along Collins street, between Queen's and Swanston, when my old eyes were made glad by the appearance of a real old Boson water cart in full operation. The streets were being watered— and 'twas amusing to see the astonished natives on each side gaping incredulously at the watering machine. No wonder—poor benighted race. It was something they had never dreamed of; they could not understand how that water, which they were paying two dollars a cask for, should be scattered up and down the street. One man, more intelligent than the rest, had presence of mind enough to climb up on the wheel and tell the driver, amid a shout from the knowing ones, that the water was all leaking out of his cart!

On enquiry, I found that an *American* was watering the street on subscription. I noticed one spot in the middle of the street as dusty as ever—while either side was carefully sprinkled. It seems that the occupant of the store adjoining declined paying for the luxury—so the driver stopped just before, and commenced sprinkling again just after having passed his door!

A company of American Californians have started a line of passenger wagons—(American, of course, made at Concord)—to Bendigo; another party have two teams running from Geelong to Balaarat; and some Cape Cod folks are doing a good business with some Yankee coaches between Sandridge and Melbourne.

There are about one hundred New York buggy waggons in and about the city—mostly owned by Englishmen, who for a long time could not believe that the tiny spokes and slender wheels and springs were sufficiently strong to carry their weight! They are much delighted with the covered buggies, and well they may be, for the sun comes down most scorchingly upon those who sport a 'dog cart!'

Some two or three Americans are engaged in catching fish, some forty miles from town, for this market; another party are cutting firewood at the Heads, on speculation—while Moss is selling American ice at the Criterion at fifty cents a-pound.

American timber (save shingles) will entirely shut out the colonial; and American mining tools have already displaced the English.

American *liquors stand no chance* here—but the American drinks [cocktails] are very popular—and now having exercised the peculiar privilege of an American in saying what he can of his countrymen, permit me to wish you and your readers as many happy returns of the new year as it may be pleasant for you and them to enjoy.

E. Daniel and Annette Potts (eds), *A Yankee Merchant in Goldrush Australia: The Letters of George Francis Train, 1853–55* (1970).

RAFFAELLO CARBONI

(1820–75)

Italian patriot, writer, and composer. The young Carboni studied for the priesthood, learned languages, and originally worked as a clerk. He joined the Young Italy movement and was wounded in the rebellion of 1849, then travelled through Europe, before sailing for Australia in 1852. His time as a digger on the Ballarat gold-fields was interspersed with periods working as a shepherd and living with local Aborigines. Although Carboni, who was a member of the miners' central committee in the lead-up to the Eureka uprising, was not actually in the stockade at the time of the attack on it on 3 December 1854, he was one of twelve diggers charged with high treason, all of whom were acquitted. He extended his stay in Australia in order to write The Eureka Stockade *(1855), which he sold on the stockade site on the first anniversary of the rebellion. After leaving Australia in January 1856, he travelled in the East for several years before returning to Italy, where he took part in the Risorgimento. After further travel in Europe, he worked as a dramatist and composer, although his efforts went largely unacknowledged.*

'A FOUL DEED' (1854)

Here begins a foul deed, worthy of devils, and devils they were. The accursed troopers were now within the stockade. They dismounted, and pounced on firebrands from the large fire on the middle of the stockade, and deliberately set in a blaze all the tents round about. I did see with both my eyes one of those devils, a tall, thick-shouldered, long-legged, fast Vandemonian-looking trooper, purposely striking a bundle of matches, and setting fire at the corner end, north of the very store of Diamond, where we had kept the council for the defence.

The howling and yelling was horrible. The wounded are now burnt to death; those who had laid down their arms, and taken refuge within the tents, were kicked like brutes, and made prisoners.

At the burning of the Eureka Hotel, I expressed it to be my opinion that a characteristic of the British race is to delight in the calamity of a fire.

The troopers, enjoying the fun within the stockade, now spread it *without.* The tent next to mine (Quinn's) was soon in a blaze. I collected in haste my most important papers, and rushed out to remonstrate against such a wanton cruelty. Sub-inspector Carter pointing with his pistol ordered me to fall in with a batch of prisoners. There were no two ways: I obeyed. In the middle of the gully I expostulated with Captain Thomas; he asked whether I had been made a prisoner within the stockade. 'No, sir,' was my answer. He noticed my frankness, my anxiety and grief. After a few words more in explanation, he, giving me a gentle stroke with his sword, told me, 'If you really are an honest digger, I do not want you, sir; you may return to your tent.'

Mr Gordon—of the store of Gordon and M'Callum, on the left of the gully, near the stockade—who had been made prisoner, and was liberated in the same way, and at the same time as myself, was and is a living witness to the above.

On crossing the gully to return to my tent, an infernal trooper trotting on the road to Ballaarat, took a deliberate aim at me, and fired his Minie rifle pistol with such a tolerable precision, that the shot whizzed and actually struck the brim of my cabbage-tree hat, and blew it off my head. Mrs Davis, who was outside her tent close by, is a living witness to the above.

At this juncture I was called by name from Doctor Carr, and Father Smyth, directed me by signs to come and help the wounded within the stockade.

The Eureka Stockade (1855).

HERBERT HOOVER

(1874–1964)

American engineer and president. Hoover travelled widely before the First World War, working as a mining engineer in various countries. From 1897 to 1899 he did 'general engineering work' for a group of mines in Western Australia. During and after the war he organised relief work in Europe and the United States. A Republican, Hoover was secretary of commerce (1921–28), before becoming the 31st president of the United States (1929–33). In old age he recalled some of his Western Australian experiences.

'OUTPOSTS OF CIVILIZATION'

Coolgardie and Kalgoorlie are among the hottest and driest and dustiest places on this earth. The temperature was over 100° at midnight for days at a time. The rain was little more than an inch per year and most of it all at once The country is unbelievably flat and uninteresting. There is not a fish in stretches of a thousand miles. In fact there are no running streams and few appearances of water courses anywhere in the great interior plain. The country is covered with a low bush eight or ten feet high with occasional eucalyptus trees so starved for water as to have only an umbrella of foliage. The roads—more properly 'tracks'—that were gradually cut through the low brush extended in straight lines for a hundred miles. They added to the monotony of life by their never attainable notches in the bush on the horizon. The vegetation was in fact up to expectations considering only one inch of rainfall. It had one redeeming feature. After the sole annual rain the whole desert broke into a Persian carpet of different-colored immortelles which lasted for weeks. When rain threatened the whole town started running for home. When water was $2^1/2$ cents a gallon the whole population quit its normal occupation to collect free water from the heavens. Roofs, blankets, buckets, tubs, were all in service.

Some of our mines lay long distances away in the interior and at that time the principal means of transportation was long strings of Afghan camels. We rode them on inspection trips and I am in a position to state authoritatively that a camel does not fulfil all the anticipations of romantic literature. He is even a less successful creation than a horse. He needs water oftener than the schoolbooks imply. His motion imparts aches to muscles never hitherto known. No amount of petting will inspire him with affection. His long neck enables him to bite one's leg unless he is constantly watched. We traveled in 20 to 30 mile daily stages, mostly slept on the ground under the cold stars and were awakened by swarms of flies at daybreak. We cooked our own food and I soon reduced my culinary operations to a diet of toasted bread, cocoa and sardines heated in the can. Sometimes we substituted baked beans by the same metallurgical processes. Flies, sand, and dirt generally were the chief undertones. Later on with the digging of more salt-wells and the establishment of crude distilling apparatus we were able to replace our camels with horses—mostly with two-wheeled carts driven tandem.

On one of these early jaunts 150 miles into the interior I camped overnight near a prospect called the Sons of Gwalia, which was being worked by a group of Welshmen for owners in Wales. After supper I called upon them and was taken over their 'show' and their small mill. I became much impressed with the evidences of a real mine and on reaching a telegraph office the next day, I cabled to Mr Moreing that I thought the prospect well worth examination, if he could get an option from their Welsh financial backers. This was done, and a few weeks later I completed the examination and recommended the purchase of a two-thirds interest for $250 000 and a provision for $250 000 working capital. It was my first assumption of responsibility for what seemed to me a huge sum of money. However, the mine turned out well. [Over the succeeding 50 years it produced $55 000 000 of gold and paid $10 000 000 in dividends.] The firm was naturally pleased with this venture. I was carried for a small percentage interest and was appointed its first manager at $10 000 a year and expenses. I built a corrugated iron residence under the shadow of Mt Leonora—one of the highest peaks in Western Australia. It rose 160 feet above the plain. I at once undertook vigorous development of the mine and the installation of a large metallurgical plant.

The sodden conditions of life at the Gwalia were perhaps expressed by a foreman who had a habit of getting blind drunk about once a month. Good foremen were too scarce to be discharged for such sins and on one occasion when I reprimanded him violently he said, 'Well, if you live in this place you just have to get good and drunk once in a while.' I inquired how he knew when he was 'good and drunk.' He replied, 'When Mt Leonora whiskey begins to taste good, then I know.'

But no one need sympathize with men engaged in constructive work at the outposts of civilization. Our staff and I enjoyed every hour of it. There were many light moments. I still recollect Ernest, the Austrian cook, serving American canned corn direct from the tin as a dessert. And the burro who ate the wax matches and had to have his internal fire put out by a bucket of water through a funnel. But to feel great works grow under one's feet and to have more men constantly getting good jobs is to be the master of contentment. And here again I had time for reading—chiefly upon Australasia and its history and government.

The Memoirs of Herbert Hoover: Years of Adventure 1874–1920 (1952).

8

Journalists

♦

FRANK FOWLER

(1833–63)

English journalist. At the age of twenty-two, suffering from consumption, Fowler decided that a 'run round the world' to New South Wales would improve his health. During his stay in Sydney, which lasted from December 1855 until March or April 1858, he gave public orations on literary and political subjects, wrote for the Empire *and* Sydney Morning Herald, *and founded a short-lived literary journal entitled the* Month. *He reputedly wrote his controversial account of colonial life,* Southern Lights and Shadows, *during a three-day gale off the Falkland Islands during the voyage home. His lack of regard for facts is reflected in the book's subtitle,* Brief Notes of Three Years' Experience of Social, Literary, and Political Life in Australia, *an odd choice of wording given that he spent closer to two than three years in the colony. He died from tuberculosis in London in 1863. Like many travellers to the Antipodes, he was much impressed by Sydney Harbour.*

IMPRESSIONS OF SYDNEY HARBOUR (1855)

It was at breakfast-time on a warm, cheerful morning in December, when *our* 'long dun wolds are ribbed with snow,' that the 'Kate' and I cast anchor in Port Jackson. Myriads of emerald cicadas were splintering the silence with their shrill, cricket-like chirruppings, as they glanced from bough to bough beneath the burning sun. It wanted three or four days to Christmas, but every tree was full of leaves, every bush afire with blossoms. Of the harbour of Port Jackson it is difficult to speak within the bounds of calm description. I have talked with travelled men—old salts who have weathered at Rio, young sprigs who have yachted at Naples—and they all agree in this, that, for scenery, capacity, and safety, the haven of Sydney is the finest in the world. It is a harbour *sui generis*. Great mouldering rocks, crowned with tall, solitary trees, stretch along the shore, while the water divides itself into a hundred streams, and runs, like the canals of Venice, along and around the greater portion of the city. Whereever you walk in Sydney, blue glimpses of the harbour are marked in the distance. In one direction you see it sheening away for miles, until it loses itself in the dim greenery of the far-off bush; in another you catch a mere shield of it set out bravely against the sun. Here it dwindles to the dimensions of a pillar of marble prone upon the hill-side; there it opens into a perfect sea, with a fleet of tapering masts cut clear against the sky. From almost any balcony in any part of the city, the eye, gazing through the torrid atmosphere, is cooled by the grateful breezes blowing off the water. For miles out of the town, too, you mark the tortuous windings of the stream. One arm of it—and it is a very Briareus in arms!—reaches up to Parramatta, a distance of about fifteen miles, and forms to my mind, and speaking so far as my narrow experience goes, the fairest river out of Eden. Its banks, from Sydney to Parramatta, are crowded with orange trees, which shoot a keen delicious perfume across the water, and through the foliage of which the golden fruit gleams out, like lamps of palest gold, or, as Andrew Marvell sings so quaintly,

'Like stars of lighte in a greene night.'

Charming villas rise from every agreeable point along the banks, while here and there is a village of neat stone houses (with little garden and orangery to each, and sometimes a landing-place of rough water-whitened stones, running out into the stream), centred and consecrated by a toy-like church, with tiny spire, bright with copper, pointing through the air. Here, too, is a fine convent, with a wealth of tinkling bells, and a magnificent erie-like property, set high on a jut of rock and surrounded by a perfect forest of white-limbed eucalypti, belonging, I was told, to a lineal descendant of one who could have sung rich music there—one, alas! who climbed a higher alp to write αθεος nearest heaven!

Rising from different parts of Port Jackson are verdant islets, singularly beautiful, and which look like bits of faërie-land—fragments of a dream—slumbrous homes for the companions of Ulysses or Mr Tennyson's later 'Lotus-Eaters.' They are edged with pendulous bushes and tropical water-plants,—which cool their brazen leaves and thirsty tendrils in the tide,—and smothered all over with a sward of matted bush-flowers, veined with the basanite stalk of the trailing melon.

Similar to these were my notes of the harbour on arriving at Sydney. Flocks of sailing-boats were hovering about the ship, and jumping into one of them, I soon found myself on the great public quay of the city. There must have been from twenty to thirty first-class vessels lying along the wharf, and scores of carts and drays were hurrying to and fro with cargo. A couple of carts, drawn by ten or twelve drowsy-looking bullocks, were going, at drowsy-bullock pace, along the wharf, each piled high with wool, and with a swarthy, heavily-bearded driver tramping at the side, whip in hand, and curt black pipe in mouth. ...

Southern Lights and Shadows (1859).

GEORGE AUGUSTUS SALA

(1828–96)

English journalist. During his lecture tour of Australia and New Zealand in 1885, Sala wrote for various newspapers, including the Argus, *the* Australasian, *the* Sydney Morning Herald, *and the London* Daily Telegraph. *Impressed by Melbourne's rapid progress and apparent prosperity in the 1880s, he dubbed the city 'Marvellous Melbourne', a term which quickly became popular. Given the subsequent turn of events, discussed at the conclusion of this extract from his autobiography, the association of his name with these words proved to be sadly ironic.*

VISITING THE ANTIPODES (1885)

It was on a Sunday morning that we arrived at Auckland. A party of journalists came off in a boat and boarded the steamer; and I was marched off to the principal hotel, the smiling landlady of which establishment informed me that Miss Geneviève Ward, the *tragédienne*, had been staying in the house, and had just left for the Hot Lakes. After luncheon, the steamer again took her departure, and on the fifth morning afterwards we entered the indescribably beautiful harbour of Sydney, and anchored at the Circular Quay. The Mayor of Sydney and Mr Alison, one of my *entrepreneurs*, were waiting for me; and I was told that my first lecture was to be delivered in the Town Hall, Melbourne, on the morrow of St Patrick's Day. After luncheon, I went to Government House; paid my respects to Lord Augustus Loftus; and was subsequently conducted to the Public Offices, where I was introduced to most of the Cabinet Ministers, including a great friend of Lord Rosebery, the late Hon. William Bede Dalley, who had been mainly instrumental in sending the New South Wales contingent to the Soudan.

Mr Dalley was one of the most cultured gentlemen and the most fluent orators I ever had the honour to meet. The Postmaster-General presented me with a free railway pass available for some months for myself and my wife; and I may here mention that every one of the Australasian Colonies showed us similar courtesy, and it never cost us a penny for railway travelling during our stay in the Colonies. Before leaving for Melbourne the members of the Athenæum Club—a society in which Lord Rosebery during his stay in Australia took great interest—entertained me at dinner, the chair being occupied by Mr Dalley. The railway journey from the capital of New South Wales to that of Victoria occupied from six in the evening until about eleven the following morning. But midway, at the frontier of the two colonies, there was an examination of luggage at a Victorian custom-house. The line of railway seemed to run principally through tractless forests of tall gum-trees. At the railway terminus at Melbourne I found my wife and Mr and Mrs George Rignold waiting for me on the platform; and we at once adjourned to Menzies' Hotel, then, and perhaps now, the very best hotel in Australia.

I found Melbourne a really astonishing city, with broad streets full of handsome shops, and crowded with bustling, well-dressed people. For two days we held almost continuous receptions at the hotel; and I wish that I had preserved the hundreds of cards of the ladies and gentlemen who were so kind as to visit us. The next evening I lectured for two hours at the Town Hall, which was crowded, and the receipts amounted to more than three hundred pounds. At the second lecture the aggregate takings were only eighty pounds. I am afraid, to begin with, that the hall was much too large for my purpose, and that my voice was scarcely audible to the occupants of the back seats. I remember at my first lecture being struck by two very curious circumstances. First, that what I intended to be a glowing eulogium on Mr Gladstone was received in dead silence; and that every allusion I made to Lord Beaconsfield was responded to by a thunderous storm of hand-clapping and cheering.

I went to Government House; was received by Sir Henry Loch, and dined with his Excellency, who, with Lady Loch, was present at my third lecture; but I must frankly own that as a lecturer I was not particularly successful in Melbourne. I realised, however, large sums in Australia. In Sydney I did remarkably well; and in New Zealand even better in a financial sense:—my agent there being the 'Little Smythe' with whom I had had the embryonic negotiations already mentioned. I earned, moreover, between March and December, something like a hundred pounds a week by the republication in the Melbourne *Argus*; the Sydney *Morning Herald*; another journal at Adelaide, South Australia; the *Auckland Herald*, and the *Calcutta Englishman*, of my letters under the title 'The Land of the Golden Fleece,' for which I was receiving another twenty pounds a week from the *Daily Telegraph*. I got four per cent. for my money on deposit in the Commercial Bank of Australia, and, in fact, by the end of the year I had realised a competence—which, for a literary man, might be considered handsome—for my old age; but within a year of my return to England I lost all my laboriously acquired shekels in one great crash.

I had my ups and my downs during my lecturing tour on the Australian continent; journeying, as my wife and I did, into the remotest 'back-blocks' of the Bush. In some towns our success was magnificent, in others the takings did not exceed ten pounds. At Adelaide, at Brisbane in Queensland, and indeed throughout the last-named colony, the money rolled in gloriously. At one township where there was a rather handsome theatre, I peeped—as lecturers as well as managers will do—through the usual orifice in the drop-curtain to see what kind of a house there was; but to my dismay the pit—there were no stalls— was tenanted only by three men and a boy. It was a case, I thought, of Hull and Lieutenant Gale's lecture on 'Aërostation' over again. But the case was pleasantly altered when the curtain rose. The most expensive seats in the house were in the dress-circle, which had been invisible to me through the hole in the curtain; and I found the boxes crowded with the 'quality' of the place—magistrates, clergymen, and wealthy squatters. We had hot roast fowl for supper that night.

Great financial success was also our lot at Wagga-Wagga, a really pretty town, with the name of which all those who remember the Tichborne trial will be familiar. The Assizes were on when we arrived; and by good luck the Crown Prosecutor turned out to be an old friend of mine. I had a capital house on that and the succeeding night—the Judge came, the Bar and the solicitors mustered in full force; the prosecutors and the witnesses were all to the fore; and I could almost have believed that the prisoners, escorted by friendly warders, were likewise present. It was at a place called Mudgee that I underwent one of the most serious snubs that I ever experienced, although I must admit that I have not unfrequently, while making a speech, been more or less 'shut up' by an unsympathetic audience. Once, taking the chair at the Holborn Town Hall, in advocacy of a movement for establishing a tram-car system in the parish of St Pancras, I began my address with—'Ladies and gentlemen. When I was last in the United States—' whereupon a gentleman in the gallery cried out: 'Why the devil didn't you stop there?' This was not very encouraging, but my rebuff at Mudgee was much more mortifying. It came from the lady who, as I have elsewhere related, exclaimed 'Rubbidge!' when I had come to the end of what I thought was a pathetic and picturesque description of the appearance of her Majesty Queen Victoria at her Coronation in June, 1848 [*sic*].

It was at Brisbane, in Queensland, that I found Miss Geneviève Ward, whose dramatic tour, in company with that excellent actor

Mr Vernon, had been one uninterrupted triumph. She made, I apprehend, as much if not more money than I did; and she had the sense, I hope and believe, to keep her winnings. We afterwards had the pleasure of meeting her both in Melbourne and Sydney. Of the many scores of places which I visited, many of them with wholly unpronounceable native names, I took count in a ledger which I have mislaid. I know, however, that in the autumn, under the auspices of 'Little Smythe,' I went to New Zealand, and lectured with bright success at Auckland, Wellington, Christchurch, Dunedin, Invercargill, and other places. At Wellington, the capital of the colony, I had the advantage of meeting the Governor, Sir William Jervois, whom I had not seen since the old Canadian days in 1864. Moreover, I received from an unknown source a hundred pounds as an honorarium for visiting the wonderful Hot Lakes district and formally opening some of the baths. I saw the marvellous Pink and White Terraces, since utterly annihilated by a succession of dreadful earthquakes.

Returning from New Zealand early in December, I lectured four or five times, but with indifferent success, at Hobart and other towns in the beautiful and hospitable island of Tasmania—the sanatorium, the Isle of Wight of Australia. In the third week of December my wife left me to go to Melbourne to pack up our things with the intent of departing for India; and three days after she left I crossed to Sydney to draw out some money from a banking-house there. I spent my Christmas Day at sea, not very convivially; there was no roast beef and there was no plum pudding, and I dined on boiled mutton and turnips, and a pint of Bass's pale ale. At Sydney I left my card with Lord Carrington, the newly arrived Governor, who at once sent down a trooper to the hotel where I was staying and asked me to dinner that same evening. At the end of the repast his Excellency, after proposing the Queen's health, told me that that was the only toast usually drunk at Government House; but that he meant to drink the health of my wife: which he did. We walked afterwards in the garden, and gazed at the blue velvet sky—not *melaina astrōn* ('black with stars'), as the Greek playwright somewhat paradoxically puts it in *Electra*—but studded almost overwhelmingly with the dazzling luminaries of the Southern Cross. 'What a beautiful country!' exclaimed Lord Carrington, 'and what a happy time you must have had.' Yes; I had had, all things considered, a happy and most prosperous time.

Next evening, having settled all my money matters, I took the train; and on the platform at Melbourne I found, not my wife, but my secretary, who told me that my dear partner had caught at chill at sea in

Bass's Straits; that she was lying dangerously ill at Menzies' Hotel, where a consultation of three physicians had just been held. It was New Year's Eve; the weather was ferociously hot, with a hotter wind, and a 'brickfielder,' or dust-storm, blowing through Melbourne's broad streets. I found my wife inarticulate, in the agonies of peritonitis. She only spoke once, when, pressing my hand, she said, 'Go to India, dear, and complete your education.' That night she died. At three o'clock in the afternoon of the next day I had to bury her. I had no mourning attire; and I was obliged to borrow different articles of sable dress from different friends. Everybody was pitiful and kind to me. The Governors of every one of the Australasian Colonies sent me condoling telegrams; and similar missives reached me from Lord Rosebery and from Henry Irving. The Bishop of Melbourne, now Bishop of Manchester, wrote me a touching letter. The Venerable Archdeacon of Melbourne, then nearly eighty years of age, and who died only a few weeks ago, came and prayed with me. Geneviève Ward was away; Mrs Menzies and her daughter were beautifully good to me; but I fancy that during a full fortnight I was more or less off my head.

The Life and Adventures of George Augustus Sala, vol. II (1895).

ANTHONY EDEN

(1897–1977)

English politician. Eden visited Australia and New Zealand in 1925, his main purpose being to represent the Yorkshire Post *at the Imperial Press Conference held in Melbourne that year. His newspaper articles formed the basis for his book* Places in the Sun *(1926), from which the following piece about Canberra is taken. A Conservative MP from 1923 to 1957, Eden was foreign secretary three times (1935–38, 1940–45, 1951–55) and prime minister once (1955–57), before being made an earl in 1961.*

'AUSTRALIA IN SEARCH OF A CAPITAL'

A country must have a capital, and a State—and so, presumably, a Commonwealth—must have a capital also. But where, and how to be chosen? Australia has found the decision and its execution a matter of difficulty.

Melbourne would seem the most natural capital. It is to-day the residence of the Governor-General, and has been the acting capital since the Commonwealth Constitution Act of 1900. But Melbourne is already the capital of Victoria and, not unnaturally perhaps, all the other States would not relish that Victoria should boast at once the capital city of the State and of the Commonwealth.

Sydney, too, had a claim as Australia's largest and first city. Here, then, lay the problem of rivalries. Inevitably a decision was difficult. The Act laid it down that:

> The seat of Government of the Commonwealth shall be determined by the Parliament, and shall be within territory which shall be granted to, or acquired by, the Commonwealth, and shall be in the State of New South Wales, and be distant not less than one hundred miles from Sydney.

Canberra was the site chosen. But Canberra was not the first choice, and so prolonged were the negotiations that it was not until January 1, 1911, that the territory finally became vested in the Commonwealth.

Canberra was not destined to rapid construction. The war further delayed building; and the need for economy after the war reduced the funds available, so that from the end of 1916 until 1921 hardly any progress was made. In recent years, however, the work has been pressed on with all possible speed, and it is hoped that Parliament may meet at Canberra, and the Governor-General take up his residence there, in 1926. With this end in view, some 2500 workmen are at work in Canberra to-day.

The setting up of a capital in a territory of its own, of 900 square miles, with no town of any size or thickly populated countryside in the immediate vicinity, is a brave undertaking, and its outcome will be watched with interest. At the date of our visit it was difficult to visualise the future city.

When Canberra ultimately takes her place, in spirit and fact as well as in name, as Australia's capital, it should rank among the fairest cities of the earth. The site chosen is beautiful—the undulating ground, the low slopes upon which the capital and Parliament House will one day stand, the vast extent of graceful rolling plains, and the abundant foliage.

No pains have been spared in afforestation. Trees and shrubs and sheltering copses have been planted, and in a nursery established at Canberra, tests have been carried out to ensure the planting of those varieties that will best thrive in the local conditions of soil and climate.

In order to enable Parliament to move to Canberra with as little delay as possible good temporary buildings are being constructed, but it must be many years before Canberra achieves the form of its original design.

The early years of Australia's capital were dogged by difficulty and misfortune. May her evil genii now be satiated and the future prove Canberra a capital city worthy of so beautiful a continent.

Places in the Sun (1926).

E. W. SWANTON
(1907–)

English cricket writer and commentator. Between 1946 and 1975 Jim (as he was known) Swanton made eight visits to Australia covering Marylebone Cricket Club (MCC) tours, during his years as cricket correspondent for the London Daily Telegraph. *In December 1974, during one of those visits, he travelled by train from Sydney to Perth.*

'THE LAST WORD'

It's the misfortune of all who travel with MCC to Australia that they are confined almost wholly to the cities and are able to see little of the out-back. I write as one who has never cast eyes on Alice Springs, or the Barrier Reef, and to whom the Snowy River scheme is only a name. We climb from city to city watching the red roofs and the green ovals recede, giving place as we reach cruising height to a huge indefinite panorama of brown and yellow splashed with green, the sun glinting now and then off blue water. It was with this vast gap in my education in mind that I planned with Thomas Cook to take the Indian Pacific train from Sydney to Perth, booking, as one needs to do, some six months ahead.

Rail travel in Australia has been hampered for generations by the variety of gauges—a strange self-inflicted disability attributable, I suppose, to early inter-state rivalry and distrust. It was only five years ago that the last stage of the standard gauge was completed and the first train made the journey right across the Continent from Sydney to Perth. The Indian Pacific now leaves three times a week each way, and the journey takes about 65 hours. One spends three nights in the train. I left Sydney on the Thursday afternoon following the Brisbane Test which had ended on the Wednesday, and got to Perth in time for breakfast on Sunday.

There is nothing scenically dramatic about the journey, but one sees inevitably a cross-section of the Australian countryside from the rich pastures of New South Wales on the east, dipping briefly down to the sea at Port Pirie, across the endless Nullarbor Plain—not a tree, not a hint of moisture—to Kalgoorlie, with its romantic Gold Rush associations, and thence by night to Perth.

One can either immure oneself in one's own snug air-conditioned coupé, emerging only for meals as they are announced over the intercom, or live a more gregarious life in the bar and lounge-car with its piano and leather armchairs. My own journey is a compromise, and I emerge at the end of it relaxed and refreshed, and with a profusion of memories: of the Blue Mountains shimmering in the afternoon sunlight; of limitless gums, red-capped, as we make the twilight ascent to Broken Hill; of the frustration of a lengthy, unexplained stop outside Port Pirie which postponed the dinner-hour almost to bed-time (we made up most of the three hours lost); of times observing the social scene in the Club Car with Harold Nicolson's *Diaries*, volume one, for company—a teenage girl playing the piano passably enough and being succeeded on the stool by a nun, rendering the tunes of her youth with a wistful smile; of an old man in braces wagging his head in appreciation.

Then comes the Nullarbor and the longest utterly straight stretch of line in the world—exactly 300 miles from around Ooldea to a point east of a halt called 'Haig'. The Aboriginal word 'Ooldea' means 'a meeting-place where water is obtainable'. It is thought to come from an underground river, and it is the very last such point before one enters this featureless expanse of scrub. The illustrated map makes the most of the variety. Some apparently is myall, some mulga, and some mallee, but to the townsman's eye it is all stumpy greyish bush.

Just on the Western Australia side of the state border with South Australia is an inconspicuous halt named after the man whose courage and initiative linked the state of which he later became Premier with the rest of the continent. In 1870 John Forrest (who was ultimately made Lord Forrest of Bunbury) crossed overland above the Great Australian Bight from Perth to Port Augusta and thence to Adelaide. Horses and camels provided his transport, and the entire 1500-mile journey took five months. Forrest's object was to join these waterless tracts by rail, and this was ultimately to be achieved within his lifetime—the longest such project to be undertaken anywhere in the world. The three thousand workers proceeded yard by yard laying two and a half million sleepers, supplied by a town on wheels which followed their progress. This was the fore-runner of the 'tea and sugar train' which today caters for the needs of the railway-workers at stations which are still called camps. We passed this train from which fresh food can be bought, and which has its mobile theatre, dentistry, and facilities for 'ministers of religion'. It was in order to labour on the railways, by the way, that the Chinese were first brought down from the north—before the White Australia policy was ever considered.

The place names, as is the case all over Australia, have three main derivations. There are the Aboriginal names, euphonious and several-syllabled; Coondambo, Mundrabilla, Kingoonya, Kellerberrin, Para-too: those imported direct from England and Scotland; Croydon, Peterborough, Penrith, Strathfield, Wimbledon, Burnley, Perth: and those commemorating people both British and colonial, from Sydney, the name of the Home Secretary at the time of the first settlement made by Captain Phillip, RN, 'dear Lord Melbourne', and Queen Adelaide to the nineteenth-century Australian pioneers. But why Haig and Kitchener for mere specks in the desert? I asked my neighbour in the dining-car, who laughed and said, 'Well, you know, we didn't feel too good about those generals of yours.' A subtle form of revenge?

The food was good on the train, the drink likewise, though the average Australian, like most of Anglo-Saxon stock, does not exactly aim to head the field as regards grace of service. We leave the refinements to the Asiatics and the Latins. In these egalitarian days it's rather that you, the customer, have to win your way into his regard, than vice-versa. This is true except in the case of the famous Australian clubs, as I will elaborate in due course.

I had an example on the train of varying standards in this respect that makes me laugh as I recall it. Before my first lunch aboard I ordered a pink gin and was politely and correctly served, the barman first rolling the angostura bitters round the glass in the prescribed manner. A day later I approached the bar with the same request which was quite differently received.

'*Pink gin?*' said the man indignantly, 'we don't have any pink gin.' It was as though I'd stepped into a small hotel and nonchalantly asked for pink champagne. I said, 'I think you'll find you have—I had some yesterday.'

'*Yesterday?*' he cried, 'that's got nothing to do with it. The New South Wales blokes were on yesterday. We've got no *pink gin.*'

I remembered that the train is staffed by different state railways as each border is passed—first NSW Railways, then South Australian (to which this chap belonged), then Commonwealth, and finally Western Australia. However, he was too aggressive for my taste, and so I said quietly, 'Look, you only had to say you were sorry that South Australia railways didn't carry pink gin, and I'd have understood.'

'*Sorry?*' he asked, 'I'm not sorry, I'm bloody glad.' E.W.S., fascinated by now, and puzzled at this: 'Tell me, why are you bloody glad?'

'Because it'd be more for me to bring on the train, that's why.'

I thought of telling him the size of a bottle of angostura, but, as I settled for a plain gin, delivered instead a few well-chosen (and no doubt horribly pompous) remarks about courtesy to the customer. This seemed to silence him, but when I asked my dining neighbour whether he'd heard this lively exchange he said as he was a bit deaf he hadn't caught it. 'But when I went up to order mine the bloke said "Cor, that Pom was a bit cranky, wasn't he? Reckon it was because England lost the Test!"' He'd had the last word after all.

Swanton in Australia with MCC 1946–75 (1975).

NERYS LLOYD-PIERCE

(?–)

British journalist. Originally from Wales, Lloyd-Pierce travelled extensively in Australia for a year during the 1980s. She began her visit by spending six months on a remote cattle station.

'SIX MONTHS IN THE OUTBACK'

Having spent four months travelling around Asia, a trip to Australia seemed a logical progression. My reasons for visiting that country were ambiguous. On a mercenary note, I knew I would be flat broke by then and had a good chance of earning money. The prospect of warm, sunny weather was also appealing after a succession of chilly English winters.

I arrived with the usual preconceptions about heat, flies and Bondi beach, but was soon to learn that Australia had considerably more to offer. My first preconception was shattered as I flew into Perth. It was green! Greener in fact than the subdued winter face of the England I had left behind.

On the flight from Bangkok I had my first encounter with Australian hospitality. The young guy I started chatting to on the plane was shocked when I remarked that I had nowhere to stay, no connections and very little money, and offered me an indefinite place on his sitting-room floor. This gave me an invaluable base from which to look for the work I now desperately needed.

Finding casual work in Australia shouldn't be a problem and the pay is good. It helps, however, to have a working holiday visa as the government is trying to clamp down on people working illegally. Those I met working without a permit hadn't had any problems, but the penalty if you are caught is instant deportation. Having enough money to tide you over does ease the pressure; I arrived at my first job with only thirty cents left in my purse.

Despite dire financial straits I really didn't want to do a mundane job like waitressing or working behind a bar. Having travelled halfway across the world I wanted to do something which was as much an experience as a job. The chance came when I saw a newspaper advertisement for a stock camp cook on a remote cattle station. I was accepted for the job with an alacrity which surprised me. Only later did I learn that the job had been advertised for three months and I was the only applicant!

To the horror of my Perth friends—urban Australians rarely seem to venture into the bush—I set off, leaving them convinced that I would loathe every minute.

The bus journey from Perth to the cattle station brought home to me the vastness of Australia: close on 2000km of open space and travel for hours without seeing a solitary sign of human habitation. The station itself was situated 260km from any town with over 60km to the nearest neighbour.

The homestead formed a small cluster of houses in a vast bowl skirted by rugged magenta hills. A deep slow-moving river curled in crescent shape around these homes, creating an effective natural fire break. Families had their own houses while the unmarried stockmen lived in bedsits. I was lucky enough to have a house to myself, which gave me both space and privacy, essential elements in what could very easily become a claustrophobic environment.

Everyone used to meet up for coffee and a chat at morning 'smoko' when I, being the 'cookie', had to produce vast quantities of cake or biscuit. Food was of great importance to people leading such active outdoor lives. There was no television and evening entertainment revolved around barbecues, fishing, playing cards and scrabble. I was always amazed how the same group of people managed to laugh and joke together in spite of seeing each other every day. On the other hand, living in such close proximity you can't afford to fall out with anyone as there's no way you could manage to avoid them.

Coming from a tiny country like England, the isolation of the outback is hard to imagine. The four-hour drive between station and town naturally made conventional shopping quite impractical; fresh produce was flown in on the mail plane every fortnight. If you ran out of anything in the meantime, too bad.

Every four months a road train brought in supplies of non-perishable goods, absolutely essential in the wet season when it was often impossible for the mail plane to land. During this period the dirt road connecting properties with the outside world would become altogether impassable, sometimes for weeks at a time.

Communications were made by means of a two-way radio with a shrill continuous call sign to clear the airwaves in the event of an emergency. In such a case the flying doctor plane would land on the nearest airstrip, but the patient still had to be transported from the scene of the accident to the waiting plane. Radio also plays an important role in children's education. The school of the air is part of their daily routine, the teacher no more than a disembodied voice. To qualify for a government governess a community must have seven or more children of school age.

The cattle station covered one-and-a-half million acres, a distance that I found hard to assimilate. Stand on a high point and literally all that the eye can see is one property. On arrival I naively commented that fifty horses seemed a lot in one paddock, only to be told that the paddock stretched over 12 000 acres.

My job out in the bush was to cook meals for fifteen stockmen, or ringers as they're known, on an open fire. We worked on the basis of three weeks mustering cattle in the bush, when we slept on 'swags' (bedrolls) under the stars, and a week at the homestead. Every day we loaded up the gear on to the creaking chuck wagon and moved to a new camp, each of which had a name: Corner Billabong, Eel Creek, Old Man Lagoon.

This itinerant lifestyle led me to discover the hidden corners of a region that might simply appear barren and hostile to the casual observer: an arid outcrop of rocks hiding a tumbling waterfall, a pool framed by the luxuriant growth of pandanus palms, the sudden blooming of hibiscus on a dry plain or the strangely contorted branches of a boab tree clawing the sky.

At first I was afraid of getting hopelessly lost between camps—after all there was no one I could stop to ask for directions—until Phil, the manager, put my mind at rest with the wry observation, 'No worries, if you've got the tucker they'll always come and look for you.'

Despite the obvious novelty of being in a new place and seeing a different way of life, being a stock camp cook was far from easy. At times I felt very isolated from anything familiar and comforting. Physically the job was often hard work and the hours were long as the cook is always the first up and last to finish. On occasions, struggling to lift billies of boiling water from the fire, sweat dripping down my face and clothes smeared in grime, I wondered why the hell I was doing it.

It's not easy to conquer the vagaries of cooking on an open fire. In order to bake a cake or loaf of bread I had to build up the fire, only to wait for it to die down to a heap of glowing coals. The temperature of these coals was all important; too hot and the cake would burn, too cool and it would simply never cook. I can't remember how many times I found myself frantically piling on more coals in an effort to cook a loaf, while the middle remained stubbornly soggy.

Having put so much effort into cooking you become strangely possessive about the results! On one such occasion I had been labouring over melting moments (biscuits which literally melt in the mouth), a task I wished I had never started, when John, the youngest of the ringers, strolled up remarking, 'These look good, cookie' and grabbed a handful. Seeing him munching so indifferently after my labours was too much and to his amazement I socked him across the back with an axe handle. Cooks are notoriously bad-tempered and I can see why.

Eight of the fifteen stockmen were Aboriginals. Relationships between the two communities on the station were amicable but distant. I found the Aboriginal men good humoured, easy-going company. The oldest among them couldn't have been more than fifty, though the deeply etched lines on his face suggested a much older person. He would tell me stories of how he first came into contact with white Australians—how, at the age of fifteen when he saw his first car, he got on his horse and chased it off his land. Despite their superficial friendship, a certain segregation clearly existed between the two communities. The Aboriginals always built a separate campfire in the evenings. This was done by tacit agreement and both groups seemed to accept the arrangement. During the twelve months I lived there I never met a white Australian who mixed socially with an Aboriginal and was shocked to find racial intolerance common, even among the educated elite.

Generally speaking women in the bush tend to adopt the conventional female roles, and male attitudes perhaps resemble those in Britain twenty or thirty years ago. It is considered unladylike for a woman to swear and, by the same token, it really isn't on to swear in front of a 'lady'. On one occasion at camp I burnt my foot quite badly on the hot coals; all alone, angry and frustrated, I let loose the tirade of swearing I had so carefully been suppressing!

The three women on the station stayed at the homestead while the men and I went out into the bush. I was worried this might cause friction, or that they might simply resent me for being an outsider intruding on their close-knit community, but nothing could have been further from the truth. I was welcomed and accepted from the beginning.

The women's role was different, though no less important than that of the men. They were responsible for the smooth running of the station during the men's absence; they organised the vegetable garden and the orchard and kept chickens. They also provided a balance in a male-dominated environment. The station manager's wife was a nursing sister and fortunate enough to be able to pursue her career as organiser of community health in outlying areas. She told me that without the job she could easily have found the lack of intellectual stimulation hard to handle.

Even though I was alone in the bush with fifteen men, I never at any point encountered sexual harassment. Both women and men went out of their way to make sure I settled in and felt happy and at home. Working on the station was an incredible experience, probably the last vestige of frontier spirit left in Australia. Several things will remain imprinted on my mind forever: the cloud of dust on the horizon heralding the return of stockmen and cattle; riding all day across that immense parched land; the sheer delight of coming across a cool shady water hole.

It was not without regret that I decided after six months that the time was right to move on. I wanted to see more of Australia and now had the finances to do so. As a leaving present the Aboriginal men gave me three boab nuts, carved with the traditional pictures of emu, goanna and kangaroo.

Returning to the city was like emerging into another world, only this time it was urban life that felt alien.

Miranda Davies and Natania Jansz (eds), *Women Travel: Adventures, Advice and Experience* (1990).

9

Writers

♦

HENRY KINGSLEY

(1830–76)

English novelist. After leaving Oxford University following some 'trouble' and without a degree, Henry Kingsley, a younger brother of Charles Kingsley, author of The Water Babies *(1863), spent from 1853 to 1858 in New South Wales and Victoria, working on the gold-fields and elsewhere. While staying on a station near Skipton, he began writing* The Recollections of Geoffry Hamlyn, *which was published in 1859 after his return to England. For years it was considered to be the 'best Australian novel' ever written. Kingsley apparently drew upon a Cornish folktale and an actual incident that occurred near Avoca in Victoria for a chapter about a lost child, part of which is reproduced below. The entire chapter was subsequently published as a cautionary children's story,* The Lost Child *(1871).*

'HOW THE CHILD WAS LOST'

Four or five miles up the river from Garoopna stood a solitary hut, snug—sheltered by a lofty bare knoll, round which the great river chafed among the boulders. Across the stream was the forest sloping down in pleasant glades from the mountain; and behind the hut rose the plain four or five hundred feet over head, seeming to be held aloft by the blue-stone columns which rose from the river side.

In this cottage resided a shepherd, his wife, and one little boy, their son, about eight years old. A strange, wild little bush child, able to speak articulately, but utterly without knowledge or experience of human creatures, save of his father and mother; unable to read a line; without religion of any sort or kind; as entire a little savage, in fact, as you could find in the worst den in your city, morally speaking, and yet beautiful to look on; as active as a roe, and, with regard to natural objects, as fearless as a lion.

As yet unfit to begin labour. All the long summer he would wander about the river bank, up and down the beautiful rock-walled paradise where he was confined, sometimes looking eagerly across the water at the waving forest boughs, and fancying he could see other children far up the vistas beckoning to him to cross and play in that merry land of shifting lights and shadows.

It grew quite into a passion with the poor little man to get across and play there; and one day when his mother was shifting the hurdles, and he was handing her the strips of green hide which bound them together, he said to her,—

'Mother, what country is that across the river?'

'The forest, child.'

'There's plenty of quantongs over there, eh, mother, and raspberries? Why mayn't I get across and play there?'

'The river is too deep, child, and the Bunyip lives in the water under the stones.'

'Who are the children that play across there?'

'Black children, likely.'

'No white children?'

'Pixies; don't go near 'em, child; they'll lure you on, Lord knows where. Don't get trying to cross the river, now, or you'll be drowned.'

But next day the passion was stronger on him than ever. Quite early on the glorious cloudless midsummer day he was down by the river side, sitting on a rock, with his shoes and stockings off, paddling his feet in the clear tepid water, and watching the million fish in the shallows—black fish and grayling—leaping and flashing in the sun.

There is no pleasure that I have ever experienced like a child's midsummer holiday. The time, I mean, when two or three of us used to go away up the brook, and take our dinners with us, and come home at night tired, dirty, happy, scratched beyond recognition, with a great nosegay, three little trout, and one shoe, the other one having been used for a boat till it had gone down with all hands out of soundings. How poor our Derby days, our Greenwich dinners, our evening parties, where there are plenty of nice girls, are after that! Depend on it, a man never experiences such pleasure or grief after fourteen as he does before: unless in some cases in his first love-making, when the sensation is new to him.

But, meanwhile, there sat our child, barelegged, watching the forbidden ground beyond the river. A fresh breeze was moving the trees, and making the whole a dazzling mass of shifting light and shadow. He sat so still that a glorious violet and red king-fisher perched quite close, and, dashing into the water, came forth with a fish, and fled like a ray of light along the winding of the river. A colony of little shell parrots, too, crowded on a bough, and twittered and ran to and fro quite busily, as though they said to him, 'We don't mind you, my dear; you are quite one of us.'

Never was the river so low. He stepped in; it scarcely reached his ancle. Now surely he might get across. He stripped himself, and, carrying his clothes, waded through, the water never reaching his middle all across the long, yellow, gravelly shallow. And there he stood naked and free in the forbidden ground.

He quickly dressed himself, and began examining his new kingdom, rich beyond his utmost hopes. Such quantongs, such raspberries, surpassing imagination; and when tired of them, such fern boughs, six or eight feet long! He would penetrate this region, and see how far it extended.

What tales he would have for his father to-night. He would bring him here, and show him all the wonders, and perhaps he would build a new hut over here, and come and live in it? Perhaps the pretty young lady, with the feathers in her hat, lived somewhere here, too?

There! There is one of those children he has seen before across the river. Ah! ah! it is not a child at all, but a pretty grey beast, with big ears. A kangaroo, my lad; he won't play with you, but skips away slowly, and leaves you alone.

There is something like the gleam of water on that rock. A snake! Now a sounding rush through the wood, and a passing shadow. An eagle! He brushes so close to the child, that he strikes at the bird with a stick, and then watches him as he shoots up like a rocket, and, measuring the fields of air in ever-widening circles, hangs like a motionless speck upon the sky; though, measure his wings across, and you will find he is nearer fifteen feet than fourteen.

Here is a prize, though! A wee little native bear, barely eight inches long,—a little grey beast, comical beyond expression, with broad flapped ears, sits on a tree within reach. He makes no resistance, but cuddles into the child's bosom, and eats a leaf as they go along; while his mother sits aloft, and grunts indignant at the abstraction of her offspring, but, on the whole, takes it pretty comfortably, and goes on with her dinner of peppermint leaves.

What a short day it has been! Here is the sun getting low, and the magpies and jackasses beginning to tune up before roosting.

He would turn and go back to the river. Alas! which way?

He was lost in the bush. He turned back and went, as he thought, the way he had come, but soon arrived at a tall, precipitous cliff, which, by some infernal magic, seemed to have got between him and the river. Then he broke down, and that strange madness came on him which comes even on strong men when lost in the forest: a despair, a confusion of intellect, which has cost many a man his life. Think what it must be with a child!

He was fully persuaded that the cliff was between him and home, and that he must climb it. Alas! every step he took aloft carried him further from the river and the hope of safety; and when he came to the top, just at dark, he saw nothing but cliff after cliff, range after range, all around him. He had been wandering through steep gullies all day unconsciously, and had penetrated far into the mountains. Night was coming down, still and crystal-clear, and the poor little lad was far away from help or hope, going his last long journey alone.

Partly perhaps walking, and partly sitting down and weeping, he got through the night; and when the solemn morning came up again he was still tottering along the leading range, bewildered; crying, from time to time, 'Mother, mother!' still nursing his little bear, his only companion, to his bosom, and holding still in his hand a few poor flowers he had gathered the day before. Up and on all day, and at evening, passing out of the great zone of timber, he came on the bald, thunder-smitten summit ridge, where one ruined tree held up its skeleton arms against the sunset, and the wind came keen and frosty. So, with failing, feeble legs, upward still, towards the region of the granite and the snow; towards the eyrie of the kite and the eagle.

The Recollections of Geoffry Hamlyn (1877 edition, first published 1859).

ANTHONY TROLLOPE
(1815–82)

English public servant, novelist, and travel writer. Trollope, who had worked in the British postal service from 1834 to 1867, was a well-known novelist, famous in particular for his Barchester series, by the time he visited all of the Australian colonies, including New South Wales where his son was living, and New Zealand in 1871–72. He also made a brief second visit to Australia in 1875. In the following extract from his two-volume work, Australia and New Zealand *(1873), which was based upon a series of letters he had written for the London* Daily Telegraph, *he records some of his impressions of a place that has since become a tourist attraction.*

PORT ARTHUR

I visited Port Arthur, and was troubled by many reflections as to the future destiny of so remarkable a place. It is in a direct line not, I believe, above sixty miles from Hobart Town, but it can hardly be reached directly. The way to it is by water, and as there is no traffic to or from the place other than what is carried on by the government for the supply of the establishment, a sailing schooner is sufficient,–and indeed more than sufficiently expensive. In this schooner I was taken under the kind guidance of the premier and attorney-general of the island, who were called upon in the performance of their duties to inspect the place and hear complaints,—if complaints there were. We started at midnight, and as we were told at break of day that we had made only four miles down the bay, I began to fear that the expedition would be long. But the wind at last favoured us, and at about noon we were landed at Tasman's peninsula in Norfolk Bay, and there we found the commandant of the establishment and horses to carry us whither we would. We found also a breakfast at the policeman's house, of which we were very much in want.

Tasman's peninsula, which has been held entire by the Crown for the purposes of the convict establishment, is an irregularly formed piece of land about twenty-five miles long and twelve broad, indented by various bays and creeks of the sea, very hilly, covered with primeval gum-tree forest, and joined on to the island by a very narrow neck of sand. Port Arthur, where are the prisons, is about nine miles from Nor- folk Bay; but our first object was to visit the neck,—called Eagle Hawk Neck,—partly for the sake of the scenery, and partly because the neck is guarded by dogs, placed there to prevent the escape of the convicts. I had heard of these dogs before I visited Tasmania, but I had thought that they were mythic. There, however, I found them, to the number of fifteen, chained up in their appointed places at and near the neck. The intention is that they should bark if any escaped prisoner should endeavour to swim at night across the narrow arm of sea which divides the two lands. In former days they used to be employed in hunting the men down. I doubt whether they are now of any service. They are allowed regular rations, one pound of meat and one pound of flour a day per dog; and I found the policemen stationed at the Neck very loud in their assurances that the business could not be carried on with- out the dogs. The policemen also have rations,—somewhat more than that of the dogs, though of the same kind; and it struck me that to the married men who have families in the neighbourhood, the rationed dogs might be serviceable.

The scenery at this spot is very lovely, as the bright narrow sea runs up between two banks which are wooded down to the river. Then we went farther on, riding our horses where it was practicable to ride, and visited two wonders of the place,—the Blow-Hole, and Tasman's Arch. The Blow-Hole is such a passage cut out by the sea through the rocks as I have known more than one on the west coast of Ireland under the name of puffing-holes. This hole did not puff nor blow when I was there, but we were enabled by the quiescence of the sea to crawl about among the rocks, and enjoyed ourselves more than we should have done had the monster been in full play. Tasman's Arch, a mile farther on, is certainly the grandest piece of rock construction I ever saw. The sea has made its way in through the rocks, forming a large pool or hole, some fifty yards from the outer cliffs, the descent into which is perpendicular all round; and over the aperture stretches an immense natural arch, the supports or side pillars of which are perpendicular. Very few even now visit Tasman's Arch; but when the convict establishment at Port Arthur comes to an end, as come to an end I think it must, no one will ever see the place. Nevertheless it is well worth seeing, as may probably be said of many glories of the earth which are altogether hidden from human eyes.

On the following day we inspected the prisons, and poor-house and lunatic asylum and farm attached to the prisons,—for there is a farm of well-cleared land,—seventy or eighty acres under tillage, if I remember rightly; and there is a railway for bringing down timber and firewood. The whole was in admirable order, and gave at first sight the idea of an industrial establishment conducted on excellent commercial principles. The men made their own shoes and clothes and cheeses, and fed their own pigs, and milked their own cows, and killed their own beef and mutton. There seemed to be no reason why they should not sell their surplus produce and turn in a revenue for the colony. But prisons never do turn in a revenue, and this certainly was no exception to the rule.

I found that there were altogether 506 persons, all males, to be looked after, and that no less than 97 men were employed to look after them. Of these 25 were officers, many of whom were in receipt of good salaries. There was the commandant, and the Protestant chaplain, and the Roman Catholic chaplain, and the doctor, and the doctor's assistant, and the postmaster, forming with their wives and families quite a pleasant little society, utterly beyond reach of the world, but supplied with every comfort,—unless when the wind was so bad that the government schooner could not get round to them. These gentlemen all had houses too. I was hospitably received in one, that of the commandant, which, with its pretty garden and boat-house, and outlook upon the land-locked bay of the sea, made me wish to be commandant myself. There would have been nothing peculiar in all this, except the cleanness and prettiness of the place, were it not that it must apparently all come to an end in a few years, and that the commandant's house, and the other houses, and all the village, and the prisons, and the asylum, and the farm, and the church, will be left deserted, and allowed to fall into ruins. I do not know what other fate can be theirs. Tasmania will not maintain the place for her own prison purposes when there is an end of the English money;—and for other than prison purposes no one will surely go and live in that ultima Thule, lovely as are the bays of the sea, and commodious as may be the buildings.

Australia and New Zealand (1873).

——

MARK TWAIN
(1835–1910)

American humorist and novelist. Mark Twain worked variously as a printer, riverboat pilot, and journalist, before becoming a popular novelist, whose works include classics such as The Adventures of Tom Sawyer *(1876) and* The Adventures of Huckleberry Finn *(1884). He visited New South Wales, Victoria, South Australia, Tasmania, and New Zealand as part of a world lecture tour that he undertook in 1895–96 to make money to stave off bankruptcy. Below are some of his impressions of New Zealand, taken from the book that he wrote about the trip.*

'JUNIOR ENGLAND'

It was Junior England all the way to Christchurch—in fact, just a garden. And Christchurch is an English town, with an English-park annex, and a winding English brook just like the Avon—and named the Avon; but from a man, not from Shakespeare's river. Its grassy banks are bordered by the stateliest and most impressive weeping willows to be found in the world, I suppose. They continue the line of a great ancestor; they were grown from sprouts of the willow that sheltered Napoleon's grave in St Helena. It is a settled old community, with all the serenities, the graces, the conveniences, and the comforts of the ideal home-life. If it had an established Church and social inequality it would be England over again with hardly a lack.

In the museum we saw many curious and interesting things; among others a fine native house of the olden time, with all the details true to the facts, and the showy colors right and in their proper places. All the details: the fine mats and rugs and things; the elaborate and wonderful wood carvings—wonderful, surely, considering who did them—wonderful in design and particularly in execution, for they were done with admirable sharpness and exactness, and yet with no better tools than flint and jade and shell could furnish; and the totem-posts were there, ancestor above ancestor, with tongues protruded and hands clasped comfortably over bellies containing other people's ancestors— grotesque and ugly devils, every one, but lovingly carved, and ably; and the stuffed natives were present, in their proper places, and looking as natural as life; and the housekeeping utensils were there, too, and close at hand the carved and finely ornamented war canoe.

And we saw little jade gods, to hang around the neck—not everybody's, but sacred to the necks of natives of rank. Also jade weapons, and many kinds of jade trinkets—all made out of that excessively hard stone without the help of any tool of iron. And some of these things had small round holes bored through them—nobody knows how it was done; a mystery, a lost art. I think it was said that if you want such a hole bored in a piece of jade now, you must send it to London or Amsterdam where the lapidaries are.

Also we saw a complete skeleton of the giant Moa. It stood ten feet high, and must have been a sight to look at when it was a living bird. It was a kicker, like the ostrich; in fight it did not use its beak, but its foot. It must have been a convincing kind of kick. If a person had his back to the bird and did not see who it was that did it, he would think he had been kicked by a wind-mill.

There must have been a sufficiency of moas in the old forgotten days when his breed walked the earth. His bones are found in vast masses, all crammed together in huge graves. They are not in caves, but in the ground. Nobody knows how they happened to get concentrated there. Mind, they are bones, not fossils. This means that the moa has not been extinct very long. Still, this is the only New Zealand creature which has no mention in that otherwise comprehensive literature, the native legends. This is a significant detail, and is good circumstantial evidence that the moa has been extinct 500 years, since the Maori has himself—by tradition—been in New Zealand since the end of the fifteenth century. He came from an unknown land—the first Maori did—then sailed back in his canoe and brought his tribe, and they removed the aboriginal peoples into the sea and into the ground and took the land. That is the tradition. That that first Maori could come, is understandable, for anybody can come to a place when he isn't trying to; but how that discoverer found his way back home again without a compass is his secret, and he died with it in him. His language indicates that he came from Polynesia. He *told* where he came from, but he couldn't spell well, so one can't find the place on the map, because people who could spell better than he could, spelt the resemblance all out of it when they made the map. However, it is better to have a map that is spelt right than one that has information in it.

In New Zealand women have the right to vote for members of the legislature, but they cannot be members themselves. The law extending the suffrage to them went into effect in 1893. The population of Christchurch (census of 1891) was 31 454. The first election under the law was held in November of that year. Number of men who voted, 6313; number of women who voted, 5989. These figures ought to convince us that women are not as indifferent about politics as some people would have us believe. In New Zealand as a whole, the estimated adult female population was 139 915; of these 109 461 qualified and registered their names on the rolls—78.23 per cent. of the whole. Of these, 90 290 went to the polls and voted—85.18 per cent. Do men ever turn out better than that—in America or elsewhere? Here is a remark to the other sex's credit, too—I take it from the official report:

'A feature of the election was the orderliness and sobriety of the people. Women were in no way molested.'

At home, a standing argument against woman suffrage has always been that women could not go to the polls without being insulted. The arguments against woman suffrage have always taken the easy form of prophecy. The prophets have been prophesying ever since the woman's rights movement began in 1848—and in forty-seven years they have never scored a hit.

Men ought to begin to feel a sort of respect for their mothers and wives and sisters by this time. The women deserve a change of attitude like that, for they have wrought well. In forty-seven years they have swept an imposingly large number of unfair laws from the statute books of America. In that brief time these serfs have set themselves free—essentially. Men could not have done so much for themselves in that time without bloodshed—at least they never have; and that is argument that they didn't know how. The women have accomplished a peaceful revolution, and a very beneficent one; and yet that has not convinced the average man that they are intelligent, and have courage and energy and perseverance and fortitude. It takes much to convince the average man of anything; and perhaps nothing can ever make him realize that he is the average woman's inferior—yet in several important details the evidences seems to show that that is what he is. Man has ruled the human race from the beginning—but he should remember that up to the middle of the present century it was a dull world, and ignorant and stupid; but it is not such a dull world now, and is growing less and less dull all the time. This is woman's opportunity—she has had none before. I wonder where man will be in another forty-seven years?

In the New Zealand law occurs this: 'The word *person* wherever it occurs throughout the Act includes *woman*.'

That is promotion, you see. By that enlargement of the word, the matron with the garnered wisdom and experience of fifty years becomes at one jump the political equal of her callow kid of twenty-one. The white population of the colony is 626 000, the Maori population is 42 000. The whites elect seventy members of the House of Representatives, the Maoris four. The Maori women vote for their four members.

November 16. After four pleasant days in Christchurch, we are to leave at midnight to-night. Mr Kinsey gave me an ornithorhyncus, and I am taming it.

Sunday, 17th. Sailed last night in the *Flora*, from Lyttelton.

So we did. I remember it yet. The people who sailed in the *Flora* that night may forget some other things if they live a good while, but they will not live long enough to forget that. The *Flora* is about the equivalent of a cattle-scow; but when the Union Company find it inconvenient to keep a contract and lucrative to break it, they smuggle her into passenger service, and 'keep the change.'

They give no notice of their projected depredation; you innocently buy tickets for the advertised passenger boat, and when you get down to Lyttelton at midnight, you find that they have substituted the scow. They have plenty of good boats, but no competition—and that is the trouble. It is too late now to make other arrangements if you have engagements ahead.

It is a powerful company, it has a monopoly, and everybody is afraid of it—including the government's representative, who stands at the end of the stage-plank to tally the passengers and see that no boat receives a greater number than the law allows her to carry. This conveniently-blind representative saw the scow receive a number which was far in excess of its privilege, and winked a politic wink and said nothing. The passengers bore with meekness the cheat which had been put upon them, and made no complaint.

It was like being at home in America, where abused passengers act in just the same way. A few days before, the Union Company had discharged a captain for getting a boat into danger, and had advertised this act as evidence of its vigilance in looking after the safety of the passengers—for thugging a captain costs the company nothing, but when opportunity offered to send this dangerously overcrowded tub to sea and save a little trouble and tidy penny by it, it forgot to worry about the passenger's safety.

The first officer told me that the *Flora* was privileged to carry 125 passengers. She must have had all of 200 on board. All the cabins were full, all the cattle-stalls in the main stable were full, the spaces at the heads of companionways were full, every inch of floor and table in the swill-room was packed with sleeping men and remained so until the place was required for breakfast, all the chairs and benches on the hurricane deck were occupied, and *still* there were people who had to walk about all night!

If the *Flora* had gone down that night, half of the people on board would have been wholly without means of escape.

The owners of that boat were not technically guilty of conspiracy to commit murder, but they were morally guilty of it.

I had a cattle-stall in the main stable—a cavern fitted up with a long double file of two-storied bunks, the files separated by a calico partition—twenty men and boys on one side of it, twenty women and girls on the other. The place was as dark as the soul of the Union Company, and smelt like a kennel. When the vessel got out into the heavy seas and began to pitch and wallow, the cavern prisoners became immediately seasick, and then the peculiar results that ensued laid all my previous experiences of the kind well away in the shade. And the wails, the groans, the cries, the shrieks, the strange ejaculations—it was wonderful.

The women and children and some of the men and boys spent the night in that place, for they were too ill to leave it; but the rest of us got up, by and by, and finished the night on the hurricane-deck.

That boat was the foulest I was ever in; and the smell of the breakfast saloon when we threaded our way among the layers of steaming passengers stretched upon its floor and its tables was incomparable for efficiency.

A good many of us got ashore at the first way-port to seek another ship. After a wait of three hours we got good rooms in the *Mahinapua*, a wee little bridal-parlor of a boat—only 205 tons burthen; clean and comfortable; good service; good beds; good table, and no crowding. The seas danced her about like a duck, but she was safe and capable.

Next morning early she went through the French Pass—a narrow gateway of rock, between bold headlands—so narrow, in fact, that it seemed no wider than a street. The current tore through there like a mill-race, and the boat darted through like a telegram. The passage was made in half a minute; then we were in a wide place where noble vast eddies swept grandly round and round in shoal water, and I wondered what they would do with the little boat. They did as they pleased with her. They picked her up and flung her around like nothing and landed her gently on the solid, smooth bottom of sand—so gently, indeed, that we barely felt her touch it, barely felt her quiver when she came to a standstill. The water was as clear as glass, the sand on the bottom was vividly distinct, and the fishes seemed to be swimming about in nothing. Fishing lines were brought out, but before we could bait the hooks the boat was off and away again.

Following the Equator (1897).

———

AGATHA CHRISTIE
(1890–1976)

English detective novelist and playwright. Agatha Christie, who had published her first novel, The Mysterious Affair at Styles, *in 1920, accompanied her first husband, Archie Christie, when he toured South Africa, Australia, New Zealand, and Canada in 1922 as a member of a mission to promote inter-imperial trade and the British Empire Exhibition that was to be held in England in 1924. She divorced Christie in 1928 and married the archaeologist (Sir) Max Mallowan in 1930. In her autobiography, the 'queen of crime' recalls her stay in Australia, which had lasted from April to June 1922.*

MEMORIES OF AUSTRALIA

From South Africa we set sail for Australia. It was a long, rather grey voyage. It was a mystery to me why, as the Captain explained, the shortest way to Australia was to go down towards the Pole and up again. He drew diagrams which eventually convinced me, but it is difficult to remember that the earth is round and has flat poles. It is a geographical fact, but not one that you appreciate the point of in real life. There was not much sunshine, but it was a fairly calm and pleasant voyage.

It always seems to me odd that countries are never described to you in terms which you recognise when you get there. My own sketchy ideas of Australia comprised kangaroos in large quantities, and a great deal of waste desert. What startled me principally, as we came into Melbourne, was the extraordinary aspect of the trees, and the difference Australian gum trees make to a landscape. Trees are always the first things I seem to notice about places, or else the shape of hills. In England one becomes used to trees having dark trunks and light leafy branches; the reverse in Australia was quite astonishing. Silvery white-barks everywhere, and the darker leaves, made it like seeing the negative of a photograph. It reversed the whole look of the landscape. The other thing that was exciting was the macaws: blue and red and green, flying through the air in great clustering swarms. Their colouring was wonderful: like flying jewels.

We were at Melbourne for a short time, and took various trips from there. I remember one trip particularly because of the gigantic tree ferns. This sort of tropical jungle foliage was the last thing I expected in Australia. It was lovely, and most exciting. The food was not as pleasing. Except for the hotel in Melbourne, where it was very good, we seemed always to be eating incredibly tough beef or turkey. The sanitary arrangements, too, were slightly embarrassing to one of Victorian upbringing. The ladies of the party were politely ushered into a room where two chamber pots sat in isolation in the middle of the floor, ready for use as desired. There was no privacy, and it was quite difficult ...

A social gaffe that I committed in Australia, and once again in New Zealand, arose in taking my place at table. The Mission was usually entertained by the Mayor or the Chamber of Commerce in the various places we visited, and the first time this happened, I went, in all innocence, to sit by the Mayor or some other dignitary. An acid-looking elderly female then said to me: 'I think, Mrs Christie, you will *prefer* to sit by your husband.' Rather shame-faced, I hurried round to take my place by Archie's side. The proper arrangements at these luncheons was that every wife sat by her husband. I forgot this once again in New Zealand, but after that I knew my place and went to it.

We stayed in New South Wales at a station called, I think, Yanga, where I remember a great lake with black swans sailing on it. It was a lovely picture. Here, while Belcher and Archie were busy putting forth the claims of the British Empire, migration within the Empire, the importance of trade within the Empire, and so on and so forth, I was allowed to spend a happy day sitting in the orange groves. I had a nice long deck-chair, there was delicious sunshine, and as far as I remember I ate twenty-three oranges—carefully selecting the very best from the trees round me. Ripe oranges plucked straight from the trees, are the most delicious things you can imagine. I made a lot of discoveries about fruit. Pineapples, for instance, I had always thought of as hanging down gracefully from a tree. I was so astonished to find that an enormous field I had taken to be full of

cabbages was in fact of pineapples. It was in a way rather a disappointment. It seemed such a prosaic way of growing such a luscious fruit.

Part of our journey was by train, but a good deal of it by car. Driving through those enormous stretches of flat pasture land, with nothing to break the horizon except periodic windmills, I realised how
frightening it could be: how easy to get lost—'bushed', as the saying
was. The sun was so high over your head that you had no idea of north,
south, east or west. There were no landmarks to guide you. I had never
imagined a green grassy desert—I had always thought of deserts as a
sandy waste—but there seem to be far more landmarks and protuber-
ances by which you can find your way in desert country than there are
in the flat grasslands of Australia.

We went to Sydney, where we had a gay time, but having heard of
Sydney and Rio de Janeiro as having the two most beautiful harbours
in the world, I found it disappointing. I had expected too much of it, I
suppose. Luckily I have never been to Rio, so I can still make a fancy
picture of that in my mind's eye.

It was in Sydney that we first came in contact with the Bell family.
Whenever I think of Australia, I think of the Bells. A young woman,
somewhat older than I was, approached me one evening in the hotel in
Sydney, introduced herself as Una Bell, and said that we were all coming to stay at their station in Queensland at the end of the following
week. As Archie and Belcher had a round of rather dull townships to go
to first, it was arranged I should accompany her back to the Bell station
at Couchin Couchin and await their arrival there.

We had a long train journey, I remember—several hours—and I was
dead tired. At the end we drove and finally arrived at Coochin
Coochin, near Boona in Queensland. I was still half asleep when suddenly I came into a scene of exuberant life. Rooms, lamp-lit, were filled
with good-looking girls sitting about, pressing drinks on you—cocoa,
coffee, anything you wanted—and all talking at once, all chattering
and laughing. I had that dazed feeling in which you see not double but
about quadruple of everything. It seemed to me that the Bell family
numbered about twenty-six. The next day I cut it down to four daughters and the equivalent number of sons. The girls all resembled each
other slightly, except for Una, who was dark. The others were fair, tall,
with rather long faces; all graceful in motion, all wonderful riders, and
all looking like energetic young fillies.

It was a glorious week. The energy of the Bell girls was such that I
could hardly keep pace, but I fell for each of the brothers in turn: Vic-
tor, who was gay and a wonderful flirt; Bert, who rode splendidly, but

was more solid in quality; Frick, who was quiet and fond of music. I think it was Frick to whom I really lost my heart. Years later, his son Guilford was to join Max and me on our archaeological expeditions to Iraq and Syria, and Guilford I still regard almost as a son.

The dominant figure in the Bell household was the mother, Mrs Bell, a widow of many years standing. She had something of the quality of Queen Victoria—short, with grey hair, quiet but authoritative in manner, she ruled with absolute autocracy, and was always treated as though she was royalty.

Amongst the various servants, station hands, general helpers, etc., most of whom were half-caste, there were one or two pure-bred Aborigines. Aileen Bell, the youngest of the Bell sisters, said to me almost the first morning: 'You've got to see Susan.' I asked who Susan was. 'Oh, one of the Blacks.' They were always called 'the Blacks'. 'One of the Blacks, but she's a real one, absolutely pure-bred, and she does the most wonderful imitations.' So a bent, aged Aborigine came along. She was as much a queen in her own right as Mrs Bell in hers. She did imitations of all the girls for me, and of various of the brothers, children and horses: she was a natural mimic, and she enjoyed very much doing her show. She sang, too, queer, off-key tunes.

'Now then, Susan,' said Aileen. 'Do mother going out to look at the hens.' But Susan shook her head, and Aileen said, 'She'll never imitate mother. She says it wouldn't be respectful and she couldn't possibly do a thing like that.'

Aileen had several pet kangaroos and wallabies of her own, as well as large quantities of dogs, and, naturally, horses. The Bells all urged me to ride, but I didn't feel that my experience of rather amateurish hunting in Devon entitled me to claim to be a horsewoman. Besides, I was always nervous of riding other people's horses in case I should damage them. So they gave in, and we dashed round everywhere by car. It is an exciting experience seeing cattle rounded up, and all the various aspects of station life. The Bells seemed to own large portions of Queensland, and if we had had time Aileen said she would have taken me to see the Northern out-station, which was much wilder and more primitive. None of the Bell girls ever stopped talking. They adored their brothers, and hero-worshipped them openly in a way quite novel to my experience. They were always dashing about, to various stations, to friends, down to Sydney, to race meetings; and flirting with various young men whom they referred to always as 'coupons'—I suppose a relic of the war.

Presently Archie and Belcher arrived, looking jaded by their efforts. We had a cheerful and carefree weekend with several unusual pastimes, one of which was an expedition in a small-gauge train, of which I was allowed, for a few miles, to drive the engine. There was a party of Australian Labour MPs, who had had such a festive luncheon that they were all slightly the worse for drink, and when they took it in turns to drive the engine we were all in mortal danger as it was urged to enormous speeds.

Sadly we said farewell to our friends—or to the greater portion of them, for a quota was going to accompany us to Sydney. We had a brief glimpse of the Blue Mountains, and there again I was entranced by landscape coloured as I have never seen landscape coloured before. In the distance the hills really *were* blue—a cobalt blue, not the kind of grey blue that I associated with hills. They looked as if they had just been put on a piece of drawing-paper, straight from one's paint-box.

Australia had been fairly strenuous for the British Mission. Every day had been taken up with speech-making, dinner, luncheons, receptions, long journeys between different places. I knew all Belcher's speeches by heart by this time. He was good at speech-making, delivering everything with complete spontaneity and enthusiasm as though it had only just come into his head. Archie made quite a good contrast to him by his air of prudence and financial sagacity. Archie, at an early date—in South Africa, I think—had been referred to in the newspapers as the Governor of the Bank of England. Nothing he said in contradiction of this was ever printed, so Governor of the Bank of England he remained as far as the press was concerned.

From Australia we went to Tasmania, driving from Launceston to Hobart. Incredibly beautiful Hobart, with its deep blue sea and harbour, and its flowers, trees and shrubs. I planned to come back and live there one day.

An Autobiography (1977).

D.H. LAWRENCE

(1885–1930)

English novelist. The son of a miner, D.H. Lawrence was educated at Nottingham High School and Nottingham University College. He worked as a schoolteacher until 1911, before becoming a full-time writer. From 1919 onwards, he and his wife Frieda mostly lived abroad, in Italy and elsewhere.

Lawrence had already published a number of books, including Sons and
Lovers *(1913),* The Rainbow *(1915), and* Women in Love *(1920), before
his visit to Australia with Frieda, which lasted from May to August 1922.
He wrote part of his semi-autobiographical novel* Kangaroo *(1923), which
has frequently been praised for its sensitive evocations of the Australian landscape, while staying at Thirroul on the south coast of New South Wales. One
famous passage sees Richard and Harriet Somers (characters based upon the
Lawrences) and Jack and Victoria Callcott travel by train from Sydney to
Mullumbimby (the name given to Thirroul in the novel).*

SYDNEY TO THE SOUTH COAST

They went to Mullumbimby by the two o'clock train from Sydney on
the Friday afternoon, Jack having managed to get a day off for the
occasion. He was a sort of partner in the motor-works place where he
was employed, so it was not so difficult. And work was slack.

Harriet and Victoria were both quite excited. The Somers had insisted on packing one basket of food for the house, and Victoria had
brought some dainties as well. There were few people in the train, so they
settled themselves right at the front, in one of those long open second-
class coaches with many cane seats and a passage down the middle.

'This is really for the coal-miners,' said Victoria. 'You'll see they'll
get in when we get further down.'

She was rather wistful, after the vague coolness that had subsisted
between the two households. She was so happy that Somers and Harriet were coming with her and Jack. They made her feel—she could
hardly describe it—but so safe, so happy and safe. Whereas often
enough, in spite of the stalwart Jack, she felt like some piece of fluff
blown about on the air, now that she was taken from her own home.
With Somers and Harriet she felt like a child that is with its parents, so
lovely and secure, without any need ever to look round. Jack was a
man, and everything a man should be, in her eyes. But he was also like
a piece of driftwood drifting on the strange unknown currents in an
unexplored nowhere, without any place to arrive at. Whereas to Victoria, Harriet seemed to be rooted right in the centre of everything, at last
she could come to perfect rest in her, like a bird in a tree that remains
still firm when the floods are washing everything else about.

If only Somers would let her rest in Harriet and him. But he seemed
to have a strange vindictiveness somewhere in his nature, that turned
round on her and terrified her worse than before. If he would only be
fond of her, that was what she wanted. If he would only be fond of her,

and not ever really leave her. Not love. When she thought of lovers she thought of something quite different. Something rather vulgar, rather common, more or less naughty. Ah no, he wasn't like that. And yet—since all men are potential lovers to every woman—wouldn't it be terrible if he asked for love. Terrible—but wonderful. Not a bit like Jack—not a bit. Would Harriet mind? Victoria looked at Harriet with her quick, bright, shy brown eyes. Harriet looked so handsome and distant: she was a little afraid of her. Not as she was afraid of Somers. Afraid as one woman is of another fierce woman. Harriet was fierce, Victoria decided. Somers was demonish, but could be gentle and kind.

It came on to rain, streaming down the carriage windows. Jack lit a cigarette, and offered one to Harriet. She, though she knew Somers disliked it intensely when she smoked, particularly in a public place like this long, open railway carriage, accepted, and sat by the closed window smoking.

The train ran for a long time through Sydney, or the endless outsides of Sydney. The town took almost as much leaving as London does. But it was different. Instead of solid rows of houses, solid streets like London, it was mostly innumerable detached bungalows and cottages, spreading for great distances, scattering over hills, low hills and shallow inclines. And then waste marshy places, and old iron, and abortive corrugated iron 'works'—all like the Last Day of creation, instead of a new country. Away to the left they saw the shallow waters of the big opening where Botany Bay is: the sandy shores, the factory chimneys, the lonely places where it is still bush. And the weary half-established straggling of more suburb.

'Como', said the station sign. And they ran on bridges over two arms of water from the sea, and they saw what looked like a long lake with wooded shores and bungalows: a bit like Lake Como, but oh, so unlike. That curious sombreness of Australia, the sense of oldness, with the forms all worn down low and blunt, squat. The squat-seeming earth. And then they ran at last into real country, rather rocky, dark old rocks, and sombre bush with its different pale-stemmed dull-leaved gum-trees standing graceful, and various healthy-looking undergrowth, and great spiky things like yuccas. As they turned south they saw tree-ferns standing on one knobbly leg among the gums, and among the rocks ordinary ferns and small bushes spreading in glades and up sharp hill-slopes. It was virgin bush, and as if unvisited, lost, sombre, with plenty of space, yet spreading grey for miles and miles in a hollow towards the west. Far in the west, the sky having suddenly cleared, they saw the magical range of the Blue Mountains. And all this hoary space of bush between. The strange, as it were, *invisible* beauty of Australia, which is undeniably there, but which seems to lurk just beyond the range of our white vision. You feel you can't *see*—as if your eyes hadn't the vision in them to correspond with the outside landscape. For the landscape is so unimpressive, like a face with little or no features, a dark face. It is so aboriginal, out of our ken, and it hangs back so aloof. Somers always felt he looked at it through a cleft in the atmosphere; as one looks at one of the ugly-faced, distorted aborigines with his wonderful dark eyes that have such an incomprehensible ancient shine in them, across gulfs of unbridged centuries. And yet, when you don't have the feeling of ugliness or monotony, in landscape or in nigger, you get a sense of subtle, remote, *formless* beauty more poignant than anything ever experienced before.

'Your wonderful Australia!' said Harriet to Jack. 'I can't tell you how it moves me. It feels as if no one had ever loved it. Do you know what I mean? England and Germany and Italy and Egypt and India—they've all been loved so passionately. But Australia feels as if it had never been loved, and never come out into the open. As if man had never loved it, and made it a happy country, a bride country—or a mother country.'

'I don't suppose they ever have,' said Jack.

'But they will?' asked Harriet. 'Surely they will. I feel that if I were Australian, I should love the very earth of it—the very sand and dryness of it—more than anything.'

'Where should we poor Australian wives be?' put in Victoria, leaning forward her delicate, frail face—that reminded one of a flickering butterfly in its wavering.

'Yes,' said Harriet meditatively, as if they had to be considered, but were not as important as the other question.

'I'm afraid most Australians come to hate the Australian earth a good bit before they're done with it,' said Jack. 'If you call the land a bride, she's the sort of bride not many of us are willing to tackle. She drinks your sweat and your blood, and then as often as not lets you down, does you in.'

'Of course,' said Harriet, 'it will take time. And of course a *lot* of love. A lot of fierce love, too.'

'Let's hope she gets it,' said Jack. 'They treat the country more like a woman they pick up on the streets than a bride, to my thinking.'

'I feel I could *love* Australia,' declared Harriet.

'Do you feel you could love an Australian?' asked Jack, very much to the point.

'Well,' said Harriet, arching her eyes at him, 'that's another matter. From what I see of them I rather doubt it,' she laughed, teasing him.

'I should say you would. But it's no good loving Australia if you can't love the Australian.'

'Yes, it is. If as you say Australia is like the poor prostitute, and the Australian just bullies her to get what he can out of her and then treats her like dirt.'

'It's a good deal like that,' said Jack.

'And then you expect me to approve of you.'

'Oh, we're not all alike, you know.'

'It always seems to me,' said Somers, 'that somebody will have to water Australia with their blood before it's a real man's country. The soil, the very plants seem to be waiting for it.'

'You've got a lurid imagination, my dear man,' said Jack.

'Yes, he has,' said Harriet. 'He's always so extreme.'

The train jogged on, stopping at every little station. They were near the coast, but for a long time the sea was not in sight. The land grew steeper—dark, straight hills like cliffs, masked in sombre trees. And then the first plume of colliery smoke among the trees on the hill-face. But they were little collieries, for the most part, where the men just walked into the face of the hill down a tunnel, and they hardly disfigured the land at all. Then the train came out on the sea—lovely bays with sand and grass and trees, sloping up towards the sudden hills that were like a wall. There were bungalows dotted in most of the bays. Then suddenly more collieries, and quite a large settlement of bungalows. From the train they looked down on many many pale-grey zinc roofs, sprinkled about like a great camp, close together, yet none touching, and getting thinner towards the sea. The chimneys were faintly smoking, there was a haze of smoke and a sense of home, home in the wilds. A little way off, among the trees, plumes of white steam betrayed more collieries.

A bunch of schoolboys clambered into the train with their satchels, at home as schoolboys are. And several black colliers, with tin luncheon boxes. Then the train ran for a mile and a half, to stop at another little settlement. Sometimes they stopped at beautiful bays in a hollow between hills, and no collieries, only a few bungalows. Harriet hoped Mullumbimby was like that. She rather dreaded the settlements with the many many iron roofs, and the wide, unmade roads of sandy earth running between, down to the sea, or skirting swamp-like little creeks.

The train jogged on again—they were there. The place was half and half. There were many tin roofs — but not *so* many. There were the wide, unmade roads running so straight as it were to nowhere, with little bungalow homes half-lost at the side. But they were pleasant little bungalow homes. Then quite near, inland, rose a great black wall of mountain, or cliff, or tor, a vast dark tree-covered tor that reminded Harriet of Matlock, only much bigger. The town trailed down from the foot of this mountain towards the railway, a huddle of grey and red-painted iron roofs. Then over the railway, towards the sea, it began again in a scattered, spasmodic fashion, rather forlorn bungalows and new 'stores' and fields with rail fences, and more bungalows above the fields, and more still running down the creek shallows towards the hollow sea, which lay beyond like a grey mound, the strangest sight Harriet had ever seen.

Kangaroo (1923).

W. SOMERSET MAUGHAM

(1874–1965)

English writer. Somerset Maugham, who lived in Paris until the age of ten, was educated at King's School, Canterbury, and Heidelberg University. He trained as a doctor but became a writer instead, ultimately writing novels, including works such as Of Human Bondage *(1916) and* The Moon and Sixpence *(1919), plays, and short stories. From about 1927 until his death, he mostly lived in the south of France. A stay at the Grand Hotel on Thursday Island in the early 1920s inspired the following short story. The hotel was destroyed by fire in 1993.*

'FRENCH JOE'

It was Captain Bartlett who told me of him. I do not think that many people have been to Thursday Island. It is in the Torres Straits and is so called because it was discovered on a Thursday by Captain Cook. I went there since they told me in Sydney that it was the last place God ever made. They said there was nothing to see and warned me that I should probably get my throat cut. I had come up from Sydney in a Japanese tramp and they put me ashore in a small boat. It was the middle of the night and there was not a soul on the jetty. One of the sailors who landed my kit told me that if I turned to the left I should presently come to a two-storey building and this was the hotel. The boat pushed off and I was left alone. I do not much like being separated from my luggage, but I like still less to pass the night on a jetty and sleep on hard stones; so I shouldered a bag and set out. It was pitch dark. I seemed to walk much more than a few hundred yards which they had spoken of and was afraid I had missed my way, but at last saw dimly a building which seemed to be important enough to suggest that it might be the hotel. No light showed, but my eyes by now were pretty well accustomed to the darkness and I found a door. I struck a match, but could see no bell. I knocked; there was no reply; I knocked again, with my stick, as loudly as I could, then a window above me was opened and a woman's voice asked me what I wanted.

'I've just got off the *Shika Maru*,' I said. 'Can I have a room?'

'I'll come down.'

I waited a little longer, and the door was opened by a woman in a red flannel dressing-gown. Her hair was hanging over her shoulders in long black wisps. In her hand she held a paraffin lamp. She greeted me warmly, a little stoutish woman, with keen eyes and a nose suspiciously red, and bade me come in. She took me upstairs and showed me a room.

'Now you sit down,' she said, 'and I'll make up the bed before you can say Jack Robinson. What will you 'ave? A drop of whisky would do you good, I should think. You won't want to be washing at this time of night, I'll bring you a towel in the morning.'

And while she made the bed she asked me who I was and what I had come to Thursday Island for. She could see I wasn't a seafaring man—all the pilots came to this hotel and had done for twenty years—and she didn't know what business could have brought me. I wasn't that fellow as was coming to inspect the Customs, was I? She'd 'eard they were sending someone from Sydney. I asked her if there were any pilots staying there then. Yes, there was one, Captain Bartlett, did I know him? A queer fish he was and no mistake. Hadn't got a hair on his head, but the way he could put his liquor away, well, it was a caution. There, the bed was ready and she expected I'd sleep like a top and one thing she could say was, the sheets were clean. She lit the end of a candle and bade me good night.

Captain Bartlett certainly was a queer fish, but he is of no moment to my present purpose; I made his acquaintance at dinner next day— before I left Thursday Island I had eaten turtle soup so often that I have ceased to look upon it as a luxury—and it was because in the course of conversation I mentioned that I spoke French that he asked me to go and see French Joe.

'It'll be a treat to the old fellow to talk his own lingo for a bit. He's ninety-three, you know.'

For the last two years, not because he was ill but because he was old and destitute, he had lived in the hospital and it was here that I visited him. He was lying in bed, in flannel pyjamas much too large for him, a little shrivelled old man with vivacious eyes, a short white beard, and bushy black eyebrows. He was glad to speak French with me, which he spoke with the marked accent of his native isle, for he was a Corsican, but he had dwelt so many years among English-speaking people that he no longer spoke his mother tongue with accuracy. He used English words as though they were French, making verbs of them with French terminations. He talked very quickly, with broad gestures, and his voice for the most part was clear and strong; but now and then it seemed suddenly to fade away so that it sounded as though he spoke from the grave. The hushed and hollow sound gave me an eerie feeling. Indeed I could not look upon him still as of this world. His real name was Joseph de Paoli. He was a nobleman and a gentleman. He was of the same family as the general we have all read of in Boswell's Johnson, but he showed no interest in his famous ancestor.

'We have had so many generals in our family,' he said. 'You know, of course, that Napoleon Bonaparte was a connection of mine. No, I have never read Boswell. I have not read books. I have lived.'

He had entered the French army in 1851. Seventy-five years ago. It is terrifying. As a lieutenant of artillery ('like my cousin Bonaparte,' he said) he had fought the Russians in the Crimea and as a captain, the Prussians in 1870. He showed me a scar on his bald pate from an Uhlan's lance and then with a dramatic gesture told how he had thrust his sword in the Uhlan's body with such violence that he could not withdraw it. The Uhlan fell dead and the sword remained in the body. But the Empire perished and he joined the communists. For six weeks he fought against the government troops under Monsieur Thiers. To me Thiers is but a shadowy figure, and it was startling and even a trifle comic to hear French Joe speak with passionate hatred of a man who has been dead for half a century. His voice rose into a shrill scream as he repeated the insults, oriental in their imagery, which in the council he had flung at the head of this mediocre statesman. French Joe was tried and sentenced to five years in New Caledonia.

'They should have shot me,' he said, 'but, dirty cowards, they dared not.'

Then came the long journey in a sailing vessel, and the antipodes, and his wrath flamed out again when he spoke of the indignity thrust upon him, a political prisoner, when they herded him with vulgar criminals. The ship put in at Melbourne and one of the officers, a fellow Corsican, enabled him to slip over the side. He swam ashore and, taking his friend's advice, went straight to the police station. No one there could understand a word he said, but an interpreter was sent for, his dripping papers were examined, and he was told that so long as he did not set foot on a French ship he was safe.

'Freedom,' he cried to me. 'Freedom.'

Then came a long series of adventures. He cooked, taught French, swept streets, worked in the gold mines, tramped, starved, and at last found his way to New Guinea. Here he underwent the most astonishing of his experiences, for drifting into the savage interior, and they are cannibals there still, after a hundred desperate adventures and hairbreadth escapes he made himself king of some wild tribe.

'Look at me, my friend,' he said, 'I who lie here on a hospital bed, the object of charity, have been monarch of all I surveyed. Yes, it is something to say that I have been a king.'

But eventually he came into collision with the British and his sovereignty passed from him. He fled the country and started life once more. It is clear that he was a fellow of resource for eventually he came to own a fleet of pearling luggers on Thursday Island. It looked as though at last he had reached a haven of peace and, an elderly man now, he looked forward to a prosperous and even respectable old age. A hurricane destroyed his boats and ruin fell upon him. He never recovered. He was too old to make a fresh start, and since then had earned as best he could a precarious livelihood till at last, beaten, he had accepted the hospital's kindly shelter.

'But why did you not go back to France or Corsica? An amnesty was granted to the communists a quarter of a century ago.'

'What are France and Corsica to me after fifty years? A cousin of mine seized my land. We Corsicans never forget and never forgive. If I had gone back I should have had to kill him. He had his children.'

'Funny old French Joe,' smiled the hospital nurse who stood at the end of the bed.

'At all events you have had a fine life,' I said.

'Never. Never. I have had a frightful life. Misfortune has followed me wherever I turned my steps and look at me now: I am rotten, fit for nothing but the grave. I thank God that I had no children to inherit the curse that is upon me.'

'Why, Joe, I thought you didn't believe in God,' said the nurse.

'It is true. I am a sceptic. I have never seen a sign that there is in the scheme of things an intelligent purpose. If the universe is the contrivance of some being, that being can only be a criminal imbecile.' He shrugged his shoulders. 'Anyhow, I have not got much longer in this filthy world and then I shall go and see for myself what is the real truth of the whole business.'

The nurse told me it was time to leave the old man and I took his hand to bid him farewell. I asked him if there was anything I could do for him.

'I want nothing,' he said. 'I only want to die.' His black shining eyes twinkled. 'But meanwhile I should be grateful for a packet of cigarettes.'

Cosmopolitans (1936).

BRUCE CHATWIN
(1940–89)

English writer and traveller. Sheffield-born Chatwin, who was educated at Marlborough School, worked at Sotheby's before becoming a journalist with the Sunday Times *from 1972 to 1975. His publications include* In Patagonia *(1977),* The Viceroy of Ouidah *(1980), and* On the Black Hill *(1982). Chatwin wrote about Australia, which he visited in the 1980s, in* The Songlines *(1987), a work about Aboriginal dreaming-tracks, which reflects his longstanding interest in nomadism. In this 'novel of ideas' he touches upon the theme of lost children.*

'THE BABIES'

When I woke next morning I was lying in the middle of the bright blue groundsheet, and the sun was up. The old men wanted more meat for breakfast. The ice in the 'Eski' had melted in the night and the steaks were swimming in blood-coloured water. We decided to cook them before they went 'off'.

I re-lit the embers of the fire while Arkady held a conference with Alan and the man in blue. He showed them on the survey map how the railways would miss the Lizard Rock by at least two miles and got them, reluctantly, to agree to this. Next, he pointed to the twenty-five-mile stretch of country through which he intended to drive.

For most of the morning the vehicles edged slowly northwards over broken ground. The sun was blinding and the vegetation parched and drear. To the east, the land dropped away and lifted towards a ridge of pale sandhills. The valley in between was covered with a continuous thicket of mulga trees, leafless at this season, silver-grey like a blanket of low-lying mist.

Nothing moved except the shimmering heatwaves.

We kept crossing the path of fires. In places, all that survived of the bushes were upright, fire-hardened spikes, which staked our tyres as we ran over them. We had three flats, and Marian had two in the Land-Rover. Whenever we stopped to change a wheel, dust and ash blew in our eyes. The women would jump down, delightedly, and go off to look for bush-tucker.

Mavis was in a very boisterous mood, and wanted to repay me for the thongs. She grabbed my hand and dragged me towards a limp, green bush.

'Hey! Where are you two going?' Arkady called.

'Get him some bush-bananas,' she shouted back. 'He don't know bush-bananas.' But the bananas, when we got to them, had shrivelled up to nothing.

Another time, she and Topsy tried to run down a goanna, but the reptile was far too quick for them. At last, she found a plant of ripe solanum berries and showered them on me in handfuls. They looked and tasted like unripe cherry-tomatoes. I ate some to please her and she said, 'There you are, dearie,' and reached out her chubby hand and stroked my cheek.

When anything in the landscape even half-resembled a 'feature' Arkady would brake and ask Old Alan, 'What's that one?' or, 'Is this country clear?'

Alan glared from the window at his 'domain'.

Around noon, we came to a clump of eucalyptus: the only patch of green in sight. Nearby there was an outcrop of sandstone, about twenty feet long and scarcely visible above the surface. It had shown up on the aerial survey, and was one of three identical outcrops lying in line along the ridge.

Arkady told Alan that the engineer might want to quarry this rock for ballast. He might want to blast it with dynamite.

'How about that, old man?' he asked.

Alan said nothing.

'No story here? Or nothing?'

He said nothing.

'So the country's clear, then?'

'No,' Alan took a deep sigh. 'The Babies.'

'Whose babies?'

'Babies,' he said—and in the same weary voice, he began to tell the story of the Babies.

In the Dreamtime, the Bandicoot Man, Akuka, and his brother were hunting along this ridge. Because it was the dry season, they were terribly hungry and thirsty. Every bird and animal had fled. The trees were stripped of leaves and bushfires swept across the country.

The hunters searched everywhere for an animal to kill until, almost at his final gasp, Akuka saw a bandicoot bolting for its burrow. His brother warned him not to kill it, for to kill one's own kind was taboo. Akuka ignored the warning.

He dug the bandicoot from the burrow, speared it, skinned and ate it, and immediately felt cramps in his stomach. His stomach swelled and swelled, and then it burst, and a throng of Babies spewed forth and started crying for water.

Dying of thirst, the Babies travelled north up to Singleton, and south back to Taylor Creek, where the dam now is. They found the soakage, but drank up all the water and returned to the three rocky outcrops. The rocks were the Babies, huddled together as they lay down to die—although, as it happened, they did not die yet.

Their uncle, Akuka's brother, heard their cries and called on his western neighbours to make rain. The rain blew in from the west (the grey expanse of mulga was the thunderstorm metamorphosed into trees). The Babies turned on their tracks and wandered south again. While crossing a creek not far from Lizard Rock, they fell into the floodwaters and 'melted'.

The name of the place where the Babies 'went back' was *Akwerkepentye*, which means 'far-travelling children'.

When Alan came to the end of the story, Arkady said softly, 'Don't worry, old man. It'll be all right. Nobody's going to touch the Babies.'

Alan shook his head despairingly.

'Are you happy then?' asked Arkady.

No. He wasn't happy. Nothing about this wicked railway was going to make him happy: but at least the Babies might be safe.

We moved ahead.

'Australia', Arkady said slowly, 'is the country of lost children.'

Another hour and we reached the northern boundary of Middle Bore Station. We now had one spare tyre for the Land Cruiser: so rather than risk returning the way we'd come, we decided to make a detour. There was an old dirt road which went east and then south and came out behind Alan's settlement. On the last lap we ran in with the railway people.

They were clearing the country along the proposed line of track. Their earth-movers had cut a sweep through the mulga, and a strip of churned-up soil about a hundred yards wide now stretched away into the distance.

The old men looked miserably at the stacks of broken trees.

We stopped to talk to a black-bearded titan. He was more than seven feet tall and might have been made of bronze. Stripped to the waist, in a straw hat and stubbies, he was driving in marker-posts with a hammer. He was off, in an hour or two, to Adelaide on leave. 'Oh boy,' he said. 'Am I ever glad to get out of here?'

The road had gone. Our vehicles crawled and slewed in the loose red dirt. Three times we had to get out and push. Arkady was whacked. I suggested we stop for a break. We turned aside into the sketchy shade of some trees. There were ant-hills everywhere, splashed with bird shit. He unpacked some food and drink, and rigged up the groundsheet as an awning.

We had expected the old men, as always, to be hungry. But they all sat huddled together, moping, refusing either to eat or to talk: to judge from their expressions you would have said they were in pain.

Marian and the ladies had parked under a different tree, and they, too, were silent and gloomy.

A yellow bulldozer went by in a cloud of dust.

Arkady lay down, covered his head with a towel, and started snoring. Using my leather rucksack as a pillow, I leaned back against a tree-trunk and leafed through Ovid's *Metamorphoses*.

The story of Lykaeon's transformation into a wolf took me back to a blustery spring day in Arkadia and seeing, in the limestone cap of Mount Lykaeon itself, an image of the crouching beast-king. I read of Hyacinth and Adonis; of Deucalion and the Flood; and how the 'living things' were created from the warm Nilotic ooze. And it struck me, from what I now knew of the Songlines, that the whole of Classical mythology might represent the relics of a gigantic 'song-map': that all the to-ing and fro-ing of gods and goddesses, the caves and sacred springs, the sphinxes and chimaeras, and all the men and women who became nightingales or ravens, echoes or narcissi, stones or stars—could all be interpreted in terms of totemic geography.

I must have dozed off myself, for when I woke my face was covered with flies and Arkady was calling, 'Come on. Let's go.'

We got back to Middle Bore an hour before sunset. The Land Cruiser had hardly stopped moving before Alan and the man in blue opened their doors and walked away without a nod. Big Tom mumbled something about the railway being 'bad'.

Arkady looked crushed. 'Hell!' he said. 'What's the use?'

He blamed himself for letting them see the earth-movers.

'You shouldn't,' I said.

'But I do.'

'They were bound to see it one day.'

'I'd rather not with me.'

We freshened up under a hosepipe, and I revived our hearth of the day before. Marian joined us, sitting on a sawn-off tree stump and unravelling her tangle of hair. She then compared notes with Arkady. The women had told her of a Songline called 'Two Dancing Women', but it never touched the line of the railway.

We looked up to see a procession of women and children on their way back from foraging. The babies swayed peacefully in the folds of their mothers' dresses.

'You never hear them cry,' Marian said, 'as long as the mother keeps moving.'

She had touched, unwittingly, on one of my favourite topics. 'And if babies can't bear to sit still,' I said, 'how shall we settle down later?'

She jumped to her feet. 'Which reminds me, I've got to go.'

'Now?'

'Now. I promised Gladys and Topsy they'd be home tonight.'

'Can't they stay here?' I asked. 'Couldn't we all spend the night here?'

'You can,' she said, playfully sticking out her tongue. 'I can't.'

I looked at Arkady, who shrugged, as if to say, 'When she gets an idea into her head, no power on earth's going to stop her.' Five minutes later, she had rounded up the women and, with a cheerful wave, was gone.

'That woman', I said, 'is the Pied Piper.'

'Dammit!' said Arkady.

He reminded me of our promise to look in on Frank Olson.

At the station-house, a large woman with heat-ravaged skin came shuffling to the front door, peered through the fly-screen and opened up.

'Frank's gone down to Glen Armond,' she said. 'An emergency! Jim Hanlon's taken sick!'

'When was that?' asked Arkady.

'Last night,' said the woman. 'Collapsed in the pub.'

'We should get the chaps and go,' he said.

'Yes,' I agreed. 'I think we'd better go.'

The Songlines (1987).

JAN MORRIS

(1926–)

Anglo-Welsh writer. Oxford-educated James Morris was one of Britain's leading journalists, responsible for the scoop that broke the news of the first ascent of Mt Everest to the world, before becoming a freelance writer in 1961. After a gender change in 1972, described in Conundrum *(1974), Morris became known as Jan. Her other books include the* Pax Britannica *trilogy (1968–78), numerous travel books including* Sydney *(1992), and a novel entitled* Last Letters from Hav *(1985). Morris, who has visited Australia many times, discusses some of her feelings about this country in her autobiographical* Pleasures of a Tangled Life *(1989).*

'AUSTRALIAN DISTRACTIONS'

I was sitting recently upon a grassy incline in a park in Adelaide, South Australia, when two small boys, one rather smaller than the other, prepared to ride down the slope on their skateboards. There were a few beer-bottles lying around, left over from the night before, and I heard the elder boy say to the younger, in an authoritative voice intended largely for my own ears: 'Please don't hit the lady—I don't mind about the beer bottles, but *definitely* not the lady.'

They were splendidly entertaining children, and they brought to a head feelings about Australia which I had been working on and worrying about for years. They were free, it seemed to me, of all inherited regret, shame, cringe or pretension. They did not give a damn whether they were or were not descended from convicts. Their racial origins seemed to be mixed—a touch of Greek, perhaps, or Lebanese?—and they certainly knew of no Mother Country but their own. They were a couple of clean sheets, and upon their personalities, I surmised as I watched them fooling about, history and geography were about to write new messages.

In 1780 the Frenchman Michel-Guillaume de Crèvecoeur introduced his readers to 'the American, this new man'. Since his time we have not really had another addition to our species, but perhaps, I thought in the park that day, one is coming up.

My first landfall in Australia was at Darwin, Northern Territory, nearly forty years ago. I had decided to jump into Australia at the deep end, and spend a week or two exploring that then benighted coast. The town was dismal in the extreme, so dismal that it has left in my memory only a blur of brick and corrugated iron, and the hotel was just as depressing: an unlovely pub-like hostelry whose dinner-table I was obliged to share, feeling extraordinarily effete and fastidious, with half a dozen homespun sons of the south. What was I then, they asked me, a rich travelling Pom come to look at the other half? 'I am a sort of a writer,' I replied with dignity. A sort of a writer! That's the truth! A sort of a writer, and they knew what sort, they'd met that sort before!

Having got through these preliminaries, conventional in the Australia of the time, we grew quite friendly, and in the end I rather enjoyed Darwin—since utterly transformed, incidentally, by a combination of hurricane and tourist trade. Nevertheless on the whole the Australia of the early 1960s was not for me. It was an extremely self-conscious country, exaggeratedly independent in some ways, preposterously sycophantic in others. Its history still split it, so to speak, into jailers and convicts—the jailers ridiculously British, monarchist, racist and snobby, the convicts contumaciously Irish in spirit if not in blood. They were united only by a common sense of social and patriotic insecurity: as an Australian novelist would put it to me much later, tugging a forelock and saying 'Fuck you!' both at the same time. Cricket, royalty, booze, beaches, the Great War, the ideal of working-class fraternity they called 'mateship', these were the national enthusiasms, and they were supplemented by crude displays of male chauvinism, ethnic prejudice and Philistinism.

It was no place for a writer of my work. When I wrote an essay about Sydney it was five full years before the last letter of complaint reached me from down under.

Look at Sydney now! No city on earth so enlivens me, the moment I set foot in it, with a sense of fresh start. It is one of the most endemically corrupt municipalities in the western world, dominated by millionaires of frightful rapacity, but this only enhances its sense of inexhaustible opportunity. I love to walk around its central waterfront on a bright summer morning, say. People are very open and natural then—the joggers smile breathless smiles, the early park workers pause for a chat, layabouts summon a phrase or two of badinage and the first commuters, disembarking from the ferries at Circular Quay, still have time for greetings. Above the scene looms the harbour bridge, a very British, very 1930-ish, very George V-like, very male, very strong, graceless and orthodox thing. When I first went to Sydney that bridge was the unchallenged symbol of the place. Now it seems almost incongruous, the waterfront's one surviving reminder of the old colonial Australia. Otherwise, it appears to me nowadays as I take my exercise towards Wooloomolloo, everything around me proclaims Sydney to be entirely self-created.

Certainly no outsider could have invented its climate, its foliage or its terrain, all of which still somehow give me the impression that Australia really is upside-down, as we used to think in childhood. Australian water does in fact go down the drain the other way round, and much else about the nature of things seems to me reversed, or at best confused. The trees seem to grow wrong, and bear the wrong sorts of leaf. The birds fly with weird flapping motions and make unknown cries. That lovely harbour, with its steep banks and myriad inlets, always suggests to me a fjord in a continent of ice, the sort of place Atlantic expeditions winter their ships in, except that it has miraculously sprouted green woods and gardens. Above all there is something queer about the light. It is a northern, Scandinavian light, but reversed—just as the black swan of Australia is like a northern swan in negative. Where it should be moist, it is dry; where it should be pale, it is golden; and when, a cloud coming up from the south, it looks as though we ought to be expecting a snow-shower, nothing but a passing shadow momentarily darkens the scene.

Such are the primeval pleasures I get these days during my morning exercise in Sydney, but superimposed on them are pleasures of extreme modernity. The new buildings of the city glitter and strut. Hydrofoils sweep superbly, with curves of foam, away from the quay towards Manly and the beaches. I imagine a mesh of electronic beams, rays and signals crossing the sky. And presiding over it all nowadays, having displaced on every tourist poster that lumpish bridge, Sydney's Opera House spreads its wings provocatively beside the water—perhaps the most reckless municipal building ever erected anywhere, and not at all unlike, now I come to think of it, some primeval amphibious creature itself.

The elder of the two boys, whizzing down the slope once more, swung around to stop with a glorious flourish at my feet. 'What skill!' he observed with a winning smile.

He did not say it boastfully—ten years old though he was, at the most, he was amused at himself. One of the things I like best about contemporary Australia is its frank and entertained self-admiration. The pride of this country, when it was not chip-on-shoulder, used to be a derivative, second-hand pride, and the capital city of Canberra was designed as a pompous declaration of such sentiments, built to European patterns to represent imported values. The new Parliament Building, however, is exactly the opposite. Built within the mass of a hill, it is an assembly chamber quite properly inside-out; a recognition of the fact that the nature of Australia is almost inconceivably strange, and that its original inhabitants are as close to the earth as the kangaroos and platy-puses themselves. Without the aborigines, however sad they are, however misused, Australia would not be half so interesting. The glimpses one has of them almost everywhere in the country, if only sloping hang-dog through city streets, enhance the science-fiction quality of the country, but also give it historical authenticity. They are essential to the national meaning. Their fretful figures are evidence that Australia does have a pedigree of its own, and soon enough, I venture to prophecy, Australians of all sorts will be finding it fashionable to claim aboriginal blood.

The swift absorption too of Greeks, Italians, Lebanese, Germans, even Chinese and Japanese into the national mainstream has released the Australians from many of their old hang-ups. I remember years ago being astonished by the spectacle of an Australian man holding in his arms a baby, in those days almost a contradiction in terms. Approach-ing closer, I realized him to be what they then called a New Aus-tralian—not, that was to say, absolutely a proper true-blue, Dinkum Aussie Australian, whose father had fought at Gallipoli and whose great-great-grandparents were either related to the Duke of Newcastle or had been transported to Botany Bay merely for tumbling a squire's daughter in the hay—not, in short, quite the real thing, but an immi-grant from continental Europe. Today the New Australians have won the day, socially at least. Their manners and standards are supreme. I would not look twice at a man carrying a baby now, the pubs are no longer quite so grotesquely macho and a vast corpus of nostalgia, based upon Britishness, war and class, has been expunged from the national psyche. Robert Menzies, a particularly resilient Prime Minister of Aus-tralia, once told me that whenever he arrived over London, and looked down from his aircraft to see old grime of the place vaporized into black smoke above the capital, he felt a tremor of pride and inherited loyalty. I imagine that few Australians would get such a thrill now, and several million of them indeed have no connection with the British Isles whatever.

Not long ago I went to an ethnic parade in Melbourne, in which all the different racial groups of the city presented themselves in tableau, float or marching band. It was raining, and the festivities had a slightly muted air, the canopies, feathers and papier mâché of the floats wilting a little in the damp, the more elderly of the marchers looking resolutely rather than spontaneously cheerful. Yet the message was easy to read. Those old people were people like the rest of us, and showed in their faces more or less the same experiences, of climate, of history, of diet, that have moulded the faces of half the world. But their sons, daughters and grandchildren were the New People. Looking down from those lurching floats, dressed up as they were in Greek skirts, Ukrainian caps or Sicilian sabots, their faces of brown and gold sailed through the rain with an air of revelation, like evangelists riding by.

The skateboard boys stopped for a chat. 'At the corner of our road there's a house full of aborigines,' the younger one told me, 'and one day the aborigine lady knocked on our door and her head was all bleeding and now her husband's gone to prison.' 'For a long time?' I inquired. 'For a very, very long time,' he said.

I detected no *schadenfreude* in his reportage—they were kindly children—but all the same the anecdote gave me a jolt, as I lay there in the benign sunshine, and reminded me that Australia without its streak of malice would not be Australia at all. Even there in Adelaide, the most gentlemanly of Australian cities, where never a convict was transported—even in Adelaide a strain of bitterness surfaces. Crime there is often bizarre, as though the impulse to violence has twisted its way out of the national subconscious, and I sometimes think that the Australian gift for malignant abuse springs not from history at all, but is a product of the country's very substance, so bitter, so brooding, so full of grudge. They say the koala bear, that darling star of the Australian fauna, can be a horrid little beast, and a snide comment from the Australian Press, which is one of the most mischievous in the western world, is not unlike a nasty nip from an emu.

It strikes me as essentially a malice of the past, part of the old Australia. When I hear some middle-aged citizen, wearing shorts and long stockings, loudly calling his companion 'Mate', or even 'Cobber', I feel always that this traditional bonhomie, now beginning to seem unnatural or defensive, could easily be soured into ill-will. In a cultural sense you could not, in my experience, entirely trust the Old Australian. It once fell to me, long ago, to propose the toast at the Anzac Day dinner at Oxford. I gave a speech in what was I hoped the true Oxford vein, making the conventional fun of Australian manners, concluding with expressions of admiration which were, as it happened, perfectly true. To my horror I found that the guest delegated to respond to my toast was an Old Australian of the most utterly short-trousered and long-stockinged kind; not indeed the Mate or Cobber kind because he was immensely grand, being at once a General and a Judge of the High Court, but certainly imbued with just the same values. I expected the worst, and got it—not a fancy of mine but was cruelly demolished, hardly a joke but was taken with offence, and all the nice things I had said about Australia were rejected as ignorant or impertinent.

I suppose such old stiffs still stalk the Australian landscape, responding to toasts and rebuffing upstarts, but fortunately I do not meet them. Young people run most aspects of Australian life today, and Australia is one country where the young people are more dignified, more courteous and more sure of themselves than the old.

Perhaps even the innate malevolence will fade with time. In the park that day I observed, sitting on a nearby bench, a couple in late middle age who were clearly British immigrants—I could tell that by their stooped postures and their air of complaint. I would guess they had come to Australia in the 1950s, and had brought with them something of their mean frustrated homeland, where backs were still stooped by the effects of history, and attitudes were soured by social system. As they sat there smoking their cigarettes (ash drooping at the tip), two young mounted constables passed by, one male, one female, both of supernal handsomeness, high on white horses in the sunshine. As they rode past the English couple they smiled down at them dazzling smiles of benevolence; the old people nodded subserviently in reply, dropping ash on their laps.

It was like seeing evolution actually happening—the immigrants so ineradicably rooted in their origins, the passing cops so radiantly of a developing species that I thought they might easily prove, if stripped of their uniforms, actually marsupial. Even in Australia, though, there can be no such thing as an entirely clean break. History cannot be cancelled. Soon afterwards the younger of the two skateboard boys, pausing once again, told me that his father had lately taken part in a military parade. 'What kind of a hat did he wear?' I asked for something to say. One of those hats, he said, which were flat on one side, but turned up on the other. 'I know,' I said, 'like they used to wear in the Great War.'

There was a silence for a moment, and then the boy spoke. 'I *hate* the Great War,' he said: and my heart turned.

Pleasures of a Tangled Life (1989).

10

Political

and social

commentators

◆

THERESE HUBER

(1764–1829)

German writer and intellectual. Huber, who was described by one of her contemporaries as 'one of the most remarkable women of her age', did not visit Australia herself, but used the account written by her first husband, Georg Forster, of James Cook's second voyage around the world (1772–75) and the journals of Arthur Phillip, John White, John Hunter, and Watkin Tench as the basis for her Adventures on a Journey to New Holland *(1801), said to be the first novel set in the Australian penal colony. She wrote the novel in 1793, by which time she was living with her lover Ludwig Huber, who was to become her second husband and under whose name she published it. She uses the work as a vehicle to debate the subject of revolution, especially the French Revolution, of which she was critical. In the following extract, one of the book's main characters, Randolph, a French ex-revolutionary and traveller, describes Sydney Cove in a letter to friends in Germany.*

SYDNEY COVE

Sydney Cove

Greetings, dear friends! We are now in the harbour of Sydney Cove. The new Heavens and the new Earth are here before my very eyes, dear Reinette, but the sixth day of Creation that you promised me has not yet dawned, nor is there yet any real sign of the New Man in me! May the old one continue to thrive! And indeed as long as a man is unwilling to exchange his feelings of pain for another's happy rejoicing, all misfortune is based on a false conception of joy and suffering. So I greet you today from New Holland for the first time, heartily contented with my lot and sometimes even a little proud of it.

The last part of our journey was very pleasant, partly because of the weather and partly because of the quiet, friendly relationship between Frances, Sidney and myself. Sidney seems to have valiantly pulled himself together since that conversation and his cheerful frankness brings him closer to me with every day that passes. However, a most unpleasant incident took place immediately after our arrival, which disturbed the tranquillity of us all.

The day after the prisoners had all been disembarked and Frances on the recommendation of the worthy Captain, had been lodged with a corporal's wife, a great commotion suddenly arose because a chest of linen had been broken into and its contents plundered. The linen itself had been found in the possession of two of the female convicts but these shameless creatures had cited Frances as their accomplice. I was sitting with her beneath a tree and Betty was busy looking after her small sister when Sidney came up in great distress and informed Frances of the malicious slander. At the same time he begged her to go without delay to Government House before she should be summoned there. She went pale and said bitterly:

'This is a terrible revenge.'

However, obedient to Sidney's counsel, she hurried away to forestall the court's summons. As you can imagine, not the remotest suspicion sullied either my concern or Sidney's. We were present at the trial and the examination was very brief because the stupid malice of the accusation became apparent at once. Frances spoke modestly and her answers were clear and convincing, though I could see from her manner that she was terribly tense. As soon as the judge had dismissed her with the friendly injunction to keep on being so honest, Sidney and I hastened to her and warmly besought her to regain her spirits.

'Dear Frances, calm yourself! You have taken this too much to heart.'

She went slowly over to the children who were playing in the grass, took Betty by the hand and Clara in her arms. But as she departed she said in a voice dulled by despair:

'Whosoever has once encountered disgrace will be pursued by it as the body by its shadow.'

She said no more but went wearily on her way without looking round at us; we remained behind sad and dismayed. Sidney's mournful expression finally roused me. I said with composure:

'Dear friend, is she less good or less unfortunate because these words seem to declare her guilt beyond all doubt? Come, we shall in the end succeed in removing this shadow from her life.'

But our cheerful evenings have been disturbed. Frances is more melancholy and reserved than ever. Meanwhile her gentle and noble conduct has already gained her the great benefit of exemption from public labour. The Governor whose humane and wise rule has endeared him to all who are still capable of feeling goodness, has put her in the care of the oldest preacher in the colony, to serve there as his housekeeper.

I have wandered through some of the newly cultivated areas and have found everywhere the loveliest natural paradise, one that rewards

European diligence with interest. But a lamentable race of men disfigures it. They lack every impulse to be virtuous. It is not enough for one of these hardened souls to know himself an honest man among rogues, and even to receive praise for this—and no other reward is available to them. But they must needs find excitement in something or other and the majority for whom life had lost most of its savour, have found some of it again in a wretched religiosity. Others are just as bad here as they were in their homeland or have become still worse because they no longer have the hope of one day making their fortune at a single stroke. The best are those who have already been released for some years or who have served the whole of their sentence. In the latter the sense of honesty seems to return along with the right to own property.

Tomorrow one of the transports is going to Norfolk Island with all sorts of essential goods brought by our small convoy. I want to take advantage of the opportunity to get to know this island for it is supposed to be the paradise of this region.

Adventures on a Journey to New Holland, trans. Rodney Livingstone (1966, first published in German 1801).

———

CHARLES WENTWORTH DILKE
(1843–1911)

British politician and writer. Dilke read law at Cambridge before being called to the bar in 1866. He 'followed England round the world' in 1866–67, in the company of historian and traveller William Hepworth Dixon, visiting English-speaking or English-governed lands, including Australia and New Zealand. He reasoned that if two islands made up Great Britain, then America, Australia, and India added up to 'Greater Britain'. Therefore he used the latter term as the title of his 1868 account of the trip. A Radical MP for Chelsea from 1868 to 1886, Dilke's public career ended abruptly after a divorce scandal. In his travels, he found odd disparities in the position of women.

'WOMAN'

In one respect, Victoria stands at once sadly behind and strangely in advance of other democratic countries. Women, or at least some women, vote at the Lower House elections, but, on the other hand, the legal position of the sex is almost as inferior to that of man as it is in England or the East.

At an election held some few years ago, female ratepayers voted everywhere throughout Victoria. Upon examination, it was found that a new Registration Act had directed the rate-books to be used as a basis for the preparation of the electoral lists, and that women householders had been legally put on the register, although the intention of the Legislature was not expressed, and the question of female voting had not been raised during the debates. Another instance, this, of the singular way in which in truly British countries reforms are brought about by accident, and, when once become facts, are allowed to stand. There is no more sign of general adhesion in Australia than in England to the doctrine which asserts that women, as well as men, being interested in good government, should have a voice in the selection of that government to which they are forced to submit.

As far as concerns their social position, women are as badly off in Australia as in England, Our theory of marriage—which has been tersely explained thus: 'the husband and wife are one, and *the husband is that one*'—rules as absolutely at the antipodes as it does in Yorkshire. I was daily forced to remember the men of Kansas and Missouri, and the widely different view they take of these matters to that of the Australians. As they used to tell me, they are impatient of seeing their women ranked with 'lunatics and idiots' in the catalogue of incapacities. They are unable to see that women are much better represented by their male friends than were the Southern blacks by their owners or overseers. They believe that the process of election would not be more purified by female emancipation than would the character of the Parliaments elected.

The Kansas people argue that if you were told that there existed in some ideal country two great sections of a race, the members of the one often gross, often vicious, often given to loud talking, to swearing, to drinking, spitting, chewing; not infrequently corrupt; those of the other branch, mild, kind, quiet, pure, devout, with none of the habitual vices of the first-named sect—if you were told that one of these branches was alone to elect rulers and to govern, you would at once say, 'Tell us where this happy country is that basks in the rule of such a godlike people?' 'Stop a minute,' says your informant, 'it is the creatures I described first—the *men* who rule; the others are only women, poor silly fools—imperfect men, I assure you; nothing more.'

It is somewhat the fashion to say that the so-called 'extravagances' of the Kansas folk and other American Western men arise from the extraordinary position given to their women by the disproportion of their sexes. Now, in all the Australian colonies the men vastly outnumber the women, yet the disproportion has none of those results which have been attributed to it by some writers on America. In New South Wales, the sexes are as 250 000 to 200 000, in Victoria 370 000 to 280 000, in New Zealand 130 000 to 80 000, in Queensland 60 000 to 40 000, in Tasmania 50 000 to 40 000, in West Australia 14 000 to 8000, and 90 000 to 80 000 in South Australia. In all our Southern colonies together, there are a million of men to only three-quarters of a million of women; yet with this disproportion, which far exceeds that in Western America, not only have the women failed to acquire any great share of power, political or social but they are content to occupy a position not relatively superior to that held by them at home.

The 'Sewing Clubs' of the war-time are at the bottom of a good deal of the 'woman movement' in America. At the time of greatest need, the ladies of the Northern States formed themselves into associations for the supply of lint, of linen, and of comforts to the army: the women of a district would meet together daily in some large room, and sew, and chat while they were sewing.

The British section of the Teutonic race seems naturally inclined, through the operation of its old interest-begotten prejudices, to rank women where Plato placed them in the 'Timæus,' along with horses and draught cattle; or to think of them much as he did when he said that all the brutes derived their origin from man by a series of successive degradations, of which the first was from man to woman. There is however, one strong reason why the English should, in America, have laid aside their prejudices upon this point, retaining them in Australia, where the conditions are not the same. Among farming peoples, whose women do not work regularly in the field, the woman, to whom falls the household and superior work, is better off than she is among town-dwelling peoples. The Americans are mainly a farming, the Australians and British mainly a town-dwelling, people. The absence in all sections of our race of regular woman labour in the field seems to be a remnant of the high estimation in which women were held by our German ancestry. In Britain we have, until the last few years, been steadily retrograding upon this point.

It is a serious question how far the natural prejudice of the English mind against the labour of what we call 'inferior races' will be found to extend to half the superior race itself. How will English labourers receive the inevitable competition of women in many of their fields? Woman is at present starved, if she works at all, and does not rest content in dependence upon some man, by the terrible lowness of wages in every employment open to her, and this low rate of wages is itself the direct result of the fewness of the occupations which society allows her. Where a man can see a hundred crafts in which he may engage, a woman will perhaps be permitted to find ten. A hundred times as many women as there is room for invade each of this small number of employments. In the Australian labour-field the prospects of women are no better than they are in Europe, and during my residence in Melbourne the Council of the Associated Trades passed a resolution to the effect that nothing could justify the employment of women in any kind of productive labour.

Greater Britain (1870 edition, first published 1868).

––––––

JAMES ANTHONY FROUDE
(1818–94)

English historian. With works such as his twelve-volume history of England, published between 1856 and 1870, Oxford-educated Froude gained a reputation as a great writer of prose last century, but he is perhaps best known now as the literary executor and biographer of the famous essayist and historian Thomas Carlyle. He visited Australia and New Zealand as part of an 1884–85 tour that also took in South Africa and North America, before becoming regius professor of modern history at Oxford in 1892, a position that he held until his death. In his account of the journey, he tells of how he 'did' Auckland while awaiting advice from Sir George Grey about what else to do and see in New Zealand.

'DOING' AUCKLAND

Auckland itself might be 'done' meanwhile. There was the original Government House of New Zealand close to the Club, where the Governor lived before the new constitution removed him to Wellington. There was Bishop Selwyn's unpretending 'palace' and chapel, which the present bishop kindly invited us to see. The city was not too large to walk over. The situation is picturesque, and the ground has been skilfully laid out. There are now 30 000 inhabitants there, and they multiply like the rabbits in Australia. Wooden houses spring up like mushrooms on every vacant spot—decent always and sometimes smart. They cost of them is about 250*l.* and they are generally occupied by their owners. Here as elsewhere the labourers crowd into the town, for the high wages, the music halls, and the drink shops. The municipality finds them unlimited employment, by raising loans cheerfully in England in hopeful confidence of being able hereafter to pay them. Public works form the excuse for the borrowing; and there are works enough and to spare in progress. They are laying out a harbour—cutting down half a hillside in the process—suited for the ambitious Auckland that is to be, but ten times larger than there is present need of. They are excavating the biggest graving dock in the world (the 'Great Eastern' would float in it with ease) preparing for the fleets which are to make Auckland their head-quarters. All this was very spirited, yet I did not find it wholly satisfactory. The English race should not come to New Zealand to renew the town life which they leave behind them, with a hand-to-mouth subsistence as earners of wages on improved conditions. They will never grow into a new nation thus. They will grow into a nation when they are settled in their own houses and freeholds, like their forefathers who drew bow at Agincourt or trailed pike in the wars of the Commonwealth; when they own their own acres, raise their own crops, breed their own sheep and cattle, and live out their days with their children and grandchildren around them. Fine men and fine women are not to be reared in towns, among taverns and theatres and idle clatter of politics. They are Nature's choicest creations and can be produced only on Nature's own conditions: under the free air of heaven, on the green earth amidst woods and waters, and in the wholesome occupation of cultivating the soil. The high wages are the town attraction now, but it cannot remain so for ever. 'Non his juventus orta parentibus.' The young men bred in such towns as Auckland will be good for little. Country children alone can be reared up in simple tastes and simple habits; can be taught to obey their parents and speak the truth, and work in the working hours, sing and dance when work is over, and end and begin their day with a few words of prayer to their Maker. All this is out of fashion now. The colonies are not alone in their ways. In England, in France, in Germany, in America, the town and its pleasures are the universal magnet; the newspaper and the debating club are the mental training schools; and obedience and truth and simplicity do not flourish in such an atmosphere. Is this centripetal tendency to last for ever? or has our kind schoolmistress Nature provided for us some rude awakening?

The city authorities were proud of what they were doing. They took us round in a steam-launch, showed us their vast excavations, showed us their big dock, and left us astonished at the money they were spending. The colony collectively and the municipalities separately seem contending which can borrow the most handsomely. The State debt is between thirty and forty millions. The debts of the municipalities are a startling addition to it. The population, excluding the natives, is still under half a million, and prudent people are beginning to ask how the interest of all these millions is to be provided. To an ordinary observer it is not clear how. The workmen discourage immigration, as likely to lower wages. Very little is being done, at least in the Northern Island, in the way of cultivation; but they take it generally with a light heart, and economy will wait till money can no longer be had for asking. One of their chief industries is at present destructive. The Kauri pine, of which they have, or had, enormous forests, produces the best timber for all purposes which grows anywhere on the globe. It is fine-grained, tough, tenacious, does not split or splinter in working, does not warp, is extremely durable, and is as soft to the chisel as our own deal. It has supplied, and still supplies the amber-like Kauri gum—blocks of crystallised resin, found in the woods where these splendid trees have grown. I have seen ornaments cut out of it quite as beautiful as if they were made of amber. It is in consequence a most valuable article of export. The Kauri pine takes 800 years to grow. They are cutting it down and selling it as fast as axe and saw can work. We saw the huge trunks lying in the mud about the quays—clean stems eighty feet long and six to seven feet in diameter. It is counted that at the present rate of consumption they will be all gone in thirty years. New Zealand perhaps, like other countries, must suffer something for the honour of being governed by a Parliament.

The streets of Auckland were not interesting. The fruit-shops pleased me best. There were apples of many kinds, some old English sorts which are dying out at home and have revived in the new land. Melons, tomatoes, potatoes, were all large and abundant. Photography was in fashion—the mechanical form of art, which serves the purpose of a better till a better comes. There were marvellous landscapes, lakes, mountains, waterfalls, or, coming to human subjects, Maori chiefs and Maori villages. The average shops were full of English wares, noticeable for being extravagantly dear. We counted that in Auckland, as well as in Sydney and Melbourne, a florin would go no farther than a shilling at home, for everything except the necessaries of life. Of native manufactures we saw none, save a few Maori weapons and trinkets.

Oceana, or England and her Colonies (new edition 1886, first published earlier that year).

BEATRICE WEBB

(1858–1943)

English Fabian writer and social reformer. Beatrice Webb and her husband Sidney (1859–1947), founders of the London School of Economics and Political Science (1895) and joint authors of The History of Trade Unionism *(1894) and* Industrial Democracy *(1898), visited America, New Zealand, and Australia in 1898. Surprisingly, they were ill prepared for their visit to Australia and, in the words of the editor of their Australian diary, 'allowed a holiday visit to become a botched investigation'. The following diary entry was written by Beatrice.*

A VISIT TO THE BLUE MOUNTAINS (1898)

October 5th.
… Five days in the Blue Mountains—the Jenolan Caves, Katoomba and Govet's [*sic*] Leap. A somewhat weary drive from Mount Victoria to the Caves, along the ridges of the mountains surrounded on all sides with the forest of gum trees. Our journey in an uncomfortable wagonette, to and fro, taking up the whole of the day, was made interesting to us by the companionship of a shrewd successful farmer of the north coast of New South Wales who was giving his wife and two children an outing. He was an ugly common-looking man, sturdy and squat in build, native born, (his father and mother having emigrated from England in the early days of settlement) with the dress and manners of the English lower middle class, but with a quite admirable capacity for expressing concisely both facts and arguments, and with that curious sort of tolerance for political opponents which seems characteristic of these colonies. His wife was a little servant, but unlike a good many Australian women, a well-conducted little servant; the boy was a stalwart little fellow at the Sydney Grammar School and going on to the Hawkesbury Agricultural College; the little girl, a pasty little person, who despised farm-work and, though brought up at a State school over the way, had aspirations to be genteel and none whatever to be useful. Certainly these colonial women are in an unpleasant stage of development; the whole duty of woman consists in keeping house, and if the husband is rich enough, then even this duty is shoved on to servants. The low tone of all classes of colonial society in all that concerns

private life is to my mind mainly the result of the lack of education, strenuousness and refinement of the women.

Our friend was a member of the Land Board in his district, a body consisting of two local residents and a paid official acting as chairman. He approved emphatically of the regulations imposed on farmers with regard to the conditions of their dairies, yards and animals, and stated that these conditions had helped to raise the capacity of the farmer and had positively increased the productivity of the land. He gave us a clear account of the alterations in the land-laws since he had been in active life: how in the first days of settlement the Squatter reigned supreme and considered that the country he had opened was inalienably his; how in the reaction against this claim the free-selector has been allowed to take what he chose and leave what he liked, frequently obliging the squatter to buy him off. The present law, by which a specified half of the Squatter's estate can be resumed for free selection, whilst giving the squatter security of tenure for the other half, was to his mind the finest compromise. He was a typical New South Wales citizen. Whilst he was interested in every political problem—the land question, free trade versus protection (he was a mild protectionist) federation &c. and could discuss all with intelligence and information, he was not a party man or at any rate was not a partisan; he could see Reid's good qualities, he gave the present government 'credit' for honesty and efficiency, but on the other hand he thought Barton a finer influence in political life, and agreed more nearly with his views. His name was Matthews, but we always called him 'Benjamin Jones' for he had exactly the same sturdy sense, capacity for clear expression and lack of refinement and charm.

We spent Sunday and Monday at Katoomba with J. Ashton, and were more than ever impressed with the charm of his character, and his general intelligence. We discussed vigorously with him colonial society and politics, and our form of collectivism, and I think we succeeded in very largely changing his point of view. It is curious that the Henry George propaganda out here meant an access of individualism instead of as in England an increase of collectivism, and Ashton, like Wise and Ward (Brisbane editor) had regarded the single tax as the *one* instrument of reform. He won't in the future.

A.G. Austin (ed.), *The Webbs' Australian Diary, 1898* (1965).

EGON KISCH
(1885–1948)

*Czech communist writer and activist. Prague-born Kisch became the centre
of a controversial diplomatic incident, usually known as the 'Kisch affair', in
1934–35. He was invited to speak at the Melbourne Congress of the Movement Against War and Fascism in 1934, but the Australian government
denied him entry to Australia on his arrival in Fremantle in 1934. When his
ship subsequently reached Melbourne, he jumped ashore, breaking his leg in
the process. The multilingual Kisch failed the immigration test that he eventually sat for in Sydney, but the High Court later found it to have been
invalid because of the particular language involved. He finally left Australia
in 1935. In his book* Australian Landfall *(1937), Kisch (or 'our man' as he
calls himself) gives some details about the test.*

DICTATION TEST

'You will now be submitted to a Dictation Test,' Inspector Wilson
announces. 'Write down what Constable McKay will read to you in the
Gaelic language.'

'In Gaelic language?' our man shouts loudly, so that the public
behind the windows may know what is going on—a procedure known
in Drama as a mural or teichoscopy. 'In Gaelic language? It's true I
speak a little Celtic, I was once in Strathnaver' (reminiscence of the
boring conversation with the Scottish cabin companion) 'but it is stupid and unfair to test me with this. You will make the whole of Australia a laughing-stock.'

Whether this seems inconceivable to Inspector Wilson, or whether
he doesn't care if Australia is made a laughing-stock, whichever it is, he
gives a sign to Constable McKay. McKay prepares to read from a thick
book, and our man, who has been given a fountain pen, a sheet of
paper, and a pad to write on, prepares to write. But not what is read
out, however. He will write his above protest. Unfortunately, the fountain pen has the qualification of most fountain pens, it contains no ink.

'There is no ink in this! What sort of a trick is this?' Furiously our
man crumples up the paper and throws it into the face of a detective
who jumps threateningly towards him; an impertinence which let's
hope does not come to the notice of the Berlin *Angriff.* Our man is

brought another fountain pen, which he does not take. Constable McKay reads, our man turns away, but this does not prevent him from exclaiming that the Gaelic words now sound quite different from the first time. So! This fellow does not know Gaelic himself!

A form is made out stating that our man has not passed the test. 'You are under arrest,' proclaims Mr Wilson, and immediately three policemen seize our man, to carry him away. At this moment, Mr Phil Thorne, managing clerk of Jollie Smith, forces his way into the room and offers bail.

'Bail refused,' is the last our man hears, as he is borne away as if on wings.

Australian Landfall, trans. John Fisher and Irene and Kevin Fitzgerald (1969, first published in German 1937).

————

SHIVA NAIPAUL
(1945–85)

Trinidad-born writer. Educated at Oxford University, Shiva Naipaul settled in London, where he wrote both fiction and non-fiction. An experienced traveller, he visited Australia in 1983 as preparation for an intended book, which was never completed because of his death, at the age of forty, from a heart attack. His views about Australian Aborigines were controversial, as can be seen from these comments.

'THE GREAT AUSTRALIAN CONFUSION'

When, in 1872, Anthony Trollope visited Australia, the Aboriginal presence had shrunk to the margins of consciousness. For triumphant settlerdom, the derelict remnants of the dispossessed race no longer constituted a 'question' or a 'problem'. They did not even arouse curiosity or wonder. At best, they were the objects of morbid anthropological scrutiny. The Great Australian Silence had closed in about them. What the gun had started, indifference was bringing to completion. In scattered, isolated reserves out in the sticks, a handful of missionaries was doing what little could be done for the blackfellows, performing, it could be said, the obsequies for a race assumed by most to be doomed to extinction.

In 1872 imperial confidence, vigour and righteousness were in full flood. What would now be referred to as race relations seemed to have been arranged for all time. It was not a good time for those on the lower reaches of the evolutionary scale. Trollope wrote a big, tedious book about the Antipodean colonies. A modest chapter is devoted to the Aborigines. Their fate stirred in him neither compassion nor solicitude. ('The Aboriginal ... whom you are called on to kill,—lest he should kill you or your wife, or because he spears your cattle,—is to be to you the same as a tiger or a snake.') He mocked at those who, surrendering to vague sentiment, praised the dignified bearing displayed by many of the blackfellows. That alleged dignity of deportment, he retorted, represented nothing more than the trickery of a 'sapient monkey'. He was not moved by stories of faithfulness and devotion to duty: exceptional cases of constancy only served to highlight the innate worthlessness and shiftlessness of the race. The Aboriginal, the lowest of the low, was good for nothing; he was not even fit to be a servant, being 'infinitely lower' than the African Negro. The latter, in the cotton and sugar-cane fields of the New World, had demonstrated— under the firm governance of firm masters—his capacity for sustained manual labour. He had shown that he could be civilised into usefulness.

Trollope concedes, without a tremor of discomfort, that the land now so ripe with abundance was, in effect, the booty of dispossession; that Australia was no Terra Nullius, no empty quarter devoid of titles to ownership previous to the appearance of the Europeans. But then— so what? Could—should—what passes for natural justice be allowed to stand in the way of the expansion of the civilising instinct? Should Light, out of a nervous niceness about trespass, shrink before Darkness? The answer was obvious. The Aboriginal, condemned by his own degradation, impervious to improving influences, had sentenced himself. He had to go.

In Trollope's digressions on the Aborigines we see the civilising mission, the dogma of progress, in its most naked aspect. Theirs was to be a defeat without honour or remembrance, with no hint of possible redemption. His bland, brandy-and-water bonhomie adds to our unease. This prolix herald of Anglo-Saxon destiny is the most genial of exterminators—and not without a touch of philanthropy: the blacks, perish though they must, should, he avers, be allowed to slide into distinction 'without unnecessary suffering'.

If Trollope, a century ago, threatened to make the blacks the victims of his imperialist presumption, there are those in our own time who, moved by principles apparently in direct contradiction to those just outlined, are in no less danger of doing something similar. The contemporary mania for preservation, for the restoration of the timeless verities of culture and identity, is as disconcerting as Trollope's genocidal urges. In our day the Aboriginal has been costumed in the haute couture of prevailing intellectual fashion. He has been hailed as an ecological saint, obdurate freedom fighter, mystical dandy. Clothed in the garments of modish fantasy, he has emerged from the mists of forgetfulness.

Last year, towards the end of October, the discovery of a 'lost' Aboriginal clan was announced. Just how lost they actually were is debatable: one of the boys in the group was called Thomas. The excitement generated by this find would, one imagines, have appalled Trollope. The Central Land Council responded with militant rapture—it threatened to prosecute sightseers; anxiety was voiced about the clan's exposure to strange germs; it was rumoured that they were to be honoured by a visit from no less a personage than the Minister of Aboriginal Affairs. The anthropologists responded with caution (that boy Thomas!), sceptical about their scientific value. A reporter—the first on the scene—became almost lyrical in her attempt to describe these lost folk. They were, according to her, both statuesque and delicate of build, with skin of a translucent texture and eyes like deep pools. In a word, they were beautiful—ineffably so. Their nakedness contrasted favourably with the clothes worn by their domesticated brethren living in the out-station to which they had come. These newcomers of lustrous eye and skin had yet to be 'taught shame by the white man'.

Another writer, however, seemed a little piqued with the lost tribe. Their 'coming in' defied the trend towards going out. Across Australia, the Aborigines were on the move, turning their backs on the missions and stations, heading away from contact with a civilisation that had never done them any good. Only when he was allowed to do 'a bit of hunting and food-gathering' did the black begin to recover his spiritual wholeness and reality. The black, it would appear, became himself only when he was restored to some semblance of his original condition and was again a primitive. I use this last term with caution—it had got me into a lot of trouble—though I am not sure why it should be objectionable to so describe those elemental activities associated with nomadism in the desert places.

The writer's ideal Aboriginal (very sad, very lost) talks in a dilapidated patois. '…Want to go back west, me been thinking. I been worry and worry for my country …' It is odd that the quest for authenticity—at any rate in this case—should be coupled to the threadbare rags of a pidgin English which robs the individual of the power of self-expression; a self-expression no doubt available to him in his own language, whose locutions—presumably—could be rendered into grammatical English. But, I suppose, if this were done, his gain in lucidity would be balanced by a diminution of effect. The quasi-romantic belief in an ahistorical Aboriginal essence, beyond the reach of time, beyond—even—the reach of language, is well displayed in the writer's testy sentimentality.

The Great Australian Silence has been replaced by the Great Australian Confusion.

An Unfinished Journey (1986).

11

Missionaries

◆

FREDERICK MACKIE

(1812–93)

English Quaker. Mackie, who was born in Norwich, ran a nursery and later farmed, before beginning to train as a teacher. Between 1852 and 1855 he and Robert Lindsay toured Australia and New Zealand as 'travellers under concern', encouraging and instructing other Quakers. After continuing on to South Africa, Lindsay went back to England, but Mackie returned to South Australia where he married a fellow Quaker. He remained there for much of his life with the exception of a period in Hobart, where he and his wife established a Friends School. He also undertook another mission, this time to India, in 1862. In these entries from Mackie's diary of the 1852–55 Australasian tour, first published in 1973, he writes of his initial New Zealand port of call.

WELLINGTON (1853)

30th. [January] Thankful that we have at length arrived safe at Wellington. Many have been the delays not without danger that we have experienced in making our port. After approaching it again and again, we were becalmed and by the tide carried far away, but the 2nd time of our approach we were becalmed towards evening close in shore, shortly the tide turned and the rapid current drifted us nearer and nearer land, till we were in imminent danger of striking upon rocks. A boat was lowered, the captain thinking that it could tow us off, but it was quite in vain; the anchor was then let go and it held us in 19 fathoms of water off Cape Sinclair though in very uncomfortable proximity to rocks. The wind which for two days had been from SE had it continued from that quarter must to all appearance have driven us upon them, but providentially it sprung up from the contrary direction, NW, though very light. At midnight passengers and crew exerted themselves heaving the anchor, setting the sails and with a boat towing her out to sea, and thankful we were to see her slowly moving from her perilous situation. We gradually lost the unwelcome sound of breakers, and the wind freshening about daylight we entered Wellington Heads. A pilot boarded us and we were safely conducted into a noble land-locked harbour. The land on each side is bold and precipitous, singularly bare of trees but covered with grass and a few low shrubs. The sides of the hills are so steep that land slips are of continual occurrence and there are marks of them in every direction. Behind us on the Southern Island at a distance of about 80 miles, Kaikora, a mountain of about 9000 ft high, was distinctly visible. The summit of its softened outline was whitened with snow and the first rays of the sun shining upon it reminded me of frosted silver.

The town is on the west side of an almost circular harbour and close to the water's edge; so close indeed that there is not more than 20 ft between the houses and the sea. The whole is surrounded by an amphitheatre of hills and these are for the most part bare of trees though green with grass. The hills beyond are densely covered with forest. The houses, all fully exposed to the rays of the sun are mostly built of wood and roofed with shingles, a very few are slated and the slates are brought from England. The want of trees is very striking. The wind was blowing violently when we arrived, and distressing clouds of dust were sweeping along the roads. These high winds we understand are prevalent. We are more forcibly reminded that we are in a foreign land than when we were in VDL by seeing and hearing the natives who are numerous. A custom house boat came off to us manned by N. Zealanders or as they are called here Maoris (pronounced Mouries). They were clothed like English sailors and appeared quick and intelligent. Two of them were tatooed round the mouth and nostrils. One of them had a ribband suspended from his ear with the tooth of some animal attached to it. They make much use of gesticulation even when speaking among themselves. We are now comfortably accommodated at the Wellington Hotel kept by a German Baron von Alzdorf, a very substantial moustachioed looking person. This place, after the privations and discomforts we have experienced on board the Mumford, is quite luxurious, though in England we should look upon the accommodation as somewhat poor and mean. The luxury of cleanliness, pure air and wholesome food, I was never before so capable of appreciating.

Wellington has been colonised thirteen years and contains about 5000 inhabitants. It has had many difficulties to contend with which has very much impeded its advancement. Its first site was on the opposite side of the bay towards the valley of the Hutt, but repeated floods compelled them to remove. A violent earthquake seven years ago, throwing down houses, terrified the settlers and some left in consequence. Then six years back disturbance with the natives placed the lives of many in jeopardy. A good understanding now exists and nothing is to be apprehended from them. One of our friends it will be remembered lost his life about this time in the valley of the Wairau. It contains many agreeable residences and appears to be well supplied with places of worship of various denominations. The gold diggings have produced their effect upon this colony. Many have been induced to leave for Melbourne and great has been the disappointment of some and but few appear to have gained more than they might have done if they had staid with their families, as their labour is exceedingly wanted to get in the harvest.

31st. Yesterday was 1st day. Having had previously a sleepless night and being much exhausted, perfect rest and quiet was needful. This morning after breakfast we called on Daniel Wakefield, the Attorney General, to whom R.L. had a letter of introduction. He lives in a very humble place for such a functionary, but it is only in keeping with an infant colony. His house like almost all others is a one story wood building. It is situated in a small garden sadly wanting a little labour bestowed upon it, but English neatness is never looked for in the colonies, labour is too scarce an article and often not to be bought. He and his wife received us very kindly, and he expressed a desire to do what he could to forward R.L.'s views.

Walking about the town today I noticed several natives. One was dressed in a cloke such as we often see in our museums, of a light colour covered with short black strings. One woman I observed with bare feet, a gown on and a blanket over her head and shoulders. Most of them are tatooed but it is a practice they are beginning to give up. It is supposed that few if any above 30 years of age have not partaken of human flesh, and some are not ashamed to speak of it.

I took a short walk into the bush and was quite astonished at the exuberance and variety of the vegetation; ferns are especially numerous. I soon saw two species of tree ferns. They are graceful trees with trunks 20 to 30 ft high, the fronds of the finest, from 10 to 12 ft long. One has the under side of the frond of silvery whiteness—Cyathea dealbata. Solanum liciniatum [Solanum laciniatum] is common. The hills exposed to the sea are often green with Myoporum laetum and Leptospermum scoparium. An epiphyte—Astelia Banksii is common on the upper branches of the trees and at a distance presents much the appearance of a rookery. The trunks of others are almost enveloped in firns and a grassy leaved plant Freycinetia Banksii. Very few plants are in flower, but almost all are strangers to me, and such as are not cultivated in England. The hillsides are abounding in springs so that the ferns, mosses and lichens are numerous.

We had the pleasure to meet with Thos. Mason in the town in the course of the morning; he had come to Wellington on business. We hope to visit him at the Hutt tomorrow. We have also heard of two others, more or less connected with our society living in Wellington, Edw.ᵈ Catchpool and James Stoddard.

> Mary Nicholls (ed.), *Traveller Under Concern: The Quaker Journals of Frederick Mackie on His Tour of the Australasian Colonies 1852–1855* (1973).

———

LUCY BROAD
(dates unknown)

English temperance worker. Lucy Broad grew up in a Cornish village where she worked for the Band of Hope. After her mother's death she accompanied a friend to the French Riviera in 1897, then rode her bicycle to Italy. In 1898, with her bicycle in her luggage, she went to South Africa, where she spent some three years as a Methodist missionary and Woman's Christian Temperance Union lecturer. After returning to England via Madagascar and Mauritius, she cared for her sick sister for two years. This 'zestful missionary', as historian Jane Robinson calls her, with a 'thirst for speed' and a love of 'escapades', visited Australia (where she spoke at many meetings and services) and New Zealand in 1904–06, before further travels in Samoa, Fiji, the United States, Japan, and Korea. Here she writes about some of her 'wanderings' in New Zealand.

'SCENIC PARADISE'

I always endeavour 'to get even with things,' and so next year I had a try at the track again; a watery world first we found it in the dreary coach drive, then cold on the lake, all lowering above the snow peaks and steep wooded sides. After that, off for the tramp—for the real track must be walked—and surely never could the bush be so lovely but for that *same* rain. Trees are draped and wreathed, branches and trunks cushioned in swaying ferns, and such mosses, hanging off a good foot long of daisy fringe. In dry weather these long lines lightly swaying, have a cordy, frippery look, but when soaked with rain it is a fairy palace of delights; the rich golden green a setting for sparklets, the twisted gleaming branches a frame for loveliest ferny nooks; transformation scenes indeed, when rain or snow gives dignity and depth to them!

And so we found the Clinton Valley on the downward track, its snow-dressed peaks up to Balloon Mountain and the Pass, shutting in this realm of beauty with massive walls and uprisings of rock, all laced with watery ribbons of crystal springing over in every direction. Over the Pass, in the snow, we found a white world and a wet one; paths crumbling, rocks slipping, feet deep in the under ooze, and here and there the pure, serene of the Mountain Lily! Dainty, delicate, queenly, standing well above the globular, flashing leaves are the flowers in clusters of anything up to a score, the snow-white petals slightly crinkled and scalloped, surrounding their golden, central eye. A dream of pure, unsullied loveliness; and we found thousands of them scattered on the mountain side, later when the snow was gone.

The Sutherland Falls are like certain long-necked youngsters, who find merit enough in being an inch or two above their fellows, and so stretch their limbs in everybody's way with no other redeeming feature. But his Majesty (whether he knows it or not) has so many other aqueous rivals on the track. Lake Ada, seen through a gleaming of great tree fern plumes, from the terrace walk, is all that is sweet, that a lake should be; and then for waterfalls, streams, and rivers! We looked into the depth of the snow at the Pass and said, 'It really is blue, there is a dash of the blue-bag down through the clefts'; and here the Arthur River, as it seethes over great boulders, cools its masses of lather-foam in lakelets of delicious green. Oh, fair, sweet world, and to think of a thousand miles of it—trackless and unsurveyed—stretching away and away here!

Oh, if you go to an evening party, you only speak of three or four who were the belles of the evening—how they looked, what they wore—that is what I am doing, there are hosts of other beauties about that you can just suppose are there; I give them a nod in passing. Some of 'em ain't beauties, there are the sand-flies that pounce on you as soon as you leave the boat, and stick by every step of the way; you may think you are clear of them, but only you sit down for a lunch or a loving look, and there are twenty of them hovering round your nose and looking for a favourite pitching place. By this time you have a necklace and bracelets of ugly bites, each with an irritating head, besides sundry reminders elsewhere; but these are trifles, you must always suffer for the cause somehow.

One gets some curious experiences at the rest houses, especially of some people who do nothing but car and drive at home, and yet think they can tramp it here. Such a party came up when I was on the backward track, the ladies in trimmest of tailor-made short skirts and high-topped boots—lightness and ease are my essentials. But, alas, they had found blistered feet already, and one exclaimed, despairingly, 'Why did I ever leave my comfortable home? and how am I to get back there again from these wilds?' Another good gentleman disgraced the visitors' book with the words, 'Track beastly.' They had only gone part way, and his wife had been so distressed at the broken pathway down from the Pass, that she told me she had stretched by its side and cried.

Memories of 'The Scenic Paradise of New Zealand' throng on me, but I will only speak of our experiences at the Otteira Gorge. There had been heavy rains, and when we arrived at Springfield it was to find the river running like mad. 'She's rising now,' said our driver, as our coaching party started; and so it proved, and we were ordered back again.

On the next morning we set out for a second try with a smaller party in two coaches. But, indeed, the river looked weird and wild, with its brown surge tearing away over great drifts of cobbles and pebbles in two or three divisions. The ordinary ford, which is made by banking up and levelling a ridge of stones, was all swept away. The coaches are strongly built with great tiers of springs, that allow of their tilting to an extraordinary degree; but when, with rattle and bounce they took to the water, swing they did, and no mistake! Two smart whips had come down on horseback to see us through, and there was the road-man on his white pony, prodding about and trying the depth. A grand excitement it was, and I closed my eyes the first time at the critical point, not wishing to see us go over.

Then followed a short distance over the oozy sloppy roads, and we had the river to cross again, and after that hills to climb up and up to the highest, inhabited point. Then another spread out series of roaring rivers to tackle. We were barely through one when our spring bolt snapped; there was a rapid halloo to the front coach, and we were all turned out, blessing ourselves that it did not break in the middle of the current, and admiring the celerity of the repairs. But certainly our fourth crossing was the worst. *We* had the experience of the first coach to profit by, and away they went, bounding, swaying into the torrent; the driver calling, the brave horses straining, the outriders hovering on the watch! But, alas, there was an ugly rise and a horrible jolt to go up, and the upper part of the coach rose almost to the perpendicular. We depended they were over, and so, in turn, did they us a little later.

Then followed a hurried consultation, and our driver set his face to try further down stream, and as he says, 'always means to do a thing when he goes for it,' and done it was, but by a near shave we knew. It is just the keeping going that saves them at the critical juncture, and I did not know which to admire most, the men or the horses. They did it well and no mistake! Our coachee was an illustration of the all-round life of the colonial. First for eighteen years a chemist, which nearly killed him; then working ironmonger, and finishing up with this tough work before his pension comes.

After this it is away and away for the wonders of the gorge itself. There is the head-long declivity where you are threatened with being engulphed by the hillside sliding off in patches to the far-away bottom. Waterfalls poured over these steep hillsides in threads and veils of foam; but the trot swung us on, and corner after corner was rounded just in the nick of time and space. The road we were to reach in the bottom looked like the veriest sheep track, and our front line of vision taking in the horses tails and the front-rows back hat brims. Quiet for the most part were we, save for the hoof-beats and the flying stones; and then would come a deep breath, and remarks flew round again. How poor we are in adjectives; but this was supreme of its sort!

A Woman's Wanderings the World Over (1909).

———

JESSIE ACKERMANN

(*c.* 1860s– ?)

American temperance worker. Chicago-based Ackermann was a 'round-the-world missionary' for the Woman's Christian Temperance Union, helping to organise branches and their activities. A strong campaigner for woman's suffrage, she visited Australia several times between 1889 and 1912. Australian flora, among many other subjects, attracts her attention in her 1913 study of Australia.

AUSTRALIAN FLORA

There are few really striking features in an Australian landscape. The mountains are scarcely more than one line after another of foothills, with the exception of two or three ranges, which, at most, fall far short of mountain heights elsewhere. These stretch themselves along in the general direction of the coast-line, breaking the monotony of the flat plains, and lend a fine setting to cities snuggled away in the valleys. This leaves the interior a great flat basin, awesome to behold, but, like all weird solitudes, it is wildly fascinating.

The Blue Mountains of New South Wales are the most imposing, both in relation to elevation and variety of vegetation. The highest point of this glorious range has been chosen by about half a dozen retired squatters as a summer resort from the busy world, and it is truly another world from that of the plains. The rain, snow, and cold are too severe for winter residence. One need not dwell upon the details of sunrise and sunset, lights and shadows, spring and autumn colouring; they are common to mountains everywhere, but seem to reach a climax under these clear southern skies and vaulted heavens. As the greatest height is barely above 7000 feet, perpetual snows are unknown. In the sheltered gullies a remarkable tree, semi-tropical in appearance, flourishes even in the snow regions. The huge fronds, feathery and graceful, look out through the light snows with a majestic air of conscious beauty, while almost every other tree is denuded of summer garb.

For centuries Nature has been silently constructing show places beneath these mountains that rival anything human genius has been able to produce. The limestone caverns are marvels of delicate loveliness, such as nothing but the ages could create. Vivid recollections of my first visit to the Jenolan Caves twenty years ago come to mind as I write. The trip was a long, hard one, made by private conveyance. Upon reaching the Cave House, I was ushered into the bridal-chamber—lonely quarters for a bachelor girl—where reposed a suit of men's apparel in which to array myself for an underground expedition. The blue cotton trousers reached only to my shoe-tops, and there was an absence of the usual gearing which must lend a sense of security to that cut of garment. We carried torches, and provisions were also necessary, as the trip required either a full day or the entire night. Never shall I forget how the guide pointed out all sorts of fierce, weird, and unearthly things which took shape and form according to the degree of individual imagination. It was hard work, this wriggling along narrow passages and crawling snake-fashion through others, emerging with blistered hands, red face, and disordered locks; but such was the price of 'seeing the caves' in those early years.

Much of this real enjoyment and wholesome fatigue has vanished. The Government has thrown up great highways, constructed railways, and hewn out motor-roads to facilitate travel for those attracted by this form of natural beauty. It has become a popular honeymoon trip, but the abbreviated garments of my first visit are no longer necessary. The present-day bride returns from her subterranean exploits free from any evidences of the trip. The caves are now well lighted by electricity, which reveals much that was formerly hidden. The colouring is so vivid that a fertile imagination may weave the fantastic forms into both the grotesque and beautiful.

In some sections of the island the timber forests are so dense and dark that it would be no misnomer to designate them the Black Forest of Australia. Gippsland is said to produce the tallest trees in the world. So huge are they that I hesitate to deal in dimensions, fearing the charge that they are of mental growth, created to fit imaginary figures.

Of the hundreds of families of trees, the outstanding, ever-present one, which looms large upon the horizon at every turn and takes rootage where the slightest nourishment is found, is the gum, or eucalyptus family, including over three hundred varieties. Some of these are among the most beautiful specimens that soil could produce—rich in foliage, glorious in boom, and valuable as timber. The white blossoms attract thousands of swarms of bees, both wild and from domestic hives. The flower is sweet, and adds great medicinal value to the honey. At eventide and early morning, the air is scented for miles around with the rich and refreshing perfume The red blooms are most vivid in colour, hang in great clusters, and are much used for decoration. Flowering trees are a feature of the winter season, and are far too numerous to name. Bright yellow, all shades of red, and many tints peculiar to this climate dot the plains, presenting a sense of real life in desert places, where they also abound.

On the west coast a most peculiar small tree, known as the 'Black Boy,' flourishes on the hillsides, and forms a fascinating feature of ugliness. It has no market value, but lends a picturesque touch to the landscape, which otherwise is bleak and sterile. The trunk is perfectly black, barren of growth except at the extreme top, where a long fringe of narrow leaves droops towards the ground, forming a more complete skirt than any garment ever worn by the natives.

As the island extends into the tropics, and through the semi-tropical and temperate zones, it is easy to imagine that climatic conditions would produce an endless variety of tree life, which must, of necessity, create a beauty not to be despised, although of an unusual character.

In the North-West the whole aspect of the country changes. Large trees vanish. The sand plains are covered with bushes, most of which are ablaze with tiny flowers of every possible shape and shade. They are really the 'saving clause' of many a mile through the weird 'Never-Never', and are the redeeming feature of 'No Man's Land.' Some of the small trees on the plains produce wooden fruit. I have gathered these products in both Western Australia and New South Wales, as perfect in shape as the rarest table fruit ever produced. In the former State I made a fine collection of wooden peaches. These were not like Yankee nut-megs, made by hand, but are a genuine growth of the trees upon the sand plains.

A great drawback to Australia, not only from the natural aspect point of view, but, more important, from that of cultivation, is the lack of rivers and the uncertainty of rainfall, upon which all agricultural development depends. There are a number of rivers, but none of them is to be compared with the great waterways of other countries. The water question will always remain one for the most serious considera-tion, chiefly because the mountains follow the coast-line. For some years the rainfall in the most populated places has been equal to requirements. This has brought unprecedented prosperity, and the country has forged ahead in leaps and bounds.

No mind can imagine what the calamity of a drought is like. I chanced to be in the country some years ago during such a period. Thousands and thousands of sheep lay dead upon the plains. From every direction droves of cattle, almost obscured by clouds of choking dust, tottered their famished way toward some coastal water supply. Men and women, hopeless with a despair which 'maketh the soul sick,' fled, leaving their possessions behind, and endured the long march over hot, cracked, baked, and burning earth in search of life-giving water. Those soul-stirring words of Longfellow, descriptive of a famine, could well be applied to the situation:

> 'Thirsty was the air around us,
> Thirsty was the sky above us,
> And the thirsty stars of heaven
> Like the eyes of dying men glared on us.'

Oh, the horror of it!—a horror which entered my very soul; the memory of it is graven upon my consciousness, never to be obliterated. To this day, when I see a patch of dry earth, the cry for water is so painful that I long and long to drench it until not another drop can be absorbed. It is years since the people have suffered the visitation of a drought; but the natural conditions render them as possible in the future as they were certain in the past.

During a later visit, when on the eastern coast, an awful flood sub-merged a vast section of the Newcastle district; I witnessed the devasta-tion at close range The water rose so high that people rushed to the house-tops, and fled to the hills for safety. I joined a Government relief steamer that visited the spot. In sending out small boats with food to the people on the hills, we frequently rowed over the buildings, only the extreme top of a chimney indicating where a house stood. The desolation was heart-sickening. Houses were swept away and came floating down the river with furniture, hay-stacks, dead sheep, horses, cattle, and, occasionally, a human form—man, woman, or child. The calamity that threatens from an excess or the lack of water is almost unthinkable.

Like America, the size of the country affords scope for great happenings. A disaster which reduces one section of it to a camp of misery and want may be utterly unfelt in other parts. There are floods, cyclones, earthquakes, and fires which are most shocking, and yet so purely local as not to make an impress on the country generally.

A short time ago, when a howling wind was blowing at a fierce pace, the cry of 'the mountain is afire' was heard in the watches of the night. We all rushed to the nearest window, and no pen or words could describe what we saw. A bush-fire had broken out on one of the foothills. At every fresh gust of wind, the flames rolled upward like unbroken waves of the sea. They mounted higher and higher, spreading wider and wider, until the very heavens became like a sheet of moving lava. The morning saw only the charred and blackened stumps of the few remaining trees. Horrible as it was, it was merely local, and created no special stir, although the capital city at one time seemed threatened with sure and certain destruction.

During the summer months the country, in aspect, reaches the very acme of all desolation. Every blade of grass withers to a dismal and forlorn yellow; not a real yellow, but burnt and hopeless, a sort of this-is-the-end-of-me shade. Flowers disappear, and the very stalks drop off at the roots; disagreeable sand-storms smite one right and left; the hot winds, like an escaped breath from the nether world, circle about in fiendish delight. This, however, is greatly to be desired—even at 108 or 114 degrees in the shade—when compared with the humid parts where the wilted people droop with the whole surroundings.

This may all seem most uninviting, but the very vastness of it is compelling. I have stood under the blighting sun when the semi-tropical rays get into the very blood and bones, with dead sheep and dying cattle on every hand; when the over-heated sand came stinging its way over hands and face, until I seemed rooted to the place, unable to move. This awful warring of the elements carries a strange spell in its track. The possibilities of it all are overpowering. Comparatively few people have been in those places where Father Time whets his scythe and Death is double-armed with fatal darts, for such scenes are limited to certain sections, and are not liable to frequent recurrence.

It is rather remarkable how soon the discomforts of the dry season are forgotten with the coming of the rain. The feeling which prevailed among the ancient Egyptians at the moment of the overflow of the Nile, and prompted long watches, which were spent listening for the voice of the Sphinx, is, as it were, reflected in Australia when the rains, which alone assure a bountiful harvest, set in. I have known members of a family to wire the news to others of the household travelling thousands of miles away, 'It rains! It rains!'

In a single week of rain the whole country begins to burst into life— and such life! Never was a greater transformation brought about in less time! A month later, no one would recognise a single locality. Everything springs into beauty. Shrubs, plants, grasses, creepers, and carpet upon carpet of endless variety of wild flowers, colour the earth from one end of the island almost to the other. In fact, wild flowers in winter are the great feature of Australia.

Scientists declare that most of the flora is distinctively Australian. These primitive types exist elsewhere in fossil form only, as belonging to the past ages of a country. Bacon says, 'God Almighty first planted a garden.' Perhaps this was the spot! There are three thousand families, not to speak of family branches of wild flowers, and nearly three hundred known specimens of orchids, which, although delicate and fragile to look upon, seem hardy and vigorous. The colouring is faint and tint-like rather than decided, and the fantastic-fringed forms are among the wonders of the floral kingdom. Then there are the rugged, sturdy, almost bold families which fairly force themselves upon notice, and demand attention whether one will or not. The Kangaroo Paw is a compelling, saucy-looking, haughty-headed flower, with monkey-like hair—a real outstanding growth upon the stem, which shades into grey as it nears the blossom. Hair is not peculiar to it alone, for there are many hairy plants to be found, especially in desert places.

The sand is as productive of plant-life as the richer forms of soil. In the northern part I have seen miles and miles literally covered with pink, yellow, red, blue, and variegated flowers, some of which take rootage in cracks in the rocks, where they thrive in a scanty supply of yellow sand. At a picnic not far from a large city, I gathered nearly two hundred varieties of flowers without leaving one hill.

The people are flower enthusiasts—not one class, but almost everybody. Children roll in flowers, caress, fondle, and gather them from the beginning to the end of the season. Flower excursions are arranged by the Government and form a most popular outing. These take place on the half-holidays, and frequently are repeated on Sundays, when whole families leave the city and spend the day with the flowers in the country. I never saw such a sight in my life. I have spent hours at a time at stations, merely watching the crowds, trying to study the relation of flowers to the people. What a day they have had! The older ones read or visit; but the children! The joy and happiness of those droves of youngsters as they romp and roll and tumble about amongst a multitude of blossoms is a delight simply to contemplate. A flower show in a great city can in no way compare with these open-air, admission-free exhibitions, where every flower-voice invites the weary and heavy laden, the toilsome and discouraged, to come and rest in Nature's bowers. By night the baskets are filled, bunches are tied up, and men and women are decorated with them wherever a stem can be thrust or a festoon hung. These gay, happy crowds plunder the fields, but soon every trace of their pillage will be covered with brighter freshness, and the scene repeats itself, until the earth refuses, for a time, to array herself in her festive garb.

Australia from a Woman's Point of View (1913).

FREDERIC C. SPURR

(dates unknown)

British Baptist minister. Spurr was a Baptist minister at Cardiff (1886–90), the missioner for the Baptist Union of Great Britain and Ireland (1890–1904), and the pastor at Maze Pond, Old Kent Road (1904–09), before spending five years as the minister of the First Baptist Church in Melbourne (1909–14). He was also president of the Baptist Union of Victoria (1913–14). In his book Five Years Under the Southern Cross *(1915), which is based upon articles that he wrote for the English* Christian World *about life in Australia, the Reverend Spurr reflects upon the influence of climate on religious customs.*

CHRISTMAS IN AUSTRALIA

But the British who first came out also brought with them a set of traditional sentiments associated with their religion. December 21 was known to them as the shortest day of the year. Christmas was observed in a setting of ice and snow. Santa Claus was a creature of the cold, and appeared enveloped in furs. The Watch Night service was celebrated in the gloomiest time of the year. Advent was the ecclesiastical season appropriate, by reason of shortening days, for meditating upon the end of all things. On the long and dismal nights of December, Spohr's 'Last Judgment' seemed a fitting work to be performed. And last, the pioneers—many of them Scotch—brought with them the Puritan spirit and austerity.

And the climate mocked these traditional sentiments. December 21 turned out to be the longest, the brightest, and often the hottest day of the year. Christmas fell in the midsummer, when frequently the heat is almost unsupportable. The familiar ice and snow were entirely absent. Santa Claus in furs appeared ludicrous. December was far too cheerful a month for the encouragement of gloomy thoughts upon the end of all things. The cricket and the frog, the 'possum and the jackass, the mina and the thrush, all threw out their defiant challenge to Spohr and his awe-inspiring work.

And the climate is triumphing. It is true the traditional 'Father Christmas' appears in more than one place in Australia. But a new 'Father Christmas' is arising. He does not descend chimneys, nor shiver with the cold, nor affect snow trappings. He drives along the streets in a bush wagon drawn by bush ponies. The new 'Father Christmas' is an Australian, pure and simple. The children understand him and revere him— so far as Australian children revere anything. He is essentially modern. He has no ancient history behind him, and in this particular he matches the country. The new 'Father Christmas' is a product of the climate. A new Christmas Day has also dawned. The dear old Christmas 'at home' is—or was—a time of reunion. It was essentially a domestic festival. In Australia it is a holiday, pure and simple. Thousands of people take their annual vacation at Christmas, and thousands more leave home for mountain and seaside. The coastal steamers are crowded with passengers. At Christmastide the churches in the city are thinly attended; most of the regular worshippers are away on holiday. Again the climate has triumphed. Turkey and plum-pudding still garnish the tables, but they are doomed. It is only a question of time, and there will be celebrated underneath the Southern Cross a Christmas festival as different from that which is known 'at home' as the poles are apart from each other.

A new 'Watch Night' service has been created. Through dismal streets, with snow or sleet, and in the teeth of a biting wind, the old folk in the Old Country trudged to the warmed church on the last night of the year. When the clock sounded the hour of midnight everybody felt relieved. The tension was over. The corner had been turned. From that moment the days would lengthen until the height of summer. But in Australia there is nothing to suggest solemnity. The last night of the old year is a warm, delightful summer night, redolent with the perfume of a hundred balms and the stifling scent of a thousand flowers. Do what one will, it is impossible, in these conditions, to impart reality into a hymn which speaks of 'Days and moments quickly flying.' It is the fault of the climate. The Puritan spirit is departing—yea! has well-nigh departed. A handful of folk are left who would in no wise travel on the Sabbath nor permit the piano to be used for secular purposes. The pioneers were severe, austere, rigid in their Puritanism. The original 'Scots' Church' resembled a barn. The present 'Scots' Church' in the city is a cathedral, containing one of the finest organs in Victoria—or anywhere else. The contrast between the two buildings marks the difference between the Puritanical spirit of seventy years ago and the light, gay spirit of to-day. Fathers who would on no account pay visits on the Sabbath have begotten sons who go to church when they please—which is not often—and who spend the majority of their Sundays on the golf course or on the bay. The temper of the people has entirely changed. And the climate has done it.

Five Years Under the Southern Cross (1915).

———

ARTHUR CONAN DOYLE
(1859–1930)

British doctor and writer. Doyle, who was born in Scotland to parents from Irish Catholic families, trained in medicine at Edinburgh University. Between 1887 and 1927 he published numerous stories featuring his very popular fictitious private detective, Sherlock Holmes. Doyle's other publications include The War in South Africa *(1902), which he wrote after serving as a doctor in the Boer War. His longstanding interest in the supernatural intensified after the deaths of his eldest son and youngest brother in the First World War. In 1920–21 he visited Australia and New Zealand to lecture on the subject of spiritualism. While in Australia he reputedly addressed 50 000 people at twenty-five meetings. His reception in Melbourne in October–November 1920 was particularly noteworthy.*

THE 'GENERAL PSYCHIC CONDITIONS OF MELBOURNE'

But these be deep waters. Let me get back to my own humble experiences, these interpolated thoughts being but things which have been found upon the wayside of our journey. On reaching Melbourne we were greeted at the station by a few devoted souls who had waited for two trains before they found us. Covered with the flowers which they had brought we drove to Menzies Hotel, whence we moved a few days later to a flat in the Grand, where we were destined to spend five eventful weeks. We found the atmosphere and general psychic conditions of Melbourne by no means as pleasant or receptive as those of Adelaide, but this of course was very welcome as the greater the darkness the more need of the light. If Spiritualism had been a popular cult in Australia there would have been no object in my visit. I was welcome enough as an individual, but by no means so as an emissary, and both the Churches and the Materialists, in most unnatural combination, had done their best to make the soil stony for me. Their chief agent had been the *Argus*, a solid, stodgy paper, which amply fulfilled the material needs of the public, but was not given to spiritual vision. This paper before my arrival had a very violent and abusive leader which attracted much attention, full of such terms as 'black magic,' 'Shamanism,' 'witchcraft,' 'freak religion,' 'cranky faith,' 'cruelty,' 'black evil,' 'poison,' finishing up with the assertion that I represented 'a force which we believe to be purely evil.' This was from a paper which wholeheartedly supports the liquor interest, and has endless columns of betting and racing news, nor did its principles cause it to refuse substantial sums for the advertising of my lectures. Still, however arrogant or illogical, I hold that a paper has a perfect right to publish and uphold its own view, nor would I say that the subsequent refusal of the *Argus* to print any answer to its tirade was a real breach of the ethics of journalism. Where its conduct became outrageous, however, and where it put itself beyond the pale of all literary decency, was when it reported my first lecture by describing my wife's dress, my own voice, the colour of my spectacles, and not a word of what I said. It capped this by publishing so-called answers to me by Canon Hughes, and by Bishop Phelan—critics whose knowledge of the subject seemed to begin and end with the witch of Endor—while omitting the statements to which these answers applied. Never in any British town have I found such reactionary intolerance as in this great city, for though the *Argus* was the chief offender, the other papers were as timid as rabbits in the matter. My psychic photographs which, as I have said, are the most wonderful collection ever shown in the world, were received in absolute silence by the whole press, though it is notorious that if I had come there with a comic opera or bedroom comedy instead of with the evidence of a series of miracles, I should have had a column. This seems to have been really due to moral cowardice, and not to ignorance, for I saw a private letter afterwards in which a sub-editor remarked that he and the chief leader-writer had both seen the photographs and that they could see no possible answer to them.

There was another and more pleasing side to the local conditions, and that lay in the numbers who had already mastered the principles of Spiritualism, the richer classes as individuals, the poorer as organised churches. They were so numerous that when we received an address of welcome in the auditorium to which only Spiritualists were invited by ticket, the Hall, which holds two thousand, was easily filled. This would mean on the same scale that the Spiritualists of London could fill the Albert Hall several times over—as no doubt they could. Their numbers were in a sense an embarrassment, as I always had the fear that I was addressing the faithful instead of those whom I had come so far to instruct. On the whole their quality and organisation were disappointing. They had a splendid spiritual paper in their midst, the *Harbinger of Light*, which has run for fifty years, and is most ably edited by Mr Britton Harvey. When I think of David Gow, Ernest Oaten, John Lewis and Britton Harvey I feel that our cause is indeed well represented by its press. They have also some splendid local workers, like Bloomfield and Tozer, whole-hearted and apostolic. But elsewhere there is the usual tendency to divide and to run into vulgarities and extravagances in which the Spiritual has small share. Discipline is needed, which involves central powers, and that in turn means command of the purse. It would be far better to have no Spiritual churches than some I have seen.

The Wanderings of a Spiritualist (1921).

12

Sightseers

♦

WILLIAM ARCHER

(1856–1924)

British drama critic. Scottish-born Archer studied at Edinburgh University before undertaking a year-long world journey in 1876–77 during which he visited Australia and America. While in Australia he spent time with his parents, who then were living on a family property, Gracemere, in central Queensland about eleven kilometres from Rockhampton. According to the editor of Archer's account of his Australian journey, which was written in late 1877 but not published until 1977, 'Australia seems to have made little lasting impression upon Archer', despite his family's continuing links with that country. Although Archer, who settled in London in 1878, subsequently trained as a lawyer he never practised, becoming instead a respected drama critic, credited with raising the standard of the English theatre. Well known for his translations of Henrik Ibsen's plays, he also wrote one successful play himself, a melodramatic work entitled The Green Goddess *(1921). Archer, who claimed in February 1876 to have 'a travelling mania', includes his impressions of Rockhampton in his Australian narrative.*

ROCKHAMPTON (1876)

Rockhampton is not one of those towns which impress the traveller at first sight. Its inhabitants are very proud of its beauty, whence it may be presumed that after a time it 'grows upon one'—but as my stay in it was not long enough to produce that effect, I must continue to regard it as one of the least beautiful places it has been my fortune to visit. The principal part of the town is situated on the south bank of the Fitzroy. Opposite it, on the north side of the river rise two of the aforesaid woolly mountains known as Mount Archer and Mount Berserker, forming part of a short chain called the Berserker range. These hills partially obstruct the sea breeze, and Rockhampton has deservedly gained the reputation of being one of the hottest places in the colony. There is a popular legend to the effect that its deceased inhabitants, though departing as a rule to regions supposed to be unpleasantly sultry, are obliged to *send up for their blankets* in order to maintain the degree of warmth to which they have been accustomed on earth. The Rockhamptonites therefore regard this life as strictly and literally a 'preparation for the next' or, in other words, a sort of acclimatization process.

The ground on which the town is situated is almost perfectly level. Some of the outer streets are subject to inundation, but no flood as yet on record has reached the inner portions. It is quite possible, however, that some tremendous flood may one day or other do terrible damage to the town. Barely twenty years have elapsed since the first white men settled in the district, and the oldest black inhabitants tell stories of enormous inundations before the arrival of the earliest settlers. 'Bime-by', says the patriarch of the region, 'plenty big water come up. White fellows' humpies', with an expressive gesture and a grin of quiet satis-faction, 'all go 'way down.' The warnings of this swarthy Cassandra have hitherto been systematically pooh-poohed, but it is by no means impossible that Rockhampton may one day meet with the fate of Gundagai and many other Australian towns. Such of the inhabitants as have any apprehensions, trust to being able to take refuge on the 'Athel-stane Range', a line of ridges at the back of the town, on which the Hospital, the Orphanage and the houses of some wealthy inhabitants are situated. This place of retreat would probably prevent any great loss of life, but the destruction of property would be enormous.

Like all Australian towns, Rockhampton gives the traveller fresh from home an impression as if it were flattened down. There are not, I should think, twenty two-storied buildings in the whole place. As the value of land increases the height of the houses is naturally increasing along with it, but as yet Rockhampton is distinctly a one-storied town. The post office, the court house, one of the newspaper offices, one or two of the banks and some large shops are as yet almost the only two-storied buildings. At home twenty or thirty thousand people would be accommodated comfortably in the same space which here supports seven thousand. Another feature which strikes the visitor forcibly at first is the almost exclusive prevalence of corrugated iron roofs which glare hotly in the sun and from a distance give the town somewhat the appearance of one of our great factories where the work is carried on in separate buildings. This system of iron roofing has its advantages and its disadvantages. In a climate like that of Queensland it makes a house almost unbearably hot, whereas the ordinary 'shingle' roofing is several degrees cooler. But, on the other hand, an iron roof is always watertight, and affords a means of obtaining pure rain-water, which is by far the best for drinking water obtainable in Australia. The rain-water which comes from the shingles is always discoloured and has an astringent taste which renders it unpleasant, though not, I believe, unwholesome.

The streets of Rockhampton are laid out at right angles to each other and are all wide, well laid thoroughfares. Verandahs project almost everywhere over the side walks and afford a much-needed shade and shelter to the foot passengers. The principal business street is named East Street and contains, besides the post office and one of the newspaper offices, a number of really handsome and well-provided shops and stores. Most of the shops are now, so to speak, 'specialized', that is, devoted to the sale of one particular class of articles, but there are still several 'stores' at which anything may be obtained, from an anchor to a darning needle, from a Turkey carpet to a pot of marmalade. The liquor-trade is unfortunately by far the most flourishing of all. At one place where two streets cross each other, each of the four corners is occupied by a public-house. It is said that there is one public-house for every seven houses in Rockhampton. The words 'public-house', 'tavern' and 'inn' are, however, quite unknown in Australia. Every little grog-shop is a 'Hotel', generally rejoicing in the most high sounding and aristocratic title. Each little township in the colony has its 'Criterion', its 'Metropolitan' or its 'National' Hotel. I was once forced to pass a night at an establishment called the 'Mulgrave Hotel'—not in Rockhampton, but in another town of considerable size. The stock of silver in the hostelry consisted, if the Hibernianism may be allowed, of one Britannia-metal teaspoon, with which the dirty servant-girl stirred each cup of tea before handing it round, sublimely oblivious of differences of taste with regard to sugar and milk. In Rockhampton, I believe, there are two or three excellent inns, but the rest of the 'Hotels' are drinking shops of the most pronounced description. The good burghers of the town are by no means behindhand in supporting these institutions, but the 'bushmen' who visit the town in large numbers form another great source of wealth to them. These dashing individuals, after a year or two in the bush away from public-houses and their delights, have usually accumulated a considerable 'pile'. As soon as this pile is large enough to make it worth while they come down to one or other of the towns to 'knock down their cheques'—a proceeding which consists in handing over their wealth to some publican, who then provides them with lodging and drink—food being of minor importance—until the value of the 'cheque' has been consumed, or until the caterer chooses to assert that it has. Thereupon the bushman returns to his shepherding, droving, or fencing as the case may be and proceeds to get together another pile with which to do likewise. I have seen one man who is said to have 'knocked down' £500 (a remittance from home) at one public-house in a bush township, and who is consequently regarded with respect mingled with awe by all his comrades, whose debauches seldom exceed £40 or £50. This form of 'enjoyment' is, it is true, more common in the smaller bush settlements than in Rockhampton, but it is by no means unknown even in that centre of civilization.

In the society of Rockhampton there are three grades, or even four if we reckon the numerous 'squatters' who come in from the surrounding stations and answer, as it were, to the 'country people' of a country town at home. The aristocrats of the town itself are the government officers, bankers, lawyers, doctors, and 'agents'—in short, all who are not actually engaged in retail trading. Then come the large and prosperous shop-keepers and their employees, and lastly the small shop-keepers, mechanics, manual labourers, etc. Each of these charmed circles, besides possessing numerous minor cliques within itself, is as haughtily exclusive towards its inferior caste as it could possibly be in a country of the most aristocratic institutions. It is only natural that democratic political organization should be accompanied by a plutocratic form of society, but in the smaller towns of a new country this defect is always exaggerated. To an outsider a study of the graduations of caste, so impalpable to himself, so painfully palpable to the initiated is always both instructive and amusing. I was present at a ball in Rockhampton given by the Volunteer Corps. As these gallant defenders of their country do not necessarily belong to the *élite*, the invitations issued were naturally not quite so select as they might have been. Consequently, a dire struggle went on in the minds of those who considered themselves the *crème de la crème*. The monotony of existence in Rockhampton is not so often broken as to render it an easy matter to resist the temptation of a ball merely because there is a danger of meeting at it people whose income is a hundred a year less than one's own. Yet the risks to be run were enormous. It was rumoured that even butchers and bakers might be expected to be present, and there was almost a certainty of being brought into contact with booksellers and apothecaries—not to mention their wives and daughters. Very few, however, resisted the temptation. Many quieted their conscience by professing that they went only to look on, and would by no means join in the Terpsichorean barbarities of the vulgar herd. It ended, I am happy to say, in everyone dancing and enjoying him or herself as much as possible under the circumstances, for the evening was swelteringly hot, and the music, which was discoursed by the volunteer band, was not of the first quality; but, on the whole, the ball was voted by everyone a decided success.

Raymond Stanley (ed.), *Tourist to the Antipodes: William Archer's 'Australian Journey, 1876–77'* (1977).

RICHARD TANGYE

(1833–1906)

*English engineer. A member of a Cornish Quaker family, Tangye was origi-
nally a teacher. He successfully developed a Birmingham engineering firm
that he joined in 1855, building new works near by in 1862, in Belgium in
1863, and in London in 1868. A leading community figure, he founded the
Birmingham* Daily Argus *in 1891. He visited Australia several times, on
one occasion in search of health, apparently having become the victim of
overwork. Here he reminisces about an excursion that he once undertook
from Melbourne.*

TO THE BLACK SPUR AND BACK

A favourite excursion from Melbourne is to the Black Spur Mountains,
about two days' drive from the city. Leaving Melbourne the route passes through some miles of suburban villa residences with beautiful gardens. After about ten miles 'the bush' is reached, and continues for the
remainder of the journey, relieved here and there by a clearing or by a
little village. The term 'bush' must not be understood as scrub, furze,
etc., but all kinds of uncultivated land, thick forests, and open country.
A curious feature of colonial life is to see in full operation the old stage
coaches, so long ago discarded in England. They are painted a brilliant
red, and indeed appear to be the veritable machines used in the 'good
old days when George the Third was king.' They are frequently drawn
by six or more horses, and, true to their ancient traditions, now and
then have a spill, for roadmakers in the Colonies have the same habit as
their English brethren of making short 'right about turns' at the bottom of steep hills. We drew up at a small wayside inn, intending to bait
the horses, but found it was closed, owing to the death of the landlord.
This man was a large wine grower, and his vineyards extended for a
considerable distance round his house. After passing through many
miles of country under vine cultivation we pulled up for the night at a
little village called Healesville, where a very miscellaneous company sat
down to a substantial repast, ending with what the waiter called a
'soafler.' The light being dim it was difficult to see what the dish really
was, and curiosity being awakened, inquiry elicited the fact that it was
intended for a *soufflé.* The hotel being quite full of visitors, two of our

party had to sleep in the parlour on sofas of the horse-hair order. The landlord, coming in to see if we were all right, informed us we could not have our boots cleaned in the morning, as his man was just then out on a boose. A colonial friend travelling with us remarked that it was 'awkward when master or man took to boosing.' Our friend had previously told us that the landlord was generally 'on that line.' 'You never saw me boosy!' said he. '*Never!*' retorted our friend, with peculiar emphasis, which summarily stopped the discussion. We were awakened early in the morning by the screams of laughing jackasses and the crowing of cocks. Our toilette was performed somewhat under difficulties, one of us having to use the piano as a washstand, and another being constrained to go through the same operation in the open street under the hotel verandah. Our route now lay over a steep hill, through a forest of gum trees, the fragrance arising from the latter in the early morning air being delightfully refreshing. The main roads are kept very fairly, a certain number of men being told off for each section at 9s. per day wages. The old corduroy roads, formed by laying trees across the track and filling the interstices with earth, are being gradually superseded by Macadam. The men seemed to work in very leisurely fashion. We were to have breakfasted at a cottage on the road, but when we arrived there found that the old lady who kept it had gone to a ball at some village public-house, several miles away, as also had the owners of all the other cottages along the route. A little girl left in charge told us that after the ball all these good people were going to the funeral of the wine grower and innkeeper previously mentioned, and our friend told us they would doubtless stay there to comfort the widow as long as there was any wine left in the house. We soon after entered the region of the big gum trees and of the tree ferns, and a wonderfully beautiful sight it was.

The whole valley is filled with tree ferns, and the fronds, in many cases being new, with the sunlight falling upon them, formed a picture not soon to be forgotten. Some of the gum trees were enormously large—we saw several 15ft in diameter and over 200ft in height—but these were small when compared with some found in the less frequented parts. In the midst of such surroundings lies the pretty little village of Fernshaw. When we were first invited to spend a week at the country house of our friend we rather unreasonably pictured in our minds an English country or seaside residence, and anticipated much pleasure in the change from dusty Melbourne. Our surprise was great, therefore, when after jolting over some half-formed roads we came upon a clearing among the gum trees, and were told that the wooden shanty before us was the Melbourne citizen's country house. We were not disposed, however, to be very critical, for the sixty miles drive in the mountain air had made us hungry, and we were quite ready to respond to the invitation to the evening meal. But our dis-illusion was complete upon entering the sitting room and finding that no provision had been made for the satisfying of our keen appetites. By some accident the supplies from Melbourne had not arrived; the rough table was covered with a couple of towels, and on it was spread a repast consisting of some bad bread and sour raspberry jam, while the 'cup which cheers but not inebriates' was innocent of milk and sugar. It was Saturday evening and we were 'out of humanity's reach,' being many miles from any source of supply, so had to content ourselves as best we might with this Spartan fare until the Monday, when our host proposed an excursion to a distant part, involving the staying a night at an hotel. We gladly embraced the proposal, and finding that the hotel was a comfortable one I determined to excuse myself from joining in the excursion on the following day in order that I might have the opportunity of recruiting nature's exhausted powers by an extra meal, a resolution I had much satisfaction in carrying into effect. Our friend and his sons own about one thousand acres, at present covered with trees, with the exception of a small clearing round the house. When a piece of land is taken, the first care is to fence it, which is done with logs, at a cost of £25 per mile, including the cutting of the logs. The next step is to 'ring' the trees—that is, to cut a deep groove round them, and so by killing them prevent any further exhaustion of the soil. The trees being dead, vegetation rapidly springs up, and there is soon abundance of food for cattle. Clearing the ground of trees and stumps is a very costly operation, and takes many years to finally accomplish. The Government with a view of preventing the accumulation of lands in a few hands, refuse to sell more than 320 acres to one person, but of course this is easily evaded. At the time of our visit the price was £1 per acre, payable in ten years by equal instalments, a condition being that some one should reside upon the allotment. At the end of three years the owner can obtain from Government a lease of the land, and can then pay up the full value, which leaves him at liberty to sell if he wishes to do so. Of course the building up of large estates is thus encouraged, but this could, perhaps, be prevented by imposing a tax on every acre. The 20 000 acre men would soon be compelled to dispose of some of the land which they hold in the expectation that it will increase in value. Such a plan has been proposed, but it naturally met with great opposition from the landed interest.

Leaving our friend's house a drive of a few miles through the bush brought us to the picturesquely-situated village of Marysville. This little village lies in a deep hollow surrounded by fine ranges of tree-clad hills of extreme beauty. A pleasant hour's walk from the village, under the shade of the tree ferns, took us to the Stephenson Falls. The principal fall is 80ft, and the volume of water is unusually large for an Australian waterfall. Close to the fall are some magnificently large tree ferns, and while sitting here enjoying the lovely view some little birds came flitting about, one of them hopping on to the shoulder of one of our party, attracted, doubtless, by the aroma of a fragrant 'weed' which at the time he was enjoying. English visitors to Australia, especially those in search of health, would find the conditions existing at Marysville most conducive to their restoration. The air is bracing, and as before stated, the scenery most delightful. A tolerably good accommodation is to be had at the inn, which will doubtless be improved as the place becomes more widely known.

Returning to Melbourne, we stayed another night at Healesville, arriving at 7.30, and as we had fared badly during the day we were quite ready for a substantial dinner, and from our previous experience of the house made no doubt of obtaining it. But unfortunately for us, there had been a chapel tea-party during the afternoon, at which a large force of parsons had been present. We had therefore to be content with a tough, woody steak, a wild duck of ancient and fish-like smell, varied by salted mutton. The butter was rancid and full of dead flies, and the bread appeared to have been cast upon the waters. We had to go to bed feeling quite faint, but hoping for a better breakfast. The beds were good, and we should have had a good night's rest, which we sorely needed after the twig beds of the previous night at the Marysville Hotel, but the partitions between the rooms being only of half-inch plank everything passing around us could be heard all too plainly. A little after midnight some fellows came in from night-fishing, and going into the room next ours woke us up by a great noise. One old donkey was telling the two younger ones he had had a deal of experience among snakes, killing as many as eight a day for many years, and that as the result of a series of experiments during that time he had found an infallible cure for snake bites. He had offered his discovery to the Government for £1000, and his partner offered to be poisoned by the most deadly snakes to test its efficacy, but all to no purpose. So he had determined to let the secret die with him. The others asked if the sovereign remedy was to be swallowed. 'Oh, no,' said the old fellow, 'for it is composed of five deadly poisons.' 'You must first cut out the wounded part, and rub the antidote in.' 'But,' added he, 'the secret shall now die with me.' 'But how about your partner?' asked the others. 'Won't he tell the secret?' 'Oh no,' was the reply; 'he's safe enough, for he's dead.' Then we heard the voice of the landlord's pretty daughter telling them it was time to go to sleep, upon which the old boy growled, 'I wonder people can't go to sleep without bothering me.' The rest of the night was made miserable for us by the two 'night fishers,' who, rising long before dawn, went prowling about the different rooms, ours included, collecting their tackle for a shooting expedition, but leaving behind them, as we found afterwards, their percussion caps.

We returned to Melbourne by another route, affording us some fine views of the plains called Yarra Flats, and the Marysville Hills in the far distance.

Reminiscences of Travel in Australia, America, and Egypt (1884 edition, first published privately 1883).

ELIM H. D'AVIGDOR
(1841–95)

British writer. The author of such long-forgotten works as Fair Diana, Glamour, *and* A Loose Rein, *D'Avigdor visited Australia briefly, and New Zealand for a longer period, during a nine-month world tour made in 1887, and subsequently published* Antipodean Notes *in 1888, under the pen-name 'Wanderer'. He was greatly impressed by the sounds of New Zealand.*

'THE SOUNDS'

The Captains of ocean passenger steamers are generally the most obliging and even-tempered of men. Perhaps they would not obtain a command if they were subject to the fits of impatience, and even anger, which the incessant questions of idiots, the misbehaviour of ruffians, the complaints of idlers, and the responsibilities of the position would certainly induce in any ordinary mortal. The Captain of the steamer *Mararoa*, which carried us from Melbourne to New Zealand, was as thoughtful and kind as most of his profession. The vessel is the largest of the Union Company's fleet, and was put on specially on account of the Christmas holidays, during which the Australians fly from their heated deserts to milder climes. Conveying, as she did, merely pleasure-seekers, it was announced that the *Mararoa* would run into Milford Sound, the most celebrated of those fiord-like inlets which cut deeply into the south-western coast of the Middle Island of New Zealand. So far, the programme was an official one; but when we had run into Milford Sound and out again, it was found that we were seven hours before our time, and would arrive at the first New Zealand port in the middle of the night, if the steamer kept up her usual average of thirteen knots an hour. Instead of 'slowing down,' our Captain steamed into several other fiords, each more beautiful than its neighbour, and thus spent the spare time in showing us what but very few even of the Colonists have seen, and which can, as a rule, only be seen either by a lucky fluke or by the possessor of a large steam-yacht.

From the pictures, photographs, and descriptions of the finer Norwegian fiords, I should think Milford Sound resembles them somewhat; but, as I have not been in Norway myself, I can only state, on the authority of an 'old traveller,' that there is nothing on the North Sea half so magnificent. For more than an hour you see a deep blue band on the horizon, exactly ahead; this band grows wider and wider, and at last you make out its serrated upper edge, and see that it is a lofty chain of mountains. The vessel approaches at full speed; gradually the lower portion of the band becomes brown and green instead of blue, and the rugged outlines grow more distinct. While some of the mountains are bare, and seem to fall vertically into the sea, others are only a trifle less steep, and clothed to the heights of many thousand feet with the most luxuriant vegetation. Soon the steamer appears to be close under the cliffs; but she still holds her course, though no inlet appears, no opening by which that great wall will admit her. At last, when the more timid of the passengers fancy she must be touching the rocks, a gap appears on the starboard bow—a gap so narrow that it might only suffice for a mountain torrent. But the height of the mountains is so great that the steamer seems to be much nearer to their foot than she really is. The helm is ported slightly, and the *Mararoa* enters an opening, of which you may form some idea if you remember the narrows of Dartmouth Harbour, and multiply the height of the hills on either side by twenty, leaving the width of the waterway as it is. The vegetation of South Devon is luxuriant, but the black birches, silver pines, and splendid tree-ferns, which seem to hang on the sides of the Milford Sound Mountains rather than to grow on them, far surpass even the vegetation of Mount Edgcumbe. One huge rock, of which the summit towers right over our foremast, falls sheer into the sea, offering no foothold even to the bold trees of New Zealand. This is Mitre Peak. It is nearly 8000 feet high—no great height perhaps when compared to the giants which Alpine Clubmen conquer, but truly formidable when seen, as this is, from the sea-level to its spire. As we steam past it, a white speck—a mere dot—appears on the narrow beach behind its huge shoulders. This is a house, the only one in the Sound, and it enables us to apply some sort of scale to the huge mountains round us. A speck only is it in the mass of rock, forest, and glacier. For on the port side, opposite the Mitre, and apparently a few yards only from the ship's side, a mountain torrent falls into the creek, descending in a succession of steps. When we look up the wild, weird ravine down which flows this silver thread, we see far above us the deep blue of glacier ice, and above this snow-covered peaks rearing their summits against the blue sky. Then, again, in a few minutes we round a projecting cape; the rocky valley and the glaciers are shut out, and the mountains are again covered with trees and grass of the brightest green. Now, on our starboard side, we pass what looks like a low cliff. A stream leaps over its edge, but, like the Staubbach of Switzerland, dissolves in spray before it reaches the sea at the bottom. We are told, however, that the 'low' cliff is 700 feet high; and glancing back to the tiny white house, now only just visible, we see no reason to doubt the statement. Here the solemnity of the scene is suddenly spoiled by the hideous screech of the steamer's 'siren,' of which the horrors are re-echoed with tenfold force from the surrounding mountains. It is part of the programme to let the passengers hear the echo; but why should this dreadful, nerve-destroying echo be called forth over and over again, till the more sensitive fly to the lowest deck, holding their ears, and the serene enjoyment of Nature's beauty is entirely marred by man's horrid contrivances? Do Colonists, like Cockney 'Arrys, really love such discordant yells and screams? Would they not admire the glaciers, nor gaze with awe at the stupendous precipices, unless their ears were roused by this modern Siren? Some of us at last implored the Captain to order the steam-whistle to cease, and he was good enough to comply, though he told us that it was usual to keep the infernal invention at work all up and down the Sound. Then the engines were stopped, and a little boat came alongside. She was manned by three men, the occupants of the one house on Milford Sound. They are employed by Government to cut tracks through the dense forest and up the mountain sides for the purpose of survey. They looked extremely well and strong, and were dressed with great neatness in a sort of sailor costume; but they told a piteous tale of privations, and were supplied with bread, meat, and whisky out of the ship's stores, for which they forgot to pay, although, as I understood, their wages are at the rate of 3*l.* a week each. Here the Sound opened out a little, and was sufficiently wide for the *Mararoa* to turn easily; she soon sped back past the Waterfall, the Glaciers, and Mitre Peak, out again to sea.

On that same day we ran into Break-Sea Sound, which is about forty miles farther south, and then through a wonderful succession of passages, between sheer rocks and tree-clad mountains, into Dusky Sound, emerging again into the ocean by another channel of a totally different character. This was, in fact, a huge bay, dotted with thousands of islands of all sizes, from a mere mound just big enough to carry a single tree, to a great park-like expanse of several hundred acres. On Break-Sea Sound is one tiny settlement, but the many islands with their fertile soil and rich vegetation are uninhabited, and even unexplored. Here is a fine opportunity for a man who wishes to retire from the world, and yet enjoy Nature's bounty to its fullest extent. His garden on one of the fairy islands would supply all English and many subtropical products; within reach of his home he could obtain shooting and mountain-climbing; while fishing and sailing could be followed up under all circumstances of wind and weather, since there are thousands of acres of land-locked salt water as well as many mountain streams. I can imagine a far worse fate than to be settled near Dusky Sound, harder pursuits than to stalk the wild pig in its forests, or plant its grateful soil with fruit-trees and flowering shrubs.

Antipodean Notes (1888).

———

ARDASER SORABJEE N. WADIA
(1882– ?)

Indian teacher. Sometime professor of English and history at Elphinstone College, Bombay, Wadia was inspired to visit Australia and New Zealand after having read, 'as a boy', of Louis de Rougemont's exciting adventures during some thirty years of living among Aborigines in the 'Wilds of Australia' after having been shipwrecked, which were published in Wide World Magazine *(1898–99). He seems to have been blissfully unaware of the fact that de Rougemont had soon been exposed as a Swiss hoaxer, who had lived an unspectacular life in Australia between 1875 and 1897. Wadia also had a strong desire to 'see the Empire' and had already travelled throughout India, Britain, and Canada. He made a four-month tour of Australia and New Zealand in 1929–30.*

'IN WEST AUSTRALIA'

One of the charms of travelling, as all who have travelled know, is the happening of the unexpected. And I had an immediate experience of it, and a pleasant one at that. I had read in newspapers and in books on Australia that an Australian was too independent-minded ever 'to touch his cap,' and far too democratically-inclined to address any one as 'Sir,' no matter what position he held in society or what influence he commanded in life. Before leaving home I had, therefore, wisely put away all ideas of expecting in the Colonies anything in the nature of old-world graces and courtesies of life and had, in consequence, prepared myself not only to do without them but also to get along good-humouredly with the rude habits and crude ways, the brusque manners and rough and ready speech of raw, immature humanity. Imagine, therefore, my surprise to find Cook's man, the first Australian to address me, doing both those highly undemocratic things which I had been led to believe no self-respecting Australian would demean himself to do. That, however, was no solitary incident, but the first of a series of systematic experiences I underwent throughout my long-extended tour of both the Southern Dominions.

It was this man from Cook's who arranged for a motor-trip to Perth from Fremantle; and it proved a twenty-five-mile drive of sheer delight. Being penned up in a boat for well-nigh eight days with nothing but sea and sky to see, the first morning out motoring in a new land, presenting new sights and new sounds, with the Australian sun shining bright and clear, was an experience never to be forgotten. Scarcely had we left the precincts of Fremantle when we came upon a row of newly built cottages with its front and side hedges and backyard all filled with geranium climbers. We of the Northern Hemisphere see the geranium grow only in pots or beds, but here it ran wild everywhere, and grew in all shades of red and pink and white, and in such profusion that it left not a foot of bare patch anywhere. Yet wild as the geranium grew, it was nevertheless a cultivated flower. But what shall I say about the wild flowers of Australia? Scarcely had we left the cottages and entered the wide spaces of the open country when fields after fields of wild flowers ran past us on either side of the road till they burst into one culminating grandeur as we entered King's Park. With justifiable pride a West Australian remarked to me that there was no prettier landscape under the

Southern Cross than that of their great National Park. Here a thousand acres of virgin woodland have been reserved for all time for the free use and enjoyment of the people of Australia. For two miles the Park over-looks the blue waters of the Swan and Canning Rivers, presenting a daz-zling panorama of Perth and its suburbs with the hazy grey outline of the Darling Ranges in the far distance. Except in Switzerland and Kash-mir, such wild flowers and in such variety and profusion I had not seen anywhere. But the wild flowers here were of a species totally unknown in the Northern Hemisphere, and went under such strange names as *pig-face, donkey orchid, smoke,* and that pride of West Australia—the *Kangaroo-paw.* In her *Travels in Western Australia,* May Vivienne goes to the extent of calling it 'the most wonderful flower of the Southern Hemisphere.' I do not know much about its wonders, but it was cer-tainly the quaintest wild flower I had ever seen: in colour dark green, tipped with deep crimson, and shaped exactly like the foot of that Aus-tralian marsupial after which it takes its name. As I wished to have a few *Kangaroo-paws* to press and send home and to my friends in England, the taxi-driver risked a fine of £10 to let me have my wish in the matter. For King's Park is under the protection of a special law that suffers no wanton, spoliating hands to be laid on the floral treasures of the nation-al reserves: a fine of ten pounds has often been imposed for the picking of a single wild flower. Besides the floral feast and scenic grandeur of King's Park, there was another feature that struck me as unique and worth imitating in every other part of the Empire. It was the Heroes' Avenue. A long line of hardy trees at regular intervals has been planted on either side of a well-made road with a brass tablet at the base of each tree bearing the name of a West Australian soldier who fell in the Great War and to whose memory that particular tree is dedicated. The Avenue, though planted but recently, yet makes a most impressive, I might almost say, a solemn sight. Anyway it must have particularly struck the imagination of the worthy Councillors of Perth Corporation, for one afternoon they assembled in solemn conclave in their City Hall and passed a resolution with becoming gravity that their own memo-rable services to the City of Perth should likewise be perpetuated in the form of a circle along with those of the heroes who had laid down their lives for the Empire and civilization. When I walked through the Heroes' Avenue and came on the central promenade of the Park I found this notable Councillors' Circle, with trees duly selected and solemnly planted by each Councillor, and brass tablet firmly fixed at the base with his own hands proclaiming to generations yet unborn their long and meritorious services to the city of their birth and fame.

This Councillors' Circle came as a comic relief to all the serious thoughts the Heroes' Avenue had awakened in my taxi-driver's mind, and in that happy, jesting mood we trundled down the hill on which the Park is situated. We passed Claremont and through Peppermint Grove, in which are situated 'the red-roofed houses of Perth's fashionable suburbia,' as a local guide-book proudly proclaims them. The houses without doubt make a very attractive sight with well-laid-out gardens in front and well-timbered heights in the background. We motored by this fashionable quarter lying along the river-bank to the city itself. Here again another surprise awaited me, for being told that Perth was the youngest of the Australian cities and built within the memory of the oldest of its citizens, I had pictured it to be, after the manner of its suburbia, composed of wooden structures. Imagine, therefore, my surprise when I entered its famous St George's Terrace and found it lined on either side with buildings of solid stone masonry, soaring high and of pleasing design, with broad concrete roads filled with constantly moving motor traffic and tram-cars, while people, modishly attired, strolled up its pavements and down its shopping side-streets. But for the clear, bright golden sunshine and the wide-brimmed colonial hats of some of the men, I could have fancied myself walking in one of the shop-lined streets of London. That evening when I returned to my boat, I brought back with me such a strong and vivid impression of Australia, of her men and modes, of her scenic ambitions and architectural aspirations, that I found later on that all my many weeks of touring in her vast domain was but a filling-in and an elaboration of the picture my mind had limned of it that bright, sunny day in Perth and Fremantle.

The Call of the Southern Cross (1932).

V. C. BUCKLEY

(1901–)

English traveller. Buckley includes a chapter about his 1931 visit to Western Australia, South Australia, Victoria, and New South Wales, apparently his second trip to Australia, in his popular book about his travels in many countries. While in Victoria, he spent some time on a station.

A VISIT TO A VICTORIAN STATION (1931)

It was just dusk when I found my destination, the homestead situated in a valley with great wooded mountains on all sides. This actual station, the word used for large properties (which would be called a ranch in Canada), was anything but flat, as people are apt to suppose the whole of Australia is. In point of actual fact there is practically every sort of climate and scenery one can think of in Australia—tropical deserts in central Australia, alpine sports in the winter at Mt Kosciusko, while parts of the Western District of Victoria resemble England in scenery and atmosphere. Then there are surfing beaches as fine as anywhere in the world, vineyards in South Australia, thousands of miles of flat veldt country, and rugged hills recalling Scotland.

The actual house at this station was of the general up-country type, a large bungalow with a wide creeper-covered verandah. There was a tennis court, small garden, garage and stables. The household consisted of my host and hostess, my host's brother and a 'jackaroo.' At first I was puzzled by that term; it is *not* a kind of animal as I at first thought it might be, but a word used for an apprentice on a sheep station. A young man who wants to gain practical experience of the running of a property goes as a 'jackaroo' to some station, large ones having three or four at a time; they are paid a purely nominal wage, but often live in the house as a member of the family, having only breakfast and lunch down at the shed with the station hands.

On this particular station, which was not considered large, the two owners and the 'jackaroo' did all the work. After giving them news of England, talking over old times, as both my host and his brother had been at school with me, they warned me that they would not have much time during the day to entertain me, but that if I liked I could ride round the paddocks with them whenever they went.

While I was there they were mostly yarding and drenching the sheep, which meant catching hold of each one by the head and opening its mouth to squirt down its throat a disinfectant fluid for its inside. I offered to help but felt that I should be no earthly use as they seemed to have the exact knack, and I should most likely have wasted all the stuff, squirting it in the sheep's eyes and all over myself, so I stood around the yard and watched.

Making a really early start, they would usually come back to lunch. The property not being very large permitted of this, but on large stations the 'jackaroos' and station hands often took their lunch out with them, if they were going into distant paddocks. About five in the evening they would knock off, but then there were odd jobs to be done in the garden and around the house, and they would probably not be finished much before they dressed for dinner.

One day we went out to ride over the property, as they wanted me to see it all; my mount was very quiet, thank goodness, for we rode over some very rough country, as it seemed to me, who had ridden only in Richmond Park and round a polo ground in India. There were endless gates to open and shut. I have always thought that Bateman ought to do a drawing entitled 'the man who left a gate open on a station in Australia,' a crime that cannot bear thinking of, as the stock would get mixed—with disastrous results. I remember we came to the foot of a very steep little hill almost completely covered with boulders, and, turning to my host, I said: 'How do we get round this hill?'

'We don't,' he replied, 'we ride up to the top and down the other side as I want you to see the view.' 'Thank you very much,' I replied. 'I could never ride up this. Was my mount crossed with a fly? It's nearly perpendicular.'

'Come on,' he shouted, and before I knew what was happening my horse had started the ascent, picking his way carefully between the boulders, and in no time we were at the top. I couldn't believe we were there, nor could I say that I fancied the look of the descent, but the view was magnificent. The little homestead nestled in the valley and all round, about ten miles away, were great wooded mountains. My host told me if the lost 'plane had crashed in them, there was little hope of ever discovering it, as a man once made a forced landing in a small 'plane on the side of one of the mountains, and after walking about 20 miles to the nearest township for help to salvage the 'plane that was stuck in the branches of the trees, returned shortly but could never locate the place where his 'plane was, although he had made careful notes as to its position.

During the week-end we motored to a small local bush race-meeting. The little course was on the side of a hill and had something of the look of a miniature Goodwood, save that the grass was burnt brown and there were gum trees in the little paddock. The attendance was about 300 in all, composed of local tradesmen, small farmers, and a few of the near-by station owners and their families. Everyone seemed to know everyone else, and what with the shouting of the bookies and the chatter of people this corner of the bush was far from silent.

There was a small tin shed where the jockeys were accommodated, and after one of the races in which there had been an objection to the winner, we happened to be walking past this shed and saw the two jockeys settling the question of the objection by the means of a good stand-up fight before an enthusiastic audience of bookies, and other jockeys, until the local policeman came along and separated them.

Not so like Goodwood after all!

The race-courses just outside Melbourne at Caulfield and Flemington are most palatial, as is also Randwick at Sydney, and these three rival any tracks I have ever seen. The crowds that attend the meetings are enormous, the more so when one considers the population of the country. On Melbourne Cup Day, during the first week in November, business is practically suspended everywhere in the city.

Australia is pre-eminently a sport-loving nation—racing, cricket, and tennis all attract large crowds. I noticed many hard tennis courts in Melbourne, lit by electric light, so that the business man could play in the evenings—and there is an amazing number of good golf courses.

The 'bush' is a term used for practically all interior parts of Australia, whether plains, wooded country, or fertile farm lands.

Picnics in the bush (consisting of making tea in a billy can and cooking chops on a camp fire) are, largely owing to the lovely climate, not the sad affairs that we have so often to embark on in England, with the rain dripping on to ham sandwiches and plum cake. We went for a picnic while I was staying on this station, but just as one would never think of going to the Tower of London unless it was to take a stranger, so those who live up-country said that they seldom picnicked. We put the lunch basket containing chops (to cook over a camp fire), billy cans, fruit and home-made bread in the car, also some rods, as we were going to the Delatite river, where there was good trout fishing.

The roads were fairly primitive, but the scenery was gorgeous, rugged purple-looking hills, tall gum trees, and little streams sparkling here and there in the warm sunshine with the uncanny stillness of the bush on all sides broken only once or twice by the almost human laugh of the kookaburra, or laughing jackass. Here, from Mansfield to Jamieson and Woods Point, used to be a great gold-mining centre, and even now any old inhabitant will tell you that there is still gold in the hills. The dense scrub through which we passed made me think of the bygone days of 'bushrangers' who would hold up and rob those carrying their findings of gold to the nearest township.

We soon left the road, opening a gate leading into a paddock, and just motored from there across country. This seemed strange at first, bumping along between the tall gums. All the while we went very slowly to avoid old tree-stumps which were half-hidden in the grass. I was glad to be in someone else's car, as my little Morris would never have had the clearance to have gone where we did.

We came to the ruins of an old farm down by the river, deserted most likely in the days after the gold rush. It seemed strange in this new country actually to see a picturesque old ruin, all overgrown and standing in this deep valley. My host said that there were some very good quince trees in the old garden, so we stopped to gather some of the fruit. Quinces, which on the trees look like large green apples, are most delicious when cooked, tasting rather like stewed pears. They are, however, uneatable raw. There was a most eerie atmosphere as we wandered about picking as many as we could carry back to the car.

Round the tumbled-down old house and the overgrown garden I imagined some pioneer having slaved to build a home, but not finding gold, just packing up one day and leaving, as it was in a useless out-of-the-way spot with no land for cultivation. So it had just remained empty and gradually tumbled down. While we fooled around, throwing quinces at each other, we suddenly came on the remains by one of the walls of a recent fire, where no doubt some poor 'swag man' had spent the previous night.

A 'swaggie' or 'sundowner' is the word used for a tramp. The latter is rather descriptive, these men just spend their lives walking from one station to another, and at sundown they call at the nearest for a night's shelter. These men are not to be confused with men out of work; they have been doing it for years and it is almost a profession, so much so that most stations keep special huts for them to sleep in and a small quantity of rough food is given to them; it is almost an unwritten law that they should be so treated. Someone told me that if a station owner should turn them away or treat them badly, they might set light to his country in the summer, thus starting a bush fire by way of revenge. On large stations there are sometimes as many as six men in the hut at night.

Every time I drove away from staying with someone in this country I felt more than usually sad at saying good-bye, because they so take you into their family life that even after only a week's stay, you feel just as if you were leaving your own home.

With a Passport and Two Eyes (1932).

13

Sporting figures

◆

W.G. GRACE

(1848–1915)

English doctor and cricketer. Grace, who studied medicine in Bristol and London, was a surgeon in Bristol from 1879 to 1899. The best-known cricketer of all time, he played for England (which he led thirteen times), Gloucestershire, and London County. At the request of the Melbourne Cricket Club, 'W.G.', as he was known, visited Australia for the first time in 1873–74 with an English team of his choice. During the trip, which was also an extension of Grace's honeymoon, his team played fifteen matches, most of which they won, in Victoria, New South Wales, Tasmania, and South Australia. He also visited Australia for a Test tour in 1891–92. An extraordinary batsman, but also an excellent bowler and fielder, he played his last Test at the age of fifty. In his memoirs Grace remembers playing cricket in the Victorian country town of Stawell during the 1873–74 visit.

'A LUDICROUS FARCE'

Our match against twenty-two of Stawell began next morning under conditions by no means inspiriting. The ground was in a deplorable condition. Here and there were small patches of grass, but the greater part was utterly devoid of any herbage. We were not surprised to hear that the field had only been ploughed up three months before, and that the grass had been sown in view of our visit. The wicket was execrable, but there was no help for it—we had travelled seventy miles through bush and dust to play the match, and there was no option but to play.

Of course the cricket was shockingly poor, and the match a ludicrous farce. How bad the ground really was may be judged from the fact that one slow ball actually stuck in the dust, and never reached the batsman. It was ridiculous to play on such a wicket, but we were in for it and went through with it. Jupp and I batted first, and adopted slogging tactics. There was really nothing else to do, but the result was that in seventy minutes we were all out for 43 runs. If all the catches we gave had been held our total would have been still smaller. We were not sorry when our innings ended, as the wicket was one of the class which I have described, as bringing all players, good and bad, down to one level. Our opponents, who were more accustomed to such wickets, kept us in the field for a couple of hours, and made 71. McIntyre did the bowling for us, taking nine wickets for 10 runs. It is scarcely worth while recording the progress of the play, though it should be stated that we were beaten by ten wickets. A plague of flies, which swept over the field while play was in progress, added to our discomforts in this remarkable match.

As the match finished in two days, a single wicket match between six of our professionals and twelve of the Stawell team was arranged for the third day. The wicket was worse, and the cricket more grotesque than ever. In response to the 29 made by the twelve the six English professionals scored 2—made by McIntyre with one hit. I went off for some more shooting in the bush, along with one or two of the other members of the team, and we were not surprised, though we were amused, to hear on our return what had happened during the day. Some of the Stawell people apparently thought that our men did not try to do their best; but with the ground in such a state, it was almost astonishing that any runs were scored at all. If the ball was hit in the air it travelled all right, but if it was sent along the ground it could not possibly reach the boundary.

'W.G.': *Cricketing Reminiscences and Personal Recollections* (1899).

ZANE GREY
(1872–1939)

American writer and deep-sea fisherman. Zane Grey practised as a dentist in New York until 1903, before becoming a full-time writer. Total worldwide sales of his books, many of which are cowboy novels set in the American west, were estimated at more than 40 million by the early 1970s. The holder of a number of big-game fishing records, Grey visited New Zealand in order to fish several times between 1926 and 1932, and Australia in 1935–36 (as a result of which he wrote An American Angler in Australia *in 1937 and 1939. In the book he wrote about the New Zealand visit he describes a place at which he camped in the North Island.*

'CAMP OF THE LARKS!'

Deep Water Cove Camp, about fifteen miles from Russell, was the rendezvous where anglers stayed while fishing the waters adjacent to Cape

Brett. It accommodated ten or twelve anglers. I decided to follow my usual plan of being independent of every one and having a camp of my own. We had brought our own tents, and we bought blankets. What wonderful blankets they were, and cheap! I never saw their equal. We outfitted at Russell, and soon were ready to start for Orupukupuku, an island belonging to Mr Charles F. Baker, one of the leading citizens of the town, and said to be the most beautiful of all the hundred and more in the Bay of Islands.

As we ran down the bay, which afforded views of many of the islands, I decided that if Orupukupuku turned out to be any more striking than some we passed, it was indeed rarely beautiful. Such proved to be the case. It was large, irregular, with a range of golden grassy hills fringed by dark green thickets and copses, indented by many coves, and surrounded by channels of aquamarine water, so clear that the white sand shone through. We entered the largest bay, one with a narrow opening protected by another island so that it was almost completely landlocked. The beach of golden sand and coloured sea-shells stretched in graceful crescent shape. A soft rippling surge washed the strand, and multitudes of fish, some of them mullet, splashed and darkened the shallow waters. The hills came down to enclose a level valley green with grass and rushes, colourful with flags and reeds. A stream meandered across the wide space. On the right side were groves of crimson-flowering trees, the *pohutukawa*, in Maori. This tree was indeed magnificent, being thick, tall, wide-spreading, with massy clumps of dark green foliage tipped by crimson blossoms. Beautiful as was this side of the bay, I decided to pitch camp on the other.

The hill-side there was covered with a wonderful growth of the tree ferns, which plant has given New Zealand the name Fernland; a tall palmetto-like tree which the men called cabbage trees; and lastly tall marvellous *ti* trees. These stood up above close-woven thickets of the same flora. The foliage was very fine, lacy, dark green, somewhat resembling hemlock, and having a fragrance that I can describe only as being somewhat like cedar and pine mingled. How exquisitely strange and sweet! Trees and their beauty and fragrance have always been dear to me. The hills back of the bay were mostly bare, graceful, high, covered with long golden grass that waved in the wind.

These were my first impressions of our camp site on Orupukupuku. How inadequate they were! But first impressions always are lasting. These of mine I gathered were to grow.

When Mr Alma Baker arrived, he pitched his camp under the crimson-flowered *pohutukawas* across from our place at the edge of the *ti* trees. We worked all day at this pleasant and never-wearying task of making a habitation in the wilderness. Never am I any happier than when so engaged. This nomad life is in the blood of all of us, though many comfort-loving people do not know it.

After dinner we climbed the high hill on our side. Fine-looking woolly sheep baa-ed at us and trotted away. The summit was a grassy ridge, and afforded a most extraordinary view of islands and channels and bays, the mainland with its distant purple ranges, and the far blue band of the sea. It was all so wonderful, and its striking feature was the difference from any other place I had ever seen. Seven thousand miles away from California! What a long way to come, to camp out and to fish, and to invite my soul in strange environment! But it was worth the twenty-six days of continuous travel to get there. I gathered that I would not at once be able to grasp the details which made Orupukupuku such a contrast from other places I had seen. The very strangeness eluded me. The low sound of surf had a different note. The sun set in the wrong direction for me, because I could not grasp the points of the compass. Nevertheless, I was not slow to appreciate the beauty of the silver-edged clouds and the glory of golden blaze behind the purple ranges. Faint streaks or rays of blue, fan-shaped, spread to the zenith. Channels of green water meandered everywhere, and islands on all sides took on the hues of the changing sunset.

I was too tired to walk further, so I sat down on the grassy hill, and watched and listened and felt. I saw several sailing hawks, some white gulls, and a great wide-winged gannet. Then I heard an exquisite bird song, but could not locate the bird. The song seemed to be a combination of mocking-bird melody, song-sparrow and the sweet wild plaintive note of the canyon swift. Presently I discovered I was listening to more than one bird, all singing the same beautiful song. Larks! I knew it before I looked up. After awhile I located three specks in the sky. One was floating down, wings spread, without an effort, like a feather. It was a wonderful thing to see. Down, down he floated, faster and faster, bursting his throat all the while, until he dropped like a plummet to the ground, where his song ended. The others circled round higher and higher, singing riotously, until they had attained a certain height; then they poised, and began to waft downward, light as wisps of thistledown on the air. I had never before seen larks of this species. They were imported birds, as indeed almost all New Zealand birds are. They were small in size. The colour I could not discern. What gentle soft music! It was elevating, and I was reminded of Shakespeare's sonnet: 'Hark! hark! The lark at heaven's gate sings.'

They sang until after dark; and in the grey dawn, at four o'clock, they awoke me from sound slumber. I knew then I had found a name for this strange new camp. Camp of the Larks!

Tales of the Angler's Eldorado, New Zealand (1926).

————

HAROLD LARWOOD

(1904–)

English cricketer. Larwood, who played for England and Nottinghamshire, was one of the fastest and most accurate bowlers in the history of cricket. He became famous as one of the English bowlers who used bodyline (or fast-leg theory) bowling against Australian batsmen during the controversial Test tour of 1932–33. In his autobiography, Larwood, who emigrated to Australia with his family in 1950, recalls the day that he hit Bert Oldfield during the third Test in Adelaide in January 1933.

'MURDER ON TIP-TOE!'

A record crowd of just under 50 000 had swarmed into Adelaide Oval on this day. It was Monday, January 16, 1933. The sun streamed down on the excited spectators, spangling the grass-verged wicket out in the middle with patches of russet brown. A faint breeze stirred from somewhere in the direction of the cathedral and helped to make it a splendid day for cricket.

But this was no ordinary day, nor was it an ordinary cricket match.

This was bodyline.

The cream of English and Australian cricketers were, in fact, locked in the most bitter combat in cricket history.

The blackest day known to cricket, one critic called it and his fellow-writers joined the chorus; the most sensational era since cricket began; the greatest upheaval the game has ever known; the most controversial— the most unpleasant; Unfair! Unsportsmanlike! Illegitimate! Disgraceful!

To bowl bodyline you had to be fast. Fast enough to make thunderbolts rear from the pitch in the direction of the batsman's ribs, shoulder or head. The faster the better. It left him with an even finer split-second to decide whether to attempt a stroke, dart out of the way or take a rib-roaster.

They said I was the fastest bowler in the world. I hurled the ball at the batsman at close on a hundred miles an hour, giving him less than half a second from the precise moment of delivery to make a decision *and act.*

Larwood the Wrecker, the newspapers called me. Lightning Larwood. Larwood the Killer. The Silent Killer. Hoodoo Larwood. Murder on Tip-Toe!

My bodyline bowling consisted of a series of short-pitched, catapult deliveries shooting up on the leg stump in line with the batsman's body. Up to six fieldsmen waited in a tight umbrella on the leg side, tensed for an easy catch that might be faint-heartedly popped up. Two fieldsmen stood on the legside boundary hoping for a catch from a hook shot.

All hell broke loose on this day when I hit Bert Oldfield. It was the Third Test and Australia were 6 wickets down for a little over 200 runs chasing England's first innings total of 341. I was not bowling to a bodyline field setting at the time. Australia's star batsmen were back in the pavilion looking on, and members of the 'hutch' were at the wicket or padded up waiting to face the Nottingham Express.

Bert wasn't a recognized batsman in the true sense, but he was a player not without style and could, on occasions, get his 50's or thereabouts. In this innings he had scored almost 40 and was settling down nicely and becoming a thorn in England's side. Now he delighted the crowd with a beautiful leg glance to the fence hit off one of my deliveries.

Running in on tip-toe I decided to drop one short to unsettle him. Oldfield swung at the ball, attempting a hook. He mistimed the stroke and as he spun round the ball struck the right side of his temple with such force that later he was found to have a fractured skull.

Critics and spectators had been prophesying that bodyline would kill somebody sooner or later. It now seemed that the dark moment had arrived.

Bert dropped his bat, clutched his head in both hands, staggered away from the wicket and fell to his knees.

As a low rumble of hooting and rage swelled from the crowd I ran up to the crumpled figure. 'I'm sorry, Bertie,' I said.

The plucky little wicketkeeper tried to collect himself as the English side, realizing how gravely hurt he was, hurried over to gather round him.

'It's not your fault, Harold,' Oldfield mumbled as soon as he was able to speak.

The scene that followed was one that had never erupted on any other cricket field and it is difficult to imagine it ever being repeated.

Woodfull, the Australian captain sitting with members of his team in the enclosure outside the dressing-room, was normally a reserved and circumspect individual, but on this occasion, still nursing bruised ribs from one of my deliveries which had hit him two days earlier, he vaulted the pickets and bustled on to the field in ordinary attire.

'This isn't cricket, this is WAR!' he boomed.

As towels and hot water were rushed from the dressing-room to bathe Oldfield's head wound, the crowd worked itself into a frenzy and with every passing moment the situation became uglier and more dangerous.

'If anybody fires a pistol they'll lynch us,' I thought.

'If one man jumps the fence the whole mob will go for us.'

I moved towards the stumps so that I might grab one in readiness if they came at us. Some of the other lads, too, moved nearer the stumps.

Thousands of almost hysterical onlookers began counting me out as Oldfield staggered groggily from the field, assisted by Woodfull. They also counted out England's skipper, Douglas Jardine.

Suddenly the editor of an evening newspaper dashed along one of the terraces under an open stand where bewildered members of the Press box were standing on tip-toe to get a clearer view of the scene.

Waving a white panama hat to attract the attention of Hugh Buggy, the newspaper's cricket reporter, he yelled: 'This is disgraceful. Put the boot into them! Put the boot in!'

Fleet Street men, riled by this display, promptly cabled back to their papers that an Australian editor had instructed his reporter to 'put the boot in' to the visiting players.

The anger of the crowd needed no stoking.

'One, two, three, four, five, six, seven, eight, nine OUT you BAS-TARD!' they bawled at me from the outer ground.

'Go home you Pommie bastards!' they yelled.

'Bastards! Bastards! Bastards!'

Although hostility had spread to every stand, this particular epithet appeared to be used only by those within the outer ring.

Although the next Australian player, Big Bill O'Reilly, had now come to the wicket to take strike, his jaw set firmly, the counting-out and hooting continued unabated.

Several police officers were rushed in and reinforcements called for by the Oval authorities. More were hastily mustered and together with mounted troopers were held in reserve at headquarters, awaiting developments.

The *Melbourne Herald* reported at the time: 'No such unrestrained hooting and abuse has ever been heard, even at a tense football match in Melbourne.

'O'Reilly missed three balls from Larwood with wild swings and each time the crowd vented its vocal fury on Larwood. No bowler in a Test has ever faced such a tornado of angry shouting. The crowd lost all interest in the Australian innings and concentrated on howling at the fast bowler.'

In an unprecedented scene rubbish galore was pelted on to the normally immaculate arena and the crowd continued its yelling and abuse until the Australian innings ended soon after for a total of 222.

More however was to come. As we left the field in silent anger, we were hooted off. Hooted, not jeered. I remember that as we walked through a crowded stand to reach the dressing-room indignant members leapt from their seats yelling insults, some shaking their homburgs and velour hats at us. This outburst was all the more amazing because cricket spectators in Adelaide, the City of Churches, had the reputation of being among the most sedate of Australian sports crowds.

The Larwood Story, with Kevin Perkins (1965).

WILLIAM F. TALBERT

(1918–)

American tennis player. Ohio-born Talbert was a member of the US Davis Cup team (1946, 1948–54) and later its captain (1953–57). In his autobiography he recalls the Davis Cup matches between the US and Australia held in Sydney in 1954, the year after the Australian 'tennis twins', Ken Rosewall and Lew Hoad, had won the cup from the Americans.

'ON TOP DOWN UNDER'

The stands at White City Stadium in Sydney were filled with 26 000 people—the largest crowd ever to watch a tennis match. I stood at attention in the limelight of the centre court while the anthems were played; shook hands with the assembled officials, the representatives of tennis and of governments; waited through the drama of Davis Cup ritual. My mind was already on the matches about to begin, trying to anticipate the situations, working out the answers.

We were in good shape. The night before, I had called in a friend to play a game of chess with Seixas, to keep Vic's mind off tennis. The luck of the draw—good luck for our side—would hold him back a little while longer now. Trabert, ready and eager to play the opener, had, in fact, drawn the first match, against Australia's Lew Hoad.

It was a contest of powerful hitters, but Tony gave it something besides muscle. A tricky wind increased the risks of a big service; we agreed that the situation called for less speed and more control. Tony, cutting down on the force of his first serve, got it in consistently. Hoad, on the other hand, faulted and was obliged to come in with an easier second serve.

From my canvas chair on the sidelines, I watched the match seesaw, first in Tony's favor, then Hoad's. Too often Trabert was being passed at the net from Hoad's backhand. I kept looking for some pattern in the Australian's game that we could anticipate. Finally, in the second set, I spotted something.

At the next change of court, I told Trabert, as I dried the handle of his racket with a towel, 'Watch that backhand. When the ball comes in high to him on that side, he's hitting it straight down the line. When it comes to him low, he drives it cross-court with top spin.'

Tony nodded, rinsing his mouth with water. When play resumed, he responded perfectly, anticipating Hoad's returns and cutting them off with a volley.

Still, Hoad held firm, and, after a grueling series of games in the third set, he led 7 games to 6, 40–30 in points, on his own serve. One more point would give him a lead of two sets to one—and that could finish Tony's chances.

Hoad served, deep and high to Trabert's backhand, and rushed to net behind it. Trabert returned sharply cross-court and also moved in. At close range they peppered each other with an exchange of volleys, before Hoad stepped into one and sent it murderously right at Trabert. Tony, flinging up his racket in self-defense, stabbed at the ball. Incredibly, it popped across the net. Hoad lunged and drove the ball beautifully down the line from his backhand—and out of court. It was one of those unpredictable breaks of the game, and Tony took full advantage of it. He went on to win the game, the set and the match.

Now it was Seixas's turn. Rosewall, his nemesis, had beaten him once again in an Australian tournament only a week or two before. But Rosewall, too, had a pattern: a tendency to hit cross-court off his relatively weak forehand. Seixas's tactic was to get to Rosewall's forehand as quickly as possible and move to the net, covering against a cross-court return.

Harry Hopman, seated down the sideline from me, evidently saw what was happening. I could see him earnestly giving instructions to young Rosewall during a break. Going back onto the court, Ken began to chip some of his forehands softly down the line. Another counter-measure was called for: Seixas had to avoid committing himself too quickly, had to hold back his move to the net momentarily, so that he wouldn't be caught going the wrong way and would be in position to take the chip shot.

The first set went to Seixas. In the second, he began to show dis-tressing signs of his old habits, missing shots he should have made without much trouble, losing leads that had seemed safe. Finally, on a crucial point late in the set, Rosewall hit a ball that looked out—to just about every one in the stadium except the linesman, who called it 'in.' Vic came storming toward the umpire's stand, clenching his fists and grimacing in protest. I started up from my chair, thinking, *Here we go again! All that work, all those calming words I've been wasting on this guy during the past weeks ...*

But Vic stopped. With a gesture of impatience, he brushed his dis-may aside, went back to work, and in two more sets put down Rose-wall.

As we came up for the doubles, on the second day, we were in the driver's seat. Not only did we have a lead of two matches to none, but we also had a psychological edge for the doubles. The Aussies, we knew, were much concerned about the signals we had used so successfully against them the previous year. They would be set for the trick this time. Knowing that, we decided to discard it—or rather, to use it only often enough to keep the opposition guessing.

The Australians put up a tremendous fight. In the fourth set, with Seixas and Trabert repeatedly on the verge of winning the match and with it the Davis Cup, Hoad and Rosewall rescued themselves time after time. But Seixas and Trabert didn't let it shake them. Vic came strolling over to me during a change of court. 'Don't worry, Cap,' he said, 'they're just delaying the inevitable.' It was positive thinking in its finest flower.

A few minutes later, Seixas and Trabert slammed the door with the winning point. They pummeled each other happily, and I ran onto the court to console the Australians and congratulate my own players for winning back the Davis Cup.

Playing for Life, with John Sharnik (1958).

MICHAEL MORRIS KILLANIN

(1914–)

Irish writer, film producer, and sporting administrator. Educated at Eton, the Sorbonne, and Cambridge, Killanin worked for various London news-papers in the 1930s before serving in the British army during the Second World War. President of the Olympic Council of Ireland from 1950 to 1973, he became a member of the International Olympic Committee in 1952 and was the latter's president from 1972 to 1980. In 1956 he attended the Melbourne Olympic Games.

'SMALL IS BEAUTIFUL'

'WHO'S WON?' I asked, just wanting the reassurance that my eyes had not played tricks. 'Your man,' replied Prince Philip from the row in front. Here, in 1956, at Melbourne, small was indeed beautiful. This was the last Games before the Olympic Movement appeared world-wide on television in drawing-rooms, burst its seams and assumed the vast complexity of today. And here was a man from a small country—my country—winning the blue riband of the track, the 1500 metres. As the Prince, who had earlier opened the Games on behalf of the Queen, and the IOC [International Olympic Committee] members around me shared my excitement, Ronnie Delany had dropped to his knees, just beyond the finishing line, in an attitude of prayerful thanksgiving.

Melbourne, on the wrong side of the world as far as the epicentre of the Olympic Movement was concerned, was bound to have a smaller representation for the Games. Ireland managed to send twelve com-petitors, but in Helsinki four years previously, which provides a better example for my comparison, there were 7500 competitors and 1863 officials, including representatives of the press and other media. At Moscow the Organizing Committee calculated, before the boycott, that there would be 14 000 competitors and 7300 media personnel alone, an enormous growth-rate in a quarter of a century.

If Melbourne ended an era there were signs of the coming changes and Delany and myself represented part of that change. Delany came to the Olympic arena not directly from Ireland but through Villanova University in the United States, to which he had won a scholarship. Many of these scholarships were frowned upon at the time as being awarded purely for athletic ability, and that the recipients were, if not pseudo-professionals, then the capitalist equivalent of state-aided athletes.

Without Villanova and Jumbo Edwards, their renowned coach, I doubt whether Delany would have mounted the winner's rostrum in Melbourne and nor would he, as a result of his education in America, have gone on to his present executive position in the British and Irish Steampacket Company. I would not have been in Melbourne either, but for commercial involvement. I could not, at that time, afford to fly to Melbourne and back and I would not have wanted to use any of the Irish Olympic funds but, as I was a director of Aspro Nicholas at the time, I was able to combine a business trip, visiting plants in Karachi and Bombay on the way. In effect, Delany the competitor and Killanin the administrator were being supported, subsidized, to realize their Olympic endeavours. So too were many other Olympic competitors, and it worried me that the Movement was not, at that time, taking proper account of the situation, and nor did it for many years as the effect of television, the growth of commercialism and nationalism took a greater hold.

I was in Melbourne again with dual responsibility as President of the Irish NOC [National Olympic Committee] and a member of the IOC and, since the Irish team was so small (the equestrian events, in which Ireland is always strong, were held in Stockholm that year), only one official went with it. He was Chris Murphy, who, unfortunately, fell ill soon after his arrival, so the team had no administrator except for the Australian attaché. I found myself commuting between IOC meetings and the Village before the Games and trying to help out during the events with all kind of items such as transportation, training and tickets for the sports. Arthur MacWeeney, the only Irish sportswriter at the Games, also buckled to.

There were high hopes that Delany would get to the final and I saw him in the team quarters before the semi-finals. We talked about his chances, and his placid attitude and belief that he could win the gold impressed me. He did not want any special treatment, just peace in which to concentrate his mind on the greatest race of his life.

After the excitement of the victory I went down to the changing-room and found the same Delany I had talked to in the Village: quiet, unexcited about it all as though it were not a great achievement. When the last newsman had departed I suggested we could both do with a drink, failing to take account of Australia's licensing laws. Anyway, we left the stadium in my car with both my lady drivers—it must have been several hours after the race because the evening paper bills were announcing 'It's Ireland's Gold'. Nowhere was open for a drink so we ended up having beers in the bedroom of my hotel.

Delany was one of the early four-minute milers. After pursuing his career, he returned to sports administration as the Chairman of the Irish Government-nominated Sports Council (COSPOIR). So many sportsmen in the Western World, devoting much time to their training and competition, are bound to neglect their working life. They have a lot of catching up to do once their international sporting days are over, and thus many are lost initially to the administration of sport.

The thought of those early days evokes a pleasing nostalgia. In recent years Mexico, Munich, Montreal and Moscow have all benefited from the Olympic Games by gaining social infrastructures, such as public housing or transport systems, which might never have been available to their people otherwise. But the Helsinki Games, the first I attended, had to make do with the existing constructions and still run efficiently.

At the previous Games in London in 1948, immediately after the war, this was even more true. There were building restrictions and only sites which had been cleared after the bombing and buildings, such as Wembley Stadium, which were constructed many years before the war, were available. Time was short and there was no demand by athletes, federations, NOCs, the IOC or the media for any extravagant facilities. At Melbourne, the last of the Games to be intimate and personal, everything except the rowing and yachting took place within easy reach of the city centre. No special stadium was built but the Melbourne Cricket Club ground was converted temporarily for the occasion, a little more accommodation was constructed and existing facilities or conversions put to use. I returned to Melbourne in 1978 to lunch with the Melbourne Cricket Union in the room where I had waited before entering the stadium to see Ronnie Delany's victory and the opening and closing ceremonies. It seemed pleasantly modest.

I also recall from those early years how light were the demands which the IOC made on the Organizing Committee as regards its own comfort. In 1952 Helsinki was a small city. IOC members had free passes on buses and all of us, except the President, travelled in this manner to sporting events. Today all IOC members insist on having their own individual cars during the Games. For some eighty members to have cars places an added burden on the resources of the hosts, who also have to provide transport for the numerous teams, competitors and officials. More recently International Federation heads and NOC heads have also had cars. All these are provided by a national car manufacturer, or agent, which means that the officials of the Olympic Movement are subsidized by commercial advertising.

At Helsinki, an extreme formality still reigned. At the receptions—and they were innumerable—white ties, orders and decorations were worn, though at least top hats and tails, which had been de rigueur before the war, had been abandoned for the opening ceremony. Instead, we were issued with little badges to put on our jackets or blazers in order to achieve some form of uniformity. In those days the members of the IOC left their stand and formed a circle before the presidential or royal box and must have looked ridiculous—a motley crew of varying ages. I was the youngest at thirty-seven except for Prince Jean of Luxembourg. Now the IOC members do not leave the stand. It would be twenty more years before I was elected President. But long before that I was to become acquainted with two of the forces which have come more and more to darken the idealism inspired by de Coubertin and put the whole Olympic Movement at risk: politics and violence.

My Olympic Years (1983).

1 4

Entertainers

♦

EMILY SOLDENE

(1840?–1912)

British singer. A mezzo-soprano, Soldene was a singer of comic opera who made her name in Offenbach's Geneviève de Brabant. *In her memoirs, she recalls the time that she spent in Melbourne during her 1877–78 tour, the first of her several visits to Australia.*

RECOLLECTIONS OF MELBOURNE

Most of the company went [from Sydney] to Melbourne by steamer, and got stuck in the mud outside that charming city, but four of us went overland. Such a journey, on a 'Cobbs' coach, drawn by six young horses, who galloped up mountains and flew down them, driven by coachmen more or less under the influence of the weather. One told us he had been out on a 'burst to a wedding, not slept for three nights,' but should be all right when he had had a 'nobbler.' We looked forward with much pleasurable anticipation to the 'nobbler,' but were horrified when we saw it—'half a tumbler of whisky.' Our driver tossed it off. He had not overstated its merits. It pulled him together splendidly, not that it made any difference in his driving, which was dare-devil and perfect, as was that of all the other boys. Fancy a track of soft sand, cut into deep ruts, piled up high in banks, winding in and out huge trees, sharp corners, unexpected fallen trunks, monster upturned roots, every kind of obstacle, six horses always galloping, the coach banging, creaking, swaying from side to side! then suddenly down we go, down over a mountain as steep as the side of a house, down into and through a rushing, roaring, tumbling, bumping, yellow river! Splash, dash. Then with a 'Houp!' 'Hi!' and a big lurch, out again and up the opposite side, galloping, always galloping, breathless; the driver shouting, cracking his whip, and the horses shaking the water from their sides, tossing their heads, and jingling their harness; then out on to the level, soft and springy, covered with mossy turf and beautiful trees like an English park; away over more sand, and leaving the mossy turf, and plunging through sharp, cutting, stiff, rusty-looking, tall grass, growing in huge tufts, far apart. At last we come to a hut, full gallop, and the driver, without any preparation, pulls the cattle up on their haunches, and you might cover them with a blanket, as the saying is. It was all lovely except for the jolting, and my hands were blistered with holding on. I liked to sit on the box, though it made one sick, not with fright exactly, but with excitement and the anticipation of some possible calamity.

My first flock of flying cockatoos disappointed me dreadfully. They looked exactly like a flock of pigeons. The driver told me that when one was wounded or hurt, and could not go on, the others despatched him, pecked his eyes out and tore him to pieces. I fancy I have seen something like that in more civilised regions. We went through groves, forests of gum trees, where there was no shade, but a delicious perfume. At night we heard the laughing jackasses, making an awful noise, but they laughed so well, that we joined in. That's another circumstance I've noticed in more civilised regions. At Gundagai there is an immensely long bridge, and we galloped over it in fine style. The approach to Gundagai, like every other mining town I have ever seen, was distinguished by a marvellous display of rubbish of all sorts, old boots, tin cans of every description (they do say the goats live on tin cans), meat cans, milk cans, oil cans, fish cans, fruit cans, old stays, old bonnets, old hats, old stockings, heaps of more cans, strewn for miles. It takes all the romance out of the scene. Gundagai was surrounded by large, middling, and small heaps of pale red sand; the place was full of 'Holes in the ground,' empty holes in the ground, as if herds of gigantic fox-terriers had been hunting out their best rabbits. This is the sign of deserted gold-diggings. Can anything be more lonely or more miserable? Nothing. I have seen them in gullies in America, in gullies and plains in Australia, in the heart of the mountains of California, in secret places of the Sierras, in little desert places in Nevada. But they are all alike—miserable, lonely, deserted, except by the wily, patient Chinaman, who goes over again the much gone over ground, making a Celestial's fortune out of the white devil's leavings, and disputing with the thin-legged, big-bellied, bearded goats, the abandoned tin cans. Still, at Gundagai there was a nice hotel. We had boiled fowls for dinner, and I left behind something I prized very much, a 5-cent palm leaf fan I had carried all the way from Cincinnati.

We opened at the Opera House, Melbourne, in 'Geneviève de Brabant,' and falsified our anticipations by making a big success. We lived at St Kilda, at Mrs Gardiner's. She was a furrier by trade, had a business in Melbourne, had prepared the furs for His Royal Highness the Duke of Edinburgh when he visited there (1868), and related the episode every day, sometimes twice a day. Some days it was very interesting, other days one found it monotonous; after many days it made one sick. She had a daughter named 'Mary Jane.' I remember it, because, when that young lady made any juvenile *faux pas*—and she was rather successful with that sort of thing—Mrs Gardiner would observe (with a decided inflexion of the voice, signifying determination), 'I'll warm you, Mary Jane Gardiner; I'll warm you.'

The St Kilda residence was a pleasant one—a long low house of one story, built on piles, with a broad passage running down the centre, and ten or twelve rooms opening off on each side. St Kilda is close to and looking over the sea, so close to the sea, in fact, that a man-o'-war practising miles away had sent a big shot through the local pianoforte shop just before we arrived. It was a delightful place, but we seemed to have a good many hot winds there. They always gave me a horrible headache. In the same house lived Mr Creswick, the Tragedian, who had just hit them very strongly in Melbourne, and was doing a great business. One night he came home in a terrible state. He had been playing 'Richard the Third,' and in the combat got cut on the head and had his teeth damaged. He was old, feverish, and fidgety. But we bathed his head, put him to bed, got his teeth mended, and he soon pulled round. During his stay in Australia he married the widow of a well-known Sydney professor. She, by the force of circumstances, had descended to keeping a lodging or boarding house. Mr Creswick lived at her establishment in Sydney, and she first attracted his attention by bringing in his tea in silence, setting it down the same, and retiring ditto. Such a woman, to a studious man, was invaluable. He felt he must possess her for his very own, and they were married.

At Melbourne we added two operas to our repertoire— 'La Perichole,' with the expurgated last act, and 'Girofle-Girofla.' During the rehearsals of 'La Perichole,' when Mr Campbell and I made our first entrance, the carpenter's dog, a fox-terrier, always accompanied us, and, wagging his tail, sat down with much gravity in the centre of the stage, with his back to the footlights, and, at one particular part of my opening song, lifted up his voice and gave a gruesome and most dismal howl. This went on for several mornings, the dog always howling at the same place, always paying the same tribute to my vocalisation. It was very funny and I thought we might utilize it. So for the performance we had a 'Toby' frill made for my appreciator. We went on as the street singers, spread our carpet, tuned our mandolins, and commenced to sing. Directly I began doggy took up his cue beautifully, howling long and loudly. It was great—terrific applause and encore. Everybody said, 'How clever! Who trained the dog?' Perhaps Mr G. R. Sims, or *The Spectator*, or one learned in dog lore will explain why this dog at that particular part howled in misery and rage, and was a silent and sniffing and sympathetic angel during the rest of the performance.

Among the many old friends we met in Melbourne were Mr and Mrs Plumpton (Mme Charlotte Tasca), and Mr and Mrs Bracy, and among the friends we made was Dr Neild, who was excessively kind, and wrote most charming notices of our performances. He had a young son (not in the best of health), who took quite a fancy to me, and we used to go out driving together.

During my stay in Melbourne, one day I got a letter from a place called 'Brandy Creek.' It was from Mr Weippert, once upon a time of Regent Street, London. It was very sad. He said he was there in that God-forsaken place in distress, and needed help to buy a piano to get his living. From his description 'Brandy Creek' seemed to me to be about the last place in the world in which a professor of the pianoforte should set up his tent.

One night I had a most delightful surprise. 'A gentleman would like to see me—a gentleman from England.' It was 'Johnny' Caulfield, one of the old Oxford chums, who since those days had married Miss Constance Loseby. But his health failing, he had come out in a sailing ship to Melbourne in search of a fresh fit out. I thought he was a ghost, but taking him home to supper we found he was not.

We had a good time in Melbourne. Mr and Mrs Saurin Lyster made us socially very welcome. We went out to their delightful place at 'Fern Tree Gully,' drove in a four-in-hand down a 'corduroy' road constructed at an angle of 45°, had a lovely dinner and a lovely day, crept down the gully and saw the huge fern trees, rode bush ponies over stumps, through and over and under the trees, emulating and nearly sharing the fate of Absalom; saw heaps of cows milked mechanically, and the fine horses sent out to sleep in the paddock instead of in stables. Then in the evening we played halfpenny nap. I lost eleven shillings. Of course; what can one expect, playing cards on a Sunday? We drove home to St Kilda by the light of the moon, and very nearly had an awful spill. But a miss is as good as a mile, they say.

My Theatrical and Musical Recollections (1897).

———

OSCAR COMETTANT
(1819–98)

French pianist, composer, and critic. Oscar Comettant was born in Bordeaux, was educated at the Conservatoire de Paris, and began his career as a pianist in 1843. After travelling in the United States and Canada in

1852–55, he returned to Paris where he taught music and became the music critic for Le Siècle. *He visited Australia in 1888 as the French member of the jury that judged the works of art at the Centennial International Exhibition, to which various countries including France sent commissions, held in Melbourne to commemorate the European settlement of Australia. Comettant, who composed his own musical 'Salute to Melbourne' while in Victoria, was a keen observer of the state of music in the Australian colonies.*

'PIANOS EVERYWHERE'

I do not believe there is a country in the world where music is more widespread than in Australia. Certainly there is none that has more grand pianos per head of population. 700 000 instruments have been sent from Europe to Australia since the vast territory became a centre of white settlement. Everywhere here the piano is considered to be a necessary piece of furniture. Rather than not have one of these sonorous instruments in the drawing-room, as a sign of respectability, they would go without a bed; they would sleep on the piano while waiting to complete their furnishings, and appearances would be kept up, which is the main thing in Australia.

It is not just in the cities and villages that custom despotically demands that there be at least one piano in every Australian home; even in the most distant shacks, away from any centre of population, the humblest farmer will have the inescapable piano. Way out in the country they are not very expert in music, and the piano that adorns the humble dwellings will be one of those cheap and nasty pieces of poor workmanship poured into the world by Germany; they are constantly going wrong, but the main thing is that they look like a piano, with vulgar moulding and ostentatious double candle-brackets; they make a noise when you strike the keyboard, and often this is all that is required.

So, I saw everywhere in Australia, in the town and in the country, pianos enhancing all the houses, and I made one observation. The oldest pianos were English makes, the newest were jerry-built German ones, designed to be exported and lacking equally in music quality and durability.

In Melbourne I saw a very beautiful Pleyel belonging to my country-men, Monsieur and Madame Duret, of Albert Park; they live with their daughter and son-in-law, a clever young doctor called Crivelli. Madame Mouchette, who runs a model institution for young ladies in St Kilda, has furnished her drawing-room with one of the grand pianos displayed (though not competitively) at the Great Exhibition; here the most famous local and transitory musicians deem it an honour to be heard. The famous composer and virtuoso, Henri Kowalski, who has settled in Sydney—to that town's greater musical glory—will not be heard in public except on a piano made by Pleyel, Wolff and Co., of Paris. Moreover, the grand piano in the main drawing-room at Government House, is a superb Erard, chosen by Lady Loch herself. This is enough, it seems to me, to save the artistic honour of our national production of pianos—until their exquisite tone and admirable construction, impervious to all climates, lead to their being used all over Australia.

With such a large number of pianos, it is not surprising that there is no lack of teachers of the instrument. In Melbourne and Sydney their name is legion. You only have to tap your foot on the ground and they come out, whether in Adelaide, Sandhurst, Ballaarat, or anywhere else—there are pianos everywhere.

In Melbourne a Monsieur Plumpton is one of the most well-known piano teachers; he also gives singing-lessons and writes the music critiques in that great newspaper, the *Age*. He has many strings to his bow, and professes an admiration for the most recent lyrical dramas of Wagner that is all the more decided for their not having being heard by him, but judged with the ears of faith; he also composes. He had an attempt at a two-act opera called *The Two Students*, if I am not mistaken, but it only ran for one night. Of course, the failure was not due to the composer, but the execrable performers, who were unable to bring out the true merits of the work. We are also indebted to Monsieur Plumpton for an ode for voice and orchestra, a mass, and several individual melodies with piano accompaniment. I did not have the opportunity while in Melbourne to hear any of these works by the artist who was my colleague in the jury judging musical instruments at the Exhibition. If then, and to my great regret, I cannot judge the merit of Monsieur Plumpton's musical creations, I have a small comment to offer about his critical qualities. Where the devil did he get the idea that my march, 'Salute to Melbourne', which he heard played by Mademoiselle Burvett at the Exhibition, during the piano recitals, resembles Kowalski's 'Hungarian March'? It is not a great crime to bear some similarity of rhythm, melody, or harmony to some master; as some one has said, to plant cabbages is to copy someone else. I am unable to discover any resemblance, however, between my Australian march and Kowalski's 'Hungarian March', and now that my 'Salute to Melbourne' has been published, I am going to send it to the *Age* critic, so that he may judge of his own pronouncement. However, I shall not ask for any recantation; my little piece has no other merit than the sentiments that gave rise to it, which are sufficiently expressed in its title. After Monsieur Plumpton I would quote the following as the most reputable piano teachers in Melbourne: Messieurs Fabet, Liede, Kelman, W.C. Russell, Gilott, Otto Linden, Summer, Guenett, and Schek, an accompanist of great talent. Among the ladies, Madam Tasca, and Mesdemoiselles Wilkinson and Burvett. If I have forgotten anyone—which is quite possible—it is accidental and I beg them to excuse me.

In the Land of Kangaroos and Gold Mines, trans. Judith Armstrong (1980, first published in French 1890).

THOMAS WOOD
(1892–1950)

English composer and writer. Wood was educated at Oxford University and the Royal College of Music, before becoming the director of music at Tonbridge School (1918–24) and later a lecturer at Oxford University. Between 1928 and 1939 his main activities were composing and writing. He published a very popular travel book, Cobbers *(1934), after spending from 1930 to 1932 as a music examiner in Australia. During his years of public service from 1939 onwards, Wood made another visit to Australia in 1944–45 to promote the war effort. After the Second World War he chaired the Royal Philharmonic Society and the Arts Council's music panel. His compositions include the cantatas* Forty Singing Seamen *(1925),* Master Mariners *(1927), and* Merchantmen *(1934).*

KOALAS

Judged by this country of distances, Phillip Island is a stone's throw from Melbourne: fifty miles. You take a train to Stony Point and go on by steamer over a strip of channel. I crossed on a day which welded sea and sky into a single sheet of polished steel. The sun was a pale golden disk showing mistily at intervals, and the air was so cold that I caught myself blowing out my breath and watching to see if it would turn to the smoky plume which comes at home in frosty weather. Phillip Island faces Tasmania across the Bass Straits; but on that day, and on many days afterwards, I was ready to believe it faced the South Pole. South Australia and its sunshine had upset my scale of values.

The island is perhaps eleven miles long by seven broad. Beaches of firm white sand surround it except at the southerly corners. Near these the sand gives way to rock, and the coast humps itself into cliffs and headlands and bastions of granite and basalt, guarded by a few outlying fangs to seaward. Elsewhere, sand-dunes run up sharply from the beach, banking an undulating plain. It is dotted with patches of oats and chicory; and in pockets and hollows stand clumps of manna gum and peppermint, bent over and twisted by the ever-blowing southerly wind. The rest is coarse grass and dark scrubby heath, a foil to creamy sprays of tea-tree blossom. It is rough country such as you can see if you think of any one of fifty islands you may know, except, oddly enough, the Isle of Wight, after whose towns—Cowes and Ventnor—two out of the four hamlets are called. But you could never imagine the native bears, the koalas.

The island is a reserve for them. They are allowed to breed, and eat gum-tips, their only food, as freely as they like. No one molests them. No one shoots them to make muffs from their thick soft fur. You might say hell itself it not hot enough for a man who would do that; but throughout Australia these little innocents are nearly exterminated. Unless you go right out into the never-never you can see them only where they exist under Government or domestic protection. On Phillip Island they enjoy the first and are not petted to death by the second. They live unmolested among the tree tops, the most enchanting little people that ever drew breath.

Koalas are on view at any hour of the day. To see them, all you need do is walk through one of the spinneys near Cowes and look up. If your luck is in, you will see half a dozen small grey forms tucked securely into the forks of the trees, peacefully asleep. The night for living, says koala, the day for rest; and his family has sat so long and so firmly among the branches that they have no tails left—a warning arm-chair critics might take to heart.

When you have found your koalas, choose the one you love the best, clap your hands, and shout 'Teddy!' Teddy wakes up, rubs the sleep out of his eyes, and turns round slowly to stare down at you in benign and gentle astonishment.

'Bless the Missing Family Tail!' he says; 'here's *another* of those long-legged bears that grow no fur. Rum: rum: em*phat*-ically rum!'

He keeps his little round eyes fixed on yours, blinking solemnly; and all you can do is wriggle with delight at your discovery that in this disillusioned grown-up world you have met the most lovable toy of your childhood come to life. Here is the very teddy-bear Aunt Alice gave you when you were three. If Aunt Alice put her hand deep down into her handbag and did you really proud, the two are the same size. Perhaps not the same colour, for koala favours grey or silver or a glossy browny-black, and goes in for white waistcoats; but otherwise, front view, they are twins. The same big bushy ears: the same trusting little face: the same absurd black button of a nose. In profile koala is slightly different from the teddy-bear you cuddled in your cot. His nose is hooky. How he got this touch of the Jew is harder to explain than how he lost his tail.

If you waken koala towards evening, he may decide it is time he roused himself and got his breakfast. If he does, you will learn, probably for the first time, what fastidiousness really means. He gets out of his arm-chair and climbs upwards, slowly and carefully, clasping the boughs with arms and feet and sticking his strong, curved, needle-pointed claws into the bark. He stretches out a hand to a leaf, pulls it gently to that ridiculous nose, and sniffs. No; too mature. He selects another: touches it with the tiniest tip of narrow pink tongue. No-o: a leetle too much body. He climbs higher. Tries again. Then again. At last! He munches solemnly, keeping even at meal-times his inimitable air of unfailing wonder, of innocent amazement, that any tree could be so crammed with surprises as the one he finds himself in at the moment.

If he decides to climb down instead of up, he does so stern first, like a seaman; and if he wants another tree, he scuttles over the ground on his way to it as though he went by clockwork. This happens only at night, so far as I saw. I stayed in a jolly house close to the shore, and nearly always after dusk there would be koalas lumbering about the garden, grunting like pigs. This noise is the only one I ever heard them make, and is called forth, probably, by the excitement of amorous adventure, into which I was too discreet to inquire. Their other noise I was lucky enough never to hear, for Phillip Island is their Eden; but if koala is hurt he will whimper like a baby: his knuckles in his eyes and tears hopping off the end of his poor little nose.

I have met only one more entrancing person than koala, and that is his wife with her baby. I lost my heart to her completely. So would you. Like all marsupials, she has a pouch for the cub to slip into; but generally she carries him on her back. She always does so when she moves about. He clings on like a burr, and looks like a tiny ball of fluff peeping over her shoulder. When she wedges herself into a fork for her daytime rest she nurses him in her arms, stroking him gently and patting him from time to time, even in her sleep. To see that alone repays a voyage to Australia. It is something no other part of the world can give.

Cobbers (1953 edition, first published 1934).

———

MAGGIE TEYTE
(1888–1976)

English singer. A soprano, she studied at the Royal College of Music and in Paris with Jean de Reszke before making her stage début in Monte Carlo in 1907. Teyte made her London début, as Cherubino, in 1910, and her American, in the same role, in Chicago in 1911. The companies with which she sang included the Chicago Opera Company (1911–14), the Boston Opera Company (1914–17), and the British National Opera Company (from 1922). In the mid-1930s she toured Australia. Teyte, who was particularly noted for her interpretation of songs by Debussy, sang her last operatic role in London in 1951 and gave her farewell concert at the Royal Festival Hall in 1955. After her retirement, she recalled her Australian visit.

WONDERS OF AUSTRALIA

A party of three of us went to Australia to give concerts—Tudor Davies, the well-known tenor, Yelland Richards, a young pianist, and myself. The journey out was a diversion in itself. I remember at Gibraltar the ship was very quiet; everyone had gone ashore, and I was alone on the deck, looking at the famous Rock, when a big, horrible black crow alighted on the deck-rail near me. Is the crow a bird of ill omen? This one exuded a most sinister atmosphere.

When we finally disembarked at Melbourne, which I remember as a charming city, it was springtime there. I was taken to play on a golf course laid out in a forest of mimosa trees—wattle, as the Australians call it. I never realised before how many varieties of this tree there are. I am very happy to have visited Australia if only to have seen its flora and fauna, which are really wonderful. One day some friends drove us out to see the panorama from the Dandenong Range—below us lay a forest of trees as far as the eye could see, and our host informed us that people did not travel very much that way, as, forty or fifty miles into the bush, the country was still inhabited by head-hunting aborigines. I found this hard to believe, but perhaps in the 'thirties it was true?

It was on this trip that I heard what I think is the most wonderful piece of synchronisation I know of in the bird world—the call of the whip birds. The male begins with two low drawn-out whistles, ending in a loud noise like a whip-crack. This is followed immediately by two notes sounding like 'chew-chew,' uttered by the female, who then descends to the low note on which the male began. The two birds synchronise like one.

I stayed at the Menzies Hotel in Melbourne, and at six o'clock one morning, the hot sun already high, I heard the most awful clatter of voices, just like a lot of women squabbling in a market square. I wasn't going to miss the fun, so quickly drew my curtains, and was surprised to see a flock of green parrots flying around the chimney-pots! John Brownlee, the Australian baritone, with whom we also took some trips around Melbourne, told me that one of the finest sights in the district was to see a flight of white cockatoos on the wing. Also from Melbourne we visited Melba's house, Coombe Cottage, at Lilydale, where I admired her lovely music-room upholstered in yellow brocade. It was walking through her garden that I heard my first kookaburra, or laughing jackass. I thought at first that the noise was Tudor Davies playing one of his tricks—it seemed impossible that a bird should laugh like that!

While Melbourne might be called the social centre of the vast Commonwealth of Australia—it has a tradition of entertainment and hospitality—Adelaide was the place where I found a more artistic atmosphere than in other parts of the country, and it was from here that I carried away one more sinister picture, which is connected in my mind with the story of Iris, the little Japanese girl, in Mascagni's opera *Iris*. In despair from the curse of her blind father, she throws herself to her death from an upper floor of the 'yoshiwara' [house of ill fame]. The transformation scene in the third act of this opera shows the iris flowers under the influence of the hot sun, blooming in the open sewers of the town. On the outskirts of Adelaide was a swamp, running along the side of the road, and from the evil-smelling mud rose, straight and tall, hundreds of beautiful white Easter lilies.

Of the other cities we visited I remember Sydney as being very beautiful, but commerce was decidedly the dominating factor there then. Brisbane was very hot and dusty when I saw it, but that being over twenty years ago now, many things will have changed. As for the musical side of our trip, while it was an artistic success, it was a financial fiasco, which I suppose was bound to colour one's impression of things

in general, but I shall never regret my visit to the great Commonwealth, and the sight I got of so many of its wonders.

Star on the Door (1958).

TYRONE GUTHRIE
(1900–71)

*English actor and theatre director. Oxford-educated Guthrie began acting at
Oxford's Playhouse in 1924, but subsequently turned to directing. After
being appointed to take charge of plays at the Old Vic and Sadler's Wells in
1933, he became administrator in 1937, a position he held until 1947. He
later worked in many countries, directing plays and founding theatres. His
theories influenced the designs of a number of theatres, including the Chich-
ester Festival Theatre (1962) and the Olivier at the National in London
(1976). In 1947, 'this sad, mad, Don Quixote of the English theatre', as
another English director, Sir Peter Hall, later described him, visited Australia for a particular reason, as he explains in his autobiography.*

A NATIONAL THEATRE FOR AUSTRALIA?

Early in 1947 I went to Australia as the guest of the British Council.
The Council had been asked to send someone to take a look at the
Australian theatrical scene and then to advise the Premier, Mr Chifley,
who was considering the possibility of an Australian national theatre.

In six weeks I visited the six principal cities, in which dwell more
than half the population of the entire continent. I attended endless
receptions and cocktail parties, met the federal Premier and the Prime
Minister of each state, and saw a great many amateur theatrical performances of widely varying quality. I did not visit a cattle or sheep station—I hardly saw a horse or cow all the time I was there—and I
would not dream of claiming that I had seen the real Australia, whatever that may be.

No traveller, however, can help getting impressions. Mine are the
rather specialized impressions of someone doing a high-pressure tour in
a purposely restricted professional field. I say this because I quickly discovered that Australians, as a whole, have an almost morbidly developed inferiority complex. 'How do you like us?' eagerly smiling

strangers would ask. 'How do you like our country?' The question was strictly rhetorical.

Naturally, after a residence of two weeks, trying manfully to be a gracious guest, I would not be likely to make any unfavourable comment. I would in all sincerity say something to the effect that, immensely as I was enjoying myself, as yet I hardly felt qualified to express an opinion. However pleasantly and warmly I tried to phrase this sentiment, it never failed to displease. Here, the smiling strangers would feel, is one more bloody Pommy, one more sneering, sophisticated, colonial-minded bloody bastard.

It was the same with food. Britain was still rationed. After five years on short commons 'my appetite, never very large, had become rather small. Hostesses with the kindest intentions would face me at four o'clock of a very hot afternoon with a plate on which in heaped profusion would be half a cow and about a hundredweight of mashed potato. Smiling eagerly, oh so kindly, they would say 'How do you like our food?'

After a party till two the night before, after three or four hours in a plane, before making a speech and in a temperature considerably higher than I am used to, I would pick and fumble at the steak, poke tunnels in the mountain of potato and pull heavily at the draughts of hot sweet tea which wash down every item of Australia's rather limited menu. 'Go on!' the host would say; 'Dig into it. There's no rationing here.' But beneath the gleaming smiles, the cordial pressing tones, it was apparent that they thought me one more bloody, sneering, sophisticated Pommy, who turns up his nose at good, plain, hearty, solid Australian food.

The anxiety to be liked by, and to impress, visitors from home— Australians even of the third and fourth Australian-born generation refer to Britain as home—is paradoxically the greatest danger to Anglo–Australian cordiality. Honest visitors cannot accord unqualified admiration and delight to every aspect of Australia. You try to concentrate upon the many things which there are to admire and like; you try to understand the rest. But right off you are put in an impossible position by this almost universal, desperate and transparent desire to impress.

If you gush and rave indiscriminately you will be taken—and quite rightly, too—either for a hypocrite or a fool, probably both. If you express even the faintest implication of criticism, immediately a wire fence springs up between you and your interlocutor, tingling with a dangerous voltage of electricity. One more unguarded word and, amid sheets of blue flame, you will fuse the mother complex. The visitor has somehow to reconcile an attitude of humility and shyness becoming to a new boy with the benign authority of one who represents home and mother. Neither attitude must be overdone—the humility can so easily seem sissy, the benignity no less easily seem patronizing; and neither attitude must be insincere.

What impressed me particularly in Australia was a rather back-handed reflection on our own society in Britain. I had been very conscious of the same thing the first time I went to Canada and the United States. You suddenly realize how tremendously important, how all-pervading in every aspect of British life is the class structure of society. Of course, class is not a static but a fluid notion; the class structure of even so ancient and elaborately stratified a society as that in England is constantly changing; in the last forty years it has undergone, under pressure of war conditions and post-war economic problems, a revolution quite as drastic as that which occurred in France in 1789.

Nevertheless, even after such a revolution, it is extraordinary to what an extent British life is still dominated by the traditions and opinions of a numerically tiny upper class. You do not realize this until you live for a while in one of the communities that have come into being since the decay of the feudal system.

Thus my dominant impression on this trip was not of Australia at all, but of home, provoked by impressions of a supposedly classless Australia. I do not mean to imply that British class-consciousness is a good thing or bad. It is both. But not till you get away do you realize how dominant it is. The English village is still, spiritually as well as architecturally, dominated, often resentfully, by the great house and the church. *The Times* is the house magazine of quite a small, exclusive, but overwhelmingly influential club. To 'get anywhere' in England—this applies much less forcibly in Scotland, Wales or Northern Ireland—it is still almost a prerequisite that you subscribe to 'establishment' conventions of speech, manners and morals. If you do not, then you must make your way in business, politics or one of the learned professions by enacting, rather cleverly, the character role of an Outsider.

Australian society is no more classless than any other. In the small towns as well as the large, the doctors and dentists and their wives dine with one another, not with the truck-drivers and their wives, for the excellent reason that, by dint of common interests and roughly similar income, the evening is apt to be easier and pleasanter. In new countries like Australia and Canada, it is, of course, very much easier to move from one class to another than in the more ancient and consequently

more rigidly stratified communities. And in countries with an expand-
ing economy, again like Australia and Canada, it is far easier to make
and to lose money, with consequent change in social position—
upwards or down.

In Australia in 1947 domestic service was still considered a degrading
occupation, although manual labour—by dint of powerful trades
unions—seemed to be rewarded, in proportion to intellectual labour,
more highly than I had ever known. But, paradoxically, this made for
more, not less, class distinction. Where nearly all homes are run without
domestic help, and on a similar scale of expenditure, the cultural standard
can still be almost always and immediately assessed; and this, rather than
wealth, becomes the distinguishing factor. Indeed, most of the more cultured people seemed to be poor. I suppose it was very snobbish and naïve
of me to be surprised, when I gave a lecture at a university, that the gentleman whose duty it was to stoke the boiler arrived in a Cadillac wearing
dirty overalls; whereas the Vice-Chancellor, whose duty it was to take the
chair, arrived on a bicycle, with clips on his evening-dress trousers.

I did not notice that spiritually the professional classes seemed
adversely affected by their low economic status. There must be less
time to read Plato if you have to dust the study and wash up lunch. But
I guess such tasks are not inimical to contemplation.

Contrariwise, I did not notice that the economically dominant workers were more happy. Nowhere, except in America under Prohibition,
have I seen such widespread and brutal drunkenness. But this may not be
a symptom of the Australian working man's malaise: for one thing, by no
means all the drunks were manual workers. Is it just possible that conspicuous insobriety is, as it was in the United States, one of the consequences of restrictive legislation in connection with the sale of liquor?

One other thing surprised me at the time: I suppose it was the influence of the immigration propaganda—all those high-coloured posters
of Sunburnt Sicklemen of Autumn Weary—but I had expected to find
Australia full of handsome, laconic men; shy but tremendously virile.
Perhaps when I was there all these types were temporarily out back.
Certainly the cities seems to be full of excitable, nervous little gentlemen with light voices and rather a lot of jewellery. It was the women
who were handsome, laconic and tremendously virile.

I have since wondered if this is perhaps a phase through which all
communities pass at a certain stage of development, a certain biological
distance from the tremendous effort put out by the pioneers. If your
immediate forbears have made a gigantic inroad upon the family's
resources of physical energy, will power and courage, it is not surprising

that for a generation or two nature should need a rest. Consider how very few of the world's great men have had sons of anything like comparable stature.

It is an ironic fact that the energy of pioneers has all to be expended upon the herculean task of just keeping alive. Consequently, these efforts are inadequately chronicled for posterity and inadequately celebrated. No one had time to record in writing, in paint, music or sculpture achievements of which, in consequence, posterity underestimates the difficulty, the glory—and the cost.

Professionally, my visit was not particularly exciting. There was one moderate semi-amateur production of *The Merry Wives of Windsor*, derivative in style from England, and one rather dreary semi-amateur production of *Rigoletto*, derivative in style from Sadler's Wells rather than Italy. There were sundry one-act plays, an amateur production of Noël Coward's *Bitter Sweet* with some superb singing but feeble acting and production, and the Australian version of *Oklahoma!* received with immense acclaim. I thought it inferior to the London production in about the same measure that the London production had been inferior to the New York original. I can remember nothing which struck me as distinctively Australian. I knew that Covent Garden and Sadler's Wells were full of excellent Australian singers; that many talented young Australians were knocking on the theatrical door in London and New York, to say nothing of slightly older people like Judith Anderson, Coral Browne, Cyril Ritchard and Robert Helpmann, who have gained honourable admittance. Therefore, it was no surprise to find Australia an extraordinary mine of talent. There was at that time no satisfactory organization for its expression, no considerable public appreciation to develop it, and little enlightened criticism to lead the public.

My report to the Prime Minister suggested that the time to *build* a national theatre had not yet arrived. But it suggested several practical ways of developing Australian talent and taste as a preliminary. It was my view that before spending great sums on a building, a much more moderate sum should be spent on equipping the human material of a national theatre. This, incidentally, should apply to the foundation of any national theatre, be it in Britain, Canada, the United States or anywhere else.

My report can hardly have reached Australia before Mr Chifley's Labour government was replaced by the Conservative government of Mr Menzies. The Menzies government took a traditionally conservative view of Art, and the report fell upon stony ground.

The suggestion, however, that Australian taste might not be entirely perfect and that Australia might, in certain matters, be a decade or two behind certain other communities, aroused a tremendous head of steam. Persons who would not otherwise have given a snap of their fingers to support a national theatre felt a passionate eagerness for Australia to possess such an institution, and a passionate rage against the sneering, bloody Pommy who dared to suggest that the time was not quite yet. This may have been of some small assistance three or four years later in the promotion of the Elizabethan Theatre Trust.

Under this trust various important interests united to commemorate the first visit to Australia of the Queen, shortly after her accession, by the establishment of a theatre and an opera company. It was a conspicuous recognition of the fact that in the new Elizabethan age Australia recognized the need for such companies as a part of the national life, and recognized, too, that the quality of such things is not estimable in solely quantitative terms; that an opera or a play must not be regarded as a failure if it fails to pay its way.

A Life in the Theatre (1960).

LAURENCE OLIVIER
(1907–89)

English actor and director. Olivier, who made his professional début in London in 1924, became famous as both a stage and film actor, noted particularly for his performances in Shakespearian roles. Generally considered the greatest British actor of his era, Sir Laurence Olivier and his then wife Vivien Leigh toured Australia for six months in 1948 with the Old Vic Company, sponsored by the British Council, appearing in The School for Scandal, Richard III, *and* The Skin of Our Teeth. *There was a poignancy about the visit for Olivier, who later wrote, 'Somehow, somewhere on this tour I knew that Vivien was lost to me.' The company also visited New Zealand, where Olivier had an operation for a torn cartilage that he had suffered in Australia. From 1963 to 1973, Olivier was the director of the National Theatre in London.*

ADELAIDE

March 31st. Adelaide. Arrived at 8 quite exhausted after a really deadly night. Straight to South Australian Hotel. Breakfast, unpacking; popped over to the Theatre Royal which is quite divine. Pretty old, lovely atmosphere, holds 1450. Very much wish we were doing 'School'. Came back to Press Conference at 12.0. When I talk slowly to the press I'm inclined to get very pompous, and I am apt to lose the trend which is faithfully quoted; when quickly, then fairly intelligently and am wildly misquoted. After lunch went to call at Government House. Sir Willoughby and Lady Norrie both charming—also the house. Dread news that 'Skin' must open Monday, May 12th, instead of Tuesday.

April 4th. Sunday. Lighting for 'Skin'—worth describing. Stage ready by 5. Quite confident all cues just had to be run through. First cue came up quite wrong with a lot of pinks in it. Thought at first colour wrong, but no. Cues came at right times but wrong things happened. I really thought my time had come. This was the *only* day when lighting could be done, so it was no use my going home and working out a new plot all night even if I had the energy. Then Bill Bunday said something about having a vague memory that at the Piccadilly Theatre, whose lighting plot we were working from, numbering went from Prompt Side to O.P. We tried plugging in all spots in reverse—it worked! We nearly died of relief. Could it be H.M. Tennent's spite against the Old Vic!

April 12th. Dress Rehearsal 'Skin'. Opening performance 8.0. It really went wonderfully and Vivien made a *very* good *long* speech. Elsie [Byer] and all stage management to supper. The end of a really hectic fortnight.

April 13th. Rather a bemused notice in the paper quoting desperately from the foreword.

April 14th. Rude letters about 'Skin' in the press. After lunch to our great joy we were taken to a private collection of white kangaroos. They are Albinos. Vivien had seen kangaroos in Perth, but these were my first and I was ravished. People pointed out joeys that had just at that moment—if only we hadn't missed—jumped from the does' pouches. Just like Ruth Draper's garden. I took photos desperately but I know the light too bad for my sort of photography.

April 16th. Sir William Mitchell (Stephen's uncle) took us round the university, 4000 students. Very impressive. Talked and answered questions to the Students' Theatre Group for about ½ hour. After lunch to Stony Fells Vineyard. Saw the crushings and had a great deal explained to us. We sampled all and sundry and thought the sherry very good. It was all delightful but we dared not enjoy it as we should have liked. Tearing ourselves away we dutifully went to Art Gallery. We flung open the door on our arrival forgetful of the flagon of sherry we had been given which was on the floor of the car and which shattered itself in the gutter directly opposite the entrance to the noble edifice. We could not face the disgrace and had to drive on several yards. The car behind was *very* angry. Correspondence has raged over 'Skin' in the papers. Those in favour being rather pushed into the background by the *Advertiser*. It has gone really wonderfully generally. I am not at all happy about Antrobus yet, feel very uneven and unfinished. The whole show makes me excessively nervous and I frankly dislike the break up bits. I've wanted to play the part so often I hate to be disappointing myself in it. V. is wonderful—better than ever.

April 17th. Two last shows and farewell to Adelaide. Vivien insisted that I make the speech—quite long. 'A picture gallery must have its Rembrandts *and* its Henry Moores'—an allusion as to why a play like 'Skin' was in our repertory. Threw a party afterwards. H.E. came and was most charming and kind, saying jolly nice things about our being good ambassadors. His small son asked why Lady Olivier called herself 'Miss Vitamin B'. 400 other people also turned up. The front of house girls gave us an enormous box of chocolates and the staff a remarkable inkwell made of Burraburraburra wood or something. Waltzing Matilda was sung.

Felix Barker, *The Oliviers* (1973).

JEAN SHRIMPTON

(1942–)

English model. One of the best-known and most beautiful models in the world during the 1960s, Jean Shrimpton was invited to Melbourne in 1965 as the guest of the Victorian Racing Club for some of the main events of the Spring Racing Carnival. Her appearance on Derby Day, 30 October, caused a furore, as she recalls in her autobiography. A photograph of her taken that day has since become one of the icons of the sixties in Australia.

'A CAUSE CÉLÈBRE'

Then Felice phoned me up one day, highly pleased with herself. She had landed me a job in Australia in November, away from the British winter.

'All you have to do is go to the Melbourne races wearing clothes made of Orlon and present the prizes for the Melbourne Cup,' she explained. 'The money is good as well. A thousand pounds a week for two weeks of appearances and all expenses paid.'

It sounded all right to me, and even Terry thought it was a good deal. Amazingly, he said he would come with me.

'Australia's a long way away,' he said. 'Let's both go. We'll come back by way of San Francisco.'

It all sounded wonderful. The company employing me paid his expenses—not because he was Terence Stamp, but because he was escorting me. I was always allowed to take someone with me on this kind of engagement.

Unfortunately, through ignorance, it was all to go disastrously wrong. I was very unprofessional. Orlon were paying me all this money, but they never bothered to choreograph me. I was not given any proper briefing and I never bothered to ask any questions. They merely sent me some inexpensive dress and suit lengths of synthetic fibres which did not impress me a great deal. My modelling work for *Vogue* had accustomed me to something rather better.

I was supposed to have some smart, race-going outfits made up from these lengths, and it was left to me to design what I wanted and arrange for them to be made. Someone told me about a dressmaker called Colin Rolfe and he did the job. That was boring enough, having to go for fittings and to be pinned. Also, there was not quite sufficient fabric. Colin Rolfe was anxious about this, but I said cheerfully: 'Oh, it doesn't matter. Make them a bit shorter—no one's going to notice.'

So he did. And that was how the mini was born.

I had settled for very simple shapes for all four outfits, and all were above the knee. It didn't seem to matter. I wore my clothes on the short side anyway and, in Britain, hemlines were beginning to creep up.

Apart from being four inches above the knee, the outfits seemed all right—though, to be truthful, rather dull. I put a large piece of costume jewellery in the middle of the little white shift dress that was to cause all the trouble—just to cheer it up.

Things began to go wrong the minute Terry and I arrived in Melbourne. We had travelled out alone, and the people who were promoting the appearance met us at the airport and took us by limo to a modern Melbourne hotel. The first panic was that our luggage—holding the Orlon dresses—had disappeared. It turned up a day late. The organizers should have been pleased at having Terry thrown in, but they didn't seem to know who he was—which, not surprisingly, didn't exactly please him. As far as they were concerned, boyfriends meant trouble. He was wearing a flowery shirt, and to their untutored eyes he looked like one of the Beatles. His hair was Beatle-length and he wasn't conventional enough for them. They did not recognize that the Beatles were Carnaby Street while Terry was Savile Row. Then, when we got to the hotel, I found they had put us in separate rooms.

'We don't need two rooms,' I said politely. 'One will be fine.'

'But you can't share a room,' one of the organizers said, and with typical Australian bluntness added: 'You and Mr Stamp are not married.'

I wasn't having that. I have never been one for hypocrisy—and besides, I was positive there was one man there in the Orlon group who was sharing with a woman who wasn't his wife. I didn't know this for sure, but my intuition told me. So I pointed an accusing finger and said: 'But he's sharing a room with a woman he isn't married to. Why do you expect me not to share?'

My intuition was spot on. After some embarrassed umm-ing and ah-ing they reluctantly agreed that we could have a double room, but the atmosphere was not good. It proved to be hardly worth the argument.

The day of the races was a hot one, so I didn't bother to wear any stockings. My legs were still brown from the summer, and as the dress was short it was hardly formal. I had no hat or gloves with me, for the very good reason that I owned neither. I went downstairs cheerfully from my hotel room, all regardless of what was to come.

The organizers were waiting in the hall.

'Where is your hat? Where are your gloves?' one of the women asked, looking pointedly at my bare legs.

'Haven't got any,' I said. No one moved. I couldn't think why everyone looked so cross. 'Isn't it time to go?' I asked as they hovered, staring at me.

In the limo that the promoters had hired to take me to the racecourse, I thought the men from the fibre company who were escorting me continued to look cross. Terry, smart in his dark needlecord suit, didn't say anything. He was used to the way I dressed. But when we arrived at the racecourse it didn't take long to realize I had committed the most terrible faux pas. The Melbourne women, in stockings, hats and long white gloves, were pointing at me and glaring. The men, as usual, didn't take too much notice.

What I had not appreciated was that the Melbourne Cup was the smartest event of the Australian year. The conservative Melbourne matrons in their somewhat out-of-date best were terribly shocked: my appearance was described as insulting and disgraceful. Opinion was that I had been rude and not bothered about an occasion that was important to my hosts and to Australian society generally. They were affronted.

I suppose it was discourteous of me, but any rudeness was unintended. I discovered too late that the sponsors expected me to go all dolled up with hat and gloves, looking like a fashion plate. I was under the delusion that they had hired Jean Shrimpton, the girl next door, the gawky waif—not a clothes horse.

I was very much mistaken—and what a target for the press photographers I was, trapped in this short skirt four inches above the knee. I was surrounded by cameramen, all on their knees like proposing Victorian swains, shooting upwards to make my skirt look even shorter. I had no idea this was going to happen—this was publicity that I certainly had not planned. Unfortunately it was not quite the sort of publicity that Orlon had in mind.

I became a *cause célèbre*. Australia was miles behind Europe in those days: the sixties as experienced in Britain had not yet arrived there. A certain section of Australian society was aghast that I had apparently thumbed my nose at all the stuffy old conservative Sheilas. Younger people, particularly those who couldn't afford to go to the races, were on my side. The newspapers got so heated that they actually said I had split Australia in two. It was ludicrous; I couldn't believe it. My picture was all over the front pages—worldwide!—and fashion editors argued for and against this rather boring little short white shift.

I was so fed up that I was on the verge of leaving, but Orlon were aware that at least they were getting a lot of publicity. They gently talked me into staying, and tried to persuade me to dress rather more suitably the next day.

I am afraid I became rather pompous. 'I will wear what I want where I want—and nobody's opinion will change me,' I declared. 'I rose to the top of my profession being what I am. And I shall continue to be just that.'

Fighting talk. But the next day I capitulated. I went to their wretched race meeting to present the prizes dressed in a slightly longer suit and wearing a hat that the sponsors had rushed out and bought me, plus gloves and stockings. I publicly complained that I did not feel comfortable with all these extras, adding defiantly that I had worn them only because the sponsors had asked me to.

It did not stop the publicity. The criticism over my appearance on the first day had not died down, yet on this second day I was described as looking 'exquisite'. That was just as much over the top as the criticisms had been the day before.

I seemed to ride out the publicity, but Terry found the sense of disapproval coming from every direction uncomfortable. That, coupled with the fact that I was getting all the attention, caused him to take off for San Francisco on the third day.

Under the rules of the contract, I had to go to the races four times. On the last day I wore a flecked off-white coat, still well above the knee, and stockings, and carried a handbag. But I did not wear gloves and I tied my hair back with a big bow. It was my last little gesture of defiance. I then fled to Sydney. Asked for a statement by the rather less conservative Sydney press I said, rather crossly: 'The trouble is they should never have asked me to come here in the first place. They wanted a mannequin, not a photographic model. I'm not interested in clothes and I hate people staring at me. I certainly didn't think I was going to cause all this trouble, and I'm sorry for the people who brought me out here.

I suppose the people who brought me out there could have said I was not exactly dragged there, screaming. I had agreed to go. But at twenty-three, you don't think as logically as that.

The end result was that all over Australia young girls started shortening their skirts. The pictures which the British newspapers used had the same results back home. Suddenly the mini, which had had a half-hearted start in Paris, became fashionable.

Mary Quant rode in on the back of it, immediately making shorter skirts. Many people gave her the credit for the new craze, but the truth was that the mini took off because Orlon had been stingy with their fabric.

As I had another couple of jobs to do I stayed in Australia for ten days more. I was miserable and kept ringing up Felice. Some long-forgotten guy took me out and showed me round, which was nice of him. I got by, but I was wondering all the time what Terry was up to and I was not happy until I caught up with him in San Francisco. He met me off the plane, and we drove to LA, where we booked into a log cabin-type hotel near Carmel that was a sort of glorified health farm.

An Autobiography (1990).

15

Expatriates

♦

BARRY HUMPHRIES

(1934–)

Melbourne-born 'music hall artiste' and writer. Educated at Melbourne Grammar School and the University of Melbourne, Barry Humphries acted with the Union Theatre, Melbourne (1953–54), and the Phillip Street Revue Theatre, Sydney (1956), before leaving Australia for England in 1959. In 1962 he toured Australia in his one-man show, A Nice Night's Entertainment, *in which two of the characters for whom he was to become most famous appeared, Sandy Stone and Edna Everage, who had made her stage début in Melbourne in 1955. Humphries continued to display his talents as a brilliant satirist, especially of the Australian middle classes, in numerous other solo shows, films, television programmes, and publications in subsequent years. In his autobiography he recalls the beginning of the 1962 visit.*

'SOLD OUT'

Although I had made some progress on my script in Cornwall before the accident, I had still a long way to go; so it was probably just as well that our voyage to Melbourne, via Rotterdam, Lisbon, Genoa and Auckland, lasted six weeks, and I could finish writing the show. We travelled on a Norwegian cargo ship with only twelve other passengers, and it was rather like being in a play by Agatha Christie. There were two nuns, an Australian honeymoon couple, and the Gillespies, a middle-aged pair migrating to Australia; a destination that we all knew they would detest. They actually began to complain about their anticipated social hardships when we were three hours out of Lisbon, and since everyone sat at the same table, the troll-like Norwegian captain had to exert great self-control in listening to this lady's ceaseless whinging. We were rather pleased therefore, when somewhere in the Indian Ocean during rough weather, poor Mrs Gillespie's chair capsized, throwing her legs over her shoulders, and she was seen by all, on that tropical evening at least, to have abandoned the humid confinements of her panties. From that undignified moment until we berthed at Auckland, Enid Gillespie never emerged from her cabin.

Also on board was an elderly German widow and her blond nephew; the son, we gathered, of a German industrialist in New Zealand. His urbane and smiling scepticism about the Holocaust was not the least of his charming attributes, though we were only privy to his political and racial views on those few occasions when he graced us with his presence. Most of his time was spent below decks providing amusement for rougher members of the Norwegian crew, who, given certain inducements, were prepared to overlook the German invasion of their country and had their own quaint methods of burying the hatchet.

In Auckland my wife was reunited with her parents, and with some success I tested my new material at a lunch-hour performance at the University. We got to know a few Kiwi poets and writers, especially Karl Stead and his beautiful wife, Kay, who to this day, remember more about my visit to New Zealand than I do …

When we finally reached Melbourne, my parents were there to greet us and there was even a family dinner party to which we were *both* invited! My sister, now living in Melbourne, had married Robert, an engineer, and already had a daughter, Penelope; my brother Michael was in his final year at school and Christopher was studying architecture at the University. They were much changed since I had seen them last and seemed to regard me with a shy diffidence. I sadly regretted that my early marriage and expatriation and the inevitable age difference had created a gulf in my relationship with them.

Although I was nervous about my opening night at the Assembly Hall, my father, it seemed, was even more apprehensive. On the day of the final dress rehearsal, the box-office lady called me over. 'Had your dad in here this morning, Barry,' she said, 'What a nice man, and thinks the world of you too.'

'What did he want?' I asked.

'Look, it was funny really, and I reckon I shouldn't be telling you this, but he wanted to buy all the seats in the house to give to his friends in the Rotary Club.'

'*All* the seats?' I asked stupefied.

'Every blessed seat,' said Joan. 'He has to be your number one fan.'

'What … what did you tell him?'

'Well, I more or less told him I would if I could but I can't. You're *sold out*, aren't you?'

I told her I hadn't known that and I asked her what he had said.

'He didn't say anything really, just looked amazed. But I found him a single for himself right up at the back on the side, and he wouldn't take a comp either.'

More Please (1992).

CHRISTINA STEAD
(1902–82)

Sydney-born novelist. Christina Stead, who was educated at Sydney Teachers' College, left Australia in 1928. For the next few decades, during which she wrote such books as Seven Poor Men of Sydney *(1934),* The Man Who Loved Children *(1940), generally considered to be her greatest work, and* For Love Alone *(1944), she lived in England, Europe and the United States. After her first return visit to her homeland, made in 1969, Stead wrote 'Another View of the Homestead', which was originally published in* Hemisphere *in 1970. She finally returned to live in Australia in 1974.*

'ANOTHER VIEW OF THE HOMESTEAD'

All night the sleeper sleeps close to a board, irons rattle, a violin played aft vibrates along the side, the body of the ship rises and falls, the engines beat on through seven hundred sleeps. The first day, yellow cliffs, blue coasts, next day, the steep green island south; a new world. Homeward bound on that ship in 1928, a Lithuanian woman in grey knitted skullcap, fifty-five, short, sour, salty; a tall English woman, eighty-four in black, small hat and scarf, who stands for hours by the lounge wall waiting for the Great Bear to rise; a missionary woman, thirty-nine invalided home, worn by tropical disease, her soft dark skin like old chamois; she is going back to the town, street, church she left eighteen years before, because of a painful love-affair with the pastor: his wife now dead, he has just married a girl from the choir, 'Just as I was then,' she says. There's an Australian girl, lively, thin, black hair flying, doing tricks with a glass of water, by the big hold aft, and around her her new nation, Sicilians, her husband one—they are playing the fiddle. There's a redgold girlish mother from the Northern Rivers, scurrying, chattering, collecting cronies. Three times she booked for England, twice cancelled; the third time, her youngest daughter brought her to the boat in Sydney. Three unmarried daughters, 'Oh, but we are not like other families; we cannot bear to part.' Before Hobart, she telegraphs that she will land at Melbourne, go home by train; but they telegraph, 'Go on, Mother, please.' 'They don't say how they are!' She is faded, sleepless, 'What are they doing now?' At Melbourne, the women dissuade her and she goes on. Across the surly Bight they make her laugh at herself; she laughs and turns away, aggrieved. As we approach Fremantle, she is dreadfully disturbed; the ship may dock in the night and leave before morning. She sends a message to the Captain. At Fremantle, she telegraphs, disembarks, her rose color all back. 'I'm going home! They'll be getting ready! Oh, what a party we'll have!' 'What about the presents?' 'I'll give them back; I did before.'

There's a country minister and his wife, two dusty black bundles who conduct services in the cabin before a number of meek, coloured bundles in Sunday hats. The couple gain in stature the farther they travel, until in the Red Sea, having lost all provincial glumness, the minister shouldering tall against the railing, arm and finger stretched, explains the texts, the riddle of the Pyramids, the meaning of Revelations.

For years, I thought hazily about returning; and like that, it would be, in just such a varied society, myself unhampered, landing unknown, 'Poor amongst the poor' (a line of Kate Brown's I always liked) and would see for myself. After I had looked round lower Sydney where I walked every morning of my highschool, college and work life, I would go out and stand in front of Lydham Hill, the old sandstone cottage on a ridge which, from a distance looks east over Botany Bay, straight between Cape Banks and Cape Solander, to the Pacific; and the other way, due west, over a grass patch and the yellow road to Stoney Creek, to the Blue Mountains. That is how it was when my cousin and I lived there with other little ones and played in the long grass and under the old pines.

I knew all that was gone; they had driven surveyors' pegs into the gardens, the neglected orchard, before we left for Watson's Bay; and a friend in the Mitchell Library archives some years ago sent me coloured slides of the house that is. But still I would go and look at the homestead.

The other place—'Watson's'? By a magic that I came by by accident, I was able to transport Watson's noiselessly and as if it were an emulsion or a streak of mist to the Chesapeake; and truly, the other place is not there for me anymore; the magician must believe in himself. And then for long years I had a nightmare, that I was back at Watson's, without a penny saved for my trip abroad, my heart like a stone. It was otherwise. I came by air, the sailor dropped by a roc, Ulysses home without all that reconnoitering of coasts, a temporary citizen of a flying village with fiery windows, creaking and crashing across the star-splattered dark; and looking down on the horizontal rainbows which lie at dawn around Athens, around Darwin.

Unlike the ship, though close-packed as a crate of eggs, we travel with people we may hear but never see. There is only one street in the flying village and in it you mainly see children conducted up and down. Beside me, is a Greek-born mother with her Australian-born son, aged seven, she talking across the alley in English to her Greek-born neighbours, about the good life in Australia, the peace, the prospects, the education. What you hear in her tones is the good news, the rich boast delivered somewhere outside Athens to the grandparents; it is a wonderful country, we are lucky to be there, no social struggle, plenty of work, success ahead, money everywhere, no coloured people. (It turns out she thinks this.) Standing now in the alley stretching, a tall Italian proud that he has been in the country forty-two years (a year longer than my absence). There are fourteen children of all ages, three high-stomached young women hurrying out to give birth in the lucky place. Few get much sleep but all are goodtempered, it does not matter; their urge and hope is on, on. 'Are you an Australian?' 'Yes.' I am looked at with consideration.

We are a day late, mysteriously stalled at Bangkok: and the talk is of husbands, friends waiting. It is a neighbourly climate—our friendships are nearly three days old; but there is no time for histories and secrets to come out. They will be met soon, go off by plane, train and car, I will never know them.

As for me, high up, almost lunar, I could not take my eyes from the distant earth, every spine and wrinkle visible in the dry air. There did not seem to be a cloud between Darwin and Sydney. Our firebird lazily paddled (so it seemed against the motionless rush of greater vessels up there) under the broad overhang and what a sight all night!—the downpour of stars into the gulf that is not a gulf. In Australia I never lived in suburban or city streets, but with wide waters and skies and this life expanded was coming home to me; you are nearer there (in Australia) to the planets. Even more now—when we have all got a bit of the astronaut in us.

At earliest dawn, the scored and plaited land, water-rivers like trickles of mercury, sand-rivers, the olive furred hide of the red eucalypt land sprawling.

Before that, at Darwin, an airfield in reconstruction. After turnstiles and a forbidding yellow plank staircase, at the top we find a large lounge and in the centre, a small trellissed horseshoe bar, a Chinese gentleman presiding. What good sense, the Australians, what humanity! It is 3:15 a.m. and we are exhausted.

It was there, over the walls, through partitions, in the women's rooms, that there came in high, tired, bangslapping voices, 'Isn't it good to be home?' 'Yes, what a relief!' 'Better than Europe!' 'Oh, yes, I had enough of Europe.' And carolling the gladness like magpies singing with parrots, strangers behind doors, 'Yes, it is good to be home.' (One comes out.) 'How long were you in Europe?' 'Three weeks—three long weeks. And you?' 'Two months.' 'How did you stand it?' (Forty years of Europe!—I left quietly.)

Novalis said, my friend Dorothy Green remarks, that you must know many lands to be at home on earth; perhaps it is that you must be at home on earth to know many lands. A child in Australia, in the home of an active naturalist who loved the country and knew scientists, nature-lovers, all kinds of keen stirring men and women who found their home on earth, I hearing of them, felt at home; this was my first, strongest feeling in babyhood. I have had many homes, am easily at home, requiring very little. My first novel (before *Seven Poor Men of Sydney*) was to be called *The Young Man Will Go Far* and then, *The Wraith and the Wanderer*, two different novels. (I still have part MSS.) The Wanderer, once he has started out in company of the Wraith, the tramp and his whisperer, does not look over his shoulder. He does not think of where to live, somewhere, anywhere; anything may happen, awkward and shameful things do happen; he does not believe it when life is good; by thirty all is not done, neither the shames nor the lucky strikes. He takes no notice, it is his equal but different fate, he marries a stranger, loves an outlaw, neighbours with many, speaks with tongues. So that if he should cross the high bridge of air sometime, going homewards, he is also on the outward path.

Now I am back in shadowy England whose pale streams are sometimes 'gilded by heavenly alchemy', they speak of 'hot summers' but there is not the pour of gold nor the fire from the open hearth. Here are white cliffs and mornings, white horses on the downs, topheavy summer trees, King Arthur in his mound, gods and Herne the Hunter in woods, green folk, little folk, squirrel-faced elves; and stranger creatures still, Langland, Wyatt, Chaucer, Ford and their pursuit of comets, the English splendour; and all this is in the people, their unconscious thoughts and their language.

Under the soft spotted skies of the countries round the North Sea I had forgotten the Australian splendour, the marvellous light; the 'other country' which I always had in me, to which I wrote letters and meant one day to return, it had softened, even the hills outlined in bushfire (which we used to see over Clovelly from Watson's Bay) were paler. The most exquisite thing in my recent life was a giant eucalypt on the North Shore as we turned downhill, the downward leaves so clear, the bark rags, so precise, the patched trunk, so bright. 'Look at that tree!' It was outlined in light. It was scarcely spring, but the lawn outside the house was crowded with camellias, magnolias in bloom, even falling; at both dawn and dusk the kookaburras thrilling high in the trees, the magpies—I had quite forgotten those musicians and their audacity—and there was even a scary fiendish cry in the bush early; it came nearer, but remained distant. It was just a bantam cockerel—I had one myself years ago in Santa Fe and had forgotten the little dawn-demon with his one-string violin. Too long in London! Everything was like ringing and bright fire and all sharpness. I was at dinner the other night, when someone said, 'What was Australia like?' 'It's the wonderful light, Bill,' I said to the Texan next to me. 'Yes,' affirmed he; and the Indian lady murmured, 'Yes.' Three exiles. No more was said; and the others, Londoners, did not even know what we had understood. It is at least the light. When people ask, I feel like saying, 'It's a brilliant country; they're a brilliant people, just at the beginning of the leaps.' I think this is true, but it may be in part the light, the broad skies, the crowded stars, that red hide stretched out so far to cover so much land; and I do not say, because I don't really understand it 'And there is the melancholy.' I knew as a girl that looking backward was not joy; I thought it was the waterlessness, the twenty year droughts, the people dead of thirst, again the hatred of England, of the hulks, our black legend. But is it like the uneasiness and loneliness felt by Russians, US Americans, Brazilians, who with, at their backs, the spaces and untamed land, seek Paris, the Riviera and New York?

This brilliance one feels is not related to the present sunnyside air common to countries having a stock exchange and business boom and with money flowing into (and out of) the country; at best, an uncritical supping of splurge and at lowest, baldly expressed, 'It doesn't matter who makes us rich, as long as we get rich.' There are people in Australia who no longer believe in poverty. It has happened elsewhere; and been followed by—but we know that.

I was not long enough there to have an opinion about many things. I know about Canberra, beautiful, desolate, inspiriting Erewhon, where one can feel 'I have awakened into the future of the world'; freer because it is unfinished and all its components not yet joined; and apart, more appealing in its upland, than Washington, DC in its swamp; younger, closer at the twenty-first century. I don't understand the settled sadness of some intellectuals, artists and academics. The heat mystery, black shadows in the tropics, the long bright road ending in a mirage? Deserts? Not belonging to ourselves? Not united with our nearest neighbours? Smalltowners in the USA leave farm for town, town for Chicago and New York, the capitals for Paris and London. Perhaps it is just *The*

Beckoning Fair One singing her faint irresistible 'very oald tune' (Oliver Onions). Well, let us be discontented then; it has never hurt art.

Ocean of Story (1985).

CLIVE JAMES
(1939–)

Sydney-born writer, critic, and television performer. After completing a BA at the University of Sydney and working as an assistant editor at the Sydney Morning Herald *in 1961, Clive James moved to England in 1962. There he worked at an assortment of jobs, completed another degree at Cambridge, and became a very successful journalist, writing for various newspapers and journals. From 1972 to 1982 he was the television critic for the London* Observer. *Since then, he has become a well-known television performer, appearing in series and specials such as* Saturday Night Clive *and* The Clive James Great American Beauty Pageant *(1984). His many publications include books of literary and television criticism, volumes of poetry, autobiographical works, and novels. In this 'postcard from Sydney', originally published in the* Observer, *James records his feelings on first revisiting Sydney.*

'HOME, JAMES' (1976)

Chugging through the stratosphere for twenty-four hours from London to Sydney, the Qantas Boeing 747 *City of Newcastle* did its best to keep us all happy, but apart from watching *The French Connection Part II* and consuming the numberless meals delivered to one's lap by the hardest-working cabin staff in the history of aviation, there was little to do except make increasingly feeble attempts to keep one's children out of mischief and go to the toilet.

This every single one of the several hundred passengers did at least a dozen times on the voyage, making a total of many thousands of separate visits. Queues for the loo stretched down every aisle. It was somewhere between Bombay and Perth that the vision hit me. Our enormous aircraft, the apotheosis of modern technology, was filling up with gunk! Converted into chemical inertia by the cobalt-blue reagent in the flushing water, the waste products of our skyborne community were gradually taking over the plane!

I adduce the above fantasy only to demonstrate the intensity with which one hallucinates after nearly a full day in the sky on the long haul out to one's homeland. I had been fifteen years away from Australia. While I had been gone, the whole of the modern phase of Australian politics had taken place. The Gough Whitlam revolution—often called a 'renaissance', to emphasise its air of cultural euphoria—had been and gone. The same conservative forces were now back in power as had ruled the country so suffocatingly when I left. How much had I missed out on? And what if, despite my unfortunate timing, the place had indeed altered past recognition? Trepidations about culture-shock were eased only by the knowledge that the captain of our aircraft was called Barry Tingwell. The sheer Australianness of that name was as antipodean as a sand-fly bite or a sting from a jelly-blubber.

In fact culture-shock had already begun a few nights before I left London, when I had seen the National Theatre's *Hamlet* and Barry Humphries' opening night as Edna Everage in the same thrill-packed evening. From the *Hamlet*, an austerity production in British Army standard-issue boots, to Edna's non-stop spectacular, with its voluptuous wealth of sequins and gladioli, had already been a large step from the old rigour to the new expansiveness. As Hamlet, Albert Finney had lacked lustre. As Edna, Barry Humphries had had lustre to burn. Edna's Proustian savouring of the *things* in her rich life—the gaudy catalogue of Australiana she carries in her dizzy head—was a call from the homeland as imperative as Penelope's sigh. Thus it was that Barry Tingwell steered me south-east around the curve of the world.

The first view of Australia was the coast near Perth: reefs, white beaches, shallow water like the juice of emeralds. In the suburbs, hundreds of swimming pools the colour of Paul Newman's eyes attested to affluence. But then, I had never seen Perth before. Perhaps it had always been like that. The transcontinental haul was fascinating to one who had never flown over Australia before in his life. (I had come to Europe by ship: a five-week voyage costing about £60 sterling. In those days everybody you knew was too poor to fly.) Look at those circular salt lakes, each a separate colour like the little tubs of paint in a child's paintbox! But an Australian businessman in a short-sleeved suit who had got on with a blast of reminiscent heat at Perth explained that this was nothing—the really fantastic scenery was further north. I should try it some time. Perhaps I should, and one day shall: but I felt resistant. For this trip, the eastern seaboard would be enough, and I wasn't even sure I could manage that. For the first time I was becoming physically aware of how far-flung the land was into which I had been born. There had been another change of pilots at Perth. Where was Barry Tingwell? Help.

At Sydney the 747 made its landing approach low over the suburb where I was born and grew up—Kogarah, on Botany Bay. It was night. Sydney was a vast field of lights: since the Aussie's ideal is to own his Own Home, the cities sprawl inordinately. Not all that much less than London, Sydney filled the sky with costume jewellery as the 747 heeled over, shaken by a great inner surge of cerulean goo. The flaps jacked out. The turbofans lapsed from a whine to a grumble. Like a winged supertanker full of odoriferous amethystine ordure the colossal machine brought me back to my roots.

Next morning the roots were on display in bright sunshine. Whatever overtones of unease eventually accrued to my four-week stay in Australia—and I should say in advance that I ended the trip feeling even more of an interloper than when I began—nothing should be allowed to detract from a proper celebration of that first, and continuing, impression of Sydney and its harbour. It remains one of the Earth's truly beautiful places. Apart from the startling Manhattanisation of its business district, the city was more or less as I remembered it, except that for the twenty-one years I lived there I never really appreciated it—one of the big things that can be said in favour of going back, partly offsetting the even bigger things that can be said for remaining an expatriate once you have become one.

The late Kenneth Slessor, in his prose as much as in his poetry, probably came nearest to evoking the sheer pulchritude of Sydney harbour. But finally the place is too multifarious to be captured by the pen. Sydney is like Venice without the architecture, but with more of the sea: the merchant ships sail right into town. In Venice you never see big ships—they are all over at Mestre, the industrial sector. In Sydney big ships loom at the ends of city streets. They are parked all over the place, tied up to the countless wharves in the scores of inlets ('You could hide a thousand ships of the line in here,' a British admiral observed long ago) or just moored to a buoy in mid-harbour, riding high. At the International Terminal at Circular Quay, the liners in which my generation of the self-exiled left for Europe still tie up: from the Harbour Bridge you can look down at the farewell parties raging on their decks. Most important, the ferries are still on the harbour. Nothing like as frequent as they once were, but still there—the perfect way of getting to and from work.

Some of the big Manly ferries have been replaced by hydrofoils, but there are a few of the old ones left. Always the biggest ferries on the harbour, they were built strongly to sail unperturbed through the pelagic swell as they crossed Sydney Heads to Manly. Poems in blond wood and brass fittings, they were named after surfing beaches: Dee Why, South Steyne, Curl Curl. Now there is a fund being raised to save the *South Steyne* from the breakers' yard, while the hulks of some of the others are to be seen lying derelict against the Pyrmont wharves.

Riding across to Manly in the Forties, we used to lean perilously over the balustrade of the open engine-room and watch the reciprocating whatchumacallits clonk and gwerp—'we' being children in English-style school uniforms of flannel short-trousered suits and long socks. The smell of the machine-oil and the sensual heave of the ferry in the Pacific waves is an abiding memory, which I found unimpaired by repeating the experience as an adult. Towards sunset, when the light strikes the harbour at a shallow angle and turns the water silver, the ferries, their setting deprived of all perspective, hang in space, like long-lensed photographs of themselves: dream-boats.

But where the ferries somehow survived, the tram did not. Melbourne keeps its trams but Sydney had got rid of them long before I left Australia. The toast-rack tram—open to the sun and breeze, full of character and incident—was the best form of street-transport ever invented. Unfortunately it sorted ill with the motor car, which since the early Fifties has ruled the city father's dreams, as if Sydney might be a new Los Angeles horizontally, just as it aspires to be a new New York vertically. It was in this spirit that the Cahill Expressway—a flyover of heroic ugliness named after the same politician who gave birth to the Opera House—was built over Circular Quay, almost totally destroying the atmosphere of what had, after all, once been Sydney Cove, the site of the First Settlement.

Almost, but not quite. More by luck than judgment, Circular Quay kept some of its character, and while I have been away has even increased in interest, due to the effects of an unequivocally positive addition to Sydney's life—immigration. The cosmopolitan, or ethnic, influence on Sydney first of all becomes visible when you notice the amount and kind of fast foods on offer. At the Circular Quay milk bars, where once the most you could hope for in the way of takeaway food was a lethal meat pie and a cream bun, you can now take your pick from kateifi, baklava, syrup rolls, honey and almond triangles, Turkish delight and fruit slices. One of the indisputably beneficial European influences—food—has been added to one of the most enduring Australian traditions—the milk-shake. And, as long as you are content to drink your milk-shake on or near the premises, it is still possible to have it prepared as it should be, in a dented silver container battered around the rim from being clipped a million times into the mixing machine.

The completed milk-shake should never be tipped into a glass, but consumed direct from the container, either through a paper straw (with a resonant slurp to mop up the frothy dregs) or by applying the loose mouth to the cold metal and tilting until the blob of ice-cream collides with the top lip. The conflict involved in choosing between these two methods almost always necessitates the purchase of a second milk-shake. While drinking it and eating your pastries, you can lean over the railings between the wharves and watch the sprats feeding underwater around the pilings. At such moments, Sydney offers a *petite bonheur* comparable to anything obtainable in, say, Paris, where there is seldom anywhere comfortable to eat your crêpes, no matter how delicious the chocolate sauce. Stay on, or near, the water and Sydney's version of the Little Happiness can be very near to Heaven.

When Australians talk about Culture they seldom mean honey and almond triangles. Perhaps they ought to, though. It's in the ordinary facts of everyday life that culture is to be measured—which is why Edna Everage reigns supreme as Australia's greatest cultural commentator, the Raymond Williams of the South Pacific. Australians talk in the one breath about the giant strides made in wine and poetry, but the awkward truth is that while the advance made in Australian wine is beyond dispute, to claim an advance in Australian poetry is largely meaningless. In the minutiae of existence Australia has changed in all sorts of ways since I left home. But in the large abstractions it seems to me to have stayed roughly as it was.

Turn back from leaning over the rails at the Quay and you are looking at Sydney's answer to Manhattan. The tallest building in Sydney when I left is now one of the shortest in the skyline. Photographs of this upsurge had disturbed me in exile but brought up against it I was less impressed. Some of the straining shapes on view are at least original, but even those are usually hideous, and on the whole I'm afraid the vaunted progress of Sydney's business architecture ('Ar, Sydney's coming on,' my old friends have been telling me for years: 'Ya wooden wreckingnise it') bears out the Italian proverb about fifty skyscrapers screwing a city. To the extent that the tall buildings have created space around their podiums they represent what Raymond Williams (the Edna Everage of the North Atlantic) would call a Clear Gain. But on the whole, the city's human scale has been destroyed for the sake of physically reflecting an exultation which was always more like arro-

gance than self-confidence and which was already fading before Whitlam toppled. Large areas of office-space in the new towers are still for
rent and will for a long time stay as empty as Centrepoint in London or
the Trade Center in New York.

Such conspicuous waste represents the self-destructive element in
the burgeoning national consciousness. There is a creative element too,
but it works within a more modest range. The care with which the
Rocks area of Sydney has been preserved is a good example of the creative element in action.

By now the awareness that there are things to be cherished is widespread, like a taste for wine, which is no longer restricted to the travelled minority. (Nor, of course, is travel.) The wine buff can order his
tipple at 30 dollars a dozen before the grapes are picked, with right of
refusal at the first tasting: it's like putting your son down for Eton. But
even the uninstructed are not likely to pass the stuff up when flagon
wine at least as good as what goes into the carafes in a restaurant in
Italy works out at 20 cents a bottle. In other words, it's free.

It's in these things—in food and drink and places to be and ways
to behave—that Australia has come on since my time. But in more
grandiose matters—matters where national consciousness is really self-
consciousness—the results are more equivocal. Culture with a small c is
doing all right. Culture with a capital C has lost its erstwhile diffidence,
but in many instances seems to have replaced it with a bombast equally parochial. The Sydney Opera House is a case in point. *The* case in
point, because in daring to suggest that there is something wrong with
the Opera House, you run the risk of appearing to deny the whole
country its right to an identity—a slur not easily forgiven.

Back in England and safe from physical reprisal, it now seems possible to say aloud what I scarcely dared breathe in Australia, even to my
relations: that the Opera House is a dud. In the matter of its appearance I have no very strong opinion. To me it looks like a portable type-
writer full of oyster shells, and to the contention that it echoes the sails
of yachts on the harbour I can only point out that the yachts on the
harbour don't waste any time echoing opera houses. But really it is
quibbling to talk about the way the thing looks. What matters is the
way it works. And for its nominal purpose it doesn't work, and never
can.

During the time that I was in Sydney there were no operas sched-
uled, but I did see a ballet—*The Sleeping Beauty*—sufficiently big to
test the opera auditorium's facilities. (There are two auditoria: the
smaller one for opera, and the larger one for concerts, including con-

cert versions of those operas too large to fit into the smaller one.) They failed the test. It was embarrassing to see the *corps de ballet* queueing up to get off, there being very little wing-space for them to disappear into. The flimsiness of the décor and the tension in the dancing could all be traced to simple lack of room.

The effort which was poured into finishing the edifice after its architect was fired should not be discounted, even though the American Beauty upholstery in the concert hall (in the opera hall it's tomato red) might not be to one's taste. But similarly it is foolish to suppose that all would have been well had Utzon remained in charge.

The farce began at the beginning, in that first flush of enthusiasm at Utzon's preliminary designs. The judges fell in love with an idea without grasping its substance, thereby acting out in little—or, financially speaking, in large—the Australian attitude to Culture. That attitude is likely to go on generating unintentional humour in large amounts. But since to some extent I once shared that attitude myself, I'm not entirely whole-hearted about joining in the laughter.

June 20, 1976

Footnote—By now I feel much more affectionate about the Opera House but the first impression recorded above is probably the more objective. If a Wagner orchestra has to be reduced in size to fit the pit, what you have got is an edifice which does less than the one at Bayreuth at a thousand times the cost. But it looks better: there is no denying that.

Flying Visits (1984).

———

GERMAINE GREER
(1939–)

Melbourne-born writer and feminist. Educated at Melbourne, Sydney, and Cambridge universities, Greer has lived away from Australia, mostly in England, since the mid-1960s. A lecturer in English at the University of Warwick from 1967 to 1972, she wrote one of the most influential works to come out of the international women's liberation movement of the late 1960s and 1970s, The Female Eunuch *(1969). Her career since then has included periods as a freelance journalist, visiting professor at the University of Tulsa, Oklahoma (1979), and professor of modern letters at the latter institution (1980–3). In this extract from her study of her father,* Daddy, We Hardly Knew You *(1989), Greer, one of Australia's best-known and most controversial expatriates, recalls coming back to Melbourne for a visit in December 1986.*

RETURNING TO MELBOURNE

Twenty-two hours later by my watch and two days later by the calendar, my airliner crossed the rim of the island continent. Flying northwest to south-east, our day had been telescoped; as we crossed the coast of the biggest island in the world, not a pin-point of light pierced our second night. Unseen around us and above us were threatening pinnacles of cloud, spun off the monsoon winds. Inside our aluminium and plastic cocoon, the passengers lay like larvae, twitching slightly. Those young enough or drunk enough to find sleep lay with their mouths open, like victims of some poison gas. The kerosene fumes we were all obliged to breathe were being enriched with the effluvium created by a party of rich Italians who, unable to stop smoking, stop talking or stop running around, spread their stink as effectively as possible, to the toilets, the corridors and the galleys, in concerted defiance of the IATA regulations. In its curtained alcove, the Italian cabin crew was concentrating on growing its own cancers.

By holding my pillow up to the porthole I could see out into the Australian night, where some titanic electrical commotion was brewing. Far to the west, great bursts of sulphur-yellow, blood-red and a sort of fizzing purply-orange light would boil up out of the black velvet and spill on to the horizon, backlighting tiers of cloud hanging in great slabs. A trickle of magnesium white would slip down them and bounce to earth, then all would vanish and the blackout would be seamless once more.

The storm system was hundreds of miles across. The 747 scuttled down its eastern flank as the horizon turned gun-metal grey, then indigo, then RAF blue and suddenly the cabin crew laid down their cigarettes to serve us a breakfast just as terrible as the other five meals I had already looked at. My appetite was not improved by a certain nervousness to do with something in my luggage.

My intention had been to give all my family presents of a distinctly Italian character. Mother was to have a bottle of Nocino liqueur and a real sponge, my sister-in-law Italian table linen, and for my sister, who has a rich husband, two elegant houses and is moderately interested in cooking, I had found two large white truffles. The vendor had packed them most carefully in a little aluminium pan filled with rice to absorb the odour, sealed it with clingfilm, finished it off in the shop's exclusive paper and tied it with monogrammed ribbon. I had tucked the elegant package among my underwear, with the nefarious intention of not declaring it.

As I gulped my grey coffee, a Voice intoned on the tannoy in seven languages: 'Australia is an island, free of many of the pestilences that plague other lands, and insists on staying that way. Any fresh foodstuffs or vegetable material must be declared.' The Italian pilot sitting next to me warned that not only would my truffles be confiscated if the customs officer found them, I could be fined some enormous amount of money and even sent to prison. Italian flights are carefully inspected, for a single salami could introduce foot and mouth disease or anthrax or rinderpest. God knows what grim organisms infest a truffle. Rabid snot from the truffle hound or vesicular fever from a truffle pig. By the time I got to customs control I was ready to torch the truffles myself.

The cadaverous Friulian peasant in front of me was encumbered with two phony-looking mandolins. The officers smelt them, tapped them, rattled them, and for a second looked like smashing them, to see if anything was inside.

My customs officer was Vietnamese; I had chosen him because the Vietnamese, unlike the Australians, have one of the most sophisticated cuisines in the world. I unwrapped my precious parcel and exhibited two very dodgy-looking grey blobs, charmless as turtle testicles. The smell filled the entire customs hall. The supervisor was called. He poked at the truffles with the tip of his pencil. 'No, no, no,' he said, with the kind of extreme patience one shows to a child. He flicked a grain of rice on to a sheet of newspaper. 'You can't have that.' He rolled the truffles over with his pencil and flicked off every grain of rice, and he poured the rice out of the pans on to his piece of paper.

'You eat these, do you?' he asked, rolling the truffles with his pencil. 'All of them?'

I gave a quick lecture on the use of the white truffle in Italian cooking, wishing that the wretched fungi would pull themselves together and try to look worth the considerable sum I had paid for them. The officer was unimpressed. 'Take them,' he said and pulled away the paper with the rice. I looked at him stupidly. 'You weren't gunna eat the rice, were you?' Only then I understood; the uncooked rice was the prohibited import. (You are supposed to use the scented rice in a risotto but I had left that out of my lecture.) I scooped the truffles up and put them naked into my pocket.

This little episode struck me as seriously odd. I would have been more able to read the situation in the airport at Addis Ababa or

Guatemala City, than I was in my home town. I still felt quite disori-
ented sitting behind my Greek taxi driver, who chatted amiably in a
combination of accents which I found considerably more difficult to
understand than Greek. The roadscape was as anonymous as airport
motorways usually are. To re-embody myself I spoke to the driver in
Greek. The back of his hairy neck suddenly glowed with hostility. Did
I think he couldn't understand English or something? Impossible to
explain that it was I who couldn't understand Australian.

Daddy, We Hardly Knew You (1989).

———

PETER CONRAD

(1948–)

*Tasmanian-born writer and academic. After completing a BA at the Uni-
versity of Tasmania, Conrad left his island state in 1968 for further study at
Oxford University. In 1973 he began teaching English at Christ Church,
Oxford. His publications include works of fiction, literary and musical criticism, and autobiography. In his book about 'revisiting Tasmania' in the
1980s,* Down Home *(1988), he includes these comments about the 'brutal,
bad-tempered eminence that 'overshadowed' his childhood, Hobart's Mount
Wellington.*

MOUNT WELLINGTON

Emotions about mountains have a complicated history. Superstition
has always viewed them as deformations of earth, Gothic horrors. In
the late eighteenth century, that changed. High mountains, according
to the romantic poets, were 'a feeling', serener in their silence than the
hubbub of cities. The change in taste happened just as Australia was
being settled, and the country's landscape followed it. At first the terrain looked eerie, ghastly, all palsied trees and agonised squawking
birds: a Gothic mystery. Then, in the course of the nineteenth century,
it was romanticised. Instead of locating topographical spots on a map
of mental terror—Mount Despair, Mount Warning, Cape Grim, Hell's
Gates, Devil's Kitchen—imagination began to see Australia sunnily, a
blazing noon of optimistic waratah. But the ancestral identity of the
country, as a place to be feared not loved, wasn't forgotten. Mount

Wellington can still commute between these meanings. One day it's as alarming as Mussorgsky's bald mountain, or the shaggy, witchy peaks where Mephistopheles leads Faust; the next it's benign, draping itself along the haze of the horizon like a dozing sun-bather.

I had both experiences of it when I was back. Within the same week, I went to the summit twice. I'd only ever been there once before, on a school excursion. Though we spent our days looking up at it, and during the summer could see the glint of cars toiling round the bends to the peak, no one thought of looking down from it. Like a cathedral spire, it observed you from its lofty height; you weren't supposed to use it as your own eyrie. So, returning, it was one of my first ambitions to see Hobart from up there. For days I kept watch, waiting for the clouds to clear from the mountain's head. Then one morning, though batteries of grey vapour were still pushing the sunlight across the sky, I decided to risk it.

The result was an hour in a Gothic climate. By the time I got there, a cloud had muffled the top of the mountain; inside it, a blizzard hung suspended above the summery city. From the road to the top, the sky looked like boiling broth. Wind scourged the creaking trees, and the boulders on the slopes could have been strewn by landslips that morning.

The mountain's face is an Aeolian orchestra: the sharp-edged columns which slide down from the top are locally known as the organ pipes. To name them is to tame them. The metaphor pacifies the geological hazard, and romantically pretends that nature is sounding a solemn diapason. Driving beneath the cliff of stone pipes, you can watch the image go in and out of focus. Close up, the simile is seen to be a deceit: this is just a chaos of cracked facets and broken ledges. It's the same with the Sleeping Beauty, on the other side of the range. Seen from the south in the Huon Valley, she is a drowsy anthropomorph, the giantess who bars the hero's advance with that body which she stretches along an entire horizon. The foothills are her unbound hair, and thanks to two hillocks she can cross her hands on her chest. But see her from another angle, further towards Hobart, and the gentle metaphor crumbles. The profile doesn't hold together; it furrows, turns knobbly, erupts in warts. The princess has aged unflatteringly in her paralysed sleep. The mountains, under that thick turbulent sky, change their expressions as you advance through them. The face that first day scowled, wrinkled in hostility. Mount Wellington is a goblin of rock; the organ pipes actually house a population of leering gnomes, robbed from suburban gardens and planted there for a prank by climbers from the university. Their bright complexions weathered and eroded, they now look as if they have grown from the shelves where they are set. Climbers tell gruesomely funny stories about them: the wind keening, the city beneath you, you fumble for support, pull yourself up a precipice, and let out an involuntary screech as a plaster dwarf stares you in the eye. Van Diemen's Land retains its demons.

The summit that day was an arrival at extinction. Erased by the frozen air, the city had ceased to exist. A map at the lookout directed attention to the absent places beneath; the view was of nothingness. This alp, swallowed by the sky, had become a site for death first by heat, then by cold. The wood of the bent shrubs beside the road was burned black, then lit with a bleak white halation of ice, as if solarised. Where the gale caught branches, it stiffened them in quills of ice as prickly as razor blades. Snow doesn't soften the world, swathing things in cotton wool; it is cutting, crystalline, and here it exposed the eldritch forkings of the battered trees. The television towers disappeared inside their fence of mesh which the ice had barbed. When the wind struck at them, frigid planks clattered down from the girders to crash as brittly as glass on the road. I had always wondered what was happening inside those clouds which drifted round the mountain. Now I knew: they were capsules of nuclear winter, in transit above us.

On my next trip, the mountain had banished its phantoms. Now it was tropically dry, the peak a desert of blue crags with lizards like flicking shadows between the roots. A currawong, coal-black except for a yellow eye and a white fan of feathers in its tail, flapped across the road, wheeling in a cavern of air to settle on a young gum. Perched there, it twisted its neck in a circle to study the view. All the world lay beneath it, bared in the lucid air. Before Hobart had been wiped away by cloud; today it was lost in the landscape. After the thin strips of settlement along the harbour and the river, it ran out so soon. Here was Australia in little: a society gobbled up by an allocation of earth too large for it, clinging in trepidation to the shore. The perimeters of my life could be clearly made out from up here, a patterned algebra—the straight line of the highway, the oval of the race-course, the concentric circles of our suburb—but none of them mattered. They were scratches on an old, forgetful surface, too callous to feel them. And inches beyond what was supposed to be our street, that surface began to buckle and fold, wandering off in tangled valleys and amorphous hills. At this southern extremity, land itself was running out. The bottom of Tasmania trails fronds and fringes along the ocean. Water invades everywhere, wearing down those crooked arms and peninsulas, leaving only threads like Eaglehawk Neck to connect one mass with another The island, here at its terminus, looks from above as if it's fraying into an archipelago of stranded islets. The mountain on which you stand marches across the skyline towards the south and west, merging with others into ranges which fade in a silhouette of crested waves. The view extends not only as far as the eye can see, but as far as the earth can travel. The world is about to end.

Above too there is a glossy emptiness. The pylons in the Telecom compound, blotted by the snow before, listen to the sibillations of the sky. On top of one tower is an elongated barrel with a blunt pencil protruding from it—a missile? A satellite dish, a sparking red bolt of electricity painted across it, takes dictation from the air; another tower wears a brass band of surveillance instruments, their music as silent as that of the organ pipes beneath—a grey kettledrum, and a pair of cymbals. Though there's a shed, no one's about. The hibernating gadgets have their own lives up here. Dwayne has carved on a boulder his love for Elaine, but even though their names rhyme, this hard, arid place has little tolerance for human affections. The mountain like the desert is a location for the ascetic. I see now why those who live under Mount Wellington don't come up it: its lesson is disillusionment, the reduction of individual existences to specks and our brave little social camp to a brief sprinkling of dust.

Down Home (1988).

———

JOHN PILGER
(1939–)

Sydney-born journalist and writer. Pilger was educated at Sydney High School before becoming a cadet journalist with the Sydney Daily Telegraph. *Employed by the London* Daily Mirror *from 1962 to 1986, he gained a considerable reputation, especially for his work as a foreign correspondent in Vietnam and Cambodia. His films include* Year Zero: The Silent Death of Cambodia *(1979), his books* Heroes *(1986) and* A Secret Country *(1989). Pilger wrote the following piece about Aboriginal rights, one of his major concerns, in 1992, at which time he was based in London.*

'THE WHITE MAN'S TUNE'

Sydney

Walking from the Opera House to the ferry jetties of Circular Quay, one of the most spectacular short journeys on earth, I came upon a white man playing a didgeridoo: the long Aboriginal instrument whose haunting woodwind sound speaks for black Australians in a way that some whites understand. That is to say, it reminds them that their country is not quite theirs: that it has a rapacious, secret past; that it is half won and its story half told.

Even the inept playing of a white busker surrounded by tourists had this effect on me, especially as tangible evidence was close at hand. Standing in the busker's audience you had only to raise your eyes to see the figure on the street corner opposite: that of a black man slumped in the gutter, around whom people walked, as if he was a hole in the ground. The irony would be searing were it not an everyday matter.

In Australia, such matters are 'everyday' once again. For almost four years, following the setting up in 1987 of a Royal Commission of Enquiry into black deaths in custody, the conditions and rights of Aboriginal people were issues. Newspapers published stories of atrocities against blacks as if they represented a phenomenon, rather than an historical pattern of events. In particular, the frequent, violent death of black Australians in prisons and police custody at last became news; and the news was shocking to many white Australians who will tell you that they seldom lay eyes on their black compatriots.

When the Royal Commission was appointed by the then prime minister, Bob Hawke, the former chief psychiatrist at Bargwanarth Hospital in Soweto wrote to the *Sydney Morning Herald* to point out that the rate of black deaths in custody in Australia was thirteen times higher than in South Africa.[1]

Comparison with South Africa is beyond the pale in Australia; it offends the nation's self-image of 'fair go'; and the Royal Commission was undoubtedly meant to deal with that. Royal Commissions are common in Australia. One of them is almost always in progress. They are like the teams that paint the Sydney Harbour bridge; once they finish one end, they must start again. Asked to describe the purpose of a typical Australian Royal Commission, the former judge and Royal Commissioner James McClelland called it 'a device employed by governments to sweep under the rug a problem which they either could not or did not want to solve'.[2]

Because there is guilt about the Aborigines, and because Australian governments have sought to persuade their Asian and Pacific trading partners that racism is no longer condoned, as it was under the White Australia Policy, there was some hope that the Royal Commission enquiring into the deaths of black people in custody would take a high moral stand and make its recommendations so tough they were unsweepable. The chief commissioner, Elliott Johnston, declared his shock at what he found. 'Until I examined the files of the people who died [in police custody],' he said, 'I had no conception of the degree of pin-pricking domination, abuse of personal power, utter paternalism, open contempt and total indifference with which so many Aboriginal people were visited on a day-to-day basis.'[3]

The Commission spent almost four years and $A30 million in its investigations and deliberations. When it reported last year, it made 339 recommendations. Not one of them was a call for criminal charges against police or prison officers or a conclusion of foul play, regardless of overwhelming evidence to the contrary. Instead, changes in policing and custodial methods, education and poverty, were to be left to the same state authorities that have been the main oppressors of black Australians. In the case of John Pat, who died in a police cell after a 'fight' with four police officers (who were subsequently acquitted of his manslaughter), Commissioner Johnston commented, 'I do not accept as necessarily true much of the evidence of the officers relating to this incident.'[4] Yet he proposed no action.

One of the Commission's main recommendations was that Aborigines—a small minority who in many towns make up the majority of prisoners—should be jailed only as a last resort. This statement of the obvious had been the Commission's theme since its inception. The response of state governments has been equally clear: more Aborigines have been sent to prison than ever before. A study last month by the Institute of Criminology at Sydney University found that the number of Aborigines jailed during and since the Royal Commission had risen by a quarter. In New South Wales—regarded as the most progressive state in its treatment of Aborigines—the increase was by 80 per cent. The author of the report, Chris Cunneen, said, 'This shatters the illusion that New South Wales is a more civilised state. It is now a leading "redneck state"— second only to Western Australia in its imprisonment of Aborigines.'[5] In July 1992 the Queensland Government announced, apparently with pride, that Aboriginal prisoners who tore up blankets in a bid to hang themselves, would no longer be charged with 'wilful damage'.

In the meantime, according to a report by the Human Rights Commission, police systematically torture young Aborigines to get them to confess to crimes.[6] Another report concludes that if you are black and seriously ill, you are unlikely to get an ambulance to come and get you. Aboriginal health levels are described as 'shameful'. The death rate of black children is two and a half times that of white children; for adults, the rate is three times higher. Diseases considered preventable in white Australia ravage Aboriginal communities; tuberculosis is an epidemic.[7]

As if this wasn't enough, a study by the World Council of Churches says the impact of such manifest racism is 'genocidal' and accuses the Australian Government of finding an 'institutionalised way of underdeveloping Aborigines'. For me, the Council's most telling observation was that a 'conspiracy of silence surrounds the plight of Australia's Aborigines ...'[8]

This is both true and remarkable—remarkable because the reports mentioned above, and numerous others, were all published widely. And there will be more of them, filling columns of space in the Melbourne *Age* and the *Sydney Morning Herald*. It is as if they are part of the veneer of civilised behaviour: to be accepted with due solemnity, then disregarded.

This has not always been the case. Twenty-five years ago a national referendum was held in which more than 90 per cent of the Australian electorate voted to give the federal government the constitutional right to legislate justice for the Aboriginal people. No referendum anywhere in modern times had produced such an overwhelming, positive result. The prime minister and his ministers could override the states on all questions relating to Aborigines; they had been handed an 'historic mandate'. The Whitlam Government drew up comprehensive land-rights legislation, part of which was made law in 1976 by the Fraser Government—but only in the Northern Territory, which the federal government administered. Redneck states were allowed to proceed with redneck policies.

When the Hawke Labor Government came to power in 1983, the minister for Aboriginal affairs, Clyde Holding, said that a national land-rights policy was 'the only restitution' for crimes that he compared with Hitler's persecution of the Jews.[9] Nothing happened. Bob Hawke dropped land rights from his government's agenda. He cried in public for the victims of Tiananmen Square in China and he damned apartheid; Australia led the campaign for sanctions against South Africa.

The tragedy of this betrayal and hypocrisy is that the coming generations of young black Australians will discard the generosity that has marked Aboriginal attitudes towards white Australia. They will see themselves as an enemy within; and they will fight back, as blacks in South Africa have fought back, disturbing more than the silence and the guilt.

In 1971, one of them wrote the following:

> *At the white man's school, what are our children taught?*
> *Are they told of the battles our people fought,*
> *Are they told of how our people died?*
> *Are they told why our people cried?*
> *Australia's true history is never read,*
> *But the blackman keeps it in his head.*

March 13, 1992

Distant Voices (1992).

1   The *Sydney Morning Herald*, October 11, 1986.
2   Ibid, May 22, 1991.
3   Ibid, May 8, 1991.
4   Ibid.
5   Ibid, February 18, 1992.
6   Ibid, April 18, 1992.
7   Ibid, February 12, 1992.
8   Ibid, February 4, 1991.
9   Ibid, March 30, 1985.

BIBLIOGRAPHY

Bail, Murray, 'Imagining Australia', in *The Times Literary Supplement*, no. 4417, 27 November–3 December 1987, pp. 1318, 1330.

Brissenden, Alan, and Higham, Charles (eds), *They Came to Australia: An Anthology* (F.W. Cheshire, Australia, 1961).

Buzard, James, *The Beaten Track: European Tourism, Literature and the Ways to Culture, 1800–1918* (Clarendon Press, Oxford, 1993).

Cowley, Des (guest ed.), *La Trobe Library Journal*, vol. 11, no. 41, autumn 1988, special issue, *The Great South Land*.

Dunmore, John, *Utopias and Imaginary Voyages to Australia* (National Library of Australia, Canberra, 1988).

——, *Who's Who in Pacific Navigation* (Melbourne University Press, Carlton, 1992).

Friederich, Werner P., *Australia in Western Imaginative Prose Writings 1600–1960: An Anthology and a History of Literature* (The University of North Carolina Press, Chapel Hill, 1967).

Fussell, Paul, *Abroad: British Literary Traveling Between the Wars* (Oxford University Press, New York, 1980).

—— (ed.), *The Norton Book of Travel* (W.W. Norton & Company, New York and London, 1987).

Gibson, Ross, *The Diminishing Paradise: Changing Literary Perceptions of Australia* (Sirius Books, Angus & Robertson Publishers, Australia, 1984).

Goodman, David, 'Reading Gold-Rush Travellers' Narratives', in *Australian Cultural History*, no. 10, 1991, *Travellers, Journeys, Tourists*, pp. 99–112.

Hanbury-Tenison, Robin (ed.), *The Oxford Book of Exploration* (Oxford University Press, Oxford and New York, 1993).

Harman, Kate (ed.), *Australia Brought to Book: Responses to Australia by Visiting Writers 1836–1939* (Boobook Publications, Balgowlah, 1985).

Lansbury, Coral, *Arcady in Australia: The Evocation of Australia in Nineteenth Century English Literature* (Melbourne University Press, Carlton, 1970).

Leed, Eric J., *The Mind of the Traveler: From Gilgamesh to Global Tourism* (Basic Books, A Division of HarperCollins*Publishers*, United States, 1991).

Mackaness, George, *Some Fictitious Voyages to Australia* (Review Publications, Dubbo, 1979, first published privately, 1937).

Martin, Stephen, *A New Land: European Perceptions of Australia 1788–1850* (Allen & Unwin Pty Ltd, St Leonards, 1993).

Mayne, Alan, 'An Italian Traveller in the Antipodes: An Historical Rite of Passage', in *Australian Cultural History*, no. 10, 1991, *Travellers, Journeys, Tourists*, pp. 58–67.

Moyal, Ann, *A Bright and Savage Land* (Penguin, Ringwood, 1993, first published by William Collins Pty Ltd, 1986).

Newby, Eric (ed.), *A Book of Travellers' Tales* (Picador in association with Collins, London, 1986, first published by William Collins Sons & Co. Ltd, 1985).

Oldham, John, and Stirling, Alfred, *Victoria: A Visitors Book* (The Hawthorn Press, Melbourne, 1969, first published 1934).

Oliver, W.H. (ed.), with Williams, B.R., *The Oxford History of New Zealand* (Clarendon Press, Oxford, Oxford University Press, Wellington, 1981).

Pearson, Michael, 'Travellers, Journeys, Tourists: The Meanings of Journeys', in *Australian Cultural History*, no. 10, 1991, *Travellers, Journeys, Tourists*, pp. 125–34.

Robinson, Jane, *Wayward Women: A Guide to Women Travellers* (Oxford University Press, Oxford, 1990).

Salmond, Ann, *Two Worlds: First Meetings Between Maori and Europeans 1642–1772* (Viking, Penguin, Auckland, 1993, first published by Viking, 1991).

Smith, Bernard, *European Vision and the South Pacific 1768–1850: A Study in the History of Art and Ideas* (Clarendon Press, Oxford, 1960).

Webster, Hilary, *The Tasmanian Traveller: A Nineteenth Century Companion for Modern Travellers* (Brolga Press, Canberra, 1988).

SOURCES AND
ACKNOWLEDGMENTS

The editor and publisher thank copyright holders for granting permission to reproduce copyright material.

Anon., *Fragmens du Dernier Voyage de La Pérouse*, ed. and trans. John Dunmore, vol. 2 (National Library of Australia, Canberra, 1987, first published in French 1797), pp. 35–7. Reproduced by permission of the National Library of Australia.

Jessie Ackermann, *Australia from a Woman's Point of View* (Cassell Australia, North Ryde, 1981, facsimile, first published by Cassell, London, 1913), pp. 6–15.

William Archer extract: Raymond Stanley (ed.), *Tourist to the Antipodes: William Archer's 'Australian Journey, 1876–77'* (University of Queensland Press, St Lucia, 1977), pp. 16–21. Reproduced by permission of Raymond Stanley.

David Attenborough, *Quest Under Capricorn* (Lutterworth Press, London, 1963), pp. 29–33. Reproduced by permission of the Lutterworth Press.

Miho Baccich extract: letter to his parents, Fremantle, 16 May 1876, reproduced in Gustav Rathe, *The Wreck of the Barque* Stefano *off the North West Cape of Australia in 1875* (Farrar, Straus & Giroux, New York, 1992), pp. 92–5.

Lucy Broad, *A Woman's Wanderings the World Over* (Headley Brothers, London, nd [1909]), pp. 126–31.

V. C. Buckley, *With a Passport and Two Eyes* (Hutchinson, London, undated reprint, first published 1932), pp. 155–60.

Samuel Butler, *Erewhon: Or Over the Range* (Jonathan Cape, London, 1926, reset and reprinted 1927, first published 1872, new and revised edition 1901), pp. 298–304.

Lord George Campbell, *Log-Letters from 'The Challenger'* (new edition, Macmillan and Co., London, 1881 first published 1877), pp. 181–4.

Raffaello Carboni extract: Carboni Raffaello [*sic*], *The Eureka Stockade: The Consequence of Some Pirates Wanting on Quarter-Deck a Rebellion* (Dolphin, Melbourne, 1947), pp. 113–15. This is republished from the original edition published by the author, Melbourne, 1855.

David W. Carnegie, *Spinifex and Sand: A Narrative of Five Years' Pioneering and Exploration in Western Australia* (Penguin, Ringwood, 1973, facsimile, originally published by C. Arthur Pearson Limited, London, 1898), pp. 109–15.

Robert Cecil extract: Ernest Scott (ed.), *Lord Robert Cecil's Gold Fields Diary* (Melbourne University Press, Carlton, second edition 1945, first published 1935), pp. 12–18.

Bruce Chatwin, *The Songlines* (Jonathan Cape, London, 1987), pp. 114–18. Reproduced by permission of Jonathan Cape.

Agatha Christie, *An Autobiography* (Collins, London, 1977), pp. 293–7. Reproduced by permission of Hughes Massie Ltd.

Mrs Charles Clacy, *A Lady's Visit to the Gold Diggings of Australia in 1852–53*, ed. Patricia Thompson (Angus & Robertson, London, 1963), pp. 72–6. This follows the text of the second edition of 1853. The book was first published in 1853.

Kenneth Clark, *The Other Half: A Self-Portrait* (Hamish Hamilton (paperback), London, 1986, first published 1977), pp. 154–5. Reproduced by permission of John Murray (Publishers) Ltd.

Alan Cobham, *Australia and Back* (A. & C. Black, London, 1926), pp. 96–9. Reproduced by permission of Jeffrey Cobham.

Oscar Comettant, *In the Land of Kangaroos and Gold Mines*, trans. Judith Armstrong (Rigby, Adelaide, Sydney, Melbourne, Brisbane, 1980), pp. 136–9. This book was first published as *Au Pays des Kangourous et des Mines d'Or* (Librairie Fischbacher, Paris, 1890). Reproduced by permission of Judith M. Armstrong.

Joseph Conrad, *The Mirror of the Sea* and *A Personal Record*, edited with an introduction by Zdzisław Najder (Oxford University Press, Oxford, 1981), pp. 121–8. *The Mirror of the Sea* was first published in 1906.

Peter Conrad, *Down Home: Revisiting Tasmania* (Chatto & Windus, London, 1988), pp. 32–5. Reproduced by permission of Random House UK Limited.

Henry Cornish, *Under the Southern Cross* (Penguin, Ringwood, 1975, facsimile of second edition, Higginbotham & Co., Madras, 1880), pp. 21–5.

William Cuff, *Sunny Memories of Australasia: Places I Saw and People I Met* (James Clarke & Co., London, 1904), pp. 99–103.

William Dampier, *A New Voyage Round the World* (Adam and Charles Black, London, 1937, reprinted from the edition of 1729, first published 1697), pp. 312–14.

Charles Darwin, *The Voyage of the 'Beagle'* (Heron Books, np, 1968), pp. 446–9. Darwin's *Journal of Researches into the Geology and Natural History of the Various Countries Visited by H.M.S. Beagle,* as the work was originally entitled, was first published in 1839. This is a facsimile of a later edition, *c.* 1845.

Wanderer [Elim H. D'Avigdor], *Antipodean Notes: Collected on a Nine Months' Tour Round the World* (Sampson Low, Marston, Searle & Rivington, London, 1888), pp. 39–45.

Gabriel de Foigny, *A New Discovery of Terra Incognita Australis, or the Southern World...* (Printed for John Dunton, London, 1693), pp. 122–6.

Rose de Freycinet extract: Marnie Bassett, *Realms and Islands. The World Voyage of Rose de Freycinet 1817–1820* (Oxford University Press, London, 1962), pp. 5–6. Reproduced by permission of Oxford University Press.

Charles Wentworth Dilke, *Greater Britain: A Record of Travel in English-Speaking Countries during 1866 and 1867* (fifth edition, Macmillan and Co., London, 1870, first published 1868), pp. 347–9.

Arthur Conan Doyle, *The Wanderings of a Spiritualist* (Hodder and Stoughton, London, 1921), pp. 88–91.

Anthony Eden, *Places in the Sun* (John Murray, London, 1926), pp. 80–2.

Robert Elwes, *A Sketcher's Tour Round the World* (Hurst & Blackett, London, 1854), pp. 245–7.

Antoine Fauchery, *Letters from a Miner in Australia,* trans. A.R. Chisholm (Georgian House, Melbourne, 1965), pp. 56–8. The original French edition was published in 1857.

Frank Fowler, *Southern Lights and Shadows,* with an introduction by R. G. Geering (Sydney University Press, Sydney, 1975, facsimile, first published by Sampson Low, Son, and Co., London, 1859), pp. 6–9.

James Anthony Froude, *Oceana: or England and her Colonies* (new edition, Longmans, Green, and Co., London, 1886, first published earlier that year), pp. 211–14.

Penryn Goldman, *To Hell and Gone* (Angus & Robertson Limited, Sydney, 1932), pp. 121–5.

W. G. Grace, *'W.G.': Cricketing Reminiscences and Personal Recollections* (James Bowden, London, 1899), pp. 77–8.

Germaine Greer, *Daddy, We Hardly Knew You* (Penguin, Ringwood, 1990, first published in Great Britain 1989 by Hamish Hamilton Ltd), pp. 26–8. Copyright © Germaine Greer, 1989. Reproduced by permission of Hamish Hamilton Ltd.

Zane Grey, *Tales of the Angler's Eldorado: New Zealand* (Hodder and Stoughton, London, 1926), pp. 48–52.

Tyrone Guthrie, *A Life in the Theatre* (Columbus Books, London, 1987, first published by Hamish Hamilton Ltd, 1960), pp. 247–52. Copyright © Tyrone Guthrie, 1959, 1960.

Joseph Hall, *The Discovery of a New World*, trans. John Healey (*c.* 1609*)*, ed. Huntington Brown (Harvard University Press, Cambridge, Massachusetts, 1937), pp. 71–2. This was first published in English *c.* 1609 and in Latin as *Mundus Alter et Idem, c.* 1605.

Robin Hanbury-Tenison, *Fragile Eden: A Ride Through New Zealand* (Arrow Books Limited, London, 1990, first published by Century Hutchinson Limited, 1989), pp. 108–10.

W. H. Harvey extract: Sophie C. Ducker (ed.), *The Contented Botanist: Letters of W. H. Harvey about Australia and the Pacific* (Melbourne University Press, Carlton, 1988), pp. 169–74. Reproduced by permission of Melbourne University Press.

James Holman, *A Voyage Round the World Including Travels in Africa, Asia, Australasia*, vol. IV (Smith, Elder, & Co., London, 1835), pp. 448–51.

Herbert Hoover, *The Memoirs of Herbert Hoover: Years of Adventure 1874–1920* (Hollis and Carter, London, 1952), pp. 32–4.

Therese Huber, *Adventures on a Journey to New Holland* and *The Lonely Deathbed*, trans. Rodney Livingstone, edited, with preface and notes, by Leslie Bodi (Lansdowne Press, Melbourne, 1966), pp. 47–9. *Adventures...* was first published in 1801 and *...Deathbed* in 1810. Reproduced by permission of Lansdowne Publishing.

Barry Humphries, *More Please: An Autobiography* (Penguin, Ringwood, 1993, first published in 1992 by Viking), pp. 207–9. Copyright © Barry Humphries, 1992.

Clive James, *Flying Visits: Postcards from the* Observer *1976–83* (Picador, London, 1985, first published as a collection by Jonathan Cape Ltd, 1984), pp. 15–22. Reproduced by permission of Jonathan Cape.

Lord Killanin, *My Olympic Years* (Martin Secker & Warburg, London, 1983), pp. 29–32. Reproduced by permission of Reed Consumer Books.

Henry Kingsley, *The Recollections of Geoffry Hamlyn,* from J.S.D. Mellick (ed.), *Henry Kingsley* (Portable Australian Authors) (University of Queensland Press, St Lucia, 1982), pp. 258–60. This latter publication includes a complete facsimile reproduction of the Chapman and Hall 1877 edition of ... *Geoffry Hamlyn,* a book that was first published in 1859. The chapter from which this was taken was published separately by Macmillan in 1871 as a children's book entitled *The Lost Child.*

Egon Erwin Kisch, *Australian Landfall,* trans. John Fisher and Irene and Kevin Fitzgerald (Australasian Book Society, Sydney, 1969, first published in German 1937), pp. 73–4. Martin Secker & Warburg Ltd, reproduced by permission of Reed Consumer Books.

Thomas W. Knox, *The Boy Travellers in Australasia: Adventures of Two Youths in a Journey to the Sandwich, Marquesas, Society, Samoan, and Feejee Islands, and through the Colonies of New Zealand, New South Wales, Queensland, Victoria, Tasmania, and South Australia* (Charles E. Tuttle, Tokyo, 1971, facsimile, originally published by Harper & Brothers, New York, 1889), pp. 361–4.

Harold Larwood with Kevin Perkins, *The Larwood Story* (W. H. Allen, London, 1965), pp. 9–12.

D. H. Lawrence, *Kangaroo* (Penguin in association with William Heinemann Ltd, Harmondsworth, 1986, first published 1923), pp. 85–9.

Nerys Lloyd-Pierce, 'Six Months in the Outback', in Miranda Davies and Natania Jansz (eds), *Women Travel: Adventures, Advice and Experience* (Rough Guides, London, 1993, first published by Harrap Columbus, 1990), pp. 24–7.

Carl Lumholtz, *Among Cannibals: An Account of Four Years' Travels in Australia and of Camp Life with the Aborigines of Queensland* (ANU Press, Canberra, 1980, first published by John Murray, London, 1889), pp. 220–2.

Mackie extract: Mary Nicholls (ed.), *Traveller Under Concern: The Quaker Journals of Frederick Mackie on His Tour of the Australasian Colonies 1852–1855* (University of Tasmania, Hobart, 1973), pp. 71–4. Reproduced by permission of the Department of History, University of Tasmania.

[James Matra], *A Journal of a Voyage Round the World in His Majesty's Ship Endeavour* (printed for T. Becket and P. A De Hondt, London, 1771), reprinted as *The Anonymous Journal* (Antonio Giordano, Adelaide, 1975), from the original first edition copy in the Mitchell Library, Sydney, pp. 97–9.

W. Somerset Maugham, *Cosmopolitans* (William Heinemann Ltd, London, 1938, first published 1936), pp. 143–51. Reproduced by permission of Reed Consumer Books.

Jan Morris, *Pleasures of a Tangled Life* (Arrow Books, London, 1990, first published in Great Britain in 1989 by Barrie & Jenkins Ltd), pp. 135–41.

Shiva Naipaul, *An Unfinished Journey* (Abacus, London, 1988, first published by Hamish Hamilton, 1986), pp. 11–14. Copyright © the Estate of Shiva Naipaul, 1986.

Eric Newby, *The Last Grain Race* (Picador, London, 1990, first published by Martin Secker & Warburg Ltd, 1956), pp. 163–6. Reproduced by permission of Reed Consumer Books.

Marianne North extract: Helen Vellacott (ed.), *Some Recollections of a Happy Life: Marianne North in Australia & New Zealand* (Edward Arnold Australia, Caulfield East, 1986), pp. 43–5. North's text is reproduced from her *Recollections of a Happy Life* (1892).

Carol O'Biso, *First Light: A Magical Journey* (Paragon House, New York, 1989, first published 1987), pp. 44–7. Reproduced by permission of Paragon House, New York.

Olivier extract: Felix Barker, *The Oliviers* (Hamish Hamilton, London, 1953), pp. 274–6. Reproduced by permission of A. P. Watt Ltd on behalf of Felix Barker.

Mary Ann Parker, *A Voyage Round the World* (Hordern House and the Australian National Maritime Museum, Sydney, 1991, facsimile, originally published by John Nichols, London, 1795), pp. 85–94.

Sydney Parkinson, *A Journal of a Voyage to the South Seas in His Majesty's Ship The Endeavour* (Caliban Books, London, 1984, reprint, originally published by C. Dilly, London, 1784), pp. 134–6.

François Pelsaert, *The Voyage of the Batavia* (Hordern House, Sydney, 1994), pp. 90–6. This book includes a facsimile of the account of Pelsaert's journal by Jan Jansz, which was first published in Dutch as *Ongeluckige Voyagie, Van't Ship Batavia* in 1647 and Willem Siebenhaar's English translation of *Ongeluckige...*, which appeared in the *Western Mail* as 'The Abrolhos Tragedy' in 1897. The extract is taken from 'The Abrolhos Tragedy'.

John Pilger, *Distant Voices* (Vintage, London, 1992), pp. 353–7. Reproduced by permission of David Higham Associates.

Harry Price, *The Royal Tour, 1901, or, The Cruise of H.M.S. 'Ophir': Being a Lower Deck Account of their Royal Highnesses, the Duke and Duchess of Cornwall and York's Voyage around the British Empire*

(Webb & Bower, Exeter, 1980), no page numbers given. Reproduced by permission of Webb & Bower (Publishers) Limited.

Mrs A. Prinsep (ed.), *The Journal of a Voyage from Calcutta to Van Diemen's Land: Comprising a Description of that Colony, during a Six Months' Residence* (Melanie Publications, Hobart, 1981, facsimile, originally published by Smith, Elder & Co., London, 1833), pp. 83–7.

Francis Ratcliffe, *Flying Fox and Drifting Sand: The Adventures of a Biologist in Australia* (Pacific Books, Sydney, 1970, first published in Great Britain in 1938, published in Sirius Books, 1963), pp. 12–14. Reproduced by permission of HarperCollins*Publishers*, Australia.

George Augustus Sala, *The Life and Adventures of George Augustus Sala*, vol. II (Cassell and Company, Limited, London, Paris & Melbourne, 1895), pp. 422–9.

John Sherer (ed.), *The Gold-Finder of Australia: How He Went, How He Fared, and How He Made His Fortune* (Penguin, Harmondsworth, 1973), pp. 313–15. This is a facsimile of the original book, first published by Clarke, Beeton, & Co., London, 1853.

Jean Shrimpton, with Unity Hall, *An Autobiography* (Sphere Books Limited, London, 1991, first published 1990), pp. 140–5. Reproduced by permission of Century Hutchinson and Random House UK Ltd.

Joshua Slocum, *Sailing Alone Around the World* (Dover Publications, Inc., New York, Dover edition, first published 1956, an unabridged republication of the work originally published by the Century Company, 1900), pp. 192–3. Reproduced by permission of Dover Publications, Inc.

Emily Soldene, *My Theatrical and Musical Recollections* (Downey & Co. Limited, London, 1897), pp. 213–21.

Frederic C. Spurr, *Five Years Under the Southern Cross: Experiences and Impressions* (Cassell and Company, Ltd, London, 1915), pp. 243–6.

Christina Stead, *Ocean of Story: The Uncollected Stories of Christina Stead* (Penguin, Ringwood, 1986, first published by Viking, 1985), pp. 513–20. Reproduced by permission of Penguin Books Australia Ltd.

E. W. Swanton, *Swanton in Australia: With MCC 1946–1975* (Fontana/Collins, Glasgow, 1976, first published by William Collins Sons & Co. Ltd, Glasgow, 1975), pp. 27–30. Reproduced by permission of HarperCollins*Publishers* Limited.

Jonathan Swift, *Gulliver's Travels* (Penguin Classics, London, 1985, first published 1726), pp. 54–60.

William F. Talbert with John Sharnik, *Playing for Life: Billy Talbert's Story* (Little, Brown and Company, Boston and Toronto, undated reprint, first published 1958), pp. 287–90.

Richard Tangye, *Reminiscences of Travel in Australia, America, and Egypt* (Sampson Low, Marston, Searle, & Rivington, London, 1884, first published privately 1883), pp. 50–9.

Maggie Teyte, *Star on the Door* (Putnam, London, 1958), pp. 139–41.

George Francis Train extract: E. Daniel and Annette Potts (eds), *A Yankee Merchant in Goldrush Australia: The Letters of George Francis Train, 1853–55* (Heinemann, London and Melbourne, 1970), pp. 93–5.

Anthony Trollope, *Australia*, vol. 1 (Alan Sutton, Gloucester, and Hippocrene Books, New York, 1987), pp. 231–4. The contents of this and a second volume published simultaneously are drawn from Trollope's *Australia and New Zealand*, first published 1873.

Mark Twain, *Mark Twain in Australia and New Zealand* (Penguin, Harmondsworth, 1973), pp. 297–304. This book consists of the first half of Twain's *Following the Equator* (The American Publishing Company, 1897).

Jules Verne, *Twenty Thousand Leagues Under the Sea* (Wordsworth Classics, Ware, Hertfordshire, 1992, first published 1869), pp. 100–5.

Ardaser Sorabjee N. Wadia, *The Call of the Southern Cross: Being Impressions of a Four Months' Tour in Australia and New Zealand* (J.M. Dent & Sons Ltd, London and Toronto, 1932), pp. 13–19. Reproduced by permission of J. M. Dent.

Beatrice Webb extract: A.G. Austen (ed.), *The Webbs' Australian Diary, 1898* (Sir Isaac Pitman & Sons Ltd, Melbourne, 1965), pp. 46–8.

Richard Whately extract: Mary Fox (ed.), *Account of an Expedition to the Interior of New Holland* (Richard Bentley, London, 1837), pp. 83–8.

Thomas Wood, *Cobbers: A Personal Record of a Journey from Essex, in England, to Australia, made in the years 1930, 1931 and 1932* (Seal Books, Rigby, Adelaide, 1978, first published by Oxford University Press, London, 1934), pp. 145–8. This text is from the third edition, 1953. Reproduced by permission of Oxford University Press.

INDEX